The Tented Field

The Tented Field:
A History of Cricket in America

Tom Melville

Bowling Green State University Popular Press
Bowling Green, OH 43403

Copyright 1998 © Bowling Green State University Popular Press

Library of Congress Cataloging-in-Publication Data
Melville, Tom.
    The tented field : a history of cricket in America / Tom Melville.
      p.   cm.
    Includes bibliographical references (p.) and index.
    ISBN 0-87972-769-1 (clothbound). -- ISBN 0-87972-770-5 (pbk.)
    1. Cricket--United States--History.   I. Title
GV928.U6M45   1998
796.358'0973--dc21   98-4030
                                                                                       CIP

Cover design by Dumm Art

Contents

Acknowledgments	vii
Introduction	1
1. Cricket "In a Way": The Reluctant Tradition	5
2. The "Useful" and the "Ornamental": The Beginnings of Organization and the Ambiguity of Identity	11
3. A Game, a Sport, but Not a National Institution	21
4. The All-England Tour of 1859 and the Insufficiency of Imitation	43
5. The Retreat from Cosmopolitanism and the Fallacy of the Chadwick Thesis	53
6. Cricket "For the Courteous": The Untenability of Elitism	73
7. "A Place for Every Man Who Will Come and Take His Part": On the Periphery of Late Nineteenth-Century Popularism	93
8. A "Most Exigent" Sport: Philadelphia and the Struggle with Structure	119
Conclusion	147
Photographs	150
Glossary of Cricket Terms and Phrases	161
Notes	163
Bibliographic Essay	209
Appendix Directory of American Cricket Clubs, 1837-1914	211
Index	269

Acknowledgments

This work would not have been possible without the help and assistance of many people and organizations, far too many, regrettably, to acknowledge individually.

Special thanks, however, must be extended to Mr. Paul Lewis of Ridley College for kindly loaning his college's holdings of the *American Cricketer;* to Amar Singh for loaning his personal copies of this publication; to George Rugg of Notre Dame's Joyce Sports Research Collection for the close personal attention he gave to my requests; to Dave Barrow for helping convert the manuscript to a computerized format; and to the late Murray Haines and other staff members of the C. C. Morris Cricket Library at Haverford College for all their help in making available the material in this valuable collection.

Finally, special thanks must again go to Georgia Jung and the staff of the Cedarburg Public Library for their dedicated and attentive interlibrary loan service.

Introduction

It is not without a touch of irony that the history of cricket in America has, over the last two decades, emerged as one of the more important subjects of attention among sports historians.

Ironic not only in the sense that the subject represents a sporting tradition that has effectively long been extinct from America's sporting culture, but because this historical discontinuity has brought sports historians to the realization that American team sports developed as they did through a complex, dynamic process that only reached a consensus and direction over a lengthy period of cultural debate.

Today most scholars believe American team sports evolved as part of the country's mid-nineteenth-century urbanizing process, even though there may be no unanimity about what the precise mechanism within this complex process specifically accounts for the rise of modern team sports.[1]

To some scholars, such as Benjamin Rader, sports represented a specific social response to forces of urbanization, such as an urban populace's "quest for sub-communities," while for others, such as Steven Gelber, the appearance of organized team sports represented a specific extension, into America's leisure life, of emerging corporate and workplace values and patterns.[2]

These and other schools of thought immediately recognized that cricket was one of the earliest beneficiaries of this complex urban process. The game prospered earlier and, for a period, more vibrantly than any other American team sport during the antebellum years, and for good reason.

The appearance of early American cricket fits well into just about every subtheory within this broader analysis of sport's urban development. The game's appearance could be interpreted as an historical example of a direct social response to urbanism, an extension of urban values, as well as an expression of urban class or ethnic influences.[3]

If the appearance of early American cricket could be used to support just about any theory of modern sport's urban origin, it also presented at least one serious challenge to all these theories. If both baseball and cricket represented one of the earliest and most logical responses to mid-nineteenth-century America's changing attitudes toward sports in an urban environment, why then did these two games take such dramatically different paths? "Modernization" is inherently an expansive and inclusive process that tends to break down traditional or ethnic cultural patterns. Why was it then that cricket, the first team sport in America to respond to these forces of urban modernism, not only quickly declined over this period but eventually failed to maintain anything more than a nominal presence on the late-nineteenth-century American sports scene?

A proper and thorough explanation of why cricket failed as an American institution, therefore, emerges as far more than a matter of historical curiosity. It becomes critical to the very validity of any theory that purports to explain the urban origin and subsequent development of American team sports.

Melvin Adelman and, to a lesser extent, George Kirsch, were the first scholars to recognize the importance of this point and the first to systematically attempt to explain why cricket, the first "modern" sport, failed to thrive in the "modernizing" process. Going on the premise that the "need to establish rational order" upon America's leisure culture was the seminal force behind the rise of modern American sports, Adelman believed the different destinies of baseball and cricket could be adequately explained as a logical and consistent development of this process. Cricket, it was true, may have been the first American team sport to respond to this process, but it was quickly eclipsed by baseball because the American game best "fulfilled the requirements of the new sporting universe created by the changing social and urban environment of the antebellum period." Specifically, baseball quickly asserted itself over cricket because the nine man game was a cultural expression more responsive to the needs of a broad, participant sport within this urban landscape. The great strength of Adelman's analysis is the recognition that the rise of early American sports wasn't merely an inevitable, impersonal, process but a dynamic interplay between emerging sports structures and individual behavior that involved human choice and cultural preference.[4]

Valuable as these studies were, both worked within self-imposed limitations. Both concentrated upon the large metropolitan areas of the American northeast, and restricted their time spans to the years between 1820 and 1870. While acknowledging cricket's presence in America before and after these dates, both Adelman and Kirsch assumed premodern American cricket had no more than a negligible influence upon the game's subsequent development and that cricket, by the 1870s, had reached a largely terminal state of influence upon America's later sports culture.

This study will attempt to present a definitive and analytical explanation of why cricket failed as an American sporting institution unrestricted by these previous scholarly limitations. While devoting considerable attention to the rise of organized American sports immediately before and after the Civil War, this study will also attempt to interpret this phenomenon in the context of its premodern American history and will also examine its subsequent development up to the First World War.

The decision to terminate the study at this latter point was not arbitrary.

Although cricket was still being played in America at that time, and has continued to be played here ever since, the few Americans who were still playing cricket (primarily in Philadelphia) were leaving the game with no others taking their places. More significantly, however, was the fact that the "cultural dialogue" over cricket's place in American culture had effectively come to an end by the second decade of the twentieth century.

Despite a modest post-Reconstruction level of actual participant popularity, cricket, throughout the latter half of the nineteenth century, was still viewed by most American sports observers as a sporting activity fully worthy of a place on the American sports scene, as either an alternative to mass sports interests or as an expression of America's international sporting commitments.

By the end of the First World War, however, this perception had all but been abandoned. Sports observers now dismissed cricket as nothing more than an alien, un-American pastime, suitable, perhaps, for commonwealth immigrants, but totally inappropriate for Americans in any form, a cultural judgment that has remained relatively intact up to the present.

This work will also extend its geographic and sociological parameters beyond those of Adelman and Kirsch. While concentrating upon cricket's development in the larger urban areas of the Atlantic seaboard, this work will also examine cricket's development in other areas of the United States, both urban and rural. This work will also attempt to examine cricket not only in its traditional nineteenth-century context—as a sport for America's middle and upper classes—but also as a working-class phenomenon. It will also examine cricket's role within the leisure life of sporting America's Victorian "underclass," women and minorities.

In sum, this work is presented more as a thematic, rather than strictly chronological, history of American cricket, an attempt to seek an explanation for the game's decline within the context of not only broad historical trends but also more specific cultural influences.

For this, after all, is the historian's—as distinct from the chronicler's—role: to explain not so much what and when something happened but why it happened the way it did.

1

Cricket "In a Way": The Reluctant Tradition

Contemporary historians have characterized premodern American sports as informal, regional, and nonquantitative, played, prior to the mid-nineteenth century, without universally established rules or organization.[1]

What evidence there is of cricket playing in America during this premodern period is, at best, ambivalent about these assumptions.

Certainly the cricket that was played by William Byrd, the colonial Virginia planter, with his tidewater neighbors in the early years of the eighteenth century—the earliest documented evidence we have of cricket playing in America—would have to be characterized as premodern. Here the game was little more than informal, private, four-a-side matches, played by Byrd and his neighbors, usually for a wager, as part of the isolated social life of the colonial Virginia aristocracy.[2]

Other documentary evidence of cricket from the pre-Revolutionary era, such as the "servants vs the inmates" match, reportedly played in Georgia around 1737, or the match between teams selected from residents "north" and "south" of the bridge at Hartford, Connecticut, played on election day, 1767, also portray an informal game played on irregular occasions by nonspecialists, selected on the basis of occupation or residency.[3]

But even during this period, a good two generations before the traditionally assigned "jumping off" stage of modern American team sports, cricket was exhibiting a number of distinctively "modern" sporting characteristics.

The existence, as early as 1779, of two geographically identifiable cricket clubs, the Brooklyn and Greenwich (presumably Greenwich, New York, then a fashionable section of Manhattan), clubs that were playing matches at the Ferry House Tavern on Fulton and Elm streets in Brooklyn, a site that would long be associated with cricket playing, seemed to indicate the game was enjoying a moderately advanced state of organization.[4]

In all probability this was the Brooklyn club that was reportedly holding regular practices "near the Jews burying ground" every Monday in New York during 1780, an organizational arrangement that may have been shared by other immediate post-Revolutionary War New York clubs, if the notices of formal club meetings and cricket equipment vendors that appeared at that time in a number of contemporary newspapers are to be believed. The cricket club that existed in Richmond, Virginia, in 1795 was formal enough to even publish a list of its members and playing rules.[5]

If the establishment and adherence to standardized, uniform playing rules are also an important prerequisite for modernity, American cricket seems to have also satisfied this condition well before the Revolutionary War. This can be conjectured from the match reported in the *New York Weekly Gazette and Post Boy* on April 29, 1751, between teams of local New Yorkers and resident Englishmen, which was explicitly played according to the "London method," most likely a reference to the cricket laws that south England cricket authorities had formally set down in 1744.[6]

Increased formalization in both rules and organization in themselves, however, would have been insufficient for the rise of modern team sports without a number of important cultural changes in the way early American society looked upon sports participation. But here as well, there is evidence that cricket playing in America, at least by the end of the Federalist era, had passed two historically significant milestones of social acceptance: (1) the game had become identified as an acceptable recreational activity for adults, and (2) it had been recognized as an activity worthy of participation by the more "respectable" segments of American society.

Though largely anecdotal, contemporary evidence for these claims is fairly consistent. The New Orleans *Picayune* seemed to be speaking for its readership at large when it declared in 1841 "Who has not played 'barn ball' in boyhood, 'base' in his youth and 'wicket' in his manhood?" (wicket, as we shall discuss shortly, was a regional American adaptation of English cricket). Of the numerous games he observed being played in New England in 1831, Horatio Smith found only young men playing cricket. And of the American adults who did play cricket, some were clergymen, such as those in Massachusetts who reportedly played the game all year long in 1785, while others were among the "most eminent citizens" of New York, who supposedly had a cricket club of their own shortly after the turn of the century.[7]

Cricket also seems to have come to terms with the moral strictures of New England's puritan heritage by the turn of the century, at least according to the by-laws of the Boston Cricket Club that existed in that city in 1809. This document, which seems to have come into the hands of a member of the Lowell Cricket Club in 1863, reveals a code of strict behavior expectations for its members, along with a specific set of fines for those members remiss in their duties and obligations to the club, perhaps the earliest acknowledgment, so critical to the rise of later American team sports, of society's right to impose standards of individual obligations upon sports participation.[8]

But who was actually playing cricket during this period of American history? This is an important question, not the least because cricket's history in America would center around the game's success or failure as a specifically American, rather than English, institution.

We know that much of the cricket played in colonial New York was identifiably English. British soldiers frequently played the game at the Ferry House Tavern in Brooklyn, a popular social center for the British army during its occupation of New York, and one that, from that time, seems to have become a focal point for cricket playing among the city's English residents. It was, in all likelihood, the "old grounds" mentioned in the newspaper reports of 1789 and again during the "short revival" in cricket playing that occurred in 1799. It was also most probably the "favorite piece of ground" selected for the June 1, 1820, match between teams of New Yorkers and English residents, as well as the approximate location of the first cricket match of the "modern" era played by English residents in 1838.[9]

In these instances cricket seems to have served as a social outlet for expatriate English residents, played in segregation from the American populace, as it also was with the English university graduates who organized a club in New York early in the nineteenth century, and the English immigrants who had been settled in the planned communities of southern Illinois in 1818, who kept up their cricket under the watchful eyes of their curious American neighbors.[10]

It would be wrong, however, to presume that few Americans played cricket during this period, or only did so under English influence.

Several firsthand testimonies have come down to us of cricket and wicket playing among continental soldiers during their encampment at Valley Forge, as well as among American soldiers in South Carolina and Boston. The American challenge issued to the British occupation force in Brooklyn in 1779 seems to have been a hoax, but the game seems to have established itself as a traditional part of the Fourth of July festivities for at least some Baltimore residents by 1825.[11]

Both literary and nonliterary evidence also confirms that cricket was a part of early student life at several American colleges. A number of engravings have come down to us portraying cricket playing at Harvard and Dartmouth Colleges in the 1790s. Harry Crosswell found his fellow students at Yale also playing cricket in 1818, as did Richard Henry Dana among his classmates at Harvard a decade later.[12]

All this raises the intriguing question, Was there a "folk" tradition of cricket playing in America independent of direct English influences similar to such premodern American ball games as two-old-cat or townball? This is an important point because Adelman believes cricket failed as an American sport because its well-developed English rules, playing technique, and customs made the game "prematurely modern" for Americans only familiar with their own undeveloped ball-playing culture. According to this theory, Americans eventually adopted baseball because they were more willing to develop and adapt this simpler ball-playing tradition than accept a more advanced, but culturally unmalleable, ball game.[13]

Supporters of this theory might even point out that the cricket that was apparently played by Americans in a spontaneous manner may have actually been inspired by the many English sports books that proliferated in America during the early nineteenth century. The most popular of these publications, the *Boys Own Book*, which provided extensive instructions in cricket playing, for example, was an American adaptation of an English publication. According to Edward Everett Hale, virtually every boy of his era took his inspiration from this publication for their outdoor games, including cricket, which, according to Hale, "we had—in a way."[14]

Certainly such an explicitly didactic chain of cause and effect was at work in some areas of America, but it hardly seems to be a sufficient explanation for all instances of cricket playing among early nineteenth-century Americans. The youngsters Emerson observed playing cricket in his educationally preoccupied Boston may have picked up their cricket from literary sources, but could this be realistically have been the case with the "forty or fifty" boys Ebenezer Davies observed playing cricket in New Orleans in the 1840s? Where could the American youngsters portrayed playing cricket in front of the Philadelphia State House in 1800 have learned their cricket, or the young men of Portland, Maine, who played cricket, football, and prisoners base interchangeably during the 1820s?[15]

To what extent a "folk" tradition of cricket playing actually existed among Americans is, at best, problematic. Much more important, however, is the question, Why did English residents, rather than Americans, organize the first identifiably "modern" American cricket clubs that appeared in New York during the late 1830s? Even if American youngsters had to rely upon such nonindigenous sources as one-off English sports manuals for their knowledge of cricket, why didn't they organize cricket clubs when they became adults, or if they had played the game in college, continue playing after their student days? Even more perplexing, why didn't the Americans who had been educated in England, such as the early New York Cricket Club member, Judge Church of Elmira, a Harrow graduate and reportedly a cricket player "for half a century," organize clubs among their friends anytime prior to the appearance of the first New York clubs? In short, why didn't a "Knickerbockers" type cricket club ever appear among young Americans motivated to keep up a game they had known in their youth as Alexander Cartwright and his young American friends did in New York when they established their famous baseball club?[16]

Here Adelman's thesis, in a way, makes more sense. Perhaps it was not that Americans had no cultural exposure to cricket so much as that this exposure was culturally too weak and geographically diverse to assert itself in the face of the technical and organizational superiority of newly emerging English clubs. Rowland Bowen, in his well-researched history of cricket, presents an interesting theory something along these lines. According to Bowen, Americans did have an indigenous tradition of cricket playing in the game of wicket, which, Bowen contends (correctly, I believe), was an archaic version of English cricket that survived in certain regions of America even after the major structural changes of the early nineteenth century had been adopted by English cricket. To support this view, Bowen points to Benjamin Silliman's observation, made during the American's visit to England in 1810, of how different the cricket was in that country from the game he had played as a youngster in New England (decades later some observers would, in fact, refer to wicket as an "American improvement on cricket"). According to Bowen, the structural changes that English cricket underwent in the early nineteenth century (a higher wicket, etc.) effectively "doomed" cricket in America by relegating this American variation to an unofficial and illegitimate status.[17]

Clever as Bowen's theory is, it poses several problems. First, wicket, far from disappearing after the early nineteenth century, actually experienced an upsurge in popularity during the late 1850s, especially in, but by no means restricted to, its traditional stronghold in central Connecticut. As George Seymour pointed out in his still valuable historical study of the game, wicket continued to be played in some areas of the country up to the end of the nineteenth century.[18]

Yet, nineteenth century sports observers never, at any time, seemed to have looked to wicket as a viable cultural alternative to either baseball or cricket, even though the game certainly reached a level of technical sophistication equal to these two sports. This was clearly demonstrated during a wicket match at Waterbury, Connecticut, in 1860 when a team of local wicket players easily defeated a team of experienced local cricket players.[19]

The reason why Americans looked to baseball, rather than wicket, as their truly indigenous bat-and-ball sport was probably because wicket wasn't all that different from cricket in its basic playing structure, despite the major changes cricket underwent in the early nineteenth century. Although wicket could be played by more participants, and seemed to allow more turns at bat than standard English cricket, both games still took a long time to play and often led to "drawn out" games. Here, for once, it seems that chronological priority didn't lead to cultural preference.

What I have been trying to show in this chapter is that there were two traditions present in premodern American cricket; a tradition of "standard" English cricket that was fairly advanced in organization, rules, and social standing, though largely supported by English residents or immigrants, and a less clearly defined tradition of indigenous cricket, exemplified in the game of wicket but also standard cricket as played by American youths and college students.

That neither of these traditions effectively asserted themselves in the premodern era of American sports seems to indicate Americans were not unfamiliar with cricket, or its native variation, wicket, or that they felt the sport was too advanced or improper for them. Instead, it seems to indicate Americans were poised to assert baseball as their culturally dominant ball-playing tradition because they had, even in this premodern era, already made a preliminary judgment against cricket as an expression of their culture.

2

The "Useful" and the "Ornamental": The Beginnings of Organization and the Ambiguity of Identity

To the sporting press of the nineteenth century, organized cricket in the United States began with an intrasquad match played between English residents from Sheffield and Nottingham on September 20, 1838, for a wager of $100, near the Ferry House Tavern in Brooklyn, a location already noted for its long association with cricket playing.[1]

In actuality, the Brooklyn match was most probably inspired by a number of informal matches that had been played among teams in the Albany/Troy area of upstate New York a year earlier. At least we know some of these upstate players were acquaintances of their New York counterparts and even participated in a number of New York matches the following year.[2]

Though the Brooklyn match was hardly the first organized cricket match played in New York, it was the first to lead to the formation of anything like a permanent club, a purpose that had been specifically expressed in the advertisement for the match that had appeared in the July 7 issue of the *Albion*. In a rematch, played on October 22, this time for a wager of $400, the participants, though basically the same as in the September match, were now playing under the names of "New York" and "Long Island," the names they also assumed during the "anniversary" match played a year later in October 1839.[3]

On April 23, 1840, however, the "New York" club officially changed its name to the St. George Cricket Club, having relocated in 1839 to a playing ground of its own at the corner of Manhattan's Bloomingdale Road and 42nd Street, at that time a small, rather isolated location "on either side of which were vegetable gardens."[4]

Sports historians have routinely interpreted the St. George's adoption of such an overtly nationalistic name as a deliberate attempt by the English community of New York to isolate its cricket from American influences. However, the possibility should also be considered that this move may have been as much an attempt to maintain the class distinc-

11

tions common in English cricket at this period as it was to assert a nationalistic identity.

Little is known of the St. George's early history, but this interpretation seems to be supported by Thomas Picton Milner's invaluable firsthand account of the club's early years that appeared many years later in the October 5, 1878, issue of the *Clipper*. According to Milner—who seems to have led a rather checkered career as editor, author, sometime soldier of fortune, as well as secretary and playing member of the rival New York Cricket Club during these years—the St. George had been organized by well-to-do English importers and businessmen, such as Robert Bage, an insurance executive, Henry Jessup, an iron merchant, and John Taylor, a wool merchant, though the club also enrolled a number of working-class players to maintain a high competitive standard, a practice common in English cricket at that time.[5]

If true, the St. George's move to Manhattan could be explained as an attempt to disassociate itself from the cricket fraternity of Brooklyn, many of whose numbers seemed to have been either working-class immigrants or individuals of lower socioeconomic standing.

By taking the name of England's patron saint, the St. George club may not have been so much declaring itself as the upholder of English nationalism as it was asserting that the cricket organized in New York must strictly follow an English pattern of class subordination. This seems further supported by the St. George's attempt, some years later, to organize an exclusive "gentleman's" match in the city, an attempt that did not seem to be particularly well received by other New York cricketers.[6]

More important to the country's leading sporting journal, the *Spirit of the Times*, was the hope that the establishment of the St. George club would at last "procure a permanent footing for this favorite game" in the United States. The immediate consequences of these expectations, however, were hardly encouraging.

With the exception of an informal intrasquad contest in 1840, no other matches were played that year, nor during the following year, even though the St. George issued a public challenge to any cricket club in the United States and Canada, a challenge that remained unanswered even after the St. George had sweetened it with a $100 prize offer. The situation had not improved by 1842, the St. George that year having to again settle for only a few intrasquad matches, all of which seems to confirm the *New York Morning News* assertion that "their [St. George's] play has been but little regarded by the American public" during this period.[7]

All this changed, however, once the first matches between New York and Canada were arranged. To Milner, these contests were the real beginning of popular interest in cricket and, for the most part, this claim seems to be fully supported by contemporary reports.[8]

The very first contacts between American and Canadian cricketers had come about in 1840 under "embarrassing circumstances," when the St. George, on the invitation of a mysterious "Mr. Philpotts," journeyed north for a match with Toronto, only to discover they had been the victim of a hoax. An impromptu match was hastily arranged by the Toronto club, but the misunderstanding seems to have left some lingering distrust between the St. George and Toronto cricket authorities.[9]

Following a number of failed attempts to arrange matches in 1841 and 1842, the Canadians were eventually induced to make a belated return visit to New York in 1843. Difficulties again arose during the St. George visit to Toronto the following year, the Canadians this time refusing to play the New Yorkers because they had enrolled onto their team a number of "honorary" members from Philadelphia's Union Cricket Club.[10]

By now relations between the two clubs had apparently so deteriorated that the St. George played its 1845 matches against Montreal, and relations took a further turn for the worse the following year during Toronto's visit to the Red House Tavern in Harlem, to which the St. George had recently relocated. This time the match was abruptly disrupted when a St. George fielder deliberately hit one of the Canadian batters with the ball for allegedly interfering with a catch. With neither side willing to accept blame for the incident, the match was abandoned, leaving such an intense state of ill-will between the two sides that seven years would pass before the two clubs would play again.[11]

Whatever antagonism these incidents aroused among the players did not seem in any way to adversely affect public interest in the matches themselves. When the Toronto club came to New York in the Fall of 1844 to fulfill the competitive obligations it had not honored earlier that year in Canada, close to 3,000 spectators were in attendance at the Bloomingdale ground, with wagers in excess of $100,000 reportedly exchanging hands on the outcome.[12]

Public interest in the following year's match against Montreal ran even higher, the event attracting an estimated 5,000 spectators, among them former New York congressman Ogden Hoffman, all of which seemed to justify the *New York Morning News* claim that "seldom have we known a [cricket] match to create so much excitement."[13]

More significantly, these international matches seemed to have been the initial catalyst for attracting direct American interest in the game. New Yorkers had reportedly first taken notice of the cricket being played in their city during the North vs South of England match held in 1842, but they only began to actively participate in the game following the 1843 U.S.-Canada match, soon after which the *Anglo-American* announced the establishment of a "new cricket club."[14]

This was the New York Cricket Club, founded on October 11, 1843, by John Richards, printer for the *Spirit of the Times*. An "enthusiastic" player, Richards no doubt lent an air of importance to the young club, though it probably was not until the *Spirit*'s influential owner-editor, William Porter, assumed the club's presidency later that year that the organization began to attract many members.[15]

Later observers always looked back upon the New York club as the country's "pioneer" cricket club, primarily because it always claimed to be the first club that actively encouraged Americans to take up cricket.

According to Milner, it was something of a precursor to Philadelphia's Young America club, trying to counterbalance the St. George's growing reputation as an organization "exclusive to Englishmen" by restricting its own membership to native born Americans.[16]

If this, in fact, was the intent of the club, it seems to have been compromised quite early. From the very beginning the New York Club had to rely upon a number of experienced English players, such as the Sussex bowler named Sawyer, to maintain a respectable competitive standing, a dependence that seems to have increased over the years.[17]

Although the *Albion*'s assertion that the club was, by 1855, "all English" was clearly untrue (among its members at that time was the famous American sports scene painter William Ranney and a prominent American from Yonkers, E. F. Shonnard), its presidency was, by that time, held by Delancy Barclay, the son of New York's British consul, a clear indication of how far the New York Club had moved away from its founding purpose.[18]

If the New York Club could not be said to represent a purely American interest in cricket, it did seem to represent an American attempt to control the game's growing commercial potential. It cannot be taken as completely coincidental that the New York Club headquarters, set up in 1844 at McCarty's Tavern in the Elysian Fields, a fashionable recreation area for antebellum New Yorkers just across the Hudson in Hoboken, New Jersey, was on property owned by Edward A. Stevens, the most prominent American sports promoter of that era. According to Milner, Stevens at that time "entered into a scheme to Americanize cricket," not in the sense of promoting American participation but by monopolizing the growing spectator interest in the game's more important matches. To this end Stevens seems to have been fairly successful. In exchange for the token $50 fee he charged the New York Club for using the playing area inside his racetrack, Stevens received a steady flow of paying customers for his ferry service between Manhattan and New Jersey, no doubt a highly profitable business during important match dates.[19]

Though still in its organizational infancy at this period, cricket did seem to be showing promise for future growth. Although the New York *Herald*'s proclamation, in 1845, that cricket was "fast progressing throughout the land—in every city, town and hamlet are clubs formed," was probably the first of what would be many overexaggerations of cricket's popularity, the game was beginning to attract some popular interest. That same year the *Herald* announced the formation of "two or three" new clubs within New York alone, among them a team of 16- to 18-year-olds in Bedford, Long Island. Cricket clubs were also appearing in other areas of the country, such as Charleston, South Carolina (where the local club seems to have been associated with that city's prestigious Jockey Club), Rochester, Cincinnati, Natchez, Mississippi, and Syracuse. The game was also being played in Chicago as early as 1840 and in Macon, Georgia, by 1845.[20]

What the sporting press seldom mentioned, however, was that many of these clubs were being set up not by Americans but expatriate Englishmen. At least one New York area club, the Jamaica, a club reportedly organized with the assistance of the New York Club, was predominantly American, but this seems to have been the exception rather than the rule. The Newark Club, for instance, was composed largely of Yorkshire immigrants under the guidance of former St. George cricketer George Wheatcroft. Another New York club, the Washington, was largely composed of "out of practice" north Englishmen, while the Syracuse club owed its existence to the initiative of the former Brooklyn Englishman, Henry Pearson. The situation seems to have been the same outside New York, with the two clubs organized in Cincinnati in 1845 staffed predominantly by Sheffield mechanics and a number of immigrant English Jews.[21]

In only one area were Americans beginning to take up cricket in significant numbers during this period: Philadelphia.

Cricket had reportedly been played in this city by immigrant English mill workers as early as 1841, but this activity did not reach a state of stable organization until English importer Robert Waller drew together the English mechanics in the Kensington neighborhood with the "Hardy Tavern" group that played on George Tichnor's farm in west Philadelphia, to set up the Union Cricket Club in 1843. This club seems to have been specifically organized as a direct rival to New York's St. George club, a status it had successfully achieved by 1846, the year it managed to beat its famous New York rival in what the *Spirit* claimed was "the greatest game ever played in the United States."[22]

Like other urban cricket clubs of this period, the Union was a predominantly English organization, but it did have among its members at least two Americans, William E. Whitman, a lawyer, and John K. Mitchell, a prominent Philadelphia physician who had been educated in Scotland.[23]

Though he does not appear to have been a playing member, Mitchell proved to be an important link between the club and a number of young men from Philadelphia's more prominent families, such as William Rotch Wister, who was encouraged, in 1845, to form a cricket club among his Germantown friends, most of whom were students at the University of Pennsylvania. The match among these young men on September 20, 1845, was, in all likelihood, the first cricket match of the modern era played exclusively among Americans.[24]

Historians have offered several explanations why the Americans in Philadelphia, rather than those in New York, began to take up cricket during this period in significant numbers, Adelman suggesting it was because Philadelphia's upper class was more willing to involve themselves in the game.[25]

Although there is certainly some truth to this, a more important reason why cricket developed differently in Philadelphia than it did in New York was because Philadelphians, unlike New Yorkers, were willing to accept English assistance only on condition that they, and not the English community, would control the cricket in their city.

Evidence for this claim appeared many years later in a letter Waller himself sent to the *American Cricketer*, a document that sheds light on the early years of Philadelphia cricket. According to Waller, it was he, and not earlier English residents such as the Tichnors, who provided cohesion and leadership to the predominantly working class English members of the Union Club. It was probably Waller's intention to impose a St. George-type leadership scheme upon the Union Club—subordinating the working class players to the captaincy and control of "gentlemen" players—that attracted Mitchell to the organization, and, indirectly, other upper class Philadelphians. This arrangement, however, apparently broke down soon after Waller relocated to New York, the Union Club eventually breaking up, by the late 1840s, due to the animosities that existed among its working class members.[26]

As a result of this experience, upper class Philadelphians never again seemed willing to tolerate English control of the cricket clubs to which they belonged. On the evidence of another contemporary of this period, Barnet Phillips, who published a reminiscence of early Philadelphia cricket in the September 22, 1894, issue of *Harpers Weekly*, it seems that this was the direction Philadelphia cricket was heading even during its earliest years. Phillips also credits early English mill workers with encouraging the game among his young Germantown friends, youngsters who eventually became proficient enough at the game that they were soon able to beat their more experienced English neighbors in a match in 1845 signifying to Phillips the "true beginning of American cricket."[27]

Phillips believed the score to this match was lost, but in all probability, it was the match reported in both the *Spirit* and the *Anglo-American* (this seems certain because the published score confirms Phillips's statement that one side was captained by William Rotch Wister, against a team that went by the name of "Germantown"). Far from revealing a contest between American and English players, the match rosters show, instead, that both teams were predominantly American, the supposedly "English" Germantown team having among its players Jones Wister, William Rotch's brother, and even one player, a B. Richard, who had been an earlier member of Phillips' own junior club.[28]

The organizational impetus for cricket in Philadelphia during the mid-1840s may have been the same as it was in New York: resident Englishmen trying to encourage Americans to take up the game. But whereas the American cricket response in New York remained weak and subservient to English control (indicated by the failure of the New York Cricket Club to assert itself as a viable focal point for American interest), the Americans in Philadelphia who took up the game were, from the start, beginning to resist English control, by either segregating themselves from English players (the case with Phillips and his friends), or subordinating to their control the English influence on the clubs to which they belonged. As we shall see, both trends would powerfully affect the character of Philadelphia cricket over the following decade.

Despite the publicity that had been generated over the U.S.-Canada matches, and the support of such influential publications as the *Spirit*, it is doubtful cricket was arousing any more than lukewarm interest from the average American during this period. In the New York area cricket interest still centered around only two clubs, the St. George and the New York, a situation that offered such limited competitive opportunities that some local players, in the late 1840s, resorted to the old North vs South of England, or married vs single, formats for their matches.[29]

Over the next few years a number of new clubs did appear in such locations as Boston, Connecticut, Pittsburgh, and Milwaukee, but these were offset by declines, at least temporarily, in the cricket activity that had existed earlier in such locations as Syracuse, Albany, and Cincinnati.[30]

Even in Philadelphia, the initial burst of interest in the game during the mid-1840s soon waned. In the seven years following the demise of the Union Club, cricket activity in that city seems to have been limited to a few informal matches among Americans and Nottingham youngsters, a level of interest so anemic, even William Rotch Wister admitted cricket in Philadelphia was "as dead as a door nail" during this period.[31]

It shouldn't be particularly surprising that cricket was unable to secure a significant place in the leisure life of New Yorkers or Philadelphians during this period. Most Americans who took an interest in the game probably did so out of curiosity, rather than from any compelling attraction to the game. The New York press may have proclaimed cricket to be "fashionable" and "much in vogue" to its readers in the mid-1840s. To other Americans, however, it was probably, at best, little more than a "novelty," as it was in Pittsburgh in 1850 or, at worst, something as strange "as some Hindoo sacrifice," which seemed to be the judgment of many of the Bostonians who attended a match between their city's club and the St. George in 1850.[32]

From its earliest appearance as an organized sport, cricket was struggling to overcome the "incorrect opinion" most Americans had of the game, a perception that seemed to insist that this game, for all its recognized values, must be specifically accommodated and adjusted to American's cultural life. Even the *Spirit* couldn't let its admiration for the game obscure its own concern about this, querying, almost from the time of its first cricket reports, "What can be done to naturalize this beautiful game in America?"[33]

It would be a question critical to the subsequent history of American cricket, and one that, interestingly, could possibly have been addressed during this important juncture in the game's history by one New York cricket club in particular: the Union Star of Brooklyn.

This club seems to have been organized in 1844 around the English immigrant community of Brooklyn, some of whom had been involved with the earliest organized matches of the late 1830s. In the beginning, the Union Star seems to have had same overlapping membership with the St. George (the Union club's founder, Henry Russell, and his brother William were on the St. George team that played in Toronto in 1840, while another of its members, Rouse, was on the St. George team that played in Canada in 1846) and even used the St. George ground at Bloomingdale Road before securing its own playing area, in 1845, near Ft. Greene in Brooklyn.[34]

At first glance it would seem that the Union Star came into existence as a matter of convenience, the cricket-playing English residents of Brooklyn preferring to have a club in their own neighborhood rather than belonging to one in Manhattan. Other evidence, however, seems to indicate the Union Star may have been set up as a result of some fundamental differences between itself and the St. George. The most compelling evidence for this lies in the fact that the two clubs, despite their proximity and personal familiarity, never played each other, even though the Union Star once traveled as far as Syracuse for a match.[35]

If, in fact, relations between the two clubs were strained, what were the reasons? My own feeling is the Union Star had organized itself to counter the St. George's attempt to impose an old-world class structure upon New York cricket. We know that the Union Star founder, Henry Russell, an English Jew and popular ballad singer, was "quite a lion in a certain circle" of New York society during this period, a religious and occupational background out of line with the Christian-mercantile elite of the St. George. What's more, Henry, and his brother William, a florist who was reputed to have been "the most scientific and finished cricketer of his day," seemed to have shown much greater willingness to promote the game among Americans than the St. George. Henry reportedly helped coach the New York Club during its early years, while William would later win acclaim as the person who was most responsible for introducing cricket into New York.[36]

The Union Star's greater openness with its cricket did not go unnoticed by the local press, the *Herald* going out of its way to point out, during the club's match with a team of Sheffield players in 1845, that this Brooklyn club was far more accommodating than other "would-be-aristocratic clubs" in New York, no doubt a veiled reference to the St. George.[37]

The Union Star's apparent unwillingness to play cricket under traditional English class constraints may have had a further, unforeseen benefit: it put the club in a position to appreciate and understand that cricket, to be popular with Americans, would have to be brought into closer conformity with America's own ball-playing traditions.

Adelman has pointed out the Union Star's close contacts with the Brooklyn baseball club, one of New York's earliest organized baseball clubs. The two clubs shared the same grounds and seemed to have some overlapping membership. At least four members of the Union Star were in the Brooklyn lineup during that club's historic matches with the New York Baseball Club in the Fall of 1845, widely recognized as the first baseball games of the modern era.[38]

Did the Union Star's contact with early New York baseball in any way influence its perception of what American cricket should be? From contemporary reports we only know the Union Star's playing style was uncharacteristic of more orthodox cricket and that the club seemed to exhibit a very nontraditional, confrontational attitude in some of its matches. More revealing evidence of possible transcultural sensitivity appeared years later, through William Russell's concern over the direction cricket was taking during the game's upsurge in popularity in the mid-1850s. At a time when underhand pitching was making baseball a more attractive and accessible game for novice Americans, Russell was upset that the faster, harder to hit (and, in some instances, illegal) roundarm bowling he was seeing in local cricket was turning Americans away from cricket, a situation further aggravated by what he saw as an unwillingness of experienced English players to stand aside for the benefit of more inexperienced Americans.[39]

Did the Union Star club have the potential of becoming the "Knickerbockers" club of American cricket, one that, through its direct contacts with early baseball and resistance to English traditionalism, could have assumed a position of leadership in "naturalizing" early American cricket?

Intriguing as this question is, it must be left to historical conjecture. The Union Star seems to have passed out of existence after 1847, though a number of its early members would resurface among later Brooklyn cricket clubs (Henry Russell himself was still playing for the Long Island Cricket Club as late as 1860).[40]

The demise of the Union Star club underscored the major difficulty early American cricket was facing during this period: a sport Americans seemed to recognize as having some core value and appeal, but one that must conform directly to, rather than demand, as a condition for its acceptance, any modifications in America's own ball-playing culture. Even John K. Mitchell, despite his strong sympathy with the game's English traditions and cultural prestige, knew quite well that with cricket, as it must be with all other institutions that aspired to become part of America's cultural fabric, "the useful must first take place in a new country before the ornamental."[41]

3

A Game, a Sport, but Not a National Institution

As it had been in the mid-1840s, the nationalistic fervor surrounding the U.S.-Canada matches was once again the catalyst for reviving American cricket interest during the early 1850s.

Several attempts had been made to revive the series since the "unfortunate occurrence" that marred the 1846 match had brought the annual event to an end. The *Spirit* had reportedly been authorized to offer a $1,500 prize if the two sides would agree to renew the series the following year, but differences apparently remained unresolved until 1853, when a representative Toronto side agreed to come to New York and renew the rivalry.[1]

If cricket supporters were hoping this event would refocus public attention upon their game, these hopes proved to be well founded, and for several reasons. This was the first match in which teams were permitted to include players from more than one club, the "American" team in this particular match being drawn not only from the St. George but also the New York, Syracuse, and Newark clubs. It was an arrangement that seems to have infused the event with greater stability and prestige, to an extent that later observers always looked to this 1853 match as the official beginning of the U.S.-Canada series.[2]

To maximize spectator interest, the match was played on the St. George ground at the Red House Tavern on 2nd and 106th Streets in Harlem, a "fashionable resort" at that time for New York's sporting elite that also had a fine horse racing track and pigeon shooting area.[3]

By all accounts, the event was a resounding success, with an estimated 2,500 New Yorkers making their way to Harlem on match day, "by stage, railway, and all sorts of vehicles, from a milk waggon [sic] up to a trotting buggy." Public interest ran even higher during the series next two home matches. "Not less" than 7-8,000 spectators were reportedly in attendance for the 1856 match, 5,000 on the last day of the 1858 contest, both of these played on the St.George's attractive new ground in the Elysian Fields, eulogized by contemporaries as "a perfect picture of cultivated and rural pastury."[4]

To the sporting press, the public excitement associated with these matches was far more than just a passing fad. To the *Clipper* these matches were powerful evidence that a "new era in popular amusements . . . [has] set in," one that was drawing more and more Americans to the enjoyment of team sports participation. Understandably, many observers believed cricket would be the primary beneficiary of this trend. "A few more matches like the one recorded," the *Spirit* was prophesying after the 1853 U.S.-Canada match, "will make the pastime as popular here as in the mother country."[5]

These were expectations that, at the time, did not appear to be unrealistic. As a result of the same match, the *Herald* was soon reporting that cricket was "extending itself to all parts of the United States," an estimate echoed by the *Clipper* a few years later, in its claim that "throughout the length and breadth of the land clubs are being formed." No longer, it seems, was the American public looking upon this English sport as "an exclusive sort of game, with a certain air of mysterious dignity about it which prevented many from aspiring to it." Instead, cricket was now becoming, as it was in Newark by 1855, "the rage with men of health and activity."[6]

Though many of these contemporary testimonies to cricket's popularity were anecdotal, they appeared to be confirmed by what quantitative evidence is available from this period. According to the *Clipper*, the 100 organized matches played in the New York area in 1856 tripled the following year, by which time the paper was also claiming there were at least 5,000 "match playing" cricketers in the mid-Atlantic region.[7]

It was during 1857 that antebellum American cricket seemed to have reached something of a high-water mark in popularity. To the *American Cricketer*, looking back from 1879, this was the year of "the great cricket revival," a time when so many Americans were taking an interest in the game, according to the *Clipper*, that "each one must have his bat and ball, and each proclaims himself a cricketer." Even among the delegates to that year's national baseball convention there seemed to be a prevailing opinion, notwithstanding the growing presence of their own bat and ball game, that "more Americans played cricket" during this particular period than they did any other team sport.[8]

To an extent, these prognostications were self-fulfilling, since they were made by the very parties who were working on the game's behalf. Adelman has pointed out the great influence the antebellum sporting press was beginning to exert upon America's emerging sporting tastes, an influence that was clearly working in cricket's favor. In addition to the *Spirit of the Times*, both *Porter's Spirit of the Times*, which began publication in 1856 as a breakaway publication from the *Spirit*, and another New York sporting paper, *Wilkes Spirit of the Times*, started up three years later, provided extensive and sympathetic cricket reports throughout this decade. But all these publications were overshadowed by Frank Queen's New York *Clipper,* which, from its beginnings in 1853, quickly assumed the journalistic leadership in promoting team sports such as baseball and cricket, to an extent that by 1861 it could claim, with full justification, that "for the manly and invigorating sports of cricket and baseball . . . no journal in America has paid so much attention as have we."[9]

For the most part the *Clipper* was able to maintain its preeminent standing in this area of sports reporting because of one person, Henry Chadwick. An Englishman by birth, Chadwick joined the *Clipper* in 1856 as its cricket and baseball reporter, the start of a 30-year association with the publication, over which time he would establish himself as the country's most respected and influential advocate of the two sports.

As an astute and critical observer of all the sports he covered, Chadwick was always sympathetic to cricket's attempts to find a place on the American sports scene, not surprising since he himself was a cricket player who never seemed to let his commitment to journalistic objectivity compromise his love for the game. Chadwick seems to have been personally involved with the formation of the American Cricket Club in 1861, and in 1872 he persuaded a number of his fellow New York journalists to form their own recreational cricket club, the Prospect Park club. He remained an active cricket player well into his 60s and, at the age of 75, could still be found keeping score for a veterans match between New York and Philadelphia.[10]

Nor was Chadwick by any means the only American journalist who took a personal interest in the cricket he was covering.

William Lacey, proprietor of the Albany *State Register* held the presidency of his city's cricket club from its inception in 1853, the beginning of a nearly 30-year association with organized cricket. Rufus King, the influential if controversial antebellum editor of the *Milwaukee Sentinel* was "passionately fond" of the game during this period, an interest that no doubt accounts for the paper's extensive cricket reports during the early 1850s.[11]

G. T. C. North of the *East New York Journal* was a long time playing member of his community's cricket club, as was H. A. Rockafield, founder of the Lancaster, Pennsylvania, *Public Register* in 1859. The editors of at least two small Wisconsin newspapers, George Tenney of the Monroe *Sentinel* and John Parker of the *Markesan Journal,* were also the moving forces behind the formation of their communities' antebellum cricket clubs.[12]

Despite cricket's growing visibility among Americans by the mid-1850s, the game's future still heavily depended upon the English immigrant community's ability and willingness to translate the game to native Americans, a rate of success that varied widely.

Cricket clubs organized by itinerant Englishmen for the purpose of maintaining ethnic identity tended to be either unsuccessful in attracting Americans or proved to be short lived. The best example of this continued to be the St. George Club of New York. Though still widely recognized by most sports observers as the club that "stands at the head of cricket in every respect" during this period, the St. George was never really able to effectively apply this standing to the benefit of America's emerging interest in the game. The club did have American members, and always professed a sensitivity to American interests, but it preferred to staff its teams with English immigrants and strongly resisted all challenges to its authority.[13]

Outside of New York, cricket organizations that depended upon nonpermanent English residents were also generally ineffective in attracting Americans to the game, such as the short-lived Cleveland Cricket Club, which was composed largely of "old players," the Scotch Star and Thistle club of Boston, and the West Farms club of New York, whose English working class members aroused the animosity of local American players.[14]

The early cricket clubs of Chicago and San Francisco, which seemed to be centered around those cities' British diplomatic communities (W. R. Booker, San Francisco's British consul, was president of that city's cricket club before the Civil War), also had limited success in attracting significant numbers of Americans to the game.[15]

Those English immigrants, on the other hand, who became permanent residents of the communities in which they resided showed more success in winning Americans over to the game. The direct and continued patronage of the immigrant English industrialists of Paterson, New Jersey, ensured a positive community interest in that city's cricket for many years, both before and after the Civil War. In Milwaukee, the Sivyer family of Kent, some of whom had been among that city's founding settlers, remained the nucleus of local cricket activity from the early 1850s to the 1880s.[16]

Nor was local cricket interest restricted to urban areas with large English communities. The cricket organized before the Civil War by the immigrant English workers in the little Massachusetts town of Shelbourne Falls survived there for at least another two decades. A similar pattern of continuity developed in the little Wisconsin community of Sussex, where the game was long supported by members of the influential Weaver family, who had immigrated to the area from Kent in the late 1840s. In another little Wisconsin community, Mazomanie, the game remained part of community life for at least a generation after the first English farmers had been recruited to the area in the mid-1840s by the British Temperance Society.[17]

In at least one small American community, Ripon, Wisconsin, cricket underwent an almost complete transformation from an ethnic tradition into a small town American institution. Here the game had originally been organized by Henry Lambert, an Englishman who had played cricket in Syracuse before relocating his family to Wisconsin in 1856. From that time, and over the next 50 years, cricket not only enjoyed an almost unbroken presence in the community life of this little central Wisconsin town, it was accepted by a broad cross section of the community's populace.[18]

Even in Philadelphia, English influences played a more significant role in reviving American interest in cricket than later Philadelphians seemed willing to concede. The three most prominent American clubs that appeared in the city during this period, the Philadelphia, the Germantown, and the Young America, were, in all likelihood, inspired by an upsurge in local immigrant cricket activity. The Washington Club, organized in the early 1850s by English mill workers, was soon followed by the Star Cricket Club, set up by William Jarvis, an Englishman from Leicestershire who had played in Pittsburgh before relocating to Germantown where he ran the Star Tavern. A highly accomplished player, who epitomized in his playing style, "perfection in the art of batting," Jarvis reportedly coached the Newhall brothers, the foremost American cricketers of this era. Another resident Englishman, James Thorp, reportedly coached the prominent antebellum Philadelphia player Jones Wister.[19]

In a way, the difficulties American cricket faced under the guidance of an English community uncertain of its exact responsibilities toward this emerging American cricket interest could be best seen in the many candidates nominated for the title "Father of American Cricket" during this period.

In later years, when Philadelphia held undisputed sway over American cricket, this honor was universally accorded to William Rotch Wister. To earlier observers, however, it was no American but a handful of Englishmen who were deemed worthy of this title.[20]

According to Picton Milner, the "Father of American Cricket" was Henry Tinson, the "overbearing captain" of the St. George Club during the 1840s, while to the *California Spirit of the Times* it was Harry Groom, a standout player for the St. George Club before relocating to

California in the late 1850s, who had "done more than any other to establish the game in the United States." Perhaps in recognition of their role in Philadelphia cricket, this honor was also bestowed upon both William Jarvis and the English player/coach of the Philadelphia Cricket Club, William Bradshaw.[21]

The claims of all these men were based largely upon their organizational contributions to the game. If, on the other hand, a more sympathetic understanding of the needs of American players is taken into consideration, then Henry Sharp, president of the New York Cricket Club during the 1850s, was probably the worthiest recipient of the title "Father of American Cricket." A Chartist from Derbyshire who had left England and come to New York at the height of that movement's political turmoil in 1849, Sharp ran a glass staining business while maintaining an active role in New York area cricket. Unlike most immigrant Englishmen of his era, Sharp seems to have been deeply appreciative of the differences between American and English sporting tastes. Open-minded and sympathetic toward baseball, which he recognized for its unique appeal to Americans, Sharp was never reluctant to compromise ethnic interests if it would further cricket's cause among Americans. He seems to have been the organizing force behind the first American vs English match in 1856, advocated the inclusion of Americans in the U.S.-Canada matches and even organized a cricket team among his employees, certainly all strong testimony to his expressed belief that "to be a thorough cricketer is to be a thorough man."[22]

Sharp wasn't the only member of the English cricket fraternity who sensed an obligation to interest Americans in the game. The *Albion*, the voice of New York's immigrant English community, expressed a hope that the renewed U.S.-Canada matches would act as "an inducement held out to our American friends to join heart and hand" in the pleasures of the game, an offer more and more English-dominated clubs were beginning to put into practice.[23]

By the mid-1850s, membership in the Paterson Club consisted of not only "old players" but also "many Americans" and "other players of less pretensions," a composition that also seemed to characterize Buffalo's cricket club. As early as 1855 all but four members of the Franklin, New Jersey, club were Americans, and within a few years of this, Americans were in the majority at both the Rumford Club of Waltham and the Lowell Cricket Club, though the best players on the latter club were still English. In its efforts to attract more Americans, the Newark Club even adopted the somewhat controversial policy of giving preference to its younger American players over its older but more experienced English members.[24]

More significantly, more and more Americans themselves were beginning to take the initiative in organizing cricket clubs. Some of these clubs were organized around individuals already familiar with the game, such as the New York Cricket Club member Edward F. Shonnard, who established a club in his home town of Yonkers. Many other clubs, however, were set up by rank beginners. Novices organized the Poughkeepsie, New York, and Rochester clubs in 1856, while "green hands" were responsible for the Bloomington, Illinois, and Richmond, Virginia, clubs, both organized in 1857.[25]

Largely inexperienced Americans also set up their own clubs in Albany (the Excelsior), Warren, Massachusetts (the United) and Detroit (the Pontiac). The young Americans in the last mentioned club evidently progressed so rapidly at the game that the *Spirit,* for one, was quite convinced these were no "backwoods Yankee cricketers."[26]

In a few locations, Americans even took up the game on a more extended, regional basis. The little eastern Pennsylvania coal mining communities of Pottsville, St. Clair, Port Carbon, and Schuylkill Haven (the last mentioned known for its "fighting men, big pigs and little children") were all supporting cricket clubs by 1858, as were the little upstate New York communities of Gloversville, Johnstown, and Amsterdam. To the American players on the Amsterdam club (which included Nicholas E. Young, who would later gain fame as the long-serving secretary and president of the National Baseball League), cricket interest exceeded, on a proportional basis, that of even the largest metropolitan areas. "Cricket in Amsterdam," local cricket club president Isaac Jackson claimed, "in reference to advancement, certainly has the superiority over Philadelphia when compared as to the respective sizes of the two places, boosting of some five different clubs in a village whose population does not exceed three thousand."[27]

This comparison to Philadelphia was, however, an open acknowledgment that the Quaker city, by this period, was beginning to stand apart for its unusually high level of American cricket interest. Here the game was attracting more American players than anywhere else, an interest that grew "like wildfire" throughout the mid-1850s, to a point that by 1857, one could find "on all the vacant lots of the city and suburbs . . . cricket matches daily."[28]

For the most part, the pattern that had emerged in Philadelphia cricket a decade earlier—a reliance upon the English community for competitive guidance but not organizational control—asserted itself even more forcefully during the 1850s. A number of the city's more prominent clubs during this period were set up by Philadelphians who had learned their cricket in the 1840s, such as William Rotch Wister, who, with a number of players from the old "junior club," set up first the "American gentlemen" club in 1853 and then, on February 10, 1854, formally organized the Philadelphia Cricket Club. Younger relatives and friends of these players organized their own club, Germantown, on August 10 of that year, while the still younger friends and relatives of these players, denied membership because of their immaturity, organized, on November 19, 1855, their own club, the Young America.[29]

As was the case in other areas of the country, many Philadelphia clubs of this period also relied heavily upon resident Englishmen for coaching and playing assistance. What competitive success the Philadelphia club enjoyed during its early years, for instance, was largely due to the contributions of its more experienced English members, such as William Bradshaw and Tom Senior. But while an English presence remained proportionately high with American clubs in most other areas, it steadily diminished in Philadelphia throughout the decade, due, no doubt, to the large influx of American players, more and more of whom, like the players on the Young America Club, were largely self-taught and did not belong to organizations that had any English members. As a result, Philadelphia cricket gradually shifted from its early English vs. English competitive makeup to American vs. English (seen in such matches as the "Boys of Philadelphia" vs the Philadelphia Cricket Club in 1856) to, eventually, a predominantly American vs. American character. As Jable has pointed out, this progression reached a point that, by the time of the Civil War, very few Philadelphia cricket clubs even had English members.[30]

For at least one segment of American society (the one always most insistent upon moral propriety), its educational institutions, an established old-world tradition of respectability worked very much to cricket's advantage. The American educational establishment, or at least that segment willing to assert the importance of physical education, had long been aware of cricket's pedagogical value, the *American Journal of Education* declaring, as early as 1827, that the game was the "best exercise" available for student's physical well-being.[31]

Perhaps the administration of New York's Free Academy, that city's first publicly supported high school and the forerunner of today's City College of New York, was sympathetic enough to these ideas to permit organized intra-class cricket playing among its students in the early 1850s, an example the *Herald* believed could be "successfully practiced in all the colleges and common schools and educational institutions in the United States."[32]

For the most part, however, it was not administrative bodies but enlightened individuals who recognized and promoted the educational benefits of cricket during this period. The Cambridge-educated English immigrant Samuel Robert Calthrop gained a measure of notoriety for organizing a cricket team among the students at his small private school in Bridgeport, Connecticut, in 1856, something the *Clipper* heralded as "opening a new field" for cricket's advancement in America. Less well known were the efforts of such farsighted educators as Nathaniel Allen, who encouraged the game among the students at his private school in Newton, Massachusetts; Myron Hazelton, who supported the game at New York's Clinton Institute; and William C. Anderson, president of Ohio's Miami College, who personally recommended the game to his students.[33]

Efforts like these received a helpful, if fortuitous, boost with the publication in 1857 of Thomas Hughes's *Tom Brown's Schooldays*, whose idealized portrait of life in the English public schools drew attention to the character building value of sports, particularly cricket, in the education process.[34]

There is little doubt Hughes's novel, which was immensely popular in America, had a direct and beneficial impact upon Americans' perception of school sports. Within a year of the book's appearance, students at Harvard (which Hughes would later criticize for its neglect of athletics) were "playing at cricket . . . in a manner that would excite the admiration, even if it shocked the taste, of Tom Brown." Although no direct causal connection can be proved, it certainly was not completely coincidental that within a year of the novel's publication cricket clubs had also appeared in such far-flung American educational institutions as Princeton University; the University of Pennsylvania; Assumption College in Sandwich, Massachusetts; Phillips Academy in Andover, Massachusetts; and the Kentucky Military Institute near Frankfort.[35]

Though both Adelman and Kirsch have demonstrated, through their extensive sociological analysis of antebellum American cricket and baseball players, that cricket was played by all social classes, contemporary evidence leaves little doubt the cricket "boom" of the mid-1850s was very much a middle-class phenomenon that relied upon the most achievement-oriented strata of American society, such as the "influential gentlemen" of Albany, the "influential and enterprising citizens" of New Brunswick, New Jersey, and the "first citizens" of St. Louis, all of whom were the moving force behind the antebellum cricket clubs in their respective communities.[36]

By looking more closely into their personal backgrounds, we can get an even clearer idea of just who these "influential" people were who were attracted to cricket during this period.

Among the New York cricketers portrayed in the lighthearted article submitted to the *Spirit* in 1849 by "Gruel," himself a poet and the "embodiment of enthusiasm for cricket," we find "Diapason," an organist, "77th Street," a downtown businessman, and "Hoboken," most likely a reference to the prominent American painter William Ranney, who, as a cricket player, was talented enough to occasionally top score for his New York Cricket Club, for which he also, reportedly, acted as record keeper.[37]

Both P. H. Reid of the East New York Cricket Club and A. A. Rockafield, of the Lancaster, Pennsylvania, club had wide-ranging literary and scientific interests, the former as founder of the East New York literary society, the latter as founder of his city's Linnean Society. Charles Mayers, a member of the Madison, Wisconsin, cricket club in the late 1850s, went on to enjoy a long and successful career as that state's assistant superintendent of public instruction and later as its state librarian. In addition to his interests as an amateur archeologist, doctor William Sweney, of the Redwing, Minnesota, cricket club, also served as the president of that state's medical society.[38]

As cricket began to reveal its potential as a focal point of mass appeal, it even began to attract the involvement of individuals who made a career of gauging popular sentiment. Buffalo aldermen Thomas Merrigan and A. S. Plumley, along with ward supervisor John Hines and city treasurer Joseph Churchman, all belonged to their city cricket club in the 1850s. Cricket's growing public visibility was also used to advantage by Chicago alderman William Carpenter, who was the moving force behind the formation of his city's Union Cricket Club in 1858.[39] Francis B. Phelps, an early member of Detroit's Pontiac Cricket Club, went on to serve as that city's acting mayor during the Civil War, an office Redwing, Minnesota, cricketer Charles McClure was also elected to in his small town.[40]

At least three other cricket players from this period, J. Frank Crockett, a member of the Boston Cricket Club who also served as the president of the Massachusetts cricket convention; Richard Weaver, a member of the Sussex, Wisconsin, cricket club; and William Webster, a member of the Milwaukee Cricket Club, all went on to later serve as representatives in their respective state legislatures. C. P. E. Johnson, an antebellum member of St. Louis's Jackson Cricket Club, achieved the even loftier political office of Missouri's lieutenant-governorship, to which he was elected in the 1870s.[41]

By the mid-1850s then, cricket seemed well poised to come to the forefront of the "rising tide" of sports interest that was sweeping across the country's larger urban areas, a trend clearly seen in the growing popularity of not only cricket and baseball but such regional "folk" type ball games as "trap ball," wicket, and "prisoner's base," all of which enjoyed a degree of organized following during this era as well.[42]

Unlike most of these bat-and-ball sports, however, cricket enjoyed the advantages of a supportive sporting press as well as the prestige of being a well-established international sport with a proven record of character-building benefits. Above all, cricket was simply a game Americans of this period enjoyed playing, a fact thoroughly confirmed from contemporary testimonies.

To Elliot Harrington, an American who played the game in Waltham during the late 1850s, cricket was "the most absorbing and fascinating thing that could possibly come into a boy's life at that time." Sutherland Law, a prominent Philadelphia cricketer after the Civil War, was so absorbed with the game as a schoolboy that friends recalled how he "spent many an hour . . . playing cricket with a handkerchief rolled up for a ball and a copy of Caesar's *Commentaries* for a bat." Many of the University of Michigan students who joined the school's cricket club just after the Civil War soon "became so infatuated with the game that they [found] it impossible to relinquish their customary sport even for a short time." In some instances, this appeal seemed to hold up well even in the face of such competing sports interests as baseball. Looking back over his long career in Massachusetts baseball, James D'Wolf Lovett, who was the last of his peer group to abandon cricket for baseball, always claimed, "I was very enthusiastic over this game [cricket] and if it would have even held its own should no doubt have remained loyal to it."[43]

If cricket was, in fact, a sport about which it could be said, as the *Milwaukee Sentinel* did in 1855, "the more you see it, the better you like it," why then did it fail to live up to these expectations?[44]

Antebellum observers themselves generally pointed to two main reasons why cricket failed as an American sport: it was English, and it was too slow, drawn-out, and unexciting for the American "temperament."

In an era characterized by an intense Anglo-American rivalry in international politics and economics, cricket was no doubt handicapped by its identity as an English institution. But this did not seem to become an important issue until observers began to object to the right of teams composed exclusively of English residents to represent the "United States" in the highly visible U.S.-Canada matches.

The *Herald* expressed an uneasiness in seeing the Union Jack and St. George flags, rather than the Stars and Stripes, flying over the Hoboken ground during the 1845 match, but by 1856, *Porters* was openly disavowing the "American" team's very right to represent the United States; "We cannot claim the honor of the victory for Americans, the simple fact being that the victors are natives of Great Britain." This observation was no doubt further aggravated when the *Albion*, commenting on the same match, openly asserted, "We beg our colonial friends not hereupon to talk of the 'Yankees.' Every man on the American side is English born and bred."[45]

In the beginning, a systematic exclusion of native players, irritating though it may have been to nationalistic sentiment, could be justified on the ground that American players were simply not good enough. *Bells Life,* Britain's most influential sports journal of that period, simply believed the United States could not beat Canada without a predominantly English side. To the American press, this line of reasoning progressively lost its validity as more and more Americans began to show proficiency in the game, especially after 1859, when it became clear the United States' success that year, the first on Canadian soil, was due to the contributions of the team's American players. This was also the first U.S.-Canada match organized under the auspices of the New York and Philadelphia clubs, rather than the St. George (something the *Clipper* had been advocating since 1853), a shift in organizational control the *New York Times* felt was "high time" and one that probably also contributed to the United States success in the 1860 match, the first in which the U.S. team included a large contingent of American players.[46]

It was the loss of this control over the most important event in the cricket calendar that seems to have incited the St. George, still the country's most prominent cricket club, into an increasingly aloof, uncooperative, and nationalistic posture. The club refused to allow the use of its grounds in Hoboken for the 1860 U.S.-Canada match, and even organized a competing match with Montreal, "that great abiding place . . . where Americans are esteemed about as highly as the abolitionists are in South Carolina." The St. George further aroused the ire of the sports press with its decision, late that year, to charge an admission fee for all matches played on its recently enclosed ground, derisively dubbed "the ten cent enclosure" by the *Clipper*.[47]

It would be wrong to presume the St. George never acknowledged any obligation to developing or encouraging cricket among Americans. The club had long recognized the value of sports to "encourage neighborliness" with their American hosts, and took some pride in its claim that "the rights and pleasures of the . . . more inexperienced players have generally been respected." Club members had helped organize cricket among the Free Academy students and occasionally tried to organize junior matches among its members. The club could also point to a number of Americans who held office in the club by 1858.[48]

In spite of all this, the St. George couldn't shrug off its reputation as a bastion of English nationalism. This was the organization, after all, that while publicly insisting it alone was responsible for popularizing cricket, would, at its private dinner parties, hurl "the accustomed sneers" at the "blarsted country" in which it resided.[49]

Even before this time, the St. George was, in the eyes of the American press, rapidly abnegating its responsibilities toward national cricket leadership for a narrow and haughty ethnic exclusiveness. "If conceit were as expansive as steam," the *North American and United States Gazette* charged in 1857, "the St. George of New York would have power enough to propel a frigate." It was largely because of the deteriorating reputation of the St. George in particular, and the New York English community in general, that cricket took on such a nationalistically negative identity. Those who played cricket could no longer avoid being associated with the "clannishness," "selfish asceticism," and "snobbishness" of the English cricket community. Even worse, these immigrant players appeared, in some instances, to be no more than "gilt gingerbread upstarts," displaying "insufferable insolence and egotism" toward their game, while giving preference to their own members, some without even "a rudimentary knowledge" of cricket over more talented outsiders in representative matches.[50]

In time, it was only natural that sports observers would lay the blame for cricket's decline upon the doorstep of the immigrant English community, whose inflexible insistence upon controlling cricket's direction had been tantamount to a refusal "to sacrifice their national desire . . . in order that the game might be popular in America." By the late 1860s, this explanation had already reached canonical proportions, typified by the *New York Times'* insistence that if not for this English exclusiveness "we have not the least doubt that cricket would have gained much of the popularity its innate attractions make it deserving of."[51]

Adelman's claim, then, that cricket declined in America not because it was English but because it was "run for and by Englishmen" seems to be quite correct. But this also immediately begs the question: why, then, didn't Americans interested in cricket simply disassociate themselves from the English community? Contemporary observers weren't willing to go as far as the *American Cricketer* did in 1877, in openly declaring Americans and English "don't mix well" at cricket, but there was a feeling Americans shouldn't be reluctant to take for them-selves a game of demonstrated appeal regardless of its origin. "We cannot conceive what objection there can be," the *Clipper* proclaimed on cricket's behalf in 1857, "in our adoption of whatever is the good of the country, let it come from where it may."[52]

American cricketers were beginning to move toward some form of self-determination as early as 1849, the year the American members of the New York club issued a challenge to any other American team in the country. This challenge went unanswered until 1854, when the Americans of the New York and Newark clubs staged the area's first exclusively American cricket match, an event that proved to be moderately successful in attracting public attention, as did similar matches played between Americans of the Newark and Philadelphia clubs in 1856 and the Newark and Brooklyn clubs in 1860.

To achieve legitimacy in their efforts at cricket, however, Americans had to prove they could play the game as well as their English neighbors. According to Adelman, one of the main reasons why Americans were turning to the more easily learned baseball during this period was because they simply weren't able to "hone their skills" at the more technically advanced English game.[53]

But surely this cannot be correct. As more and more Americans began to take up cricket during the mid-1850s, the skill gap between them and their more experienced English neighbors began to noticeably close, the strongest evidence of this coming from the results of the English vs American matches that were becoming increasingly frequent during this period "to make a trial as to whether the game cannot be learned and played with skill by those 'to the manor born.'" Matches between English and American members of individual clubs were being played as early as the mid-1850s, the first probably being between the American and English members of the Newark club in 1854. Two years later the first match between representative American and English sides was played at Hoboken, an event that proved so popular it was held annually up to the outbreak of the Civil War, and accorded an honor "next in importance" only to the U.S.-Canada matches. Even playing at odds of 18 men against 11, the Americans lost the first four of these matches, but in 1860, at Camden, they finally managed to beat their English opponents, a result the *Herald* saw as proof of the "go ahead character of the American people."[54]

Nor could this result be taken as a single, isolated occurrence. By now American cricketers in other areas of the country were also beginning to beat English teams on a regular basis, sometimes without odds, such as the American sides in Brooklyn, Philadelphia, and Circleville, Ohio, all of which registered impressive wins over the best English players in their respective cities by 1860. The American cricketers of Pottsville, Pennsylvania, were able to easily beat the best English players in their area as early as 1859, the contest leaving little doubt, in the estimation of the local press, that "several of the American players [were] quite equals, as cricketers, to some of the English players." Even as far west as Grass Valley, California, a team of largely novice Americans, fielding "like a swarm of bees," was able to play their English members to a creditable draw in 1861, a result that seemed to fulfill the *Spirit*'s projection, made nine years earlier, that there was no reason why Americans couldn't one day play this game as well as the English.[55]

Adelman's assertion appears even more questionable when the proficiency of individual American cricketers is taken into consideration. By the late 1850s, more and more Americans were being singled out for their individual cricket abilities, such as Philadelphia's Walter Newhall, who could throw a cricket ball 113 yards and once hit a ball completely out of the St. George ground at Hoboken, "a thing which had never been done before." His younger brother, George, seems to have been just as talented, thrilling crowds, at the age of 12, with batting and bowling so advanced for his age he was dubbed "the little wonder." Two talented players also belonged to Philadelphia's other prominent antebellum cricket-playing family, the Wisters. Both William Rotch and his brother Jones were standout batters, the latter top-scoring for his side in the first American vs English match in 1856 and making the second highest score against the All-England team during its match in Philadelphia in 1859.[56]

There seemed to be no shortage of promising American cricketers in Philadelphia during this period, such as Kephardt, who outscored both Newhalls and Wisters during the American vs English match of 1860, or his teammate, Provost, whose bowling during this same match, was "as straight and swift as the celebrated [English professional] Jackson." And even all these standout Philadelphians may have been overshadowed by the talented Germantown cricketer A. Charles Barclay, who in the eyes of the *Clipper*, had "no superior among the Americans" as an all-around player.[57]

Nor were the best American cricketers playing only in Philadelphia. In the estimation of many critics, the Utica, New York, American John G. French, who bowled with a strange and puzzling "half overhand, half underarm" style, was the finest American bowler of his day. In the New York city area there seemed to be at least two standout American players, a Dr. Andrews and John Holder, the latter batting so spectacularly during a match against local Englishmen it "brought down the house." Other Americans singled out for their cricket prowess included the young New Windsor, New York, player Frank Van Buren, who exhibited "the most approved scientific method" in his batting, and the Free Academy's Davis, who batted so well during the first all-American match in 1854 that the *New York Times* concluded it "was worth going to Hoboken to see Davis alone play." It was even reported during this period that at least one American player, a Holmes, of New York, managed to parlay his cricket abilities up to a professional level, a status almost exclusively reserved for the best English players.[58]

It seems clear, then, that neither cricket's English identity nor its technical sophistication should have been insurmountable obstacles for Americans willing to directly involve themselves with the game. Yet, even with these barriers removed, cricket was not able to maintain what had appeared to be such a promising level of American interest. In time, this gave rise to the most widely accepted explanation of cricket's decline: the game was simply "at variance" with the American character. According to this line of thought, cricket was simply too "slow" and "tedious," fatal handicaps for a people who seemed to be instinctively attracted to "fast paced," "high pressure" ball play, which they could find in abundance with baseball.

From his thoughtful analysis of this concept of "action," Adelman concludes that baseball wasn't necessarily more "exciting" than cricket because it was "fast paced," but because it had more "exciting drama" than cricket. In contrast to the English game, where all players bat one after another for an indeterminate length of time, baseball, with its "three out, all out" structure exhibited more "rapid interchange" between offense and defense, something that imbued the game with an appealing "ebb and flow that is lacking in cricket."[59]

Adelman's analysis is certainly correct, but this didn't necessarily mean that cricket could not also exhibit "exciting drama," only that this excitement depended upon much more variable, nonstructural factors than it did in baseball. In baseball, for example, the batter must run when he hits a fair ball. This structurally guarantees that action will be initiated on a regular basis, the batter either getting a hit or the fielders making a put-out. This, of course, also restricts the batter's hitting opportunities, since he must run even if it's certain he will be out. To compensate for this, the batter is permitted multiple times at bat, a feature Americans as early as 1855 felt made baseball "a better game than cricket" since it permitted "more fun for all."[60]

In cricket, on the other hand, the batter doesn't have to run when he hits the ball, and can continue to bat until the fielders get him out, though once out, he cannot bat again (unless it's a two innings match, in which case he will bat, at the most, twice). This particular feature of cricket, which allowed the batter greater freedom and variety than he would have in baseball, had always been one of the game's strongest selling points, and one that was certainly appreciated by Americans. George Wright, who played both baseball and cricket interchangeably throughout his career, always insisted that in comparison to baseball "there is really more science and enjoyment for the player in cricket.

There are a hundred points in batting that one has to bear in mind, and the avoidance of a difficulty, or the accomplishment of a pet stroke gives more pleasure to the player."[61]

This arrangement, however, meant that cricket could only be "exciting" under very specific circumstances. Since the cricket batter does not have to run, action can only be initiated at his discretion, unless the bowler (i.e., the cricket "pitcher") can get him out. For cricket to be "exciting" in an American sense, then, the batter and bowler must be evenly matched, a balance that if tilted either way drastically reduces the game's level of activity. In situations where the batters are much stronger than the opposing bowlers, for instance, scores can become extremely high, unduly prolonging the game and discouraging fielders who have few opportunities to get out batters who do not have to run. The students at Wisconsin's Racine College who played the game were well aware of this drawback, having learned from their own school games that "of all uninteresting things, a one sided cricket match is the worst."[62]

A good bowler, of course, could initiate some "ebb and flow" by occasionally getting a batter out, but if he's so overpowering that he's able to get out batters one after another, for low scores, this diminishes play activity just as badly, something that became a major concern with the increased popularity of fast, hard-to-hit, round-arm bowling, which *Porter's* specifically blamed for "crushing the spirit of cricket among American cricketers," and as a result of which "the game of baseball is fast gaining ground." Although skillful bowling, like skillful pitching, was always appreciated, observers were well aware that cricket's appeal heavily depended upon the batter's ability to enjoy the excitement of making runs, the *Herald* declaring that it was far better "in seeing an inning terminate for a hundred runs than all the cricket matches put together where they are put out for twenty or thirty runs."[63]

For cricket action to develop in an "exciting" or "dramatic" manner then, there had to be a delicate balance between offense and defense, where batters could score runs regularly but where fielders could also get them out on a regular basis. Circumstances like this didn't occur very often, but when they did, they could certainly make cricket as attractive to Americans as any other sport, as indicated with the intrasquad match among members of the New York Club in 1851, a well-balanced game, with only moderately high scores and a regular fall of wickets (i.e., putouts), a type of cricket that, in the eyes of the *Spirit*, had been "conducted as American cricket ought to be."[64]

Adelman's analysis of the concept of action, as it applies to cricket and baseball, also omits the important factor of length determination. If the excitement associated with a frequent interchange between offense and defense was all that was necessary to make baseball popular with Americans, why didn't the Massachusetts version of the game prosper? As a baseball variation that recognized no foul territory, thus allowing batters to initiate action on every hit ball, the Massachusetts game, in theory, should have been much more exciting than the New York game.

The reason why this version lost out to the New York game was because it had to be played up to a set number of runs (usually between 70 and 100), rather than a specific number of outs. The drawback with such a run-specific length determination, from a participant standpoint, is quite obvious. Games between unevenly matched sides could end prematurely, since the stronger side, theoretically, could reach the winning run total without allowing the opposing team more than one or two turns at bat. By the same token, a game between evenly matched teams could go on indefinitely, neither side being strong enough to reach the winning run total in anything like a reasonable time length. This last drawback was vividly demonstrated during a championship game between the Medway and Upton clubs at Worcester in 1860. This match, to be played up to 100 runs, eventually had to be adjudicated, the teams being so evenly matched the score had only reached 50-29 after five days of playing.[65]

The New York version of baseball overcame both these handicaps during the mid-1850s, by which time the older, Knickerbockers rule of playing up to 21 runs (itself really a shortened version of the Massachusetts game) had been replaced with a total-out length determination. Under this structural arrangement, with play continuing until each side recorded 27 outs, even players on weak teams were guaranteed at least a moderate amount of playing activity, while those on evenly balanced teams were ensured a result in a reasonable length of time.

The length of a cricket match, of course, was also determined on a total-out basis (in this case, 10), as it had been throughout its history. But because cricket batters didn't have to run when they hit the ball, and could bat indefinitely, this structural arrangement actually retained, for participants at least, many of the weaknesses of a run-total length determination.

In sum, baseball didn't emerge as a more attractive participant sport than cricket because it was necessarily more "exciting" (cricket could be just as exciting), or because it was a shorter game than cricket (many early baseball games were just as long, if not longer, than many cricket matches of this period). Baseball became more popular because it was a bat-and-ball game that structurally guaranteed excitement would not only occur more regularly than it would in cricket, but that this excitement would last *only so long.*[66]

Does all this mean that Americans were, indeed, "temperamentally" disposed to a type of bat-and-ball game with only exciting, dramatic action, with a short, rapid-transition structure? Why was it that cricket's more continuous but relaxed activity level instinctively struck most Americans of this period the way it did the popular antebellum humorist Mortimer Neal Thompson, who, in his widely syndicated lampoon on cricket, viewed the game as "a solemn ceremony periodically performed with the greatest seriousness by deluded Englishmen who think they are having fun," and one that only seemed to be played by "doleful" and "disheartened" looking participants, who went about their play in such "desponding silence"?[67]

Scholars have traditionally been very reluctant to recognize "national characteristics" as a causal factor in sports development, primarily because of its imprecision as an analytical tool.[68]

Vague and imprecise as this concept may be, there seems to be little doubt that Americans, even when playing cricket among themselves, everywhere and always exuded an unmistakable impulsiveness and urgency in their approach to ball playing. The students from Princeton and Trinity Colleges displayed a marked "eagerness of carriage and astuteness of manner" throughout their cricket match in 1881, a spirit duplicated by the Germantown and Staten Island juniors, who "threw an enthusiasm into their play that much older folks cannot feel" during their 1880 match. These same Staten Island juniors, in a match against a team of St. George juniors in 1877 "were no sooner on the ground . . . than they wanted to get to work in the field at once; and when one inning had been completed, they were anxious to commence the next without delays." The story was the same between the East New York and Queens County juniors in 1862, whose match "from the time the wickets were pitched until they were drawn, was one period of excitement."[69]

Even more revealing was the way Americans always approached the most important part of cricket, batting, always and everywhere showing a predilection for an open, free swinging style rather than the careful, restrained method of orthodox cricket, as seen with the *Spirit*'s admonition, in 1852, that Americans "not hit at balls that are 'dead on the wicket' for the sake of making as many runs in ten overs as their opponents can make in twenty." There always seemed to be something of the "Fritz Fluke" (as the *Ball Players Chronicle* termed it) in every American who played the game, from the students at Racine College with their "nervous swiping" all the way up to the best Philadelphia players, whose greatest weakness, their English opponents knew, was an incessant desire "to play or score off every ball."[70]

Why didn't these distinctive cultural characteristics assert themselves in controlling the direction and development of American cricket? The *Clipper* believed that if only this American element were introduced, cricket will receive a marked impetus in its growth in this country.[71]

Kirsch believed "attempts to promote an American style cricket failed because of resistance by Englishmen." This interpretation, however, is only partly correct and seems to be based upon the failings of the national cricket conventions that were convened for a number of years before the Civil War.[72]

In the beginning these conventions seemed very promising. The delegates who attended the inaugural meeting in 1857, some from as far away as Cincinnati, seemed to work together amicably, as did those who attended the following year's get-together, considered to be "one of the most effective" in promoting the interests of the game. From that point on, however, these meetings seemed to fall into confusion and disarray, eventually resulting in their complete collapse by 1862, the frequent discord among delegates to this last convention becoming so heated it turned the meeting into a complete "farce."[73]

There is little doubt ideological differences between American and English delegates to these conventions contributed to their demise, possibly precipitated by the proposal of Daniel Baker, an American from the Newark club, that the convention take a leadership role in "Americanizing" cricket. If English delegates were alarmed over such a proposal, it's difficult to see why. What Baker meant by "Americanizing" the game amounted to little more than the "spreading of general information" about and "promoting a better acquaintance" of cricket to American novices, with no mention being made of any specific proposals to actually modify the game's traditional playing rules.[74]

Very few Americans, notwithstanding any personal sentiments, seemed willing to suggest at any time that the game be played in any manner other than what was considered "traditional" English cricket during this period. As early as the 1840s, there seemed to be a tacit understanding among Barnet Phillips and his young American friends, even when playing among themselves, that they "dared make no innovations" in the game. Likewise the members of the Amherst College cricket club believed cricket's status as a game of well-established "standard rules" was its major advantage over the many local variations of baseball.[75]

Adelman offers a more sophisticated explanation for this, claiming that cricket's institutional development, by this time, had reached such a point of cultural stasis that its codified rules were considered beyond innovation, even by Americans. This is certainly correct, but what remains to be explained was why there was such apparent inflexibility even within the official rules. Why was there no serious attempt, for instance, to mandate slow or underarm bowling, a requirement that, though considered "not at all chivalrous," would have made the game more exciting and given "more pleasure" to participants. "Suppose that more runs are made off the underarm bowling," the *Clipper* argued, "does it not make the fieldsman more alert, and give him more practice and excitement?" Similarly, the arrangement adopted by the American and Kings County cricket clubs in the early 1860s of limiting each player's time at bat to a specific number of pitches and runs, something fully in compliance with traditional rules, never went beyond local practice games.[76]

For some as yet unclear reason, American cricketers during this period allowed their basic sporting tastes to be superseded by an institutional allegiance they were, in most instances, under no obligation to honor. How sharply all this differed from the participant-centered dynamics at work within early baseball, exemplified by *Our Young Folks'* insistence that "wherever [baseball players] find a rule laid down which . . . hinders, instead of promoting, the spirit and fun of the game, they had better disregard it. The rules are made for them, not they for the rules."[77]

Was it then "inevitable" that baseball would be America's national pastime? Assertions of historical determinism are always treacherous, but the preponderance of evidence, in this instance, seems to justify an affirmative answer—with, however, some important qualifications. Within a broader cultural context, it was almost certain that some form of bat-and-ball sport would emerge as a central component of America's sporting life, just as it would in every other Anglo-Saxon (if we may use that term) culture around the world. In the narrower context of American culture, it also seems fairly certain that this bat-and-ball sport would have to assume a rapid transition structure (or "cyclical" structure, as Adelman calls it), played on a total-out length determination. That it was inevitable the "New York" version of baseball would be this bat-and-ball game is, however, not nearly as certain, as seen from the opposition this variation encountered during its formative years.[78]

Scholars have preferred to interpret baseball's early popularity to a deep and pervasive cultural "want" for a "national game," free from foreign influences. Most, however, tend to overlook that in the context of this period, a "national" pastime was a collective term for any sporting activity that could, within certain moral guidelines, strike a direct and positive emotional response among a wide range of Americans, not one that was adopted out of any nationalistic obligation, something that would appear only after the Civil War. The cultural process that was at work among Americans during this era was not one of "I specifically choose to play baseball because it is my obligation to do so as an American" (an explanation that seems to be unsatisfactorily subliminal) so much as it was, "I choose this particular game, baseball, because it appeals to me in a way no other does."

In theory, any sport could have been the "national" pastime if it could have evoked a similarly deep and unique response from Americans, even cricket, which the *Spirit* felt was fully qualified to fulfill this "want of a national pastime" as well as any other sport. *Porters* was even more general, hoping that not only baseball and cricket, but racquets, football, and all other manly sports "may become national throughout the United States of America—or its boundless 'area of freedom.'"[80]

Cricket's immediate future in America would depend upon the cultural viability of such an expectation, putting the game under an obligation to demonstrate it could evoke the depth and energy of response Americans were finding in baseball, a status that, if realized, should have been able to neutralize the game's negative foreign image.

Some observers, like the *New York Leader*, seemed to believe this was fully possible, prophesying "the success of [baseball's and cricket's] renewed introduction . . . bids fair to render their establishments as an American institution permanent, as it must be beneficial." But could America simultaneously identify with two sports so similar in their playing objective, yet different in their basic emotional appeal? Could a single culture bear allegiance to two bat-and-ball sports?[81]

4

The All-England Tour of 1859 and the Insufficiency of Imitation

Whatever detractions it may have had to baseball as a participant sport, cricket did enjoy one noticeable advantage over its American rival; it was an established international sport that presented a clear cultural challenge to an America that during this era was highly sensitive about its national image and prestige.

The U.S.-Canada matches had clearly shown that Americans still looked on cricket as a legitimate test of their sporting abilities, whose results could arouse as many nationalistic sentiments as those from such emerging international sports as boxing and yachting.

Just how powerfully these athletic challenges could impact upon the public imagination was further demonstrated over the fall of 1859, when a representative team of England's best professional cricketers, playing under the name of the All-England eleven, undertook a competitive tour of the United States and Canada, an event that, with the possible exception of the Sayres-Heenan boxing match the following year, developed into the most widely publicized sports even of antebellum America.

The idea of bringing England's best cricketers over to America seems to have been floated as early as 1855, on the initiation, it was claimed, of English cricket authorities themselves. The idea, however, was not given serious consideration until the U.S.-Canada match of 1856, when the English-born Canadian, W. P. Pickering, perhaps inspired by the public's interest in such international matches, attempted to arrange a visit.[1]

These negotiations as well apparently "ended in nothing," but when Robert Waller of New York's St. George Club became involved, plans for such a tour moved forward and were eventually finalized on June 9, 1859. Under the terms agreed upon, the English team would play matches in Montreal and New York, with two further "sub-let" fixtures to be held in Philadelphia and Hamilton. Another, originally unscheduled match, was also later played in Rochester.[2]

The English side that eventually made the trip was fully representative of English professional cricket at that time, but it was hardly the strongest possible. Along with George Parr, a standout batter from Nottinghamshire who captained the team, the squad included such notable players as John Wisden, John Jackson, and Tom Lockyer, but even the American press believed it would have been far more formidable if it had included Mudie and V. E. Walker.[3]

Throughout the summer months leading up to the tour, public interest in the forthcoming event steadily rose, even among Americans previously uninterested in cricket, to such an extent that *Leslie's Illustrated* half-sarcastically reported "men who up to that time were as ignorant of cricket as they were of the social life of the Chinese, now discussed learnedly of 'overs,' 'no balls,' 'cuts,' 'drives,' and all the technicalities of the cricket field as though the game had been their constant occupation from childhood." Just as revealing were the many bold, even shameless, efforts to get the celebrated English visitors to extend their visit to other American cities. No sooner had the Englishmen landed in Montreal than they were met by a representative from the Cincinnati Cricket Club, who had been authorized to offer three-quarters of the gate receipts if the English would come and play in that city. Just as insistent, but no more successful, were the representatives from the Albany and Baltimore clubs in their attempts to lure the English to their respective cities. Even far-off St. Louis entertained visions of hosting a match, just the distinction of having their local players on the same field as the English, in the eyes of the local press, being honor enough, "never mind the spectacles."[4]

Most of the media attention centered around the New York match, an event that from all contemporary accounts certainly must have met, if not exceeded, its organizer's highest expectations. On match day, "the largest array of spectators that had ever previously been congregated for such an object in this country" was on hand at the recently set aside area of the Elysian Fields (the match was not, as commonly assumed, played on the St. George ground itself), that had been outfitted with $2,000 worth of improvements, all at the expense of Edward A. Stevens, and on which local clubs had pitched their brightly colored tents (a common sight on the grounds of important antebellum cricket matches, and one that gave rise to the expression "the tented field").[5]

The English players were "absolutely mobbed" by the estimated 8,000-9,000 spectators in attendance almost as soon as they had stepped on the ground, to which they had been conveyed by both ferry and a "mammoth" lavishly decorated, four-horse coach. An even larger crowd, estimated at 12,000-15,000 spectators, was on hand during the second day's play, another 3,000 for the third day. Factoring in the 4,000 spectators who came for the exhibition match held on the final day, and contemporary claims that the All-England team attracted, during its New York stay, an estimated 25,000 spectators, does not seem exaggerated.[6]

Only the most optimistic observers could have believed the United States team, even when playing at odds of 22 men against 11 would be able to win the match, but the extreme ease by which the English defeated the American side came as a great embarrassment, leaving most critics at a loss for explanations. Trying to put forward a good face, *Porters* ascribed the one-sided result to the English players tactical, rather than physical, superiority over the American players, who, it claimed, "were beat as much by head work as by superiority in the game of cricket." Their English opponents, however, had a far different explanation. From their viewpoint the Americans simply did not "at all understand" such technical intricacies as lob bowling, while their own bowling was wild and inaccurate, "pace and not place." All in all, it seemed the New York side lost because they had simply played "very bad cricket."[7]

Other, more nationalistically sensitive critics didn't believe the loss was as much a failure of American cricket as it was a failure of New York's English community. These critics were not so much upset that the so-called American team was made up of predominantly English residents (though not all; there were three Philadelphians on the New York team, Walter Newhall, Charles Barclay, and William Morgan), as they were that so many of these players were undeserving of places. Observers were particularly upset that Waller, Marsh, and Comery, all so old they had played in the U.S.-Canada match of 1845, had been given places on the American side.[8]

National pride was somewhat redeemed during the Philadelphia match, played a week later, on grounds hastily set up on the Camac estate at 13th and Columbia Avenue. Here the English also won, but it would be the closest match of their tour and the only one where competitive resistance, from a predominantly American side, was at a level that "the English players felt they had anything to do."[9]

It was during the first innings of this match that the most controversial incident of the tour occurred. Having just started his innings, English batter Robert Carpenter was caught off a ball umpire Henry Sharp inexplicably declared a wide (a call only to be made for balls pitched, illegally, out of reach of the batter). Allowed to continue, Carpenter went on to score an invaluable, perhaps decisive, 22 runs. The consequence of this mistaken call was most probably not reason enough to justify Jones Wister's claim that it had cost the Americans the match, but *Bells Life* took some measure of satisfaction in claiming, as a result of the slip, that "the Britishers have, for once, stolen a march on their go ahead opponents."[10]

The All-England tour had a number of important consequences for antebellum American cricket. Not surprisingly, the intense media attention that surrounded the event translated into a noticeable spurt of grass roots interest in the game. Anticipation over the event alone seems to have incited the formation of two junior clubs in Pittsburgh, where, the local press claimed, that summer "the cricket mania seems to be growing apace." Madison, Wisconsin, was also "partaking of the fever which pervades every cricket club in the country" that summer, with the formation of two new clubs in that city. Over that summer three new clubs also appeared in San Francisco, and another in Lexington, Kentucky.[11]

By that fall, five cricket clubs were active in St. Louis, and nine in Baltimore, where local supporters claimed "cricket is becoming a regular institution." Two junior clubs, the Washington and the Independent, also sprang up in Brooklyn; two more, the Empire and the Union, were formed in Detroit and another in Davenport, Iowa. A junior club also appeared that fall in Lowell, Massachusetts, an area of the country where, it was claimed, "hardly a village is without its [cricket] club."[12]

Not unexpectedly, Philadelphia seems to have been the biggest beneficiary of the country's renewed interest in cricket, a place where, it was reported, the game had now "taken instantly a strong hold on the public favor, and its hereto unintelligible terms have become . . . familiar as household words." By the following spring, dozens of new clubs had sprung up in and around the city, probably nothing like the 100 clubs claimed by the *Clipper*, but very likely the 42 reported by the *Saturday Evening Gazette*, as many as 10 of which could be observed every weekend playing matches on the Powelton Fair Grounds.[13]

What must have been even more encouraging to cricket supporters was the number of clubs that were appearing in areas where the game had not previously been played. By the summer of 1860, Americans had organized clubs in locations as near as East New York, a popular summer resort in Brooklyn, and as distant as Maysville, Kentucky; Ripley, Ohio; and Redwing, Minnesota. By the fall, clubs had also appeared in Port Huron, Michigan; and Grass Valley, California. A match between Lincoln and Douglas campaign workers was even gotten up in Oswego that year, won by the Lincoln supporters, "which result," the local press proudly reported, "accorded with the sign of the times."[14]

It's generally been assumed that the South did not participate in the country's emerging antebellum interest in team sports. But within a year of the All-England tour, cricket clubs had been organized in Savannah, Mobile, and New Orleans, something the *Daily Picayune* had advocated for its citizens years earlier.[15]

New Orleans, of course, was somewhat uncharacteristic of the South, with its urban, cosmopolitan environment, but it would be wrong to believe cricket, like other traditional southern recreations, was not played in that city as "a gracious thing, involving careful attention to nonpecuniary values and actions in a world mad with materialistic frenzy." After the Civil War, cricket even seems to have somehow become closely identified with the Old South's now vanished "age of chivalry," as a pastime that had prospered "in happier times" but could exist no longer in a society overrun by carpetbagger mannerisms.[16]

Within America's educational institutions as well, the secular enthusiasm generated by the All-England tour seems to have both broadened and deepened the cause of organized athletics. Within a year of the tour, cricket had appeared in a number of publicly supported secondary educational institutions, such as Philadelphia's Central High School (where it was reported as many as 300 students played the game), Indianapolis's public high school (whose principal seems to have been an ex-New Jersey cricketer), and the Farmer's High School of Bellefonte, Pennsylvania, the distant forerunner of Penn State University.[17]

In private secondary schools, cricket continued to be favored by progressive-minded educators, such as Thomas P. Allen, who encouraged the game at his private school in Sterling, Massachusetts. Authorities at the Lawrenceville School near Trenton, New Jersey, along with those at two private Philadelphia schools, John Quincy Adams Grammar School, and the Protestant Episcopal Academy, also supported the game. The cricket match played between a team from the last-mentioned school and Mr. Faire's school in 1861 may quite possibly have been the first organized interscholastic sports event in America.[18]

It was also during this period that cricket began to assume an important role in two private secondary schools destined to be long known for their cricket playing: Racine College and St. Paul's School.

The former, a boys preparatory school established in Racine, Wisconsin, in 1852, only began to fulfill its expectations as a training ground for the trans-Appalachian Episcopal clergy under the guidance of James DeKoven, who became the school's headmaster in 1859. A forceful and articulate, if controversial, figure in the Episcopal Church, DeKoven was an avowed Anglo-Catholic and one of the most prominent advocates of "ritualism," the American offshoot of the Oxford Movement.[19]

Denied the Episcopal bishopric of Illinois because of his extreme "high church" stance, DeKoven would instead apply his superb administrative abilities to this small Midwestern school on which he would leave an indelible mark during his 20-year tenure as its headmaster. Through his personal efforts, the college became one of the first American schools to adopt the English public school "family" system of education, that encouraged close personal contact between faculty and students, an educational philosophy DeKoven had observed extensively during his visit to England in 1858.[20]

It was during that visit that DeKoven most probably recognized the invaluable role organized sports, especially cricket, could play in an educational scheme that appreciated there could be "more religion in laughter and a healthy body than in long-drawn faces, and bodies under the mortgage of consumption." Introduced into the school in 1860, cricket quickly established itself as an integral part of student life, "our chief glory and pride" among all the sports played at the institution. By the early 1870s it was not unusual to find, overshadowing the solitary student baseball game or two, as many as a dozen "scrub" cricket matches being simultaneously played by students during their recreation period.[21]

Student interest in the game was further encouraged by the administration's willingness, unusual at that time, to allow the college team to play off campus, something the students took frequent advantage of, arranging matches, over the years, with clubs in Milwaukee, Chicago, Sussex, and Bay View, Wisconsin. The school also kept up, for a number of years, a regular series of matches with its sister institution, Nashotah House Seminary in Nashotah, Wisconsin.[22]

In the eyes of another highly principled American educator, Henry Coit, the headmaster of St. Paul's School in Concord, New Hampshire, from 1855 until his death some 40 years later, cricket was also highly valued as "the greatest adornment and supporter of good education." Under Coit's encouragement, cricket was introduced into the school before the Civil War, and also quickly established itself as "the college game." All incoming students were automatically enrolled into one of the school's two cricket teams, the Isthmian and Old Hundred, the intraclass competition between the two teams forming the staple of the school's early athletic life.

Though a strong supporter of the game, Coit seems to have been more suspicious of its competitive benefits, prohibiting the school's cricket team from playing against outside teams until 1876. From that point on, however, St. Paul's was able to keep up a busy schedule of matches with nonschool clubs, especially against such like-minded institutions as Harvard and the Longwood Cricket Club of Boston.[23]

Cricket's popularity as a college sport also visibly increased after the All-England tour. While still maintaining its status as one of "the leading games" at such prominent institutions as Harvard, cricket was also beginning to appear at a number of smaller colleges, such as Bowdoin, Amherst, Williams, Holy Cross, Andover Theological Seminary, and the University of Michigan. At Oberlin College, the game was by this time "becoming alarmingly popular" as it also was at Wesleyan College, where, by 1860, "spirited games [of cricket] . . . may be witnessed every day upon the spacious campus."[24]

From this interest American college athletics were also able to make their earliest moves away from the archaism of strictly institutional play to the threshold of more modern, intercollegiate competition. Over the summer of 1860, at least two intercollegiate cricket matches were played, one between the clubs of Franklin & Marshall College and the Normal School of Millersville, Pennsylvania, another, played a few months later, between clubs at Washington & Jefferson College and Waynesburg College. Though a good year later than the Amherst-Williams baseball game that has traditionally been recognized as the first land intercollegiate sports event in American history, both these matches predate, by almost four years, the Haverford College-University of Pennsylvania cricket match long accepted as the country's first intercollegiate cricket event.[25]

The All-England tour, however, was not as successful in realizing its supporters' hopes of reasserting cricket's standing as a sport still worthy of serious American attention, a standing that was progressively being undermined by baseball, which contemporary observers well knew had become "a formidable rival to cricket, not only in the excellence of the game, but in the superiority of its players."[26]

Well aware, by this time, that their game could not duplicate baseball's strong participant appeal, cricket supporters must have hoped this exhibition of world-class caliber play would, nonetheless, establish a common ground with baseball, as well as overcome the "ridiculous jealousy" that was developing between the two sporting camps. Henry Chadwick, who always maintained that "we have yet to see the first American, who is practically acquainted with both games [baseball and cricket], and excels in both, that is not an admirer of cricket," was especially hopeful the play of the English professionals would make baseballers more appreciative of cricket's technical merits, especially its fly-ball out rule, whose adoption, Chadwick always insisted, was essential if baseball were to ever become a serious, manly game.[27]

And, at first, the New York baseball community did seem to show an increased interest in their local cricket. In anticipation of the Englishmen's visit, some New York baseballers began to enroll in area cricket clubs. A number of baseball officials also reportedly attended the All-England match in New York, while still others decided to drop into the national cricket convention the following spring, where they were "cordially received" by the cricket delegates.[28]

The most ambitious attempt to build a bridge between New York's baseball and cricket communities came about that fall, when a number of prominent New York baseballers, among them Harry Wright, James Creighton, Asa Brainerd, John Whitney, and Thomas Dakin, established the American Cricket Club, an organization that encouraged baseballers to not only try cricket but to do so in a way that would "infuse something of an American spirit into the game." To accomplish this, the club restricted its membership to native-born Americans (later amended to allow long-time English residents, and those intending to become U.S. citizens, to enroll), and adopted a flexible approach to its playing style, one that would still be "according to the laws," but "would make it a quick game," and avoid cricket's more "objectionable features."[29]

The "enthusiasm" generated by this sporting mission carried over into the club's early matches, which included a number of highly publicized wins over resident English teams. The organization, however, soon began to experience difficulties retaining its membership, resulting in a number of losses in its later games. With the outbreak of the Civil War, the club eventually disbanded; later efforts to revive it proved unsuccessful, though a number of its original members, most notably James Creighton, continued to play cricket with other area clubs.[30]

The American Club's failure to effect any noticeable shift in America's bat-and-ball preferences clearly underscored the growing confidence Americans had in baseball as the standard of their own ball-playing culture, though this had, in fact, been revealed earlier amid the speculations that the All-England eleven could be induced to actually play some baseball during their visit.

Rumors about a possible baseball match between the English cricketers and a team of representative New York baseballers had been circulating even before the All-England team got to New York; one such rumor claimed the Englishmen had been guaranteed the astonishing sum of $7,000 for such a match. Nothing came of these plans, but the English cricketers did play some mixed-team baseball during a break in their weather-effected match at Rochester, an event that provided the American public its first opportunity to judge baseball by the highest cricket standards. The surprisingly competent performance by the Englishmen at baseball—their wicket-keeper, Tom Lockyer, it was claimed, "with a little practice could put out of sight any catcher at base ball in America"—still precluded any convincing claim to baseball's technical parity with cricket, but the lively, alert manner in which the Englishmen had to play this game—"so unlike the solemn, monotonous manner of the Anglo-American cricket stars . . . on the New York cricket ground in Hoboken"—further substantiated baseball's participant advantages.[31]

To an extent seldom appreciated by sports historians, the All-England tour of 1859 was a vision of America's sports future. It revealed, for the first time, organized team sports' vast potential as a vehicle of mass entertainment. The English team reportedly grossed over $5,300 from its scheduled tour, with an additional £1,070 cleared from benefit matches. Organizers must have done well too, with the St. George Club reportedly taking in $1,900 on the first day of the New York match, on the basis of which it can safely be projected that total receipts for the three day event far exceeded the $3,177.35 the club incurred in match expenses.[32]

The tour also revealed the emerging association between organized team sports and civic pride, the best example of this being the Englishmen's hastily arranged final match at Rochester. In an eerily modern scenario, Rochester officials were not only readily willing to appropriate public funds to bring the English cricketers to their city—in this case, $1,500 to upgrade the city's cricket ground—the mayor himself even took a hand in promoting ticket sales, all for nothing more tangible than the right to claim "our city is thus honored and placed in the list along with New York and Philadelphia."[33]

But the All-England tour also revealed that this vision of America's sports future would hold only a limited place for cricket. Even if it was true, as the *Clipper* was claiming on the eve of the Civil War, that Americans "by the hundreds" were now playing cricket, other observers were far more skeptical about the depth and integrity of this interest. The *Boston Courier* was led to qualify this apparent popularity, claiming "the public, or a certain portion of it, is now excited about cricket," an excitement others believed would prove to be no more enduring than the recent fads in chess and pigeon shooting. Even the All-England players themselves weren't oblivious to the fact that most of the Americans who turned out for their matches were only there from a "curiosity as to the manner of playing the game of cricket," not from any personal interest in these matches.[34]

But despite this, many sports observers still assumed there was a uniformity of needs and requirements between American and English ball-playing cultures that could be satisfied interchangeably by both baseball and cricket. This was the "golden promise" John Irving spoke of during the English team's postmatch reception in New York, a belief the *Spirit* had articulated a decade earlier, envisioning a time when "England 'gainst America each season to be arrayed and that both the Prince and President are good bats 'twill be said."[35]

Over the second half of the nineteenth century, America would develop a number of its institutions and social movements along European patterns (in higher education and labor organization, for example). But the All-England tour and its aftermath clearly showed America wouldn't look to Europe, in any sustainable and meaningful manner, for developing its ball-playing culture.

The preferential interest Americans showed toward the English cricketers attempts at baseball, real or imagined, rather than baseballers attempts at cricket (seen in the fortunes of the American Cricket Club) was already demonstrating that it was unlikely America's ball playing tastes could be satisfied in anything other than a culturally specific manner. Any bat-and-ball sport that could not directly address these requirements, the New York *Herald* well knew, would simply never be accepted by Americans, no matter how strong were its claims to international prestige or technical standing: "Even if there were no baseball in existence," the paper concluded after its lengthy account of the All-England tour, "cricket could never become a national sport in America."[36]

5

The Retreat from Cosmopolitanism
and the Fallacy of the Chadwick Thesis

Scholars, both past and present, have generally assumed the Civil War dealt American cricket a fatal blow. With Lincoln's call for volunteers in the Spring of 1861, this theory goes, Americans marched off to war as cricket players and, four years later, returned home playing baseball, having discovered this new nine-man game during the lulls between battles.[1]

It is a claim, however, historical evidence hardly supports.

The outbreak of hostilities between North and South certainly disrupted cricket's antebellum routine, as it did just about every other aspect of civilian life. Delegates to the 1861 national cricket convention that convened shortly after the fall of Ft. Sumter seemed to sense that it would now be difficult to arrange anything like a normal schedule of matches, a prognostication that had turned even more pessimistic by mid-summer, with *Wilkes* reporting "an almost total suspension of important cricket matches throughout the country in consequence of the war."[2]

This, of course, was to be expected as more and more active cricket players began to answer the call to arms. Several members of the St. George and New York cricket clubs enlisted in the 7th New York Regiment soon after the war broke out. Seven members of the Germantown Cricket Club's first eleven, eight of the Philadelphia club's starting squad, and all of the Young America's first team also entered military service soon after hostilities began, as did large contingents of Chicago's Prairie Cricket Club, and St. Louis' Jackson club. In Baltimore, activity among that city's cricket clubs declined to a point that it virtually "suspended the game in the city during the war."[3]

A number of these former cricket players were fortunate enough to enjoy relatively successful careers during their military service. Several members of Lancaster's Keystone and Conestoga cricket clubs eventually rose to the officer ranks, as did the former St. George cricketer C. H. T. Colles, who ended the war as a brigadier general. Charles A. Vernou, of the Young America club, parlayed his Civil War service as a cavalry officer into a lengthy military career, which he used to good purpose advocating the benefits of cricket to the many soldiers who later served under him, from Ft. Leavenworth to San Antonio to Detroit. University of Michigan cricketer James H. Kidd probably enjoyed the most glamorous career during this conflict as a member of George Custer's command.[4]

For other American cricket players, the war had more tragic consequences. Walter Newhall, the talented Young America cricketer who served as a captain in the 16th Regiment of the 3rd Pennsylvania Cavalry, rather ingloriously drowned while trying to ford a flooded Virginia river in 1863, a manner of death that had, curiously, also claimed the life of former University of Michigan cricketer William C. Moore a year earlier. Isaac Walker, a former president of the Long Island Cricket Club, died of typhoid fever at Fort Monroe, South Carolina, in 1862, while former Amherst College cricket club president, Christopher Pennell, lost his life during the siege of Petersburg, Virginia, serving as an officer in Massachusetts' 19th Colored Regiment.[5]

As an adjunct to military life itself, cricket, though never as popular as baseball, seems to have, nonetheless, enjoyed a presence and standing roughly in proportion to its role in civilian life. Both military and quasi-military authorities certainly valued the game as highly as any other for promoting the health and physical well-being of soldiers. The *Clipper* strongly encouraged all soldiers to "take a hand at base ball or cricket" as a means of breaking the monotony of camp life, a sentiment also shared by the Sanitary Commission, a quasi-military organization that oversaw health and hygiene related matters in the military.[6]

To varying degrees during the war this advice was taken up by both Union and Confederate soldiers. The pick-up game played among the soldiers of Company E of the 12th Wisconsin Regiment "did much to establish pleasant relations between commanders and commanded" during that unit's stay at Ft. Leavenworth. Cricket was popular enough among the Union soldiers stationed at Ft. DeKalb, Virginia, that some kept up the game when they returned home to Lawrence, Massachusetts. In a few instances, interregimental matches were arranged, the most widely publicized being a contest between the 32nd New York Regiment (which seems to have had a large contingent of players from the Amsterdam, New York, area) and the 95th Pennsylvania Regiment, which was played at the Union encampment at White Oak Church, Virginia, in 1863.[7]

Other observers believed cricket could even render valuable service on the home front. The *Clipper* suggested the New York cricket community organize benefit matches to raise money for a soldier relief fund, while *Wilkes* hoped the cricket matches Oswego was keeping up with Canadian cricket clubs would help defuse the heightened political tension that existed between the two countries in 1862. One correspondent from Cincinnati, in an even more expansively patriotic mode, demanded that cricket "ought, especially in the present crisis, to be supported and fostered in every town and village of the United States as a national institution."[8]

The American Civil War may have been history's first "modern" war, (meaning the first war that directly influenced a significant proportion of the civilian, rather than just the military, populations) but the conflict certainly didn't seem to have been nearly as disruptive of the North's recreational life as is commonly assumed.

The conflict may have forced the cancellation of the 1861 U.S.-Canada match, and compelled the East New York Cricket Club to temporarily relinquish its cricket ground for military use, but it did not prevent an improvised U.S.-Canada match from being played in New York in 1862, or a meeting of the Massachusetts state cricket association that same year, developments that may have inspired the *Clipper* to optimistically declare "we will have the war put through soon enough for the cricket season to begin early."[9]

Even the hated draft apparently didn't deplete northern manpower to an extent that it prevented the students at Norwich University in Northfield, Vermont, from organizing a cricket club in 1864, or the young men of Greenfield, Massachusetts, from organizing the Monitor Cricket Club in their city that same year. The Union Cricket Club of Cincinnati expressed pride in having sent off more of its members to war than any other western cricket club, but evidently enough remained behind for the club to hold an intrasquad match at the very time the battle of Gettysburg was raging. While young men from the East, South, and Midwest were dying in far-off battlefields, the local press in the Utah territory was expressing delight "to learn of our youths and young men spending their holidays in recreative sports," playing cricket among the numerous teams that were active at that time in Salt Lake City, Springville, and Ogden.[10]

Adelman believed "the fate of cricket in America had been sealed by 1865." Accurate as this assessment may be in hindsight, it was certainly not shared by sports observers of that period, many of whom seemed to assume the end of hostilities signified a return to something of a sporting status quo antebellum rather than any significant watershed in the country's sporting patterns. Within a few months of Lee's surrender, the *Clipper* was cheerfully declaring "cricket is evidently looking up . . . in a year or two we may expect to see cricket as popular as ever." The

New York *World*'s assertion that same summer, that cricket "is becoming one of the most prominent out-door sports in this country," was no doubt unwarranted, but *Our Young Folks* claim, two years later, that cricket was still "next in favor" to baseball, was probably still valid. All in all, immediate post-Civil War American cricket probably was most accurately characterized as "not an amusement of mushroom growth . . . but its progress has been steady and uniform."[11]

In some of the country's larger urban areas, cricket seems to have emerged from the war under relatively prosperous conditions. The country's bellwether club, the St. George of New York, seems to have been in as healthy a condition in the mid-1860s as it ever was, with a "full treasury," 400 members, and three competitive elevens. In 1867 the club relocated from its old ground in the Elysian Fields to a new, spacious, seven acre site at the foot of Ninth Street in west Hoboken, which it had purchased for $35,000 and outfitted with a fine clubhouse.[12]

A long standing feud between the St. George and its old rival, the New York Cricket Club, was also finally resolved during this period, this deep and acrimonious rift having been, for many years, a public relations embarrassment for New York area cricket. The dispute had come about during a match between the two clubs in 1857, with the New York team claiming a win on a time limitation the St. George protested it had not agreed to. Unable to resolve the difference, the two clubs broke off relations and refused to play each other, despite offers to arbitrate the dispute and an authoritative ruling by *Bells Life*. Stoked by the "partisan malice" of two players in particular, James Higham of the New York club, and Robert Waller of the St. George, animosity between the two organizations simmered unabated for years, much to the annoyance and frustration of the *Clipper*, which never tired of ridiculing these "Montagues and Capulets" of American cricket.[13]

It was with some sense of relief, then, that the New York press reported the two clubs had finally resumed competitive contacts in 1866. The annual matches between these two "crack clubs" had, after all, always been looked on as the unofficial cricket championship of the United States, and now that the "hatchet" was "under ground," supporters must have hoped the "unbounded" interest that had always surrounded their antebellum encounters would once again return.[14]

In some urban areas, organized cricket appeared for the first time only after the Civil War, among them Memphis, Indianapolis, Nashville, and Louisville, a match between the last mentioned and Cincinnati, in 1869, probably drawing more spectators (some 2,000) than any played in New York that year. During this period, cricket was also played for the first time in Washington D.C., where it continued to attract the attention of former Amsterdam, New York, cricketer Nick Young, who, as a U.S. Treasury Department employee, continued to divide his loyalties between the game and his increasing duties with organized baseball.[15]

America's national game was rapidly overshadowing cricket in many areas of the country by now, but in a few status-sensitive western cities a reputable cricket club could still be as valued and desirable a symbol of civic prestige as any other sports organization. The efforts of such Cincinnati civic leaders as Aaron Champion, who would later bring about the formation of baseball's first professional team, the Red Stockings, were a direct outgrowth of earlier attempts to build up that city's local cricket club into the strongest trans-Appalachian cricket organization. Certainly no other city at that time probably expended as many resources for a baseball club as Cincinnati did for its cricket club, hiring away from New York Harry Wright to be its player/coach for a guaranteed salary of $1,200, while allocating another $5,000 to insure the local cricket ground was "not excelled by any in the United States."[16]

Cricket was also pressed into the cause of civic boosterism in what was probably the most status-sensitive of all Midwestern American cities, St. Louis, which was locked in a fierce economic rivalry with Chicago in the immediate post-Civil War years. Baseball was the main sports medium for this civic boosterism, but the local press also brashly proclaimed their city "has cricket talent second to none in the United States." It was a boast, ironically, a representative city cricket side went a long way to back up with the unexpectedly successful national tour it undertook in 1873, as a result of which the local press could also claim there "was a cosmopolitan spirit in St. Louis which did not exist in any other city."[17]

Cricket activity also resumed in a number of smaller American communities that had supported the game before the Civil War, such as Amsterdam, New York; Ripon, Wisconsin; Waltham, Massachusetts; Lambertville, New Jersey; Jackson, Michigan; and the little Wisconsin town of Mazomanie, which was still well known at this period for a citizenry "who take a deep interest in this 'noble game.'" The fierce, ideologically induced violence that had ravaged the little Kentucky town of Maysville during the war seems to have been quickly forgotten, making it possible for that town's cricket club, the "Corn Crackers," to renew its antebellum rivalry with Ripley, Ohio, and to establish a new one with nearby Vanceburg, Kentucky.[18]

Cricket clubs also appeared for the first time after the Civil War in such little communities as Nyack, New York; Orange, New Jersey; Meadville, Pennsylvania; Elyria, Ohio; and Galena, Illinois, as well as in the three little Wisconsin towns of Platteville, Sheboygan, and Oshkosh.[19]

Somewhat surprisingly, cricket, as a small town phenomenon, seems to have been most vibrant during this period in the Utah territory. Still situated well in advance of the nation's expanding baseball interest, and able to draw upon the territory's large number of English Mormon converts, the little communities of Sandy, Plain City, Wellsville, and Coalville, as well as Almy, Wyoming, all supported cricket clubs through the 1860s and 1870s, lending credence to the *Clipper*'s report, in 1879, that "nearly every town in the territory" was playing cricket.[20]

Nonetheless, there could be no denying cricket's popularity with Americans, as both a participant and spectator sport, was experiencing a steep decline immediately after the Civil War. The game virtually disappeared in such locations as Buffalo, Newark, Baltimore, Pittsburgh, Chicago, and New Orleans during this time, or could survive only on the support of resident Englishmen. It was a trend the *Detroit Free Press* had seen in its own area even as the Civil War was winding down, noting "time was when there was scarcely a hamlet but what could boast of an 'Eleven' if not a senior and junior one, but now things have strangely altered."[21]

Probably the most conspicuous indication of cricket's declining status could be seen in the changing circumstances of New York's St. George Club. No longer able to attract enough spectators to its matches to justify preferential treatment, the club lost the use of its old ground at the Elysian Fields in 1865. By the 1870s, public interest in the club's cricket activities was practically nonexistent, and even its more important fixtures, such as the one against the Philadelphia Cricket Club in 1871, were unable to attract any more than "the immediate friends of the two clubs, no cricket match now-a-days drawing as in the old days." It was a situation all too apparent to the *Sunday Mercury* as well, which could only lament in 1870, "Oh, for the times of 1856 and '7, when the spectators used to be counted by hundreds instead of now by tens." The story was the same even with the once popular international matches. Barely a tenth of the anticipated 25,000 spectators showed up for the St. George match against Wilshire's English professionals in 1868, and not many more for that club's match, four years later, against Fitzgerald's English amateurs, and even then so few were Americans that the *World* dismissed the event as little more than a "demonstration of the strength of the English colony in New York."[22]

The St. George, of course, happened to be in a location where baseball had already achieved a high level of organizational support and following. But in other areas of the country as well, local cricket interest—even fairly well-established interest—quickly evaporated once the east coast baseball mania arrived. Of the four Detroit area cricket clubs that were active in 1865, only one, the Peninsular, would survive the baseball fever that swept that city two years later. A similar pattern occurred in both Milwaukee, where an early post-Civil War cricket revival quickly gave way to baseball, and Washington, Pennsylvania, where the city's two local cricket clubs, optimistic as a result of their 1865 matches that "the next cricketing season [may] witness many such games" had, by the following year, both disappeared, replaced by local baseball clubs.[23]

Nowhere was this process of sporting displacement more dramatically evident than among the small anthracite mining communities of Pennsylvania's Schuylkill Valley. A popular area sport before the Civil War, cricket reappeared in just about every community there almost as soon as the war had ended, including Pottsville, Port Carbon, Tamaqua, St. Clair, Tuscarora, and Schuylkill Haven. Over the summers of 1865 and 1866, virtually every issue of the local paper carried at least two or three match reports, sometimes more. But then, almost overnight, cricket virtually disappeared from the valley. The number of match reports began to decline during the late summer of 1866, a decline that accelerated over the following summer until, by 1868, the local press was reporting no cricket matches at all save for a passing reference to the game at the local Athletic Club.[24]

From a twentieth-century perspective, the sheer intensity and magnitude of baseball's immediate post-Civil War growth has always been interpreted as a natural, almost inevitable, outgrowth of the game's modernizing process. To many sports observers of that period, however, baseball's dominating cultural ascension represented an unforeseen and ominous break with sport's long-accepted function as a moderating influence upon mass emotions. This assumption, on which rested much of early sports social justification, necessarily implied the popularity of a multiplicity of sports over which a people could spread and diversify its emotional expenditures rather than dangerously concentrate and intensify them in a single game. The *Spirit* was particularly concerned with this, noting in 1873 that "baseball is a truly glorious, exhilarating game, but why it should be allowed to sweep every other game of the bat out of existence we cannot see." Even amid the national excitement generated by the Cincinnati Red Stockings' famous undefeated season four years earlier, the *Cincinnati Commercial*, one of that club's strongest supporters, had to admonish its readers that "it is better that base ball should not always be deemed the only game worth playing." It was a sentiment the *Boston Globe* also felt compelled to express during the heyday of its own Red Stockings team, noting that in all sports "the main object should be to exercise moderation in its enjoyment."[25]

In its extreme form, such a single sport obsession could incite a narrowly nationalistic outlook that refused to acknowledge the value of any other athletic endeavor. "Inasmuch as several enthusiastic persons have called it the national game," the *New York Times* critically noted in 1872, "its devotees insist that patriotism demands that every American should profess an especial interest in [baseball]." *Wilkes* for one, would have nothing to do with this sentiment, asserting that "the truth is, we have no national game because we have the games of all nations." Even such an avowedly pro-baseball observer as Charles Newcomb, generally recognized as the first intellectual to take a serious interest in baseball, saw something of a cultural subversion behind baseball's self-proclamation as the national pastime, the sensitive and reclusive New Englander dismissing the title as nothing more than a public relations scheme by "penny-a-line" journalists.[26]

From a more practical perspective, critics were also concerned that this preoccupation with one sport could drastically narrow America's range of athletic development. Baseball had, by this period, developed into a sophisticated, highly skillful game, but unless Americans could demonstrate equal proficiency in other sports, they would run the risk of becoming a society known only for a game no other nation even played.

The *New York Times*, editorially not a particular friend of baseball during these years, was especially worried over the possible consequences of this, editorializing in 1872 "so long as we can only boast base-ball, we are like the man who hid his talent in a napkin and was afraid or too indifferent to put it out to usury. The man who can play base-ball can play cricket, football, golph [sic] and any other game.... They ought to be able to do so, and it is a duty to themselves that they should do it." This sentiment was also taken up by the foremost proponent of amateur sports, *Forest and Stream*, which declared in its inaugural issue a year later, "Open-air sports should never be limited to a single kind. We must not play base ball to the entire exclusion of cricket, any more than we must always pull boats, and never run foot races. We should be able to do each and all of them; giving all our attention to a single athletic sport dwarfs true spirit in the matter."[27]

It wasn't simply as a matter of national prestige, however, that some critics believed Americans were obliged to continue playing cricket. Since both cricket and baseball were bat-and-ball sports, it had long been assumed those who played both games enjoyed considerable crossover benefits in their skill development, that "excellence in one game promotes excellence in another." Despite the increasingly disproportionate level of popularity between the two games by this time, it was still widely believed, as *Wilkes* said in 1860, that "Base ball and cricket are kindred sports and the combination of the two will improve the playing of both."[28]

From his own experience with both baseball and cricket, Henry Chadwick was one of the strongest advocates of this view that the two sports developed skills interchangeably, asserting that "there is nothing better for practice for a base ball player than cricket," especially bowling, which, according to Chadwick, helped baseball pitchers by "making them drop their speed and go in for headwork."[29]

To support this view, Chadwick and other observers could point to a number of standout athletes who benefited from their experiences with both sports. Most frequently singled out were Harry Wright and his younger brother George, both of whom enjoyed notable success as both cricket players and professional baseballers over their long sports careers. Beginning as a member of the St. George Club, who "did nothing at the bat" during his first forays into baseball, Harry Wright eventually developed into one of the standout baseballers of his era as both a player and later as a coach/manager. It was Wright's ability to apply the "headwork" he had learned from cricket, Chadwick seemed to believe, that contributed to his Cincinnati Red Stockings famous undefeated season of 1869.[30]

His talented younger brother George also played cricket and baseball interchangeably over a long athletic career, from the single wicket beating he inflicted upon a taunting Englishman while with the Washington Nationals baseball club, to his tenure as the captain of Boston's Longwood Cricket Club, which Wright reportedly joined in 1880 rather than agree to unacceptable terms with his Providence Grays baseball club. To some, it was the Wright brother's proficiency in both sports that accounted for their Cincinnati Red's easy win over a team of San Francisco cricketers in 1869, as well as for their fine showing as members of the New York team that opposed Fitzgerald's English amateurs in 1872, a showing, according to the *New York Times*, far better than that of their cricket playing teammates.[31]

The Wright brothers may have been the most celebrated examples of baseballers who also excelled at cricket, but there were others. John Dickson ("Dick") McBride had been a much-in-demand antebellum Philadelphia cricketer before embarking upon a long and successful career with that city's Athletics baseball club. Two standout New York Mutuals baseball club members, Dick Higham and John Hatfield, also did double duty as cricketers, the former with the New York Cricket Club, the latter with the East Williamsburg and also the St. George cricket clubs, for whom he once scored a team high 54 runs.[32]

In the estimation of most contemporary observers, however, the most highly regarded baseballer-turned-cricketer of this period was James Creighton, a star player for the New York Excelsior Baseball Club whom history has generally recognized as baseball's first professional player. Creighton had also given strong evidence that he "had the elements of a good cricketer" from his playing days with the short lived American Cricket Club. After that organization's demise, Creighton joined the St. George club and quickly established himself as one of the city's standout cricket players, primarily on the reputation of his peculiar type of pitches, "half underarm shooters," as eyewitnesses described them, that came into opposing batters "like lightning, you know." The exact circumstances of his tragic death at the age of 21 are, to this day, still subject to debate, but it is almost certain he died from injuries aggravated during a mid-October cricket match in 1862, not a baseball game as sports historians have widely claimed.[33]

If baseball and cricket could represent individual applications of essentially the same ball-playing skills, then, in theory, Americans increased proficiency in baseball should have translated into a corresponding improvement in their cricket playing. A series of catastrophic losses to representative English teams between 1868 and 1879, however, clearly demonstrated this was not happening.

Edgar Wilshire's English professionals easily won all the matches they played against American teams in 1868, as did Robert Fitzgerald's English amateurs four years later, and Richard Daft's English professionals in 1879, the last mentioned having no trouble beating one team made up entirely of professional baseballers.[34]

Damaging as these results were to the belief that the playing skills of cricket and baseball were complimentary, this long standing assumption was further undermined by the failings of these same English cricketers at baseball. Wilshire's team never came close to winning any of the three baseball games they agreed to play during their cricket tour, against the Unions of New York, Athletics of Philadelphia, and a combined Harvard/Trimountain team in Boston, even though "the greater proportion of the spectators present [at the Boston game] had the impression that they would." Daft's team, 11 years later, fared even worse in the baseball game they agreed to play against the Providence Grays, the cricketers showing an almost total inability to master the intricacies of infielding and curveball pitching.[35]

Sports historians have taken little notice of these early competitive contacts between cricket and baseball, but there seems to be little doubt they materially influenced the future course of both games in America. Prior to the Civil War, cricket was generally believed to be a far more "scientific" game than baseball in its technical sophistication and athletic demands. Though this view was declining even before the Civil War, it was further weakened by the obvious inability of such highly trained cricketers as Wilshire's and Daft's professionals to competitively play the American game. As a consequence, many sports observers by the early 1870s were clearly convinced that baseball not only was "the equal to cricket as a scientific game," but one that now clearly surpassed the English sport in "demands upon vigor, endurance and courage of manhood." *Wilkes* was tending towards this opinion as early as 1868, specifically on its observation of the English cricketers futility at baseball; "Base ball does not differ from cricket so much that a knowledge of the one gives an idea of the other. But for all this, the Englishmen fell easier victim to the Unions at the American game than would the Unions have fallen to them at the old English pastime."[36]

This perception that the bat-and-ball skills developed from baseball could actually be more effective at cricket than vice-versa, something that represented a significant advancement for baseball's cultural standing, would gain further credence through the increasingly frequent success baseballers were enjoying against local cricket teams. *Porter's* proclamation, made as early as 1856, that baseball-trained Americans should be able to beat "old cricketers" was confirmed within four years, when a Brooklyn team that included several baseballers easily beat the Flatbush Cricket Club, a result that, in the eyes of the *Sunday Mercury*, "proved conclusively that base-ball players can successfully cope with cricketers at their own game." The Lowell baseballers who beat a team of Boston cricketers in 1870 also "seemed to adapt themselves in the new situation very readily," while the Lonsdale, Rhode Island, baseballer's effortless win over their local cricket club in 1889 was similarly viewed as a result that "thoroughly demonstrated that a good ball player could bat a cricket ball better than most of the old cricketers."[37]

By far the most significant and widely publicized of these early contacts between baseball and cricket came about during the famous Boston Red Stockings-Philadelphia Athletics baseball tour to England in 1874. Well aware that America's national pastime stood little chance of attracting the attention of the English public unless some cricket was mixed in, Red Stockings pitcher and tour co-organizer, Albert Spalding, arranged to have the American baseballers play a series of cricket matches in between their baseball exhibitions. Though most of these matches were against rather weak teams, with the Americans playing at odds of 18 against 11, the relative ease with which the baseballers won them all proved to be one of the bright spots in an otherwise unproductive tour.[38]

Baseball historians have tended to downplay the 1874 English baseball tour as little more than a publicity stunt by Spalding and Red Stockings teammate Harry Wright that contributed to the premature demise of the National Association, the country's first professional league. There were many indications, however, that the baseballer's success at cricket during this tour helped dispel the lingering perception that baseball's skill culture was still subservient to cricket's. These converted baseballers had, after all, been far more successful against the English than any previous American cricket teams, a fact not lost upon contemporary observers, who pointed to the baseballers marked superiority in throwing, catching, and fielding, so superior that their English opponents, according to Spalding, "were sick with envy." Spalding himself always looked back on these cricket matches with special pride, not unexpected for an organizer who tirelessly worked throughout his career to elevate baseball's standing at both home and abroad, though his pride seemed to have also been shared by the general public if the occasional letters the *Clipper* received on this subject over the years is any indication.[39]

Sports historians have long known how powerfully the incentive to "beat the other guy at his own game" can influence the development of sports in certain societies and cultures, especially with a sport that became so geographically dispersed as cricket. It was one of the most important factors behind the game's rise and development in many of England's former colonies, such as Australia, India, and the West Indies, all of whom built much of their national sports identity around their ability to beat their former colonial masters. Why then was this incentive so ineffective in cricket's development in the United States? Why didn't Americans, despite their personal preference for baseball, feel it incumbent upon themselves to channel some of their sporting resources toward beating England at cricket, any measure of success at which would probably have boosted national prestige far more than any success at other sports?[40]

The most obvious explanation is that baseball, with its rapid development as a professional sport in the 1870s, was simply able to attract and retain America's best bat and ball talent. This view, however, assumes that top caliber American baseballers had no contact with, nor interest in, cricket after the immediate post-Civil War period, an assumption that was far from accurate.

It wasn't at all unusual for baseball teams, during the early years of professionalism, to occasionally arrange cricket matches as a break from their regular schedule. As a result, no doubt, of their cricket experiences in England, the Boston Red Stockings seemed to be the most willing members of the baseball fraternity to do this. The club spent one of its free days in 1875 playing cricket against the St. Louis Cricket Club, and two more of its off days in 1878 playing the Milwaukee Cricket Club. On at least one occasion, in 1876, Albert Spalding's Chicago White Stockings played some cricket with their city's local club, as did John Montgomery Ward's Providence Grays, against their local cricket club in 1882, the Rhode Island baseballers showing up so well as cricket players that the local press quipped, "it would undoubtably require the professional eleven of England to defeat them."[41]

Rarely during the late nineteenth-century, it seems, was cricket ever so far removed from the public eye that some baseballers, at some times and places, couldn't "be prevailed upon to try their hand at Merry England's national game." At almost the same time that the Opposition Baseball Club of Meriden, Connecticut, was indulging in some cricket against its local team in 1873, half a continent away, the Salt Lake City Baseball Club was engaging in a similar contest against its local cricket club. The cricket match between the Lowell baseball and cricket clubs in 1877 was duplicated, seven years later, by a match between the local cricket and baseball clubs of Grass Valley, California. Cricket playing seems to have been particularly attractive to baseballers in 1878, with cricket matches between local baseballers and cricketers occurring that year in such diverse locations as Rochester, Utica, San Francisco, and Portland, Oregon. Even the venerable New York Knickerbocker Baseball Club, for a few years in the early 1870s, regularly concluded its season with a late Fall match with its Hoboken neighbors, the Manhattan Cricket Club.[42]

On an individual basis as well, it wasn't unusual for nineteenth-century baseballers—some quite prominent—to occasionally try their hand at cricket. Some did so on a strictly situational basis, such as the three St. Louis Brown's professionals, Baker, McGinnis, and Peters, all of whom were selected for the All-Midwest cricket team that was to play Alfred Shaw's English professionals in St. Louis during 1881. One of the era's most prominent professional baseballers, Cap Anson, along with his Chicago White Stockings teammate Fred Pfeffer, signed on with the All-Chicago cricket side during its match against a visiting Australian team in 1896, Pfeffer putting out the Australian captain, George Trott, with a fine running catch that was taken to "a hurricane of applause." Many of the San Francisco residents who turned out for the match between their local cricketers and Alfred Shaw's team in 1881 specifically came to see their local star, A. J. Piercy, "lower the English team's eleven wickets," and for a while this converted baseball pitcher bowled quite effectively, if not entirely legally.[43]

For other nineteenth-century baseballers, cricket turned out to be an attractive second career once their baseball playing days were over.

Joseph E. Sprague, who had been the "pitcher par excellence of the country" during his days with the Brooklyn Excelsior club in the mid-1860s, enjoyed a long and fairly successful second career as a specialized bowler for a number of New York area cricket clubs. His "swift, twisting, underarm" bowling, though "very inoffensive looking," seemed to be unusually difficult to play, even for experienced cricketers. It evidently puzzled the Australians who played against him in 1878, as well as the Irish amateur cricketers who visited New York a year later, both of whom treated with great respect this American's peculiar deliveries, every one of which, as one observer described them, "caroms over the ground with fearful hop and skip."[44]

Other New York area baseballers who turned to cricket later in their careers included the former Mutuals Baseball Club player Rynie Wolters and the former Eureka Baseball Club member R. Heber Brientnall, both of whom joined the Newark Cricket Club in the 1880s, the latter eventually rising to the presidency of that club. Former Star Baseball Club member Herbert S. Jewell and ex-Empire Baseball Club player Frank Sebring also took up cricket during these years as members of the Manhattan Cricket Club, an organization that, in 1892, also hired the former Louisville ballplayer William G. Schenck as its groundsman. Jimmy Tynge, who had been a standout amateur baseballer, also spent some time playing cricket for the Staten Island Cricket Club, where he, on one occasion, amazed a team of visiting English cricketers with an exhibition of his curveball pitching. At least one prominent baseballer outside of New York, P. R. Reese, also "came to the conclusion that cricket was a good game," and joined the Baltimore Cricket Club in 1880.[45]

It seems then that Americans refused to rise to the competitive challenge cricket represented not because they didn't have the necessary ball playing resources to "beat the English at their own game," but because they simply no longer looked upon success at cricket as a legitimate test of their sporting culture.

The perception has existed that before the Civil War, Americans only played baseball because they didn't have the ball-playing skills to succeed at cricket, a view specifically expressed by the *Sunday Mercury* in 1861, with its suggestion that unless Americans could beat the English at cricket, they should stick to baseball. By the 1870s, however, this perception had radically changed. Because of the increasingly visible instances of baseballers success at cricket, and cricketers failure at baseball, there was now little doubt that baseball was equal, if not clearly superior, to cricket in technical sophistication and skill demands. This didn't mean Americans were any more successful against high-calibre cricket competition, but these failures were no longer looked upon as a detraction to their own bat and ball culture, because their success at baseball had proved to be, in effect, success at cricket by proxy. Americans weren't really bothered that Daft's English cricketers "simply played with the base-ballers" they opposed at cricket in 1879, because they knew full well other baseballers had "simply toyed" with these same English cricketers when they had played baseball. The *Clipper* then, was quite correct in its judgment, in the wake of Daft's tour, that nothing was really gained from playing international cricket matches since they only reinforced American's cultural confidence in their own game, as seen in the *Clipper*'s own demand that the English send over a team to play baseball, rather than have Americans play cricket.[46]

As subsequent history would show, Americans didn't consider cricket to be completely unworthy of competitive attention. The American press, through the years, always expressed at least a passing pride in Philadelphia's later successes against foreign cricket team. But even these accomplishments were always looked on as something of an anomaly, just as their failures were routinely shrugged off as efforts expended upon a sports challenge most Americans just didn't recognize. Rather than express any wounded pride in Philadelphia's loss to Lord Hawke's English team in 1894, the American press simply passed off the incident with the dismissive proclamation, "England is welcome to the championship that it holds."[47]

By the late 1870s then, the cosmopolitan ideal—the old antebellum belief that Americans could, and should, play cricket and baseball as separate expressions of a unified bat-and-ball culture—had all but been abandoned. From an initial association culturally compatible enough that Rochester cricket players could proclaim in 1858, "All hail glorious cricket and noble base ball," an association still mutually respectful enough, by 1867, that the "honorable rivalry" between the two sports was, to University of Michigan cricketers, "the very best means of furthering the interests of each," baseball and cricket had, by the late 1870s, diverged into two so separate, unequal, and alien cultural expressions that the editor of Racine College's student newspaper in 1879 saw no other means of coexistence than to "let the base ball men go to their diamond, and the cricketers to their turf."[48]

Understandable and apparently irreversible as all this was, to some observers it nonetheless represented a worrisome and regrettable compromise of America's athletic potential. For all its popularity and technical advancement, baseball still remained, in the estimate of these critics, a game no one else played except Americans, that diverted an inordinate amount of attention and resources away from other, more recognized sports. In contrast to the English, who excelled at a wide range of sports during this period, "the record for us," the *St. Louis Globe Democrat* lamented in 1875, "is not creditable," pointing out that Americans could show proficiency in only two sports, baseball and trotting."[49]

Even more disturbing was the way American's exclusionary obsession with baseball was allowing baseball opportunists a dangerously free hand in monopolizing American sports sentiment to a degree that would not be possible with a multiplicity of bat-and-ball allegiances. The *New York Times* in particular had been concerned about this as early as 1872, warning Americans they had been "led off in a wrong direction" by totally rejecting cricket. Nine years later, with the abuses of professionalism now well before the public's eye, the paper went even further, insinuating, in a lengthy editorial, that baseball had secured its dominant cultural standing on false pretenses; "Certain unknown persons resolved to take the old game of rounders . . . and to make of it an easy substitute for cricket. . . . The baseball conspirators said to their fellow countrymen, 'Here is an easy game . . . play it and call it our national game.'"[50]

Like others born from frustration with the dynamics of mass sports movements, the *New York Times'* suggestion that "probably the time is now ripe for a revival of cricket" was as unrealistic a reading of America's sports culture as the nostalgic hope that Americans would return to cricket once the post-Civil War baseball "furor" had passed. "Popularity is everything," as the *American Chronicle of Sports and Pastimes* more correctly knew in 1868. This would be the criterion by which every sport in American culture would have to stand or fall without recourse, and there was little doubt it was a criterion cricket, regardless of its other merits, hadn't met.[51]

As America began to emerge from reconstruction into one of its most socially dynamic periods, American cricket supporters were rightly concerned about their game. Always a sympathetic, but never uncritical, supporter of cricket, the *Clipper* sensed as well as anyone the precarious state of the game, entitling one of its cricket columns, in 1869, "What about the future?", a state of concern it reiterated three years later with the even more fatalistic declaration, "Is cricket at a dead lock?"[52]

In trying to explain cricket's persistent unpopularity with Americans, most observers were by now subscribing to the view that the game was simply incompatible with the American "temperament," an interpretation articulated at length in an article that appeared in the *Nation* at the height of the post-Civil War baseball boom. Cricket stood no chance of becoming popular because the game was alien to those American characteristics the author identified as "being more fond of novelty, of change, of the excitement which novelty and change produce."[53]

All this, of course, was nothing new. More conscientious cricket observers had long known that their game, whose structure tended to encourage "tedious delays" and even outright stalling, was considered far "too slow" and "drawn out" for American tastes. Though a strong cricket supporter, *Forest and Stream* often expressed its displeasure on this point, declaring in 1879, "we sincerely trust that the patrons of the 'noble game' will see the necessity of doing away with an evil which has existed and been quoted long enough."[54]

To remedy this, some believed cricket's official rules would have to be overhauled, perhaps radically. To Henry Chadwick, however, cricket's "wearisome delays" and "want of punctuality," which Americans had always "shown a certain fretfulness and impatience with," were a consequence not of any defects in the game's official laws but the English custom of disregarding them. According to Chadwick, no radical changes in the M.C.C. laws were necessary to resolve the "irrepressible conflict between the waste of time in cricket and the saving of it in baseball," only a more rigid adherence to them. By strictly "enforcing promptness" on such points as match starts, time allowances between innings, and change of batters, Chadwick was convinced the frustratingly slow and leisurely English way of playing could be eliminated. For cricket to succeed in America, it simply had to be played "by English rules, not English customs."[55]

The problem was, Chadwick's proposals had been tried, unsuccessfully, by the American Cricket Club years earlier. The baseballers on this club had also believed they could make the games they played "quick" by strictly enforcing existing laws, requiring, among other things, that their members be on the field at least fifteen minutes before starting time, and that every batter be at the wicket ready to go within two minutes.[56]

The reason why this scheme didn't succeed with the American, or any other, cricket club was very simple; it fundamentally misunderstood the dynamics of cricket playing. In both baseball and cricket, all activity is directed toward the same object; to get the other team out as quickly as possible. In baseball this comes about in a fairly regular and predictable manner because the batter must run on every fair ball even if it's certain he'll be out. In cricket, on the other hand, this is much more indeterminate because the batter here doesn't have to run when he hits the ball and can continue to bat until the fielding team gets him out. Under such playing conditions it's difficult to see how there can ever be any real incentive to play "quickly."

An analogy can perhaps best illustrate this. Imagine a runner (representing the fielding side in cricket) is told he must run a race that can only be finished by passing ten designated markers (representing the ten batters the fielding side in cricket must put out before they can come to bat), which he must do in no more than three hours. The runner is not given any indication, however, where and at what intervals these markers will appear. Clearly, under these conditions it would make no sense for the runner to run such a race as fast as he could, because he doesn't have any idea where the markers are. He may reach all ten of them in only half an hour of running, but he may have also reached only two or three of them in the maximum three hour time allowance. Indeed, it would be far more logical to run such a race only at a slow, leisurely pace.

It was, therefore, meaningless to demand, as Chadwick did, that cricket players approach their game "with more promptness" since, like our hypothetical runner, doing so wouldn't in any way mean the end purpose of their play would be reached any sooner than if they played slowly.

It's difficult to understand why Chadwick supported this interpretation given his close personal association with the cricket of his era, some of which seemed to rather obviously refute his views. To Chadwick, for instance, the match between a representative Boston side and Fitzgerald's English amateurs in 1872 was as short and interesting as it was (nearly two full innings in under five hours) because the "rules were strictly adhered to." In actuality, it was the short, aggressive batting stands of the professional baseballers on the Boston side (George and Harry Wright, Andy Leonard, and Cal McVey) along with poor field conditions that kept the match as short and exciting as it was.[57]

Just as surprising was Chadwick's apparent inability to recognize this from his own playing experiences. Perhaps he did realize that factors such as the hard, true ice surface, rather than any "promptness" on the part of the players, was responsible for the fast and exciting cricket match on ice he himself played in during 1867, something *Wilkes* itself recognized; "In this respect, cricket has the advantage [over baseball], there being more sport in cricket on ice than on the field." Yet Chadwick still couldn't fully understand why the students at Brooklyn's Polytechnic School, in a match he himself arranged and supervised against the Manhattan Cricket Club in 1876, became so frustrated and openly "growled" as they were forced to passively stand and watch as the Manhattan batters blocked ball after ball.[58]

Neither these, nor any other experiences, however, ever seemed to alter Chadwick's conviction that playing cricket with greater promptness "as the professional [base] ballplayers do" was the salvation for American cricket. What's more, Chadwick's interpretation, in time, assumed almost canonical proportions among cricket supporters throughout the country. From St. Paul's School to Philadelphia to San Francisco, the problem with cricket was everywhere the same: its "lamentable waste of time," "countless delays," and "late beginnings," and everywhere there was only one remedy: to "make the game faster" by "beginning matches with greater punctuality," and playing them with more "energy and promptness."[59]

This uncritical acceptance of Chadwick's interpretation, along with the now culturally dominant judgment that cricket wasn't entirely worthy of America's competitive attention, would determine the game's direction in late nineteenth-century America. Forever gone were the old antebellum hopes that cricket would be able to appeal to the heart and soul of Americans in general, that it could, one day be "not something to be wondered at, but a reality, a living institution." Instead, cricket, at best, could now only expect to sustain itself as a segment sport, one that might be able to hold a modest popularity among that portion of society that honored its character enhancing values and had the resources and leisure now presumed necessary to participate in such a sport. In short, American supporters still held out hope that cricket could be "a game worthy to be added to their national pastimes, though not one calculated to suit the tastes of the general class of that people."[60]

6

Cricket "For the Courteous": The Untenability of Elitism

Organized sports had arisen in the United States on the premise that participation in sports would exert a socially beneficial influence upon the young men who played them. Sports advocates insisted participation in team sports not only developed a wide range of morally desirable qualities, such as discipline, courage, perseverance, and a sense of teamwork, but that it would also "tend to the closing of brothels and gambling houses of ill fame" by redirecting the energies of young men into more controlled and socially acceptable outlets.[1]

Although many sports were capable of contributing to these ends, baseball and cricket, being the two most popular team sports of this period, always seemed to assume a role of special importance in sports' perceived mission of elevating the public's moral sense. "Once make cricket and baseball and quoits and football and the rest of them national pastimes," the *New York Illustrated News* declared in 1860, "and there will be little room left for big crimes to grow among us."[2]

The rapid rise of professional baseball after the Civil War precipitated something of a crisis in this line of thinking. It soon became obvious that the emotional intensity that high-level baseball competition incited was everywhere manifesting itself in a variety of socially disturbing ways, such as crowd disorder, public drunkenness, and rampant gambling. The state of the game had deteriorated to such a point by 1874 that the *Spirit of the Times and New York Sportsman* could only lament that whereas baseball had been "originally a game as peaceful and as polite as one of our amateur cricket matches, it's now too often an exhibition of rudeness, rowdyism and violence." The consequences seemed to be just as worrisome with individual players as well, observers expressing concern that top-caliber baseball was, by now, becoming increasingly dominated by a class of talented, highly paid, but in many ways morally objectionable personalities, "not precisely a majestic object," as the *New York Times* found the typical professional baseballer to be in 1872.[3]

All this represented a very serious challenge to the accepted moral sports order of that period. If baseball playing did develop—as its supporters claimed—the more desirable social characteristics, then those who played baseball the most and played it the best should, in theory, also be the "best" men morally. Why was it, then, by the late 1860s, that those who did participate in the game strictly on its intended merits—the amateurs—couldn't play as well as those whose higher skill level evidenced little or no corresponding moral worth—the professionals? In short, the rise of professional baseball was directly challenging the very legitimacy of sports in American society, namely that physical superiority must be compatible with moral integrity.

Naive as this assumption may seem today, it was deeply ingrained in the conscious of nineteenth-century Americans. *Forest and Stream*, a harsh critic of the professional game from the very beginning, declared in 1873, "If the game [baseball] had possessed within itself any sound vital merits, the gentleman would soon have been able to play it quite as well as the professional." It was also the moral order Charles Newcomb wanted to see in his favorite game of baseball, noting in his journal, "as between two clubs of ball players, I always expect the most genteel of the two . . . to win the game." And when this didn't happen, Newcomb reassured himself this wasn't a failure of moral superiority but simply a shortage of experience. "When refined men fail in competition with coarse men, it is for want of the power which comes through practice; they have more of the power which comes through principle."[4]

The course of baseball's development, however, was clearly running counter to all this. As the game continued to professionalize, it was increasingly dominated by an ever smaller group of highly specialized—but usually morally questionable—people, eventually leading some observers to conclude baseball was abnegating its very claims as a sport for respectable society. "Our experience with the national game has been sufficiently thorough," the *New York Times* editorialized in 1881, "to convince us that it was in the beginning a sport unworthy of men, and that it is now, in its fully developed state, unworthy of gentlemen."[5]

With baseball's moral standing wounded by the more undesirable side effects of mass popularity, some observers began to look to cricket as the more worthy standard bearer of sport's antebellum social mission. Not that cricket advocates themselves had ever made any special claim to this effect. The "punctuality, energy, quickness of perception and execution and good temper" that John Irving praised as "the beautiful moral lesson" cricket was "capable of teaching" could apply to many sports. None of these games, however, seemed to share cricket's long tradition of orderly conduct and play, which seemed to instill a sense of obligation upon its participants to live up to these claims, something Rochester Cricket Club president E. P. Hall tried to impress upon his teammates, exhorting them, during a post-match dinner in 1858, to "strive not only to be good cricket players but good men—in fact gentlemen." It was on the reaffirmation of this essentially amateur sports ideal that American cricket would try to sustain itself, especially during professional baseball's more turbulent early years. At the height of the American game's professional controversy, in 1873, the *Detroit Free Press* was already noting, in its area, how this English game "numbers among its votaries . . . a great number of solid men who 'go in for it' in a spirit which tends to constantly elevate and give it tone among the better class of admirers of athletic sports."[6]

If cricket was still deserving of a place on the American sports scene "because it exercises every cardinal virtue in man," supporters could also point to the wider social benefits of this, especially in the always contentious issue of gambling, which had so deeply infiltrated just about every top-level baseball game in New York after the Civil War that the *Boston Herald* condemned them as "literally nothing more than gambling operations." By contrast, observers noted "in England, the sister game—cricket—has escaped the dangers of gambling and related evils." Just as striking was the way English cricket had been able to neutralize gambling's dangerous influence without compromising its own professional development, "professionalism is identical with the national field game of England, yet cricket seems as likely to be perpetual as it is immemorial."[7]

One sporting event in particular strongly reinforced the growing recognition of cricket as the team sport of social respectability: the tour of Fitzgerald's English cricketers in 1872.

Unlike the English teams that had visited the United States in 1859 and 1868, this one, captained by the articulate and urbane secretary of the M.C.C., Robert Fitzgerald, was an entirely amateur side, "all well-educated and refined young men," that included William Gilbert Grace, already, at this stage in his career, well on his way to securing a reputation as the greatest cricket batter of the nineteenth century.[8]

The *New York Times* went out of its way to point out that these English cricketers were all "gentlemen of independent fortune," here to play for fun rather than profit (though each player was reportedly paid $600 in gold for "expenses"). Above all, these English cricketers "will present to our people the novel feature of amateurs who have reached a point of excellence in their national game which, in our national game of base ball, is only attained by high-paid professionals. This is a feature worthy of the earnest study of our young athletes."[9]

In their appointed roles as ambassadors of amateur sportsmanship, the English tourists were eminently successful, winning all but one of their matches (the other being drawn) with a methodical and purposeful manner of play that was seen as the "triumph of discipline over a confused mass." In his highly readable account of the tour, *Wickets in the West*, Fitzgerald himself seemed to sense cricket's only feasible role in America would be as something of a countervailing presence to baseball. The English game could never hope to broadly appeal, as baseball did, to "the ultrarapidity, quicksilverosity" of the American character, but it could serve other purposes. "Americans might learn much, if they chose, from our noble game . . . it preaches and practices patience, it enforces self-control, it eliminates the irascible, it displays the excellence of discipline, it is more eloquent than Father Matthew on temperance and sobriety."[10]

On the whole, it was around this purpose that post-reconstruction American cricket would now organize itself, no longer as a sport that hoped to answer to market forces, but one that now directed itself toward a social segment morally unaligned with such mass sports movements as baseball. The clearest evidence of this could be seen in the shift away from the old antebellum competitive cricket clubs toward ones with a more pronounced social emphasis.

In the New York area this was most noticeable with the decline, after 1870, of that city's two most prominent old-line clubs, the St. George and New York.

The St. George seemed to have no difficulty attracting members during these years, including a number of Americans, such as the Oxford educated southerner, James T. Soutter, "perhaps the best all-around player in the country," who served a term as the club's president in 1877 before tragically going insane a few years later.[11]

The club's competitive standing, on the other hand, was materially deteriorating during this same period. With the better resident English players now enrolling with the Staten Island and Manhattan clubs, the St. George played fewer and fewer matches, limiting itself by the 1880s to largely practice or intrasquad games, so diminished a role that *Sporting Life* declared in 1887 that the once proud organization had now "entered its second childhood." The club seems to have played only two competitive matches in 1882, the last year it hosted an international match, and so few over the following years that "All Hoboken was astonished . . . to see cricketers wending their way to the St. George grounds" when the club tried to revive its cricket playing in 1887. The organization had a professional in 1888, but none in 1891, though we know it was still playing social cricket into the early years of this century.[12]

Even more precipitous was the decline of the St. George's long time rival, the New York Cricket Club. After its energetic and long-serving president Henry Sharp retired in 1867, the club found it increasingly difficult to maintain even a nominally competitive presence. It was still able to field a second eleven in 1870, but within a year the organization, which in its heyday of the mid-1850s supported nearly 400 members, had so faded from the local sport's scene that the *Clipper* could only query, "we scarcely know whether this old club is in existence or not." By the end of the decade it existed as nothing more than a nostalgic memory of the past glories of New York cricket.[13]

This pattern was duplicated among competitive cricket clubs in other areas of the country as well.

The old Union Cricket Club of Cincinnati, which civic leaders had vigorously tried to build up as the West's leading cricket club, also seemed to find little justification for its existence once baseball had arrived. So long as the club enjoyed the benefit of an overlapping membership with the local baseball club, it remained a viable organization, but after its player-coach Harry Wright took up baseball full time in 1867 it rapidly declined. By 1871, the total of its competitive activity amounted to a single match with a visiting opera troupe.[14]

Civic prestige proved to be no more enduring a foundation for cricket in St. Louis either. The city's surprisingly successful national cricket tour in 1873, which was optimistically expected to attract many eastern clubs to the city, only seemed to accentuate its isolation from other cricket circles. Once heralded as "the first team that has on this continent came up to the cricketer's ideal," St. Louis cricket, by the mid-1870s, seems to have become permanently incapacitated by a philosophical rift between its English and American contingents.[15]

As the old-line competitive cricket clubs went into decline, their roles were assumed by cricket organizations dedicated to providing an environment of more socially selective participation along strictly amateur lines.

The best example of this in New York was the Staten Island Cricket and Base Ball Club, which, by the late 1870s, had not only replaced the St. George as the city's leading cricket club, but had also established itself as one of the more vibrant and trend-setting athletic organizations in the metropolitan area.

Cricket of a predominantly social nature seems to have been played on this most rural of New York's boroughs as early as the 1840s, some of the St. George's more affluent members reportedly having their residence on the island. The club seems to have at least indirectly owed its existence, which came about on March 28, 1872, to a general dissatisfaction of its founders—Aymer Cater, William Davidge, Duncan Novel, and William Krebs—with the St. George, though the predominantly American Staten Island club still depended, during its early years, upon the St. George for experienced players. The club did, however, enjoy the advantage of having its own ground on the old quarantine area of Camp Washington on the island's northern end, a far more attractive location than the St. George's ground in rapidly urbanizing Hoboken, even though the Staten Island location, in its original condition, was "given over to the occupancy of vagrant cows and straying goats."[16]

By 1877, the *Clipper* could report that the Staten Island club had "declared its independence" from the St. George, and from that time the club quickly rose to a position of prominence in New York area cricket. The club hosted its first international match in 1879, as it would, with one exception, all other international matches played in New York from 1882 on. In 1885 the club relocated to the Delafield estate, a 5 1/2-acre plot on the corner of Bard and 1st Avenue, which it purchased for $40,000 and cleared of an orchard to make room for its new playing area. From an initial enrollment of 51, club membership rose to 352 by 1880, 599 by 1887. Though its cricket-playing members were "as plentiful as blackberries," it was the club's early support of such sports as lacrosse, football, and tennis (the last of which was supposedly brought to America in 1874 by Mary Outerbridge, wife of one of the club's founders, Albert E. Outerbridge) that convinced the *Clipper*, by 1879, that the organization was, by this time, New York's "model" athletic club.[17]

By now cricket was also evolving along these same lines in the Boston area. Cricket was being played as something of a status expression among Boston suburbanites soon after the Civil War, principally among the "young, gentlemanly Americans" of Newton's Nonantum Cricket Club. With a number of its members from such prominent local families as the Linders and Hodges, the club attempted to pattern itself after Philadelphia's Young America Club, at least to the extent of trying to distance itself from the area's predominantly ethnic clubs such as the old English-dominated Boston Cricket Club.[18]

The Nonantums, which merged with the Alpha Club of Salem in 1873, had established a clear tradition of exclusivity for New England cricket, but this did not take permanent form until a number of well-to-do Bostonians, among them H. F. Fay, John Hubbard, and James Farley, organized the Longwood Cricket Club in April of 1877. Starting with only a modest 25 members, and confined to a small plot on the Sears estate, awkwardly rectangular in shape because of the adjoining streets, this west Boston club was soon able to attract the area's more status-conscious sportsmen, including some from the old Nonantum club such as Charles Mixer, C. L. Bixby, and George Linder.[19]

The club's competitive standing was significantly boosted in 1880, the year George Wright retired from a long career in professional baseball and assumed the captaincy of the club's cricket team. From that point, and over the next decade and a half, Longwood would stand "preeminently at the head of New England cricket," not only in competitive strength, but wealth and quality of facilities, a standing that was sometimes resented by the many smaller immigrant working-class cricket clubs that proliferated in New England during that period, which often rallied to the cry "anything to beat the Longwoods."[20]

In some respects, however, it was neither Staten Island nor Longwood, nor even the more prominent Philadelphia cricket clubs (to be discussed in chapter 8) but Detroit's Peninsular Cricket Club that may have best typified cricket's transformation into a focal point for alternative sports interest.

Unlike either Staten Island or Longwood, the Peninsular club had begun as an antebellum competitive club that gradually implemented a self-transformation into a more exclusive general purpose athletic club. Following a period of noticeably diminished activity after the Civil War, the club was able to leverage the success of an 1878 eastern tour to good purpose, increasing its membership from a modest 70 in 1882 to 179 active members by 1886. The organization also relocated to more fashionable locations, first to a plot leased from the Detroit Sporting and Recreation Company and, in 1885, to a more luxurious site on the Detroit Recreation Grounds near Woodward Avenue, where it expanded its athletic offerings, adding tennis and bicycling for its growing female and junior membership. The club's social standing was further enhanced in 1890, when it became the cricket department of the prestigious Detroit Athletic Club, with which it shared facilities "in the heart of the finest residential portion of the city."[21]

In common with most other American cricket clubs of this time, the Peninsular always relied upon a number of English, and in its particular case, Canadian, players, but here most of these individuals were permanent residents (such as Charles Calvert and George Heigho, English immigrants who owned their own lithography companies), a situation that ensured there would be a strong social cohesion among the club's American and non-American members. Throughout most of its history, in fact, the Peninsular Club was always under the administration of prominent local figures, such as U.S. Attorney George E. Hand, and Ford Hinchman, president of the White Lead Paint Company, both of whom served terms as club president during the 1860s and 1880s.[22]

The Peninsular club could also count, among its members, one individual of special symbolic significance, George Pierre Codd. An accomplished all-around athlete during his days at the University of Michigan, where he excelled at both baseball and tennis, Codd also proved to be a talented cricket player, contributing many outstanding performances as a member of the Peninsular club during the 1890s, among them a fine running catch that put out Hugh Trumble, star batter of the Australian team that played in the city in 1893. In addition to his athletic versatility, Codd was also an individual of great social accomplishments, serving a term as the mayor of Detroit just after the turn of the century, another as the representative from Michigan's 1st Congressional District during the 1920s. Perhaps more than any other individual, Codd may have exemplified the founding purpose of these late 19th-century cricket clubs: that nonspecialized, culturally neutral pursuits were the best means of developing the whole man.[23]

The more status-conscious late 19th-century American cricket clubs probably provided an ideal atmosphere for developing athletes such as Codd, since their overriding purpose was to provide an environment that strictly subordinated professional influences to amateur athletic purposes. Membership in most of these clubs, though hardly exclusive, was, in most cases, based upon a uniformity of social outlook and values. The Chicago Cricket Club adopted a statutory requirement that "all objectionable persons making application" be screened out, a policy duplicated by the Pittsburgh Cricket Club, which saw to it that "every Tom, Dick and Harry will not be admitted."[24]

Established above all as organizations that encouraged its members to directly participate in sports, most of these clubs shared a strong distrust of professionalism of any kind. The Toledo Outing Club, which supported an in-house cricket team, was specifically set up by young men "who feel the need of outdoor recreation not subject to the influence associated too often with professionals." The view was also shared by Philadelphia's Belmont Cricket Club, which, in its early years, forbade the employment of a professional in any capacity. Most of the country's larger cricket clubs did routinely have at least one professional on their staffs, but their duties were usually restricted to coaching, umpiring, or grounds maintenance.[25]

Insofar as this arrangement was a direct adoption of English cricket practices, almost all professional cricketers in America were Englishmen specifically brought over to fill these positions. Like their counterparts in England, and to a lesser extent, in professional baseball during this period, these professionals often led highly peripatetic and frequently insecure careers. To pursue his livelihood as a professional, William

Hammond worked, at various times, in Philadelphia, Boston, and finally at Brooklyn's Union Baseball Club, where he was serving as that club's groundsman at the time of his death from typhoid fever in 1872. John Norley, of Kent, was even more far-ranging in his cricket career, holding positions, over the years, at Syracuse, Buffalo, Chicago, and even Harvard University. Tom Armitage, a Yorkshireman who played professionally for a number of Chicago area clubs, had to supplement his income as a saloonkeeper, a requirement that may have contributed to his poor mental health, which deteriorated so badly that he would spend time in a Kankakee insane asylum before ending his career as the groundsman for the Pullman Cricket Club.[26]

For other English professionals, their careers in America turned out much more favorably. George Bromhead, of Nottingham, enjoyed a long and prosperous forty-one-year tenure with Philadelphia's Germantown Cricket Club, where his coaching talents significantly contributed to that club's competitive dominance of Philadelphia cricket during the 1890s. Another Nottingham immigrant, John Isaac Chambers, enjoyed a forty-eight-year career with the Longwood Cricket Club, where he lived to see his two sons succeed him as club groundsman and a nephew become that club's tennis professional.[27]

None of these men, however, seems to have had quite as eventful a career as Tom Dale. This tall, well-built English fast bowler, nicknamed "jumbo" by his teammates, had spent time as a professional in St. Louis and Chicago before joining the Peninsular Club in 1877. He would best be remembered, however, for a series of bizarre events that unfolded while he was in England playing for a touring Canadian team in 1880. Though traveling under the pseudonym "Jordon," Dale was identified as a deserter from a British regiment that had been stationed in Canada and immediately arrested. Apparently finding even the exceedingly light one-month prison term too onerous, the former army corporal tried to elude his guards by "running down" Knightsbridge Street, only to be recaptured and have his sentence extended an additional eleven months. None the worse for the whole experience, Dale eventually returned to Detroit, divorced his wife, who, it was rumored, had betrayed him to British authorities, and evidently spent the remainder of his career in peace and quiet in that city.[28]

In marked contrast to the uncertainty and insecurity under which the average professional cricketer lived, members of the more prominent late nineteenth-century American cricket clubs expected their organizations to ensure an environment of order, propriety, and conspicuous expression of leisure time. In most instances, cricket playing was viewed more as a vehicle for maximizing social interaction among peers than as a pure test of competitive abilities. In addition to their first elevens, many of these clubs also supported second and even third elevens, as well as junior and veteran teams. Still others occasionally arranged lighthearted "ladies vs gentlemen" matches, with the male participants usually playing lefthanded or with baseball bats.[29]

The vacation month of August at these clubs was frequently given over to leisurely cricket tours to other areas of the country or to the more popular destination, Canada. The Chicago Cricket Club played in the Dominion in 1882, and the Seabright Lawn Tennis and Cricket Club in 1887, while the Peninsular club undertook late summer tours to that country on an almost annual basis during the 1870s. The most ambitious of these working vacations was undertaken by a contingent of New York and Philadelphia cricketers who spent the winter of 1887-1888 playing in the British West Indies.[30]

Typical of other organizations secure in their economic and social standing, some of these clubs also lent themselves to charitable purposes. The Newark Orphan Asylum was the beneficiary of a charity cricket match between the Staten Island and Newark clubs in 1882, as were the southerners afflicted by the yellow fever epidemic of 1878 assisted by relief funds raised from a baseball match between the Peninsular club and Detroit's Cass Baseball Club. The All-Philadelphia side that toured England in 1889 donated its proceeds to British charity, something it had the luxury of doing because Philadelphia clubs were always able to raise large subscription funds for the representative teams they sent overseas.[31]

International matches in particular proved to be the most conspicuous opportunities for these clubs to showcase the propriety and order associated with their sport. In contrast to more popular forms of recreation "the crowd at an international match," *Harpers Weekly* duly noted during an 1892 Philadelphia match, "is eminently orderly. Rowdyism has no place there." To others, these events were characterized by a distinct atmosphere of appreciative sportsmanship and nonpartisan demeanor, where "the flow of comments and explanations and good natured bantering," as one reporter noted during an international match in Detroit in 1879, "reminded one of a scene of a county fair just after the awards of premiums had been announced."[32]

When properly ordered, these matches even tended to completely obscure their competitive purposes for a higher, aesthetic rationale, which was how a match in Philadelphia struck one observer in the early 1870s:

> You will find a glorious stretch of velvet turf . . . level and green as a huge-billiard table, skirted, on one hand, by a rolling landscape and

hedged on the other by a row of primeval oaks . . . The pavilion is appropriated to the players and perchance the band. The grandstand is already filled with spectators, old men and children, young men and maidens are there . . . The whole picture is one of beauty and animation and that spirit must indeed be dull who does not yield to the exhilarating influences of such a scene.[33]

Committed as these clubs were to an environment supportive of the ideals of the "gentleman at play," they always assumed, nonetheless, this was fully compatible with high quality cricket. The larger clubs had all along tried to loosely replicate first-class English cricket's competitive structure, which allowed amateurs to compete on a fully equal footing with the best professional players without compromising amateur control of the game. With the best resident foreign players usually among their membership, and with the best cricket facilities at their disposal, these clubs always assumed they would be able to uphold the old antebellum expectations that Americans could still play cricket at a reasonably high level.

These expectations received a totally unexpected boost during a series of matches against Australia's national team, which had agreed to play in America on its way home from England in 1878. Although this was the first foreign team to visit the United States in six years, a circumstance that probably accounted for the public's high interest in a team that, it was claimed, played with "something of the dash of the New World," memories of past disasters against foreign cricket teams were still fresh enough in the minds of most observers to lead them to expect no better results against the Australians. The *American Cricketer* even morbidly declared New York would have to "play 69 men instead of 18" to have any chance against these cricketers from a land as "remote as Mars."[34]

As it turned out, the New York team that opposed the Australians on this occasion confounded even the most pessimistic critics. With Ed Sprague's underarm "dew skimmers" being well supported by fielding that up to this time had been reviled for "handling the ball generally like muffin base ball players," the New York team hard pressed the Australians throughout their first innings, which at one point stood at a near disastrous 32 for 7. Extended into a second innings, the Australians eventually won the match, but even then "the surprise and enthusiasm of the public were almost unbounded" over the American's unexpectedly strong showing.[35]

In Philadelphia, things started out even better for the local team. Buoyed by Robert Newhall's 84 run first innings stand, the Philadelphians, playing an overseas team for the first time on even terms, eleven-a-side, nearly forced the Australians to follow on. Once again the visitors recovered in their second innings and would most likely have won the match had a lengthy dispute between the two sides not lost valuable playing time. As a consequence the match unsatisfactorily ended in a draw, but even then it represented the first time an American side had not lost an international match, reason enough to make it "in every way, an exceptional event."[36]

Observers were quick to interpret these surprisingly positive results as America's much desired, if long overdue, coming-of-age in international cricket. Though holding no assurances of future success, to the *Clipper* the matches at least proved American cricket had progressed to a point that its representative teams hereafter "have no longer any reason to claim odds in a contest" against any foreign opponent.[37]

Just how mistaken were even these modest claims became painfully evident over the next four years, during which time representative American sides suffered an unbroken series of defeats against foreign teams as disastrous as any in their history. Barely eight months after their fine showing against the Australians, a representative New York side, this time emboldened to play at even odds, was easily beaten by a contingent of Lord Harris's English team that had decided to return home from Australia via the United States. Hastily arranged in early May, long before the start of the local cricket season, the match was generally discounted as little more than a "scratch match."[38]

No such excuses, however, were forthcoming for the string of losses that befell American teams later that fall against Richard Daft's squad of English professionals. Everywhere the Englishmen played they completely overwhelmed the local opposition; in Detroit, Syracuse, New York, and even Philadelphia, where they inflicted so severe a defeat upon the pride of American cricket, the Young America Club, *Forest and Steam* could only lament "the match was painfully absurd, and to an American humiliating."[39]

This sad series of events was virtually repeated two years later, when Alfred Shaw's English professionals also made a clean sweep of all their American matches, even when playing without their star batter Arthur Shrewsbury, as they did in their win against Philadelphia.[40]

Most discouraging of all were the rematches with the Australian side that returned to the United States in 1882, not the least for showing up the results of 1878 for what they really were: complete flukes. In their first innings against the Australians this time around, the New Yorkers barely eked out 25 total runs, so miserable an exhibition the Australians themselves were reportedly laughing by the fall of the last wicket. Over all, the American effort proved to be so pathetic that the *Clipper* outright condemned it as "the poorest exhibition seen in any of our international contests in this vicinity."[41]

The Australians were hardly any more inconvenienced during their rematch with the Philadelphians. This time Bonner and Massie, with only an hour of time remaining, quickly destroyed what hopes local supporters had of also drawing this match by effortlessly hitting up the required 53 runs in less than 40 minutes.[42]

These experiences must have not only effectively dispelled any hopes that American cricket would ever be able to compete on a level remotely comparable to professional level English or Australian cricket, but also underscored the impropriety of even trying to do so. With the exception of two more visits by the Australians, in 1893 and 1896, only amateur teams would visit the United States after 1882, an arrangement that clearly seemed more philosophically compatible with the character of American cricket at that time.

Certainly the amiable amateur Irish teams that toured the United States in 1879, 1888, and 1892 proved to be far more popular cricket ambassadors than their professional counterparts, the ease and openness of their play exhibiting "nothing of the wooden men about them when at the wickets," which had characterized the workmanlike intensity of the English professionals. The Irishmen's approachability and willingness to play matches in such out-of-the-way locations as Pittsburgh, Lawrence and Lowell, Massachusetts, and even St. Paul's School, along with their less consuming competitive intensity (the tour doubled as a honeymoon for one player of the 1879 team), sharply contrasted to the practices of such professionals as the Australian "sharps," who during their New York match in 1882, were suspected of artificially prolonging the game to insure an extra day's worth of gate receipts.[43]

On a purely competitive level as well, American cricket was not nearly as deeply in over its head against this caliber of opposition. The Philadelphians were clearly superior to the amateur West Indian team that toured the United States in 1886 and were also able to beat every Irish side, save one, that visited their city. These matches with Irish sides were usually so closely contested observers couldn't help noting "it would probably be hard to find teams that are more evenly matched."[44]

Because it had been the first time an American team had ever beaten an overseas opponent at cricket, Philadelphia's win over the Irish in 1879 was looked upon as something of "an astonisher." Philadelphia, however, achieved the far more significant milestone of making the English themselves "cry quits to the Quakers" when it won the first of its two matches against Rev. E. T. Thornton's amateur English side in 1885.[45]

What limited success Americans enjoyed at international cricket in other areas of the country also came against amateur opposition. Longwood's win over the Irish team it hosted in 1892 would be its one and only success against foreign opposition, as would be Staten Island's win over the West Indians in 1886. Representative New York sides briefly enjoyed a first inning's lead over E. W. Roller's amateur English side that same year and came close to beating the Irish in 1888, the locals so surprising themselves with their 202 first innings' total during that match that they "fairly hugged themselves with delight in having made such a splendid stand."[46]

Few, however, seemed to be under the apprehension that these infrequent successes against amateur foreign sides in any way "tended to improve American cricket vastly." By the late 1870s, in fact, it seemed clear that cricket in America, at least outside Philadelphia, had settled into an irremediably low and stagnant competitive level. The sole and solitary difference the *Clipper* could find between the New York cricketers who lost to Daft's team in 1879 and those who had lost to the all-England side in 1859 was that the former had suffered their humiliation exactly 20 years to the date after the latter had suffered theirs. And following the city's disastrous loss to the Australians in 1882, most observers were not willing to even give local cricket this much credit.[47]

Foreign cricket teams would continue to visit American for another quarter of a century, but from this point on most of these encounters were looked on as rather hollow exhibitions, rather than serious gauges of competitive standards. No one believed that the outcome of the New York-Australia match in 1896 would be anything but "a sure lead-pipe, dead-easy cinch" for the Australians, who themselves freely confessed this American cricket excursion was little more than a "picnic trip" not to be taken "too seriously." The *Boston Globe* probably best articulated America's frustration with this state of affairs with its cricket, noting, as Roller's English amateurs were overwhelming Staten Island in 1886, "with what ease [the English cricketers] can play the cat to the American cricket mouse."[48]

Over time, such an unmitigated string of reverses even began to negatively influence public sentiment, some American observers sensing what they believed to be a veiled condescension on the part of their foreign visitors. Some believed the star English batters Prince Ranjitsinhji and Archie MacLaren both faked illnesses so they wouldn't have to bother playing with their team against a feeble New York team in 1899. Others were convinced the Australians, having easily won their first two matches against Philadelphia in 1896, lost their final match on purpose (a charge the Australians denied), and that some of Bernard Bosanquet's English team had simply signed on to play cricket as a pretext to see the America's Cup race in 1901. Most of these accusations were probably born of simple frustration, but Lord Hawke would confess, years after losing his first match to Philadelphia in 1891, "I was glad we did not win. It would not have encouraged cricket in America had we won every game."[49]

Always reluctant to concede America's failings at cricket were due to any athletic deficiencies, observers began to interpret America's chronic inability to "develop good cricket players" as a consequence of more fundamental differences between English and American social systems. Because proficiency at cricket, it was widely assumed, required a large expenditure of time and resources, the vitality, if not the very existence, of the game seemed to "imply a leisure class," a social segment that had the requisite financial security and free time to devote to the game. America's inability to produce good quality cricket then, simply proved American society had no English-type leisure class, nor was it in any way realistic to expect this would change "until a new generation with unlimited leisure and patience" would arise in America.[50]

As proof of this, observers usually pointed to Philadelphia, whose upper-class support, it was generally believed, was most responsible for that city's high quality cricket. The *New York Times* specifically claimed Philadelphia's breakthrough win over Thornton's English team in 1885 was "disproof of the reckless assertion that we have no leisure class," while the *New York Tribune* saw in the success of Philadelphia's English tour in 1903 a strong indication that American society was experiencing an "enlargement of [its] leisure class."[51]

Throughout its modern history, cricket had always been a highly social game, one known for encouraging beneficial interaction between participants. "Cricket is . . . eminently a social game," the *Clipper* had declared well before the Civil War, "and one in which the amenities of social life are of vital importance to its existence." Equating sporting interest and proficiency with specific social conditions, however, always ran the risk of subsuming a game's competitive rationale to nonplaying purposes. This became especially apparent in the wealthier late nineteenth-century American cricket clubs, whose extravagant post-match meals, balls, and other social expressions became inextricably associated with more important cricket events. The Baltimore Cricket Club seems to have been particularly guilty of this, being known more "for the excellence of the lunch than the cricket" it played, and where social amenities became so dominant they tempted P. F. Warner's English batters to purposely get themselves out so they could dance with the Baltimore society girls rather than exert themselves in their match against the club in 1898.[52]

Disruptive photo-ops and lengthy meal breaks also became increasingly prominent at important matches, as well as bands, hired to serenade players and spectators during the game with strains from Verdi and Strauss, the chosen music for Philadelphia's match against Wilshire's English pros in 1868, a peculiar American cricket custom that even the English found to be "a downright nuisance."[53]

Within such an environment it was almost inevitable that the game, in some instances, would completely lapse into unpalatable and highly stereotypical expressions of snobbery and social posturing, played by "duffers" and "freaks of the fop" whose presence did nothing to mitigate cricket's reputation as "suitable only for the drones of society." It was a development harshly criticized by *Forest and Stream*, which lamented, by the late 1870s, that on too many American cricket grounds one was finding "gaudy, effeminate males, adorned like embroidered tobacco pouches, teetering to and fro, calling themselves cricketers—and getting out first ball."[54]

This trend appeared in its worst light during international matches, especially against English amateur sides that incited a slavish Anglo mania and contorted role-playing that critics found to be fertile ground for ridicule. Unsympathetic observers never tired of scoffing at the "Welsh Rabbits" (American anglophiles) who cozied up to the game simply because it was English, or the Baltimore society girls who were "tickled to death" just because titled individuals were on Lord Hawke's team that visited their city in 1891. Plenty of ridicule was also heaped upon the "dudenus Americanus" who took up the game just to mimic English mannerisms, one reporter mockingly predicting as a result of Lord Hawke's second visit in 1894, "All the dudes will be buying cricket outfits before the week is out."[55]

If would be easy to conclude that such overly exaggerated and conspicuous displays of status only confirmed the belief that cricket was essentially alien to mainstream American sports culture. But this conclusion would not be entirely correct. A good number of sports such as tennis, golf, and polo first appeared in elitist sports environments, some under the same negative stereotypes that plagued cricket. Yet most of these sports continued to flourish, some even becoming popular mainstream American sports.

The best example of this was tennis, which, like cricket, was also typecast in its early years as a snobbish, at times effeminate, game played only by Americans aping English mannerisms. Yet these perceptions didn't appreciably retard the game's progress, which quickly outstripped cricket in popularity even within many cricket clubs themselves. Tennis was "very popular" in the Germantown Cricket Club as early as

1877, and made its first appearance at Longwood a few years later. By the 1880s, virtually every organized cricket club had taken up tennis to some extent, from Pawtucket, Rhode Island, to Greenwich, New York, to Minneapolis and as far west as Omaha. Even in New York, the *Clipper* regretfully reported, in 1883, that "a sigh goes up because the veteran St. George club . . . seems to have temporarily deserted in behalf of lawn tennis."[56]

Nor should this have been particularly surprising. As a sport with a rapidly alternating play structure, that could be enjoyed by men and women over a relatively short period of time, tennis was a game that could provide its participants with essentially the same social amenities as cricket without cricket's unappealing play structure.

Understandably, some cricket supporters could not help but view tennis as a serious threat to their own game. The most impassioned plea to this effect came from *Forest and Stream*, which in 1880 asserted that "we have not for years worked hard to advance the interests of cricket, to now allow an innovator like lawn tennis to crowd out our manly game . . . Shall the stumps that we now firmly planted be torn out before they have taken root? Not if we can help in staying the destroying hand."[57]

The *American Cricketer*, in a lengthy reply to these concerns, was not nearly as alarmist. The publication actually welcomed tennis as an activity that could indirectly benefit cricket by providing noncricket playing club members with their own recreational outlet. Despite recurring claims to the contrary, there seemed to be little evidence that cricket lost large numbers of its followers directly to tennis. The only documented evidence of this was the Manhattan cricket club player who in 1881 actually left his team in the middle of a match to go play tennis. The *American Cricketer* itself actually saw no harm in functioning as the official organ of the United States National Tennis Association during the mid-1880s.[58]

Tennis's rapid social acceptance within an exclusive sporting environment that observers once believed could only be possible with a sport like cricket, then, represented no change in the tastes of late nineteenth-century upper-class Americans as much as it revealed their uneasiness with cricket as an elite sport.

If we mean by an "elite" sport one that is actually played by the upper class, then this was never really the case with American cricket. Only one upper-class American family outside of Philadelphia—the Carnegies—seemed to have actually participated in the game; two of Andrew Carnegie's nephews, T. M. and W. C. Carnegie, were playing members of the Pittsburgh Cricket Club in the early 1890s.[59]

Members of some of America's more exclusive social clubs did take up the game during the late nineteenth century, but in most instances, this interest was relatively short lived. Two of New York's most prestigious sporting organizations, the New York Athletic Club and the New York Jockey Club, supported in-house cricket teams for only a single season in 1892, as did Philadelphia's most exclusive social organization, the Rittenhouse Club in 1891. Only slightly more interest was shown by the New York Racquet Club, which held an annual cricket match with the Staten Island Club for a few years, and San Francisco's prestigious Bohemian Club, which entered a team into their local cricket league during the 1890s.[60]

Just as revealing was cricket's conspicuous absence from the one location supporters believed should have been the game's natural habitat: Newport, Rhode Island. Certain that the summer residents of this most exclusive high society watering hole would be "the very class likely to become interested in cricket," the *American Cricketer*, as early as 1879, was scheming to tap into this clientele by holding a number of international matches at the location. The idea, however, never seemed to strike a responsive chord with Newport society itself, which steadfastly preferred its polo, tennis, and yachting, cricket's presence being limited to a few matches played among Philadelphia vacationers during the mid-1880s.[61]

Similarly, if we mean by an "elite" sport one that is patronized by the upper class, this also was never really the case with American cricket outside Philadelphia.

Prominent Americans did, ostensibly, hold membership in a number of the country's larger cricket clubs during this period. Industrial magnate George Westinghouse and agricultural tycoon C. A. Pillsbury were members, respectively, of the Pittsburgh and Minneapolis cricket clubs during the late 1880s, while the Chicago Cricket Club could count among its members in 1890 such local movers and shakers as retailer Marshall Field and meatpacking baron Phillip Armour. Maryland governor Robert McLane and state supreme court justice Hugh L. Bond held membership in the Baltimore Cricket Club and even John Phillip Sousa was a member of the Washington, D.C., cricket club just prior to the First World War. But most of these individuals were only honorary members, who seemed to take little direct interest in cricket, with the possible exception of Phillip Armour, who permitted the Chicago club use of his personal property as a playing area, and Andrew Carnegie, who lent his signature to a petition in 1889 to build a cricket pavilion in Central Park.[62]

In only one instance, it seems, did a prominent American become extensively involved with cricket. This was Thomas McKean, the long-time patron of the Germantown Cricket Club. This wealthy Philadelphia industrialist virtually underwrote that club's entire operations for a number of years, permitting it use of his personal property at Nicetown, paying the salary of its professional, and acting as security for its debts.[63]

But American cricket never had a Lord Sheffield-type figure, someone who would lend his vast personal influence and resources to support the game on a broad front, underwriting overseas tours or encouraging domestic competitions. America's upper class instead channeled its resources and support toward horse racing, yachting, and to a lesser extent, tennis, leaving late nineteenth-century American cricket to rely upon tokenistic support from strictly local interests, such as the "leading businessmen" of St. Louis, who chipped in to help their city's cricket club get to Chicago in 1895, or the city leaders of Minneapolis, who helped "partly defray" the expenses their local cricket club incurred as hosts to a tournament in 1887.[64]

Probably more than any other episode in American sports history, cricket's failure as an elite sport demonstrated the futility of trying to culturally sustain, on purely extraneous motives, a sport with an unattractive playing structure. Late nineteenth-century Americans turned to cricket in order to maintain an environment of "gentlemanly values." In doing so, they believed they were expressing sporting tastes distinct from such mass participation sports as baseball. Their eventual abandonment of a game other segments of American society had already rejected, however, only confirmed that this range of sporting tastes was fundamentally no different from that of any other social class.

In this respect, cricket's failure as an elite sport demonstrated the true sense in which American sports were "democratic"—not on the basis of equality of access (this did not really exist, then or now)—but from a uniformity of emotional requirements that cannot be fundamentally altered by social influences. Late nineteenth-century upper-class American cricketers may have been persuaded to play this game "for the courteous" in the belief they were expressing emotional values unique to their social class (patience, discipline, reserve, etc.), when, in fact, their reluctance to continue with the game only betrayed a set of emotional values (a demand for excitement, tension, and quick action) more in common with other Americans than they may have been willing to admit.[65]

The *American Cricketer* knew very well that "we can not make men play cricket who don't feel disposed thereto," yet it still seemed to believe Americans could be induced to do just that purely on such extraneous social appeals as status, image, and international prestige. Such involvement without direct and unequivocal emotional interest, however, could only deteriorate into snobbery, role-playing, and posturing, without which, one observer was sure, this "game of antediluvian modeling would have drifted along in the wake of the ark until it stranded on the shoals of American unpopularity."[66]

Despite fears that it represented a serious deterioration of sporting values, cricket's decline as an elite sport was necessary for America to come to terms with the basic homogeneity of its sporting culture, which was proving to be highly resilient to any reorientation along the lines of "class consciousness." All this seemed apparent enough to the reporter who attended an international match in Philadelphia during 1907. Behind the facade of high society attention and interest, the reporter couldn't help sensing there was here something unnatural and contrived. "Society pretends to like cricket," he had to report, "but someday someone is going to confess in a diary that it's all an attitude."[67]

7

"A Place for Every Man Who Will Come and Take His Part": On the Periphery of Late Nineteenth-Century Popularism

Over the last decades of the nineteenth-century, organized sports began to play an increasingly significant role in the leisure lives of the average American. If not quite the era of mass participation, this period witnessed the rise of the athletic club movement, dedicated to bringing the benefits of organized sports to America's urban middle class, as well as the rise of organized school and college athletics.

It was during this period as well that organized recreation and physical education first became widely supported as public policy, through either urban recreation programs or private initiatives such as YMCAs and working man associations.

Americans also had an increasingly greater variety of sports to choose from. Tennis, golf, football, and basketball, to name the most popular, all appeared on the American sports landscape during this period, offering an expanding range of sports opportunities for men and women of all ages and social backgrounds.

Late nineteenth-century Americans were showing an increased interest in sports for a variety of reasons: a growing social acceptance of sports participation, increased leisure time, and a growing demand for greater autonomy and self-direction in the specific use of this time.

Much of this represented a natural and straightforward extension of the sports interests that had developed around America's first two organized team sports—baseball and cricket—just before the Civil War. But the proliferation of late nineteenth-century sports alternatives also represented, to a noticeable degree, a reaction to the perhaps inevitable, but nonetheless unwelcome, overspecialization and selectivity of these sports.

Baseball, in particular, was coming under increased scrutiny for this. America's national game was as popular as ever during this period, but with this popularity had come an increasingly higher skill level that some believed was making the game inaccessible to the average American. In its early days, baseball had been primarily a participant sport, but now, in an era of highly competitive standards and increased specialization, some observers, such as Philadelphia's influential publication the *American,* were beginning to conclude, "Base ball has become so scientific that it has got beyond the interest of the average man."[1]

Compounding this was the continuing social concern over the abuses that still plagued professional baseball throughout this period, such as crowd disorder, player misconduct, and heightened labor-management tension, which boiled over into the bitter and divisive Players League War of 1890. It was with some measure of satisfaction, then, that the *American Athlete,* a strong advocate of amateurism, claimed more conscientious Americans were beginning to turn away from baseball and look to other sports: "Since the late mix-up in base ball circles, there has been a gradual drift among certain classes, and the better classes of our American public, towards other sports of a more decidedly amateur character. In the fields of cycling, cricket and tennis this fact has been most decidedly demonstrated."[2]

Just as they did in the earliest days of professional baseball, some American sports observers could not help but notice how different a path baseball's bat-and-ball rival, cricket, had followed in English society. Not only had English cricket, even at its highest competitive level, avoided the abuses of professionalism that persistently plagued baseball, but its professionalism didn't seem to at all deter or adversely affect the game's participant popularity among a broad cross section of English society. "The United States today," the St. Paul *Pioneer Press* noted in 1895, "has no national game in the sense that all play it and enjoy it as the English people play and enjoy cricket. This assertion may be surprising to base ball devotees but it is a fact."[3]

Not surprisingly, some critics began to believe America's softening interest in baseball as a participant sport was now creating a ready-made clientele for cricket, as the Topeka *Daily Commonwealth* did in 1887 with its claim, "for those who do not care for base-ball and want some kind of game for exercise, the best advice we can give is to try cricket." The English game's negative reputation as a less exciting sport than baseball now began to appear in a more positive light, observers noting that this bat-and-ball game was "free from the extreme excitement that attends the characteristic sport of baseball." At a time when baseball was being increasingly perceived as a sport where "all is vanity and vexation of spirit," cricket's relaxed and leisurely pace now seemed to make it a far better game for middle-age Americans, since it could be "continued through life as opportunity offers." Whereas the typical American baseball club was an organization of young men, the *New York Times* pointed out in 1889 that "in the cricket clubs of this neighborhood are to be found plenty of men over forty years old, active in business and professional interests."[4]

It was on these growing impressions, that cricket was not only a sport where "there's a place for every man who will come and take his part," but one that could also be played to "vary the monotony" of baseball, that the game seemed poised to play an expanding role within those late nineteenth-century sports trends that were affecting a broader cross section of American society.[5]

To what extent these perceptions actually influenced the level of cricket being played in the United States is hard to determine, but both anecdotal and quantitative evidence seem to confirm that the game enjoyed a marked upswing in popularity from its low levels of the 1870s, a time when the *Clipper* believed no more than "one in ten thousand" Americans actually played cricket. This estimate was probably as overly pessimistic as the *American Cricketer*'s claim in its inaugural issue that 300 North American clubs existed, was unjustifiably optimistic. *Forest and Stream*, which claimed to speak for all cricket, even in "the by-ways, where the broomstick stumps and sting-handle bat still hold undisputed sway," was probably more reliable in its 1879 estimate of 150 active North American clubs.[6]

If cricket interest in America was characterized by an extreme irregularity, where "for years the game would waste away to a mere skeleton, and then give satisfaction to its promoters by coming hale and hearty again," anecdotal evidence strongly indicates this interest was on the ascent from the mid 1880s to at least the early 1890s.[7]

Cricket was reviving so briskly in the New York area by 1890 that the Trenton *Daily True American* was claiming "in another season this game will become a general pastime for a large number." This prognostication seemed to be confirmed by both the *American Cricketer*, which in its report the following year noted that "an immense boom has cane [sic] to the game in New York," and the New York *World*, which by 1893 believed cricket now "follows closely upon baseball and tennis as one of the principal summer outdoor pastimes."[8]

Cricket was beginning to attract a greater following in other urban areas as well. The game was "coming more and more into favor" with Milwaukeeans as early as 1883, had experienced "a reawakening interest" among Detroiters a few years later, and had "come at last to stay, and grow and prosper" in the Minneapolis/St. Paul area by 1891. Though cricket certainly never reached a point of popularity to justify the Butte *Daily Miner*'s contention that it now "promises to become almost as popular as base ball," the game had achieved such a level of acceptance in New England by 1886 that George Wright could report there were "ten players now where there was only one a few years ago."[9]

In a few instances, these highly anecdotal claims can be more precisely quantified. The number of scheduled matches in New England rose from a meager 40 in 1882, to 70 in 1883, to a hundred by the following year, evidence enough, in the eyes of the *Boston Globe*, to declare "with sixteen clubs contending for honors . . . New England cricket may be safely designated as booming." In Philadelphia, the figures are more compelling. Here the number of scheduled matches mushroomed from 94 in 1887 to 225 in 1891, to a peak of 279 in 1895. These numbers, taken in conjunction with the *World*'s claim that there were 3,000 active cricket players in the greater New York area by 1892, seem to guardedly confirm the *Illustrated American*'s observation in 1891 that cricket "seems to have struck a popular fancy" with Americans.[10]

Why were more Americans now playing cricket? In addition to its emphasis on amateur values, and its attractiveness as a lifetime sport, cricket also seems to have fit in very nicely with the prevailing late nineteenth-century trend away from sports-specific organizations to either multipurpose athletic organizations, such as athletic clubs, or social/fraternal organizations in which athletics were of only peripheral importance, such as company athletic clubs, armed forces athletics, and YMCAs.

In this context, it was quite logical that cricket, with its pronounced social emphasis, would find a place in the most conspicuous amateur sports development of this period, the urban athletic club. In a number of instances, these organizations actually began as cricket clubs, such as Albany's Ridgeland Athletic Club, or Chicago's Wanderers Cricket and Athletic Club, both of which progressed from sport-specific to multipurpose athletic clubs. The old Newark Cricket Club underwent a similar transformation, expanding into an all-purpose recreational organization that, in addition to cricket, could now offer—on the 38-acre plot it purchased for that purpose in 1885—a wide variety of activities for not only its adult male members but their families as well.[11]

More often, however, established athletic clubs simply encouraged their members to organize in-house teams to supplement their range of recreational offerings. This was the route taken by three of New York's larger athletic clubs—Berkeley, Crescent, and Columbia—as well as a number of smaller metropolitan organizations, such as the Williamsburg Athletic Club, the Staten Island Athletic Club, and Hoboken's Americus Athletic Club, all of which supported cricket teams at various times over the last two decades of the century.[12]

The most prominent of these in-house teams was associated with the New Jersey Athletic Club, a well-appointed organization domiciled in an attractive area of Bayonne. With some of the area's best resident Englishmen among its members, such as M. R. Cobb and F. F. Kelly, the club had, by the early 1890s, eclipsed Staten Island as New York's premier cricket organization, a status it would maintain to the end of the century, and one that members felt justified the club's decision to host New York's match against the Australians in 1896.[13]

In the Midwest, the Michigan Athletic Association followed the lead of its cross-town rival the Detroit Athletic Club in setting up an in-house team during the early 1890s. Cleveland's Cricket and Golf Club and Toledo's Outing Club also supported cricket teams during this period. The game enjoyed a somewhat more privileged place at the Omaha Cricket and Athletic Association, due to the influence of club founder Arthur Spencer Treloar, a peripatetic English sports promoter who, among his other exploits, had once managed a team of English clown cricketers during their United States tour in 1876.[14]

Further west, cricket also enjoyed a fairly active and, in some instances, relatively long-lived presence in the Denver Athletic Club, the Astoria, Oregon, Football Club and in Portland's two largest sporting organizations, the Multnomah and Portland Amateur Athletic clubs.[15]

Though far less formal than the urban athletic club, the company or industry-specific athletic organization was probably a far more popular recreational outlet with America's growing urban middle class, a clientele that, in many instances, also valued cricket as a participant activity. This seems to have been especially true with employees of three traditionally clerical-intensive industries: banking, insurance, and railroading.

At one time or another, bank employee cricket teams could be found from Portsmouth, New Hampshire (the Strawberry Bank), to Chicago (the Bankers Athletic Club) to Portland, Oregon (the Associated Bank Cricket Club), teams that, in some instances, even arranged intra-profession matches, such as the one between Philadelphia's Franklin National Bank and the Commercial Trust Company in 1904.[16]

A number of insurance companies also supported employee cricket clubs, the most prominent being New York's Metropolitan Life Insurance Company, whose employee team competed in that city's cricket league for a few years in the mid 1890s. Insurance industry teams were also active in San Francisco and Milwaukee, the team in the latter city being under the guidance of Connecticut Mutual Insurance Company manager J. I. D. Bristol.[17]

Cricket was also well represented within a number of railroad industry athletic organizations. As early as 1876 employees of the Pennsylvania Railroad's Philadelphia office (perhaps on the urging of company vice president and Belmont Cricket Club officer John P. Green) had organized a company cricket team, an arrangement that was taken up a few years later by the company's repair shop workers in Altoona, Pennsylvania. On at least one occasion in 1892, the company even arranged a match with a railroad employee team from the booming railroad junction of Roanoke, Virginia.[18]

Busy railroad hubs like this, in fact, seemed to have been particularly fertile ground for industry cricket teams. The Omaha employees of the Burlington and Missouri Railroad organized a club in their rapidly growing city during the 1880s, as did the Northern Pacific Railroad workers in Brainerd, Minnesota, the location of that company's regional offices during the 1890s.[19]

American sports underwent an explosive growth in organizational sophistication over the last decades of the nineteenth century, through the establishment of a wide range of formal sports championships, qualification standards, and competitive guidelines. It was a trend also followed by American cricket, which by the late 1880s was quickly moving away from the decades-old practices of playing matches on an informal, irregular basis, to more structured league formats.

In New York, the idea of establishing a formal city cricket league, which had been raised as early as 1883, eventually came to reality on January 28, 1890, when the area's eight largest clubs formally set up the New York metropolitan District Cricket League. This was followed, a few years later, by the New York Cricket Association league, set up by the area's smaller, second tier clubs as "a sort of junior organization" to the metro league. Inevitably, a certain amount of friction developed between the two organizations, especially over player qualifications, but never, it appears, to the detriment of the game as a whole. On at least two occasions, the leagues even came together and staged interleague all-star games.[20]

A two-tier competitive format was also adopted by Chicago area cricket clubs in the early 1890s, the "A" squads of the city's four largest clubs competing for the Spalding Cup (donated by sporting goods magnate and White Stockings co-owner Albert Spalding), while its "B" teams, along with a number of smaller community clubs, competed for their own championship, the President's Cup.[21]

Nor was such organizational sophistication limited to big city cricket. The cricket clubs in the little Pennsylvania communities of Pottsville, Lebanon, Norristown, Port Carbon, Wadesville and Hazelton came together and established the Eastern Pennsylvania Cricket League in 1890. A similar competitive arrangement was set up, four years later, by the cricket clubs in the western New York State communities of

Jamestown, Auburn, Rochester, Utica, Syracuse, and Buffalo. In at least two locations, New Jersey and Maine, attempts were made to set up state wide cricket leagues.[22]

Occasionally these organizational efforts became quite expansive, the most noticeable being the Northwest Cricket Association, which attempted to bring into closer contact the cricket clubs from such far-flung locations as Chicago, Minneapolis, Milwaukee, St. Louis, Kansas City, Omaha, Denver, LeMars, Iowa, and Winnipeg, Canada. Established in 1887 as a successor to an earlier, unsuccessful, Western Cricket Association, this league managed to overcome its most serious organizational obstacle—lengthy distances between members—by inaugurating, in 1897, an annual league tournament that brought all members together at a single location for a weekend of organized competition.[23]

One of the most important reasons why sports continued to gain acceptance among America's late nineteenth-century urban populace was its perceived compatibility with the two bedrock institutions of middle-class American morality: the military and the church. This perception also applied to cricket.

Both baseball and cricket supporters had long claimed participation in their respective games was ideal for developing such traditional "military" virtues as courage, discipline, and perseverance, in a setting that closely mimicked military conflict. The *Sunday Mercury* was so convinced of this it proudly declared that among all the recruits destined for combat during the Civil War, "we will bet that our cricketers [and] base ball players . . . will be the last to give out."[24]

It always seemed harder to convince American military authorities themselves that the introduction of organized sports into their institutions would "develop the animal courage in man," but those who were convinced seemed to view cricket as fully compatible to this purpose. Captain Brewster of the U.S. Military Academy was encouraging his cadets to organize cricket clubs as early as 1847, but this recommendation seems to have struck a more responsive chord with Naval Academy cadets, who organized a number of interclass matches in 1859. The midshipmen apparently kept up the game during their school's Civil War relocation to Newport, Rhode Island, though never as an official part of the school's physical training program, as had been recommended by a number of American educators.[25]

Later military authorities seemed to value cricket more as a welcome and healthy respite from the drudgery and monotony of garrison life than as a finishing school for future officers. The *Army and Navy Journal* suggested in 1884 that army posts "obtain the rules . . . for base ball and cricket from the published professional editions," and encourage these games among their troops, "the greater the variety the better." This option, in fact, had been exercised as early as 1868 by the soldiers of the 2nd U.S. Infantry, who obliged the civilian cricket club in nearby Louisville, Kentucky, with a few matches that year. Cricket playing also served as a recreational outlet for the soldiers of Ft. Douglas, who occasionally played matches with the civilian club in nearby Salt Lake city during the late 1870s and early 1880s.[26]

Matches like these also served to improve relations between military garrisons and their often less than appreciative civilian neighbors. This was captain Charles Vernou's intention in organizing a cricket team among the soldiers at his garrison near San Antonio in 1889. The goodwill matches arranged between the garrison and the local cricket club by this former Young America Cricket Club member, who, before the Civil War, had been acclaimed as "a young, but really magnificent American player," apparently succeeded in mollifying the civilian population's persistent tendency to "look down" on the soldiers stationed in their area.[27]

In other, more far-flung, locations, American military personnel familiar with the game from civilian life were also usually the catalyst for cricket playing. Two former Philadelphia cricketers serving on the *U.S.S. Enterprise* organized an informal match between their shipmates and sailors from the British ship *H.M.S. Coquette* while both vessels were in Piraeus, Greece, in 1880. Ex-Philadelphia players arranged a similar match in Honolulu in 1895, between sailors from their vessel the *U.S.S. Philadelphia* and the *H.M.S. Nymphe*. The ex-New Jersey Athletic Club cricketer, F. C. Calder, also tried to adapt his civilian cricket experience to military life by organizing a team in 1900 among his fellow soldiers doing occupation duty in the Philippines.[28]

Cricket had ideologically been aligned with Christian morality ever since the "muscular Christianity" movement of the 1850s, more so with English supporters, but there had always been a pervasive view among Americans as well that "moralists . . . have never discovered in cricket any transgression of the decalogue."[29]

The American clergy had traditionally been slow to personally associate itself with cricket or any other type of sport, but this began to change over the later part of the nineteenth century. Henry Chadwick believed the clergymen he expected would join his Prospect Park Cricket Club in 1873 would represent "a new thing in cricket in this country," when, in fact, a number of American clergymen had been active in the game well before this time.[30]

By far the most celebrated of these athletic clergymen was Thomas Wentworth Higginson, a Harvard divinity school graduate of no clear denominational ties, who had been one of the earliest and most eloquent advocates of the social benefits of organized athletics, not surprising for someone who had excelled at a number of sports, including cricket, during his undergraduate days at Harvard. Higginson kept up his cricket as a member and later president of the Lincoln Cricket Club of Worcester, Massachusetts, where the gravity of his duties as the pastor of that city's Free Church in the 1850s did not seem to interfere with his youthful ardor for the game. This staunch abolitionist, who would later command a black regiment during the Civil War, found the experiences of his club's match against nearby Clinton "a thing I have been dreaming about ever since I was a child and found it as pleasant as I expected. We were all day in the open air, in the pleasantest green meadow—we played from 9 to 3 with short intermissions and then all took a swim in the river and went to dinner."[31]

A number of later nineteenth-century American clergymen also found their cricket interests to be fully compatible with their pastoral responsibilities. Samuel Robert Calthrop, already noted for his pioneering role in encouraging cricket as a school sport, continued to play the game during his many years of service as the Unitarian pastor of Syracuse's Mary Memorial Church.[32]

Edward R. Ward, an India-born, Oxford educated Englishman who received his theological training at Wisconsin's Nashotah House Seminary, was also able to balance his duties as pastor to Milwaukee's Christ Episcopal Church and editor of the national publication, the *Western Church*, with an active role in Milwaukee area cricket, including the presidency of that city's Young America club.[33]

For sheer longevity of interest, it's doubtful any clergyman surpassed Rev. T. Dowell Phillipps, an Anglo-Canadian, whose cricket career would span some five decades. A prominent figure in Canadian cricket during the 1860s and 1870s, Phillipps relocated to Chicago in the 1880s, where he continued to play for another ten years, and where he scored, at the age of 61, his first century (100 runs in a single time at bat). Even semiretirement couldn't dampen the enthusiasm of this participant of the 1858 U.S.-Canada match, who, at the age of 75, could still be found playing cricket with his students at the Arkansas School of Theology in Winslow, Arkansas.[34]

For other clergymen, cricket wasn't so much an expression of self-cultivation as it was a valued resource within an ever-widening range of pastoral responsibilities. This was the case with New York's most prominent late nineteenth-century advocate of the social gospel, William Stephen Rainsford, the minister of that city's St. George Episcopal Church during the 1880s. Concerned that this once prominent Manhattan parish was neglecting the social needs of its growing working-class membership, Rainsford, an immigrant Englishman who in 1891 held the honorary presidency of New York's Metropolitan District League, initiated a variety of church programs intended to improve its poorer parishioners' quality of life, especially health and hygiene. As part of his effort to "fight for healthy bodies," Rainsford personally encouraged his parishioners to become more active in sports, including cricket, which he made sure had an area on the parish athletic field specifically set aside for its use.[35]

Rainsford's example at St. George may have inspired a number of other American churches to organize parish cricket teams during this period, among them New York's St. Agnes and Brooklyn's St. James churches. Two congregations in Omaha, All Saints Church and Trinity Cathedral, actually organized an interparish cricket match among themselves in 1889. Rev. Charles Scadding, who had been a close associate of Rainsford's at St. George, also encouraged parish athletics, including cricket, during his tenure at Toledo's Trinity Episcopal Church in the 1880s, as he also later did in Oregon while serving as that state's Episcopal bishop.[36]

Cricket also found a modest following within the era's most prominent layman's organization, the YMCA, perhaps as a result of that organization's attempt during this period to distance itself from such overtly competitive sports as baseball. YMCAs in Philadelphia, Brooklyn, Yonkers, Needham, Massachusetts, and Elizabeth, New Jersey, all supported cricket teams at various times around the turn of the century. At the YMCAs in Trenton and Harlem, cricket interest was at such a level that these two chapters actually organized a match between themselves in 1890.[37]

Organized athletics were also making dramatic inroads into America's schools and colleges over this period, though not without some resistance and then only if they could demonstrate a strict conformity to the "Victorian pattern of using games to restore discipline." To those American educators who were beginning to appreciate the educational benefits of organized team sports, cricket still seemed to be one of the most highly respected for this purpose. Connecticut State Reform School trustee, Dr. E. W. Hatch, seems to have been under this impression when, in 1869, he "marched" the school's 150 pupils to a local cricket match in Meriden, evidently assuming some good would come from even an arm's length contact with the game. Similarly, the administrators at St. Louis' Christian Brothers College probably permitted, in 1891, the use of their campus for a match between their city cricket club and a visiting team from Cicero, Illinois, on the expectation that just the presence of such a gentlemanly game would have a positive influence upon their students.[38]

This view—that adolescent participation in athletics in general, and cricket in particular, was the surest "evidence of a healthy normality"—though gaining credence within a broader spectrum of educational institutions, continued to be most appreciated within private American schools, especially those with denominational affiliation. This was most probably the contributing factor behind the game's growing presence in such church-sponsored institutions as Philadelphia's Protestant Episcopal Academy, Friends Select School, Westtown School, and New York's St. Austin School.[39]

How tenuous this tie between cricket and its perceived educational mission could be, however, especially when it was the vision of a single individual, was tragically demonstrated at Racine College. Cricket playing at this school continued to be popular in the post-reconstruction period, despite the school's isolation from cricket contacts and baseball's growing presence. The game's standing was much more traumatically impacted by the premature death of the school's dynamic headmaster James DeKoven in 1879, a loss from which the institution never fully recovered. Without DeKoven's forceful leadership, enrollment at the school sharply declined over the following decades and with it an emphasis upon athletics, including cricket, which declined to such a point by the turn of the century that this once-leading school sport existed only as an intramural activity.[40]

Even in its decline as an institution, however, Racine College managed to indirectly bequeath its English public school athletic ethos to a successor institution, the Delafield, Wisconsin, boarding school St. John's Academy, which was founded by Racine College alumnus Rev. Sydney Thomas Smythe on the expressed intention of making it the "American Rugby." Smythe's educational mission was, in no small part, a tribute to DeKoven himself, under whose influence Smythe had deeply fallen during his student days at Racine College. This included DeKoven's strong belief in the disciplining influence of organized athletics, and from the time he first opened his school in 1884, Smythe systematically integrated sports into his school's educational mission, as evidenced by the institution's adopted motto: "work hard, play hard, pray hard."[41]

Being a fine athlete himself, Smythe encouraged all types of sports at his school, including cricket, which he personally supervised for a number of years, organizing matches and even occasionally playing for the school team.[42]

At the private American school best known for its cricket, St. Paul's, the game also continued to thrive over the last two decades of the century, due, at least in part, to the administration's decision in the 1880s to hire a professional coach, Sam Morley, whose technical input noticeably contributed to the school's performances against an expanding slate of outside opponents. From 1876 to at least the end of the century, the school cricket teams undertook regular summer excursions to New York, where they typically spent a week playing against the second elevens of such local clubs as St. George and Staten Island. The school enjoyed even greater success during its tour of Canada in 1889, winning all but one of its matches against Dominion school and club sides.[43]

Though still typecast as a game best suited for the more exclusive environment of the private school, cricket was also beginning to be taken up by a number of American public schools by this time. Local cricket supporters succeeded in organizing a team among the students at the St. Paul, Minnesota, high school at the end of the century, something local Milwaukee cricketers had also managed to do among the students of their city's Fourth District School in 1879. Interest in the game at Omaha's public high school seemed to have arisen in a more spontaneous manner, with the students themselves evidently being behind the 21 interclass matches that were reportedly played at the school over the 1885 school year.[44]

Not unexpectedly, public school cricket was on its firmest footing in the Philadelphia area. By the end of the century, school cricket teams from Philadelphia's Central High School, Radnor High School, along with those from the Central and Northeast Manual Training schools, were regularly competing against the city's traditional cricket-playing private schools, Germantown Academy and Penn Charter School. This interest was further boosted when the city's interscholastic sports organization, the Inter-Academic Athletic League, officially sanctioned cricket, in 1893, as one of its recognized sports, and even sponsored, in 1904, an all-star cricket match among the league's best prep players.[45]

It would seem that its reputation as the quintessential "gentleman's" game would have ensured cricket a significant role within American collegiate athletics, particularly in light of the creeping professionalism that continually threatened the amateur standing of college athletics during this period. This was the way many influential academic administrators looked upon the game, such as Harvard's Charles Elliot, who personally believed cricket was the best "of the gentlemanly games," and the one that supporters most frequently put forward on cricket's behalf, such as those at Cornell, who claimed theirs was the only collegiate sport by 1906 that still upheld the integrity of "sports for sports sake."[46]

American college students themselves, however, never seemed to be nearly as impressed with these claims and, in fact, what cricket was played at American colleges was viewed no differently than any other student activity, namely one that had to be closely monitored for corrupting influences. It was on this justification, for example, that Haverford College prohibited its college teams from playing off-campus for many years, and Princeton forbade its team from doing so except on Saturdays. Harvard authorities went even further, forbidding its college cricket team from playing with any outside clubs in 1883, and in 1885 denying the club permission to hire a professional coach.[47]

With a few exceptions then, cricket was destined to play a largely peripheral role in late nineteenth-century American college athletics and one that always seemed to be plagued by organizational insecurity and inconsistent support.

Harvard, the trendsetter in most late nineteenth-century college athletics, was perhaps the best example of this. The college had graduated up from informal, intraclass, to more distinctively modern, competitive, cricket playing by the end of the Civil War, with its win over the Suffolk Cricket Club in 1867 probably being the first against an outside club. From that time on, student interest fluctuated widely, periods of relatively low interest being interspersed by such high-activity years as 1880, when the club roster numbered an impressive 75 members, and 1891, a year the club enrolled as many members as the college baseball team.[48]

Just as unpredictable was the availability of proper playing facilities. For many years forced to play its matches at Longwood for lack of a decent on-campus playing field, Harvard cricketers were finally able to lay out a usable, if hardly impressive, ground of their own at Jarvis and later Soldiers Field, making it possible for the college club to play its first on-campus match against the University of Pennsylvania in 1888.[49]

Like other eastern collegiate cricket programs, Harvard's was heavily dependent upon the year-to-year availability of students who had learned their cricket elsewhere, principally at Philadelphia or St. Paul's School. The college cricket team enjoyed its "best season ever" in 1887 primarily because one of its members, Hazen Brown, was a highly experienced cricketer from Philadelphia. Another standout Philadelphian, Percy Clark, along with St. Paul's alumnus Eugene H. Pool, were instrumental in bringing the college its first intercollegiate championship in 1894. The college also won this championship in 1897, this time due largely to the contributions of another standout Philadelphian, John Lester, a success that even gave rise to talk of an English tour.[50]

There was always some bewilderment why Yale, Harvard's archrival, never demonstrated anything like a corresponding interest in cricket, even though suggestions to this effect were made as early as 1851. Efforts to arrange cricket matches between these two colleges, made on at least two occasions, in 1874 and again in 1887, came to nothing until St. Paul's alumnus J. K. Tibbets managed to organize a viable cricket club at Yale in 1891. That spring the first, and only, cricket match between these two renowned colleges was finally played, a low-scoring affair won by Harvard, an event that might have only been made possible because the traditional Harvard-Yale baseball game was not played that year.[51]

Cricket interest at most other Ivy League colleges also pretty much waxed and waned relative to the availability of Philadelphians or St. Paul's alumni.

A couple of former St. Paul's students, J. P. Conover and G. Hyde-Clark, got together same of their classmates at Columbia and formed a cricket club at that college in 1879. Though largely composed of novices, who exhibited an "essentially baseballish" technique, the club enjoyed a brief period of competitive success in 1880, registering wins over Harvard and a number of New York area clubs. As the only member of the recently formed Intercollegiate Cricket Association to complete all its scheduled matches the following year, the college seemed justified in protesting that it had been "defrauded" of the association championship.[52]

A number of Philadelphians seemed to have been behind the cricket clubs that appeared at Princeton in 1866 and 1874, the latter club reportedly reaching a peak enrollment of some 50 members. Another club, this one under the guidance of two St. Paul's alumni, John B. Shober and F. S. Conover, was organized in 1881, this one apparently stable enough to gain admission to the intercollegiate association. The club, however, survived for only a single season, as did the cricket club St. Paul's alumnus Richard Sherman organized at Brown University in 1885.[53]

At only two American institutions of higher learning, Haverford College and the University of Pennsylvania, did cricket enjoy anything more than an incidental popularity as a college sport, not surprising since both institutions benefited from the vast network of players, supporters, and competitive opportunities in the Philadelphia area. The two schools first played each other at cricket on May 7, 1864, though it wasn't until 1878 that these contests began to be held on anything like a regular basis. From that time on, however, the cricket rivalry between the two institutions assumed a status in American collegiate athletics comparable to the Oxford-Cambridge cricket rivalry, a flattering comparison local supporters certainly did nothing to discourage.[54]

Tradition has always claimed that the cricket team English gardener William Carvill organized at Haverford in 1834 was history's first exclusively American cricket club. There are, however, at least two problems with this long-standing claim.

Lester himself pointed out that Haverford records do not mention Carvill's employment at the college until 1842. Nor does there seem to be any evidence Carvill himself ever claimed he had been personally involved with cricket at the college during the 1830s, even though he lived in the Philadelphia area up to the time of his death in 1887.[55]

According to the earliest surviving student accounts, cricket wasn't played at the college until the late 1830s, but by this time cricket clubs are known to have existed at such geographically dispersed schools as Harvard, Fordham, and Ohio Wesleyan College, some of which almost certainly were as sophisticated in their organization as those at Haverford.[56]

Throughout much of its early history, in fact, Haverford showed few signs of its future role as the leader in American collegiate cricket. It was left to an English teacher, a Dr. Lyon, to revive student interest in the game during the late 1850s, an interest that actually seemed to lag behind that of other Philadelphia schools at that time. The early college teams also had to make do with homemade equipment, did not get around to playing their first outside opponent until 1862, and were, for years, forbidden to play off-campus. This prevented the college from joining the Intercollegiate Cricket Association until 1883, the year it also dropped its old name, the Dorian Cricket Club, and began to play under the Haverford College name.[57]

The game underwent a far more dramatic period of development with the arrival, in the late 1880s, of Arthur Woodcock, the school's first professional coach, who was able to utilize the school's indoor practice shed, erected in 1887 and expanded in 1893, for much needed off-season practice. By this period, cricket was now unquestionably ruling "supreme" in Haverford athletics, with fully 4/5 of the student body participating in the game in one form or another, students who now looked upon any underclass expressions of disloyalty to the game "as equivalent to disloyalty to the institution" itself.[58]

That good quality cricket was played at the college became evident enough in 1896, the year the college team embarked on a highly publicized English tour, the first of five the college would undertake between that time and the First World War. In most instances the American collegians showed up fairly well against their mostly English public school opponents, usually winning more matches than they lost, and convincing skeptics that, despite its wealth and prestige, English public school cricket was certainly "not . . . invincible at all points." Little wonder then, that this little Quaker institution, as a result of these extensive transatlantic contacts, was, for many years, the American college best known to the British public.[59]

The state of affairs with cricket at the University of Pennsylvania was always much different from what it was at Haverford.

With no cricket ground of its own, only limited indoor practice facilities, and a university athletic association never more than lukewarm toward cricket, the university was much more dependent upon the Philadelphia cricket community at large for facilities, coaching, and manpower. For most members of the university cricket team, in fact, their college days usually represented a straightforward progression of a cricket career that started in the junior programs of the city's larger cricket clubs and ended with a selection to their club's first or second elevens.[60]

The extent of the university's interrelation with Philadelphia cricket was no more convincingly demonstrated than during the visit of Frank Mitchell's Oxbridge side in 1895. Of the English collegians two losses in Philadelphia that fall, one was at the hands of a Philadelphia side composed entirely of active and former university cricketers, a result supporters hoped would elevate collegiate American cricket onto an international level.[61]

As would be expected, University of Pennsylvania cricket teams were never as far ranging in their travels as were their rivals at Haverford, but the one university side that did tour England, in 1907, turned out to be the most successful of any American team to play abroad, due largely to the play of Australian dental student Herbert Hordern, recognized at that time, as he is to this day, as one of the finest exponents of the recently developed googly style of bowling.[62]

It was largely through the efforts of another University of Pennsylvania cricketer, John B. Thayer Jr., that one of the country's first collegiate athletic organizations, the Intercollegiate Cricket Association, was established on April 26, 1881, among five eastern colleges: the University of Pennsylvania, Harvard, Columbia, Princeton, and Trinity College of Hartford, Connecticut.[63]

Going on the impression that cricket was "the coming college game," supporters evidently believed this interest would best be nurtured with a formal championship format, but by the end of the league's initial season, Columbia, Trinity (whose cricket club had been organized by St. Paul's alumnus Stanley Emery), and Princeton had all dropped out, even though the local press found the association match between the last two colleges "decidedly the most interesting cricket match of the season."[64]

From that point on, membership in the association (with the exception of Cornell, which entered a team for a few years in the early twentieth century) consisted of only three schools, Haverford, Harvard, and the University of Pennsylvania, certainly a modest and unimpressive state of affairs for collegiate cricket and one that got no real boost from the two all-star matches, staged in 1895 and again in 1899, between American and Canadian college cricket teams.[65]

Notwithstanding its identity as a "gentleman's" game, and all the social prerequisites commonly associated with such a title, cricket also enjoyed a reputation as a game appropriate for other social classes. In England the sport had long been valued as a social activity that encouraged class interaction, able to bring lord and laborer, master and servant together in socially beneficial contact of great potential for "both harmonizing and humanizing a people."[66]

American observers, however, always feared this old-world tradition of interclass participation would also invite the unwelcome English tradition of strict class subordination. As early as 1847, the *Spirit* was admonishing supporters that cricket playing in America must be "a purely democratic game, and those who wish to see it fully carried out, must support it on that principle."[67]

In expressing these sentiments, the *Spirit* may have had in mind the unwelcome incident of class polarization that had occurred during the U.S.-Canada match a year earlier. This contest had been disrupted and subsequently abandoned when American Sam Dudson, a working-class mechanic, hit Canadian batter and "gentleman" player T. Helliwell with the ball for intentionally interfering with a catch. The Americans were harshly criticized for their behavior, attributable, in many eyes, to the absence of any "gentlemanly" character within an American side composed almost entirely of "uneducated" mechanics. Interestingly, it was left to the normally conservative *Anglo-American* to dispel this sham aristocratism, pointing out that the Canadians, had they been true "gentlemen," would have admitted they were in the wrong, apologized, and finished the match.[68]

Specific attempts to restrict participation upon social or economic status rarely occurred in American cricket, and when they did were almost always strongly resisted. *Forest and Stream*, usually a conservative voice in cricket matters, strongly objected to the decision, in 1879, to include some players on the United States team simply because they were able to pay their own way to Canada—"it is the players, not the man with the pocket book, that should represent his side in these games." The working-class members of Chicago's Pullman Cricket Club reacted even more militantly to a similar incident of selection discrimination in 1889, protesting that "if the hard working Pullman mechanics are to be barred out of a game to help along the record of pseudo-professionals and silkstocking non-entities, then indeed is the game de-moralized."[69]

American cricket supporters may have been well within their rights in trying to maintain their game's status as a "gentleman's" game, but only on the understanding that this would have to be the new-world type of gentleman: "men of sense, moral worth and education, and not the 'gentleman' of the purse or tailor." To most late nineteenth-century cricket supporters, this seemed to be the prevailing opinion, one that, over the last two decades of the century, opened the game to a broader cross section of the American populace, typified by the Young America Club of Milwaukee, which in 1880 invited all sports-minded residents to come enjoy the game, "no matter how humble or how high his station in life may be."[70]

Though principally a late century phenomenon, this trend toward working-class cricket had been well established among some of the country's smaller, skilled labor industries before the Civil War. The English cutlery workers who organized a cricket club in Connecticut's Naugatuck valley in the early 1850s had actually preempted the *Clipper*'s 1856 recommendation that the workers in "the mills and other manufacturing establishments in New England" take up the game. This advice was, however, taken up by workers in at least two antebellum New England companies, the Wheeler-Wilson sewing machine company in Bridgeport, Connecticut, and the Hazardville, Connecticut, gunpowder works, where it can be confirmed that at least two of the company's cricket playing employees later died from accidental explosions.[71]

Other antebellum clubs were organized among the skilled workers in the Lancaster, Pennsylvania, locomotive works, the Tallcott and Underhill iron foundry in Oswego, the Watervliet, New York, woolen mills and the gunsmithing industry of Paterson, New Jersey, workers at the last mentioned evidently taking their club name, "Texas," from the popular revolver they manufactured.[72]

Workers in one New England company in particular, the American Watch Company of Waltham, Massachusetts, had a long association with the game, maintaining an employee cricket club through the Civil War and well past the reconstruction period. In 1873, the club even managed to beat, largely through the efforts of immigrant English watchmaker "Alf" Eastwood, the still formidable St. George club. Other employees of this company eventually took this legacy of watchmaker cricket to Illinois, organizing a club among the employees of the rival Elgin Watch Company, a club that remained active late into the century.[73]

American industry expanded at a rapid and almost unbroken pace over the last decades of the nineteenth century, creating such a high demand for labor that many American industries, particularly those requiring large numbers of skilled workers, such as textiles, hard-rock mining and steel rolling, actively recruited workers from overseas. Between 1881 and 1890, over 600,000 of these immigrant workers came from the United Kingdom, most attracted to the United States on the promise of high wages, steady employment, or advancement in their chosen field of work.[74]

Since many of these British immigrant workers valued their leisure time very highly, playing cricket in their new home served to reassert not only their ethnic identity but also their social self-determination. As a result of this old-world tradition of cultural solidarity through sports, working-class cricket clubs, at one time or another, appeared in virtually every American industry that employed significant numbers of immigrant British laborers, and in virtually every area of the country where these immigrants were concentrated.

Nowhere was this more evident than in New England. The cricket clubs that had been formed among the immigrant workers in the Massachusetts cutlery industry before the Civil War were succeeded in the 1870s by clubs organized among immigrant workers from the Meriden, Connecticut, silverware industry and in the 1880s by those organized by Scottish granite cutters in Quincy, Massachusetts.[75]

English hosiery workers, many from Nottinghamshire, were the mainstay of the Brockton, Massachusetts, and Thornton, Rhode Island, cricket clubs. Other employee cricket clubs were associated with the Roxbury Carpet Works, Brockton's Herbert & Rapp Company, Chelsea's Eastern Elastic Company, Holyoke's Farr Alpaca Company, and the Boston Belting Company, such a concentration of working-class interest that the Brockton, Roxbury, Quincy, and Chelsea cricket clubs in 1885 set up among themselves a commercial league.[76]

Virtually every large textile establishment in the Merrimack valley was also supporting at least one cricket club by this time, among them the Arlington Mill of Lawrence (a town with so many Yorkshire immigrants it was nicknamed the "Bradford of America") and the Merrimack and Boot Hill mills of Lowell.[77]

Outside New England, cricket seemed to be most popular with workers in heavy industry. Employees of Chicago's Bessemer Steel Company had formed a club as early as 1874. This was followed by working-class clubs associated with the Schenectady Locomotive Works, the Sanderson Steel Company of Syracuse, the George Westinghouse Electric Company, and Andrew Carnegie's Homestead Steel Mill outside Pittsburgh. Cricket also played an important part in the social life of the skilled English workers lured to Bay View, Wisconsin, in the 1870s to work that city's steel plant. Playing on grounds situated in the shadow of their mill, the club quickly established itself as Milwaukee's dominant cricket organization, due in part to the contributions of its English professional, who was paid from funds raised through a company benefit concert.[78]

Another company cricket club, the Pullman, was, for a number of years, the dominant cricket organization in the Chicago area, winning that city's cricket championship four years in a row during the 1890s. This club was organized in 1882 by employees of George Pullman's Palace Car Railroad Company, a massive industrial complex in south Chicago that encouraged, through its company athletic association, employee participation in a wide variety of sports.[79]

Cricket playing within the intensely male and often isolated working-class culture of the American mining industry, common in Pennsylvania's anthracite coal mining region before the Civil War, could be found by the 1870s as far west as the little Wyoming coal mining community of Almy, where the game seems to have been organized by English mine foreman Reuben Folkes. To the residents of nearby Coalville, Utah, it was, in all likelihood, their working-class cricket club's win over the "city jakes" of Salt Lake City that in 1878 put their little coal mining community on the map.[80]

Cornish miners seemed to have been the driving force behind much of the cricket that proliferated within several late nineteenth-century Montana copper mining communities, such as Butte, Livingston, Helena, and Marysville. The local press only hoped the working-class club that was also active in Centerville would turn out to be "as good cricketers as they are beer smugglers."[81]

Cricket was also played by the stone cutters of East Sioux City, South Dakota in the late 1880s, and the granite cutters of Redgranite, Wisconsin, at the turn of the century, as well as by some gold and silver miners in Colorado's Central City, Cripple Creek, and Nevadaville.[82]

In none of these locations, however, was cricket ever as popular as it was among the miners of Michigan's Keweenaw peninsula copper mining boom towns. In the decade immediately preceding the First World War, the game had "taken a firm hold" among the workers of virtually every one of the area's many contiguous copper mining communities: Ahmeek, Mohawk, Kearsarge, Calumet, Tamarack, Trimountain, Painsdale, to name a few. By 1909, worker participation had reached such a level that the area's organized cricket league, set up three years earlier, had to be expanded into a ten-team, two-division format, an arrangement that could bring out as many as 2,000 spectators to the league's more important matches.[83]

It was not uncommon for American business owners and managers to promote employee morale and improve management/labor relations by actively encouraging cricket playing among their workers. The East Sioux Falls stone quarry magnate, Chelsea W. Hubbard, personally encouraged his workers to take up the game during their off hours, as did Tamarack Mining Company vice president Norman Haire, who in 1908 donated, in his name, a prize cup to be annually awarded to the Keweenaw peninsula's champion cricket club.[84]

In a few instances, management even took a more personal interest in their company's cricket activities, such as Staten Islander Cyril Wilson, who played an active role in organizing a cricket team among the employees of his International Tile Company, and hosiery mill superintendent G. Sparkhawk who granted the Ashton, Rhode Island, club use of company property for its matches. William Horlick, owner of Racine's Horlick Food Company, played alongside the employees of his company cricket team, as did mine captain Ed Waters, who was a member of Tamarack's cricket club, and Pullman chief accountant Alex Harper, who rubbed shoulders with eight clerical workers on his company cricket team.[85]

Like other nineteenth-century labor-class organizations, however, these cricket clubs remained very much the domain of the working man. Their members seldom allowed gestures of corporate paternalism to obscure the fact that this was an era of deeply adversarial relations between labor and capital.

The Empire Mining Company of Grass Valley, California, may have won some goodwill by giving its workers a half-holiday to play cricket, but gestures like this were of little value to the members of the Fall River, Massachusetts, cricket club who had been laid off, or those of the Dedham, Massachusetts, club, who in 1885 disbanded their club because many of their members had to seek work elsewhere.[86]

On one occasion, the working-class cricket players from Lowell and Lawrence even used their game as an antimanagement weapon, playing a benefit match, in 1887, to raise funds for striking shoe manufacturing workers in Worcester. Ahmeek cricket club member James Paull did not hesitate to join other union leaders to authorize what would become the long and bitter Keweenaw copper mining strike of 1913, even though this strike proved to be so disruptive it practically brought the area's cricket playing to a standstill.[87]

Just how inconsequential were the ties of sporting comradeship before the harsh demands of economic necessity was most forcefully seen during the nationwide railroad strike of 1894, when a number of striking San Francisco cricketers found themselves face to face with some of their fellow cricketers among the militia called out to suppress the strike.[88]

Cricket's English identity, so often a handicap to the game's acceptance among mainstream American society, materially contributed to its standing among two members of America's late nineteenth-century sporting underclass: women and blacks.

Late nineteenth-century American sports observers were highly sensitive to charges that American women weren't as athletically active as their English counterparts. This could be seen in the frequent American reports of cricket playing among English women, such as the 1885 English actresses match, carried by the *Pall Mall Gazette* and widely syndicated in the United States, and the Original English Lady Cricketers, covered at length by American writer Elise Heaton.[89]

Not unexpectedly, these concerns struck a responsive chord among America's most status conscious social strata, which, in the case of cricket, meant the more exclusive American clubs. The first serious effort to interest American women in the game seems to have been made at New Jersey's Seabright Lawn Tennis and Cricket Club. In 1888 the wife of one of the club's more energetic cricket advocates, Herman Clark, organized a number of matches among the club's female members.[90]

Within a few years, women teams also appeared at Staten Island, the New Jersey Athletic Club, and at a number of Philadelphia clubs, most limiting their play to informal, in-house matches, though the Germantown Cricket Club by the late 1890s was playing matches with women teams from other area clubs.[91]

The most supportive environment for women's cricket during this period existed within two private girls' schools, Mrs. John Cunningham Hazen's school in Pelham Manor, New York (whose administrators were of the opinion that cricket was "undoubtedly the best game for girls"), and Rosemary Hall in Wallingford, Connecticut, whose founder and headmistress, Caroline Ruutz-Rees, was a sports-minded Englishwoman. The cricket match these two schools played in late fall 1896—a rather over-publicized and mildly sensationalized event—may very well have been the first interscholastic girls sporting event in American history.[92]

Britain's traditionally progressive racial policies within its colonies enabled late nineteenth-century American cricket to generally avoid the taint of racial prejudice that plagued so many other American sports during this period. Blacks are known to have played cricket in New Orleans and Philadelphia as early as the 1860s, though any effort to arrange interracial play during this racially charged period of American history was as strongly opposed as any other attempt to bring about closer racial contacts. In its report of one such interracial match, held in Washington, Pennsylvania, in 1869, the local press strongly objected to such a precedent, deploring the sight of "the 'proud caucasian' . . . fraternizing with the 'despised nigger' on terms of the utmost perfect equality."[93]

Cricket would prove to be most popular with black Americans of West Indian descent, an ethnic group that, by the late nineteenth century, was immigrating to America's larger east coast cities in significant numbers. As it was with immigrants from other British colonies, cricket playing within the immigrant West Indian community functioned as an important assertion of its cultural identity. New York's first West Indian cricket club actually began as an arm of the West Indian Benevolent and Social League before setting itself up as a free-standing organization in 1893. By the turn of the century at least a dozen other immigrant West Indian cricket clubs were active in the New York area.[94]

Coming from a culture more racially tolerant than the one they found in the United States, most of these West Indian players assumed their clubs would enjoy a competitive standing fully equal to the area's white clubs, and for the most part, the prevailing English character of New York area cricket ensured a relatively harmonious and open relationship between the city's black and white clubs.[95]

Only one incident ever seemed to seriously jeopardize this otherwise acceptable arrangement. In 1903, a West Indian team from Brooklyn preferred to forfeit its rematch with New Jersey's Branch Brook Club, a white team, rather than risk racially motivated retaliation for an incident that had occurred earlier between the two teams. The potentially serious situation was, in time, amicably resolved through the intervention of league officials, who also used it as an opportunity to strongly reassert the league's standing policy that "any attempt to introduce racial discord will be frowned upon."[96]

It was an unwritten policy that seems to have been honored by most American cricket clubs during this period. Oregon's Portland Cricket Club had no qualms about playing an integrated team of British sailors during their shore leave in 1901, nor did the Philadelphians who toured Jamaica in 1909 express any reservations about playing against the island's many black clubs. Even George Wright, despite a long career in unofficially segregated baseball, felt no compunction in urging West Indian George F. Samuels in 1892 to organize a West Indian cricket team and enter it into competition with other Boston area clubs.[97]

Extended social popularity has typically been one of the strongest indications of a sports cultural permanence. Why, then, did this not prove valid with American cricket, which by the late nineteenth century had made inroads into the leisure patterns of just about every segment of American society?

With working-class cricket there's a fairly straightforward explanation. Although some working-class Americans did take up cricket, the game was mostly played by English immigrant laborers as an expression of their ethnic identity. Like other ethnic customs that were not able to integrate into mainstream American culture, this one also soon disappeared once the immigrant working-class communities that supported the game either dispersed due to changing economic conditions (as was the case in such areas as the Keweenaw Peninsula after the First World War), or, in the case where these immigrants established permanent residence, were eventually absorbed into the local American culture.[98]

Cricket's failure as a working-class sport, then, demonstrates how much more powerfully cultural, rather than social, influences determine a sport's popularity. However alike American and English immigrant laborers may have been in their "class" values and outlook, these similarities weren't nearly strong enough to alter their more culturally determined sporting tastes.

American working men may have sympathized with immigrant working-class cricket as an expression of labor-class companionship and self-determination, but these Americans' own culturally defined sporting tastes would never permit cricket to become a permanent part of their own leisure culture. George Wright clearly recognized this in New England cricket, noting that the state of the game here, by 1898, had progressed no further than it had "ten to fifteen years ago," being restricted to immigrant workers with only negligible American interest.[99]

Cricket was slightly more successful within those environments that fostered more trans-national class values, specifically American schools and colleges. At some of these institutions, cricket prospered, as it did at Racine College, as "sort of a tradition" that could be "handed down from class to class," providing cohesion to a shared range of English-public-school-type social values. But this environment was very different from American society at large, as the alumni of such cricket playing schools as St. Paul's and Haverford College discovered whenever they tried to interest other Americans in their self-nurtured school game. In most instances these attempts failed, especially in American colleges, where students from these schools could only keep cricket alive as sort of an alumni activity among themselves. When sufficient numbers of these cricket-knowledgeable students were available, as they were at Harvard in 1900, the impression could easily arise that the game was "on a firmer basis ... than it ever has been." When they weren't, the game would virtually disappear, as it had at Harvard only three years after the above claim was made.[100]

With its tradition of gentlemanly play and all the status symbolism normally associated with this, cricket was always able to attract some interest among those Americans who believed they were worthy of these values. So the middle-class and upper-class American women sensitive to international social trends could be induced to take up the game as an expression of gender advancement, just as some college students at Ohio State University, Howard, Syracuse, Johns Hopkins, and the University of Virginia could be motivated, like "the kid-gloves and eye-glass student who takes no interest in commoner sports" at Columbia, to take up the game as an expression of their advancing social expectations. These may have been motives more in line with typical American sporting tastes than those of America's upper class but they were not nearly broad enough to provide cricket with a solid cultural underpinning.[101]

This probably explains why cricket was largely absent from some of the more broadly rooted late nineteenth-century American sports trends, such as the Playground Movement, a national effort to bring the benefits of recreation to urban youngsters. The game also failed to align itself with the growing Olympic movement, even though organizers of the 1904 games in St. Louis extended invitations to American cricket authorities to do so. Nor did many turn-of-the-century American physical educators seem to believe cricket held any contributing value to their profession, and those that did, like the teachers at Wellesley College in 1909, seemed to think the game was suitable only for girls.[102]

Throughout its American history, cricket always labored under the perception that participation in the game was, in ever so subtle a manner, always an alternative to, a judgment upon, or a disapproval of, broader American sporting values. For many of its supporters, this may have been cricket's peculiar strength and appeal; "It is a property of cricket," the *New York Times* pointed out in 1878, that "it arouses an enthusiasm among its devotees little affected by the claims or the popularity of rival sports." But those who persisted in believing cricket had to be played in this spirit were unrealistic to expect their game would be destined, in America, for anything except a culturally invisible existence.[103]

8

A "Most Exigent" Sport:
Philadelphia and the Struggle with Structure

"It has long been a problem for the psychologist or sociologist . . . why Philadelphians play cricket and why they are the only Americans who do play it." This sweeping statement from a *New York Times* editorial that appeared shortly after the Gentlemen of Philadelphia's unexpectedly successful English tour of 1903 puts into bold relief the uniqueness of late nineteenth-century Philadelphia cricket as a sports phenomenon.[1]

In no other area of the United States did so many Americans play cricket for so long, and with such proficiency, as they did in Philadelphia. Cricket had been played by significant numbers of Americans at other times and places during the nineteenth century, but only here did the game enjoy such purposeful attention and measurable continuity, a fact Philadelphia cricket supporters took great pride in. Surveying the healthy state of the game in 1894, the *American Cricketer* proudly declared that, outside of Philadelphia, the only place where "the growth of cricket has been more brilliant and phenomenal is Australia."[2]

Over the years, sports observers would offer many conjectures as to why cricket enjoyed the popularity it did among Philadelphians, but the answer seems to be fairly straightforward: cricket prospered here because it was supported, on a much more open and extended scale, by the same type of integrated social network that had ensured the game's vitality in such locations as St. Paul's School or Haverford College. Cricket in Philadelphia was never so much an individual, but a class, family, and neighborhood phenomenon, which proved to be a highly propitious means of expressing and perpetuating the values of Philadelphia's interrelated upper-class families.

The best example of this had always been the Germantown area of Philadelphia, where local cricket interest appeared earlier and endured longer than in any other part of the city. Though legally a part of Philadelphia proper after 1854, this old-stock, upper-class residential area, sometimes referred to as America's first suburb, always retained a unique communal identity, with an "individuality of its own, with a society and with interests of its own." A long tradition of cricket playing was part of this identity, especially among two local families in particular, the Newhalls and the Wisters. In 1859, a match was even organized between teams made up entirely of players from these two extended families. As members of this interrelated network of "proper" Philadelphia families moved or relocated to other fashionable areas of Philadelphia, such as the Main Line in the western suburbs, or Chestnut Hill in the northwest, they established similarly strong support systems for cricket in these locations.[3]

For Philadelphians of this class, cricket playing became one of the "most exigent" of all social expressions, and one of the best through which "a gentleman can show his moral character." In this context, cricket was valued not so much as a game, but as a comprehensive moral education, where participants "learn lessons of self-control, patience, endurance, and perseverance which he can obtain in no other way."[4]

This belief that "cricket alone builds up a finer man altogether," though not a particularly effective inducement to upper-class Americans elsewhere, meant more to Philadelphians because they believed that of all available sports cricket was the one that could bring out ingrained characteristics and attributes only found among higher class individuals, "as we know many other qualities, aptitudes and what are vaguely called 'instincts' to be."[5]

Above all, Philadelphians valued cricket as a tool for ensuring a cross-generational continuity of these values among extended families and peer groups. In the eyes of Philadelphians themselves, what distinguished their cricket from the cricket played elsewhere around the country was its secure foundations among young Americans, who were encouraged to take up, and were assisted in developing, the game at every turn. The *American Cricketer* could point out with pride in 1881 how the young cricketer in Philadelphia "has everything combined to make his way easy: good grounds, thoroughly provided for physical development, and competent teachers."[6]

Philadelphia's insistence that only in their city was youth served was far from accurate, but only here was the game played on a systematically intergenerational basis, "to provide a more or less primary group social world within which the younger generation is socialized." By playing their cricket alongside adults and older relatives, Philadelphia youngsters were not only shielded from the most harmful tendencies of competition, they were also made aware of their responsibilities and obligations to their peer group: ". . . in the game of cricket," the Germantown Academy school paper claimed, "boys play, a good part of the time at least, with men. Where youth are accustomed to play their games with grown men it introduces an element of sobriety, courtesy and reticence in their play and behavior.'"[7]

It was this intergenerational system of sports participation, formally institutionalized through the more prominent Philadelphia cricket clubs, as well as the city's more exclusive schools and colleges, that accounted for the peculiar strength and vitality of Philadelphia cricket over the years. Cricket playing became a rite of passage into, and one of the binding ties among, proper Philadelphia society, which began when "the grey-haired father . . . proposes his son to his club, hands over his bat to him, and watches the boy's hair breadth 'scapes thereafter with a breathless interest."[8]

It's always been tempting to construe Philadelphia's peculiar interest in England's national game as little more than an example of late nineteenth century upper-class America's tendency to look "to the British Isles for standards of culture and genteel behavior." And Philadelphia cricket did consciously adopt a number of English precedents, such as the "Gentlemen vs Players" matches that were occasionally arranged between the city's top players and their professional coaches, and the English system of competitive progression from school to college cricket, which Lester conceded "may in a remote way be paralleled with us."[9]

It may be fair to claim that upper-class Philadelphians, with their rowing and fox hunting, directly adopted many English organizational and competitive precedents, but with their cricket, most presumptions of direct English imitation seemed to have existed in the eyes of outsiders. Coming to Philadelphia from the social stagnation of reconstruction Virginia in 1876, Englishman A. G. Bradley may have found among the city's larger clubs an atmosphere "almost like that of Lords or the Oval," while P. F. Warner may have found the social whirl surrounding his English team's match at Merion in 1898 "like an Eton and Harrow match on a small scale." But Philadelphians themselves never seemed to have viewed their cricket as anything other than the expression of a specifically American spirit and probably would have been the least likely to agree with the *Birmingham Post*'s culturally inflammatory assertion in 1897 that "the game lifts its head [in Philadelphia] like a choice plant in a jungle of baseball and other barbarisms."[10]

From at least the time of the All-England tour in 1859, Philadelphia had, in fact, been motivated by a distinct and uncompromising insistence upon the nationalistic integrity of its cricket. The most obvious example of this could be seen over the issue of eligibility for the city's representative teams, city authorities expressly disbarring—as a standing policy—all foreigners from these sides, even if it resulted in less competitive teams or aroused ethnic animosity. This policy denied the talented Hargreaves brothers of Leicestershire a place on the city's representative teams for a while in the 1880s, as it did Lester himself for a period in the 1890s, a move that, in some quarters, incited charges that "there is more class and caste shown [in Philadelphia] than on the green swards of old England." This principle was also upheld over the objections of the talented Nottingham immigrant Arthur M. Wood, whose long and subsequently successful career as a member of the Gentlemen of Philadelphia was delayed for years until he had met the eligibility requirements of five years' residency, amateur standing, and intended naturalization.[11]

No other Philadelphia cricket club better typified the city's standing principle that "the English may beat us, but they may not help us," than the Young America club, which had from its inception specifically permitted only Americans to play on its sides. One member of that club in particular, George Newhall, seems to have personally dedicated himself to ensuring that Philadelphia cricket retain a distinctively American identity. As a member of a club long reputed to be "anything but old-fogeyish," and a standout player in a city where, he insisted, "there is not a dude cricketer," Newhall even seemed perfectly willing to sacrifice the game's old-world decorum to secure competitive advantages for the Philadelphia teams he captained, as he did by inciting the Australians, in their match against Philadelphia in 1878, to walk off the field in protest to what they believed was blatantly biased local umpiring. Australian manager John Conway publicly downplayed the incident as nothing more than "a little contretemps," but once outside the country he condemned it as indicative of the "blarsted Britishers" attitude he found among the Philadelphia cricket community.[12]

Newhall, however, seemed uncompromising in his views, later asserting, in the face of circulating rumors, that English, and even Australian, influences were responsible for the success of the All-Philadelphia team that toured England in 1884, "they [the English] may imagine that they made it [cricket] what it is in Philadelphia, in that they are mistaken. All the steps toward popularizing it among Americans have been taken by Americans."[13]

Foreign cricket observers, despite their many encounters with Philadelphia sides, never seemed quite able to appreciate this insistence that "a victory over our [English] cousins, to be real, must be native." English authorities were especially puzzled why Philadelphia seemed to prefer not to compete at all rather than with anything less than entirely American sides. The *American Cricketer* had to forcefully counter the English authorities who criticized Philadelphia's decision in 1894 to cancel a planned English tour rather than substitute, for their own unavailable players, resident Englishmen from New York or Boston. Only when teams like these are composed of the best Americans, and no one else, the publication asserted, could these tours work "entirely in the interest of American cricket."[14]

Only the Australians, sensitive, perhaps, to their own emerging sports identity at this time, seemed able to appreciate Philadelphia's obligation to work for a self-reliant cricket culture. After a long summer playing in England, Frank Iredale found a refreshingly different and vibrant cricket spirit while with his Australians in Philadelphia in 1896, noting "we saw nothing in England to compare with our reception in Philadelphia, and nothing else to compare with the fraternity and wholeheartedness of the Philadelphia cricketers." Arthur Mailey, while in the city with another Australian team 17 years later, would also find the atmosphere of this American city so uniquely invigorating that not even another 20 years of cricket globe-trotting would diminish his opinion that "cricket in Philadelphia took me to far greater imaginative heights than nine wickets in Melbourne or 'ten for 66' against Gloucestershire."[15]

Over the later decades of the nineteenth and early years of the twentieth centuries, dozens of cricket clubs of various sizes and organizational sophistication existed in the greater Philadelphia area. But for all practical purposes, local cricket was dominated by the five largest, wealthiest, and most organizationally complex clubs; three antebellum organizations, the Philadelphia, Germantown, and Young America, and two established after the Civil War, the Merion and the Belmont.

The oldest of the city's major clubs, Philadelphia, never seemed able to leverage the prestige usually associated with chronological priority to any appreciable advantage, either before or after the Civil War. From the very beginning the club seems to have always emphasized more of the game's social side, necessitating a greater reliance upon resident Englishmen than other area clubs.[16]

As the only major Philadelphia cricket club without a ground of its own, the organization led a wandering existence for many years after its antebellum playing area in Camden, which belonged to its professional William Bradshaw, became unavailable. All this changed in 1882 when the club merged with the Chestnut Hill Cricket Club, making it possible for the club to secure a permanent ground in this fashionable area of northwest Philadelphia being developed by industrialist Henry Howard Houston, who was well aware of how valuable a cricket club could be to the community's quality of life.[17]

Variously known in local cricket circles as "St. Martin's" from a nearby church, and "Wissahickon" from a nearby tavern-turned-fashionable-hotel, the Philadelphia club formally opened its new grounds on October 1, 1884, and by 1890 had also added an impressive all-purpose clubhouse.[18]

Nonetheless, even with these greatly improved facilities, the Philadelphia Club remained, for many years, one of the more undersubscribed (it only had 600 members in 1893, about half the number of Philadelphia's other major cricket clubs) and least competitive of the area's larger clubs, a situation that did not materially improve until 1914, when, bolstered by the addition of some standout players from the recently disbanded Belmont Club, it was able to win its first Halifax Cup championship.[19]

Both before and after the Civil War, Philadelphia cricket activity remained centered around the two largest clubs in the Germantown area, the Germantown Cricket Club and its sibling rival, the Young America Club. Both organizations continued to draw upon the area's extended social network of prominent Philadelphia families, primarily the Newhalls and Wisters, but also such "proper" Philadelphia families as the Clarks, Scotts, and Browns.[20]

The Germantown Club, originally domiciled in a small "stone house" on William Wister's property, relocated in 1865 to the Henry Pratt McKeon property at nearby Nicetown, where it would remain for another 25 years. Here the club set up the city's first enclosed cricket ground and erected the first grandstand built specifically for cricket, facilities that gave the club an almost uncontested claim to host every international match played in the city up to 1893.[21]

Despite these material advantages, Germantown, like other Philadelphia area clubs, was competitively overshadowed by its cross-town rival, the Young America Club. Through the 1870s and into the 1880s, this club was easily the strongest in Philadelphia and most likely the entire United States, a tribute to its youthful membership and conscientious application to the game. *Forest and Stream* was impressed with the way even its second eleven played with such purposefulness and resolve: "It is correct and early training that enables this team to play so charmingly together. Brains, besides muscle are used. A system is observed and a discipline maintained. There is a captain; he is their authority and his word is law."[22]

To most outsiders, Young America was always looked on as something of a role model for American cricket in general, and indisputable proof that American proficiency at the game was eminently possible. In reviewing the Young America's success against New York area teams in 1870, the *National Chronicle* expressed its admiration in the way the club "has succeeded in its efforts to show that those who love cricket and organize to make it popular, may conquer obstacles that some are disposed to think are insurmountable."[23]

By the late 1880s, however, it was becoming clear that Germantown could not support two large-scale cricket clubs. Young America was already experiencing declines from its peak enrollment of 500 by 1880, which it enjoyed as a result of its relocation to a new ground at Stenton, made possible by the club's share of the match receipts from the 1878 Australian match.[24]

Merger talks between Germantown and Young America were initiated in 1887, but were not finalized until April of 1889, when it was agreed to retain the Germantown name but adopt the Young America clubs colors, blue and white. The newly amalgamated club soon made arrangements to purchase, for its new home, the Price and Littell estate on Manheim street for $90,000, with another $100,000 going towards such improvements as a grandstand and ladies clubhouse, making it, on completion, the finest cricket facility in the United States at that time.[25]

The two major Philadelphia cricket clubs that appeared after the Civil War, the Merion and the Belmont, prospered from their advantageous locations within two of late nineteenth-century Philadelphia's growing suburban areas: the Main Line and west Philadelphia.

Originally established as little more than a "quasi-school-boy frolic" by William Montgomery and Marshall Ewing over the summer of 1865, the Merion club led a rather precarious existence during its early years on a leased plot in Wynnewood. Emerging as it did in the heyday of the post-Civil War baseball boom, the club had to turn back an early attempt to convert it into a baseball club, and was not able to secure a permanent ground of its own, at nearby Ardmore, until 1873.[26]

Even with the manpower resources available at nearby Haverford College, Merion did not begin to assert itself competitively until its relocation, in 1892, to a new 12-acre plot at Haverford Station. Here the organization grew and prospered as one of the more prominent centers of social life within this increasingly fashionable suburban area, a progress that was only temporarily set back in 1896, when its new clubhouse experienced major fire damage twice within nine months.[27]

Somewhat different from all these organizations was the Belmont Cricket Club. Founded on September 10, 1874, the club seems to have catered to a more middle-class clientele—primarily, it seems, Philadelphia's growing business and mercantile, rather than professional, classes. Under the capable management of its founder, George Wharton, and later Pennsylvania Railroad vice-president John P. Green, the club became a popular social center for residents of this respectable, though never particularly fashionable, area of west Philadelphia.[28]

By 1880, the club had over 500 members, a growth so unexpectedly vigorous it came as "a matter of surprise to older cricket organizations." Over the years, the club relocated from its original ground at 40th and Aspen Streets to progressively better locations; first to 49th and Baltimore in 1879, then 59th and Woodland in 1884, and a year later to 49th and Chester, where the club attractively situated its clubhouse in the middle of its property, straddling the cricket ground on one side and its tennis courts on the other.[29]

Reputed to be the best of Philadelphia's major cricket grounds because of its small size and fine pitch, the Belmont site became known as the city's "lucky ground" after Philadelphia's decisive win over Australia here in 1893. The club was somewhat slower, however, in its development as a local cricket competitor (in 1877 it once lost a match to New York's St. George Club by the embarrassing score of 340-27), primarily because of its early refusal to employ a professional. The club's fortunes, however, improved through the 1880s and again after 1897, when the club enrolled a number of standout players from the recently disbanded Tioga Cricket Club, such as Eddie Cregar and John B. King.[30]

As the larger Philadelphia cricket clubs increased in size and organizational complexity, it soon became necessary to replace their irregular competitive contacts with a more structured arrangement. This led to the establishment, in 1880, of a formal, round-robin competition among Germantown, Philadelphia, Young America, Merion, and Belmont, the winner of which could lay annual claim to the Halifax Cup, a trophy that had been won by a representative Philadelphia side during a tournament at that Canadian city in 1874.[31]

Intended to duplicate—as much as was practical—an English first-class level competition, the Halifax Cup was always restricted to the city's largest clubs, an arrangement that, over time, lent the competition a rather in-grown character. To remedy this, Germantown and Merion entered two teams for a few years but the *American Cricketer*'s suggestion, first raised in 1902, that the competition would be less "monotonous" if Baltimore and New York's Knickerbocker Athletic Club were admitted, was never acted upon.[32]

Mindful of the playing requirements of their younger, or less talented members, these clubs also set up in 1888 the Club Record Cup. The championship of this innovative competition (which became the Philadelphia Cup competition in 1900, the year it also opened to non-Halifax Cup clubs) went to the club that had the best combined record of its first, second, and junior elevens. This arrangement, along with a number of other second-tier competitions, such as the Inter-City League, organized among the smaller clubs in Philadelphia and west New Jersey at the turn of the century, seems to have obviated any potential friction between the "haves" and "have nots" of Philadelphia cricket. Over the years there seems to have been little disharmony between the area's larger and smaller clubs, save for the occasional complaint that too few players from the smaller clubs were being selected for the city's representative teams.[33]

More serious were the occasional disputes among Philadelphia's larger clubs themselves, especially over the distribution of the highly lucrative international matches. In particular, there had always been an undercurrent of resentment toward Germantown for its insistence, ever since it relocated to Nicetown, that all international matches be held on its grounds. This resentment intensified after Germantown merged with Young America, when the club not only tried to reassert this prerogative at its fine new facility at Manheim, but also insinuated that it alone should select representative Philadelphia sides for these matches.[34]

Philadelphia's other major clubs had previously attempted to break Germantown's monopoly of these events; most notable was Merion's attempt in 1879 to secure for itself a match with the Irish amateurs, but they were not able to effectively accomplish this objective until 1895. Coming together in a common cause that winter, Philadelphia, Merion, and Belmont threatened to bring over a foreign team under their own auspices, a move that, if carried out, would have had the financially disastrous consequences of multiple foreign teams playing in the city at the same time. Forced to deal with its sister clubs as equals, Germantown relented and agreed, in the future, to distribute these international matches among the other clubs on a rotating basis provided at least one of them be held annually at Manheim.[35]

As local interest continued to grow during these years, it was decided that Philadelphia cricket also needed a voice of its own, which came about on June 28, 1877, with the inaugural issue of the *American Cricketer*, a publication established on the rather optimistic belief that there were "thousands of persons on the continent who are more or less interested in the 'noble game.'"[36]

Originally under the editorship of Dan Newhall, Henry Brown, and Henry Cope, this "interesting little paper," as the *Australasian* called it, struggled through its early years, once even being prematurely declared defunct by the *Clipper* in 1885. The periodical, however, managed to persevere through not only financial difficulties but also editorial neglect, which had become so pronounced by the late 1890s that it even spawned a short-lived local competitor, *Cricket Club Life*. Under the more capable editorship of Sidney Young, the *American Cricketer* strongly revived during the early years of the twentieth century, enabling it to carry on as the faithful record of a local sporting interest that had, for all intents and purposes, expired long before the publication itself did in 1929.[37]

It would seem only logical that Philadelphia, being the one location where significant numbers of Americans not only played cricket but played it well, should have assumed the leadership of American cricket. But in fact, the city had to continually reassert such a claim, often to the point of putting itself at odds with the rest of the American cricket community.

As late as the mid-1860s, most sports observers, while conceding Philadelphia had the best American players, still believed New York's St. George Club was the country's strongest organization, even though it had been beaten by both the Philadelphia and Germantown clubs during this period. Not until the Young America Club, which, even in the eyes of the *Clipper* was still no more than the "strongest American eleven," was able to beat the St. George in 1865, a match in which the Englishmen were "outplayed at all points of the game," and twice again in 1870, did the sporting press finally seem willing to admit the center of American cricket had undeniably shifted to Philadelphia.[38]

The incontestable fact that cricket in Philadelphia was a good "half a century in advance of other American cities," perhaps inevitably began to arouse, from a variety of quarters, as much resentment toward as it did admiration of the city's cricket accomplishments. It was perhaps to be expected that the surprising success of the city's English tour in 1884 would be perceived as an unwelcome concentration of power in a single city. "The time is past," a letter to the *American Cricketer* admonished that year, "for the exaltation of Philadelphia cricket at the expense of . . . American cricket." Somewhat less understandable was the *New York Times* interpretation of this and later Philadelphia cricket successes as no more than self-serving civic egotism that only tended to "further inflate the monstrous conceit of that sequestered town."[39]

Philadelphia's head-and-shoulder's superiority over the rest of the country's cricket, however, always made it difficult for the city to promote the game in a constructive manner. Philadelphia always acknowledged it had a "missionary" obligation to foster the game elsewhere, sending out touring teams, over the years, to Detroit, Pittsburgh, Chicago, and Cleveland in the hope of encouraging local interest. In most instances, however, Philadelphia ended up beating the local opposition so badly (Belmont, for example, beat its host club, Cleveland, in 1899 by the spirit-killing score of 419-75) that these visits were probably counterproductive to their intended purpose.[40]

The situation was further complicated by the fact that most of the cricket outside Philadelphia was dominated by foreign residents, making it nearly impossible for Philadelphia to view any of these promotional efforts as anything more than challenges to its historic role of upholding American cricket.

The problem this presented became all too clear during the intercity championship of 1891. This competition, optimistically got up as a sort of national cricket championship, was supposed to bring the country's major cricket playing centers of Boston, New York, Philadelphia, Baltimore, Pittsburgh, Detroit, and Chicago into closer competitive cooperation. But Philadelphia so badly defeated the English-dominated Chicago team in the finals that the result aroused only resentment from the losing side and killed the competition after its initial year. To the Philadelphians themselves the championship game was not even a "national" cricket championship at all, but simply a test of American cricket strength against resident English opposition.[41]

The difficulties Philadelphia faced in trying to provide specifically "American" leadership to a cricket clientele that was predominantly non-American had actually surfaced years earlier, during the city's attempt to set up a national cricket organization. Efforts had been made to reestablish a national cricket body in 1867, but it was left to the larger Philadelphia clubs to formally establish a Cricketers Association of the United States at a meeting in Philadelphia on April 17, 1878.[42]

Almost as soon as this organization had come into existence, however, sharp divisions seemed to appear along nationalistic lines. Representatives from the English-dominated clubs, such as the St. George, were so opposed to Philadelphia's suggestion to overhaul some of the official M.C.C. rules, proposed at the 1883 meeting in New York (the first and only one to be held outside Philadelphia), they considered setting up their own national association without Philadelphia, an idea that would periodically resurface in later years.[43]

The Philadelphia controlled association was also criticized for its ineffectiveness in organizing anything but meaningless cricket events, such as the ill-fated East vs West All-Star game of 1887, which proved to be such a "failure" that a number of clubs, such as Pittsburgh, questioned the value of belonging to the organization. The Cricketers Association of the United States was, and would remain, an appendage of Philadelphia cricket, despite calls over the years from even the *American Cricketer* that there should be "a truly United States organization," a handicap that effectively reduced the organization to little more than a symbolic status, whose annual meetings, always dominated by Philadelphia clubs, amounted to little more than "social gatherings."[44]

Faced with such an unsatisfactory leadership structure, some cricket observers suggested sweeping authority be delegated to a single American club, similar to the Marylebone Cricket Club in English cricket. The names most frequently mentioned for such an exalted, if impracticable, office were the St. George, Philadelphia, Germantown, and Staten Island clubs.[45]

To complement such a single club authority scheme, the idea of laying out a national cricket ground, much like Lords in England, was also periodically floated. The Elysian Fields and Staten Island were occasionally mentioned as possible sites for such a ground, but the most widely recommended location, curiously enough, was always New York's Central Park, which, through its early history, was more closely identified with the aspirations and disillusionments of American cricket than might be imagined.[46]

Planned during the New York ball-playing fervor of the mid-1850s, Central Park was supposed to have had a cricket ground from the very beginning. Both Robert Viele's plan for the park, which was rejected, and Frederick Olmstead's, which was accepted, "mandated" an area for cricket playing—according to the *Clipper*, to have been a spacious 30-acre tract situated near the 59th Street entrance.[47]

New York cricket supporters, however, soon realized the park that was eventually laid out was often very different from the park that had been originally proposed. Neither a cricket, nor any other specific athletic ground was set aside in the park during this period, something the national cricket convention must have suspected as early as 1858, when a delegation of its members went "to wait on" park commissioners to no effect.[48]

The St. George Club tried many times to gain access to the park during the 1860s and 1870s, and, on one occasion, did gain conditional permission to use the facility, a development that, to the New York *World*, portended the park's future role as a venue for many grand international cricket matches, "such as the United States vs France, United States vs All-England, twenty-two of Scotland or Ireland vs eleven of the United States, or even eleven of London or Paris or of New York." Park commissioners, however, imposed so many restrictions upon their cricket playing that the St. George found it impossible to use the area then or at any later period.[49]

Ridiculed by *Forest and Stream* as "the Rip Van Winkles" of Central Park for such restrictive policies towards athletics, park commissioners eventually relented and, in 1885, permitted for the first time cricket playing in the park's North Meadow area, where on September 5 of that year the Riverside and Essex cricket clubs played what was in all likelihood the first cricket match in the park's history.[50]

Once opened, Central Park hardly developed into a beehive for cricket activity and never saw any "swarm of your best young men playing cricket," as a correspondent to the *Nation*, in 1869, confidently predicted would happen once the facility became available. Only the New York area's smaller cricket clubs ever used the facility, though they did so with a fair amount of regularity. It was not uncommon to find as many as a dozen local clubs using the North Meadow area during the summer weekends of the 1890s.[51]

This "sudden fit of liberality" (as the *Clipper* derisively termed it) that had moved the commissioners to open their park to cricket never seemed to have induced them, however, to assist the game in any other manner. Park commissioners did promise in 1886 to erect a clubhouse (which was never built) and to make other improvements, but in contrast to the directors of Brooklyn's Prospect Park, who by this time had already added a fine clubhouse to their park's well-maintained cricket area, Central Park authorities languished under the reputation of being the officials who "have never done more than cut the grass" for the cricket patrons of their facility.[52]

In at least one important matter, however, the Cricketers Association was successful: it managed to revive the old United States-Canada matches that had not been played, except for a single instance in 1865, since the outbreak of the Civil War.[53]

It would be wrong to presume the suspension of this series had brought all cricket contacts between the two countries to a standstill. Over this period there was still plenty of coming and going between individual American and Canadian clubs, especially those located along the northern border. The St. George club kept up its traditional contacts with Montreal over this period by hosting the Canadians at Hoboken in 1874, a hospitality the Canadians returned in 1877. The Philadelphia Cricket Club made at least one visit to Toronto in 1868, while the Peninsular club undertook several Canadian tours during the 1870s.[54]

A number of matches between representative sides were also played during these years, some of which could very easily be construed as "U.S. vs Canada" matches in their own right. The weak Canadian side Rev. T. D. Phillipps brought to the United States in 1876 may hardly have been representative of Canada's cricket strength, but in the estimation of the *Montreal Herald*, the British officers team that played in New York and Philadelphia under the "Garrison Knickerbocker" name in 1868 was the strongest cricket team that could have been assembled in the Dominion. To some observers, the match played in Philadelphia between representative Philadelphia and Canadian sides in 1875, itself a return match to the one played in Halifax a year earlier, fully qualified as an official contest in the U.S.-Canada series.[55]

The "official" series eventually resumed in 1879 with a match in Ottawa, and, just as it had before the Civil War, almost immediately became a flash point for nationalistic disputes. Both the *Clipper* and *Forest and Stream* were upset that the so-called United States team that year included two resident Englishmen, Cress of New York and Calvert of Detroit, a complaint also raised during the following year's match. The *American Cricketer*, somewhat surprisingly, did not concur with these prevailing sentiments, castigating the "know nothings" of American cricket for their narrowly nationalistic stance, which had denied places to a number of talented New York players for the 1885 match.[56]

In time, however, the United States sides would be purged of all but American players, or more correctly, all but Philadelphia players who year in and year out monopolized the American teams, a rather incestuous arrangement that was also frequently criticized. Again the *American Cricketer* took exception to hometown sentiment, noting in 1904 that "it is something of a shame that this match should be called 'Canada vs the U.S.' for neither side is ever representative of the country at large."[57]

To an extent this criticism wasn't quite fair. Philadelphia authorities knew who were the most talented American players outside of Philadelphia and always seemed willing to make room for them on United States teams. F. C. Irvine, a talented American from the Peninsular club, acclaimed as "the cricket meteor of the year" in 1875, and John Lawrence Pool, a St. Paul's alumnus who was generally recognized as the best bowler in New York, were included, respectively, for the 1881 and 1886 matches. Kelsey Warner Mallinkrodt, a talented Baltimore player, whom English batter Gilbert Jessup found to be a "genius for disguising pace" also played for the United States during the 1903 match. Philadelphia selectors were even more receptive to outside players during those years when the matches were played in Canada, inviting a number of Boston and Baltimore players to play in the 1895 match, as well as two standout resident Englishmen from New York, M. R. Cobb and C. H. Clarke, to the 1902 match.[58]

At one time a highlight of the American sports calendar, the U.S.-Canada series, in its revived form, never really came close to regaining the status it had enjoyed before the Civil War. The event could still make the front page of Philadelphia's *Public Ledger* as late as 1898, but this obscured the more obvious fact that most of these matches attracted only meager popular interest, were poorly attended, and, as was the case with the 1886 match held at the Seabright Lawn Tennis and Cricket Club, proved to be a complete "failure" as a fashionable event.[59]

The "apathy" and inability of Philadelphia organizers to get together anything like a representative side forced the outright cancellation of the 1887 and 1889 matches, not, as is commonly believed, because the best players from Canada and Philadelphia were, respectively, playing in England those years. It also became an accepted practice, on the part of both sides, to routinely field weak teams for away matches, though this didn't prevent the United States, with the exception of two three-year spells in the mid-1880s and 1890s, from dominating the series, a competitive imbalance that may have hurt, rather than helped, cricket relations between the two countries.[60]

Philadelphia could assume a posture of benign neglect not only toward its cricket neighbors to the north but also those in the United States simply because the city had reached such a high competitive level by the 1880s, that it more properly considered itself the North American outpost of the international cricket community, even though it was never quite sure of its exact place within this community.

The All-England players could already see in 1859 that the standard of Philadelphia cricket was moving beyond a merely national to a potentially international standard, inspiring what would be the first of many later prognostications of Philadelphia's impending parity with first-class English or Australian cricket. Over the next two decades, Philadelphia did give fleeting signs that it was inching toward this long term objective, such as its creditable performances against Wilshire's English pros in 1868 (a match some claimed was "the best and most hotly contested . . . in the history of cricket in this country"), and Fitzgerald's English amateurs in 1872. With their surprising draw against Australia in 1878, Philadelphia seemed fully justified, as Lester believed, in viewing their cricket, by this time, as "fully grown."[61]

This contented confidence, however, was severely shaken following the disastrous losses to Daft's and Shaw's English professionals, as well as to the Australians over the next four years, a series of reverses that forced the Philadelphians to reluctantly lower their competitive expectations, which they did *de facto* by agreeing to a slate of strictly amateur matches during their English tour of 1884.

There was little doubt the Philadelphians were here playing at their more proper competitive level. The team managed to complete the tour with a highly respectable record against amateur opponents (8 wins, 5 losses, 5 draws), results that again tempted some observers toward unrealistic assessments of American cricket strength, among them Henry Chadwick, who "tossed up my old cricket cap in exultation" on word of the Philadelphia successes in England.[62]

In reality, the entire tour had been not so much a triumphant conquest as a catechism for American cricket. The Philadelphians had proved they were "good at scoring against moderate bowling" but not at anything more. They were also unschooled in the subtleties of bowling outside the off stump, or playing back, leading one member of the team to confess that "we realized for the first time the true science of the game." In the estimation of one of the team's more observant members,

Howard McNutt, the whole experience had left little doubt that the Philadelphia cricketers of his generation would never be able to reach a level comparable to first-class English cricket.[63]

It would take only a single match, however, against Lord Hawke's English amateurs in 1891, to dramatically revive Philadelphia's long-cherished hopes of reaching first-class standards. The team Lord Hawke brought over to the United States that Fall was not a particularly strong one—Hawke himself admitted it was "not regarded as representative of our amateur strength," a glaring understatement according to prominent sports critic Caspar Whitney, who dismissed the side as "third rate"—but the Englishmen's visit came at a fortuitous time for Philadelphia cricket. It was the first international match at Germantown's recently opened Manheim ground, the first against a representative English side in five years, and the first against a side captained by a member of the nobility, all of which, collectively, fueled so much local anticipation that the *American Cricketer* claimed there had never before been "so much interest displayed in a visiting team."[64]

On the first day of the initial match, 22,000 spectators "by actual count" under the watchful eyes of some 50 policemen, crowded into the Germantown ground, where "rows of benches extended around almost to the entire circuit of the field, nearly a quarter of a mile in length, were jammed, but in addition, the crowd overran the ropes and seated itself four or five deep . . ." Certainly a more fitting setting couldn't have been imagined for an American win, which the Philadelphians actually managed to pull off by a comfortable seven wicket margin.[65]

Though this was by no means Philadelphia's first win over a representative foreign team, no other match so broadly and directly affected the immediate future of Philadelphia cricket. From now to the end of the century international cricket matches, which had been events of only moderate "fashionability," became an established feature of "proper" Philadelphia's fall social life. Here, in this city, as *Harpers Weekly* duly noted, "Fashion has set her seal upon the international match and her devotees must perforce patronize it." On the grass roots level as well, local clubs reported, as a consequence of Hawke's visit, a marked upswing in membership, match fixtures, and such an increase in junior interest that "even the small boy now wants a cricket bat."[66]

To some, Philadelphia's success against Lord Hawke's side was "the high water mark . . . in the annals of cricket in America," for others it meant a renewed confidence that Philadelphia could now produce cricket players comparable to those of first-class English cricket.[67]

There had always been many obstacles to this, not the least being Philadelphia's relatively small player pool. Even at the height of the game's popularity, Philadelphia selectors had to draw their representative sides from a talent pool that probably never exceeded some 250 candidates, this being the maximum number of active players probably available at any given time from the city's four or five largest clubs. In addition, cricket playing in Philadelphia, even at its highest level, had never been anything more than a part-time occupation that had to be balanced against business and professional demands. Philadelphia cricket history is punctuated with many instances of talented local players who had to shorten or interrupt their cricket careers because of occupational obligations, such as Joe Fox, a Germantown player of the 1880s who was "one of these men peculiar to Philadelphia cricket, where the demands of business take them away from the game just when they are in the way of becoming great players."[68]

By the last decade of the nineteenth century, however, Philadelphia was producing a number of such "gentleman" cricketers proficient enough to collectively secure the city at least a passable role in international cricket; such as Merion's Henry Scattergood, and Germantown's Frank Bohlen and Percy Clark, the last of whom, according to English critics, "would be welcomed by most of our counties [professional cricket clubs]." It was three Philadelphia players in particular—George Patterson, John Lester, and John B. King—who would most convincingly disprove the persistent nineteenth-century impression that the United States "can't develop good cricket players."[69]

The son of a University of Pennsylvania law professor and later a prominent attorney in his own right, George Patterson had quickly developed from one of Germantown's more talented junior players into Philadelphia's most consistent batter by the late 1880s, despite a highly "peculiar" batting style some foreigners found aggravating and a reputation as someone who "never exerted himself in the field."[70]

Dubbed the "W. G. Grace of American cricket" as a result of his outstanding series against Frank Mitchell's visiting English side in 1895, when he averaged better than 84 runs per match, Patterson had difficulty living up to this reputation in later years. His 33 runs-per-match average during Philadelphia's English tour of 1897, though respectable, was far short of the "sensation" Caspar Whitney was sure this star Germantown player (whom Australian George Giffen found to be "one of the most enthusiastic cricketers" he had ever met) would create against first-class English opposition.[71]

In contrast to Patterson, John Lester, in his youth, did not give nearly as much indication of his future greatness as a player. A "very indifferent batsman" during his student days at Cumberland's Ackworth School, Lester began to develop the highly polished batting style he would be known for only when he came to the United States and enrolled at Haverford College. Singled out for his high quality batting during that school's English tour of 1896, Lester attracted so much critical attention during Philadelphia's English tour the following year that several counties extended him contract offers to play in England.[72]

Lester even more forcefully asserted his standing among his Philadelphia teammates as the "one batsman who may almost [be] described as great" during his captaincy of the Philadelphia side that returned to England in 1903. He finished that tour as his team's top scorer as well as its third best bowler, an exceptional accomplishment for the university professor who according to some critics, "would soon be one of the greatest men of his day" if professional obligations hadn't prematurely shortened his playing career.[73]

The greatness of at least one Philadelphia cricketer of this period, John Barton ("Bart") King, was never in doubt. The son of a north Philadelphia dry goods dealer, King apparently took up cricket when he was 15 and then largely on a self-taught basis with one of the city's less prestigious clubs, the Tioga, where he seems to have first experimented with what would become his trademark ability to swing a cricket ball much like a curveball in baseball.[74]

In itself, this ability to bowl with an effective "curl" was even during this era of technical innovations in cricket "no new thing." The English professionals George Hurst and A. E. Relf had both developed a similar type of ball during this period. Only King, however, seemed to have the ability to swing the ball both ways without any appreciable loss of pace, not "floaters" that gently swung into or away from batters but high velocity deliveries that could sharply break over "the last yard" of their flight.[75]

Under ideal conditions—which to King was with "a gusting wind sweeping up the gulley [sic] to the right of second slip," strong enough to "flutter the left corner of my shirt collar"—the best of these "anglers" (as King termed them) could become the virtually unplayable "wild man from Borneo," of the type that bowled Sussex's Prince Ranjitsinhji during Philadelphia's 1897 English tour, a delivery match umpire Clayten claimed "would have taken out the stumps of any batsman in the world."[76]

More impressively, King seems to have been able to sustain this pace and ball movement without any noticeable compromise in line and length, a weakness P. F. Warner and Gilbert Jessop found so pervasive among other swing bowlers. Throughout Philadelphia's match against Lancashire in 1903, King's bowling "never became erratic and nearly every ball was on the wicket," leading the always critical *Manchester Guardian* to conclude this American's "capacity for hitting wickets is absolutely unrivaled. Even Richardson [the standout English bowler of that time] in his deadliest days hardly equaled it."[77]

English observers were also fascinated with King's unusual and intimidating delivery style, which, on approaching the wicket, he began by "lifting his arms like Souza [sic] conducting the opening bars of the Washington Post," then bringing them behind his head before releasing the ball at "a terrific pace," all-in-all "a most awe-inspiring spectacle" to every opposing batter.[78]

Towering head-and-shoulders above all domestic rivals (he once took seven wickets for one run in a local match, nine wickets for four runs in another), King was an automatic selection for every representative Philadelphia side from the U.S.-Canada match of 1892 up to the Australian matches of 1912, during which time the fortunes of Philadelphia cricket so often rose or fell on the individual performances of this star player. "Without King," the *Manchester Guardian* correctly noted, Philadelphia "would not be in the least formidable; with him they may beat any of the counties."[79]

By the end of Philadelphia's English tour of 1903, many critics ranked him behind only Richardson and Mold as a fast bowler, a standing that England captain P. F. Warner believed would have made the American an automatic selection for England's upcoming Australian tour had he been eligible.[80]

With their fortunes so heavily dependent upon the performances of a few top players, representative Philadelphia teams were anything but models of consistency, their international performances against the numerous foreign teams that visited their city between 1892 and 1899 varying from the appalling to the brilliant.

The euphoria surrounding the success against Lord Hawke's side quickly soured when the Philadelphians suffered what would be their first and only loss to a visiting Irish team the following year. The local press also vented its frustration over the city's failure to duplicate the success of 1891 against Lord Hawke's second team in 1894. "Rarely . . . has a Philadelphia team in an important international fixture given as poor an exhibition of batting" the *Public Ledger* proclaimed after the Philadelphians lost the first match, which it followed up with the even more stinging rebuke, "never . . . has a Philadelphia team suffered such an ignominious defeat" after the home team also lost the second match.[81]

The Philadelphia press also took its representative team to task for batting "like a lot of sheep" in its loss to P. F. Warner's English team in 1898, while *Harpers Weekly* could only quip, on watching the Philadelphians throw away an almost certain win against Frank Mitchell's weak Oxbridge team in 1895, "it required genius to lose that game."[82]

On the flip side, the local press could launch into equally overindulgent superlatives with every Philadelphia success. Reporters proclaimed the city's massive 525 first innings total against the Australians in 1893 to be "the greatest innings in the history of the world," as well as certain proof Philadelphia "can play correct and scientific cricket," choosing to overlook the likelihood that some of this was due as much to the weary, sea-legged fielding of their opponents, who by some "lively hustling" had been rushed from their boat in New York directly onto the Belmont ground. The Philadelphians' first two losses against the Australians in 1896 were also quickly forgiven after they won the final match by an even larger margin than they had in 1893, which the local press immediately trumpeted as "the greatest achievement in the annals of Philadelphia cricket."[83]

Throughout its history, in fact, Philadelphia always seemed to have considerable difficulty objectively evaluating its cricket abilities, as became all too clear from the decision to arrange a slate of entirely first-class matches for its 1897 English tour. This decision seems to have been unduly influenced by the Australians, who, following their loss to the Philadelphians in 1893, had urged their hosts to "go to England and give them a dose of the same medicine," a recommendation the Australians Trott and Iredale, in so many words, reiterated three years later, insinuating the Philadelphians should be able to beat every English country except Surrey, Yorkshire, and Lancashire. The Americans apparently chose to ignore the more objective opinion of their English opponents, such as Frank Mitchell, who was sure the Philadelphians "would not have any chance whatsoever" against English professional bowling.[84]

Just how far in over their heads the Philadelphians were with this decision became painfully apparent from just their first two encounters with the university sides. "From first to last the Americans were outplayed," was how the critics saw their match against Cambridge, followed by so poor a showing against Oxford, most observers were ominously predicting the Philadelphians "will have several long outings before the tour is ended." By the conclusion of Philadelphia's next match, a loss to Lancashire, most English critics had seen enough to realize it had been a mistake to include the Americans among their first-class fixtures. It was a view tacitly shared by many of the county clubs as well, most of whom shunted off their matches against the Philadelphians to minor grounds and routinely fielded less than full strength sides against them.[85]

There were some bright spots for the Americans, notably King's remarkable bowling against a full-strength Sussex side and a well earned win over Warwickshire, the Philadelphians "rising to the occasion in brilliant style" during that match, to pick up their second, and final win of a fifteen match schedule (four were drawn). To the Philadelphians themselves, their first innings against an admittedly weak Nottinghamshire side was "better cricket than even against the Australians in 1893."[86]

Over all, however, Philadelphia's play came up far short of first-class standards. Their batting always seemed to be "tame and uninteresting," characterized by a "general lack of life," that seemed to be saying to their opponents, "Here I am. Now try to bowl me out if you can." As an example, observers had to only point to George Patterson's innings against Yorkshire, the Philadelphia captain listlessly batting for some forty minutes before making his first run, "which evoked a cheer from the crowd."[87]

The Philadelphians themselves were especially disappointed with their bowling, which they had overconfidently assumed would be "well above the county average" when, in reality, it was, with the exception of King and his opening partner Percy Clark, "lamentably weak," lacking variety, and tending toward waywardness.[88]

Compounding these technical deficiencies were the frequently sparse, sometimes hostile, English crowds, like the one the Philadelphians ran into at Yorkshire, which "hooted the visitors whenever they came near the boundary." The Philadelphians were also critical of the English umpiring, pointing in particular to their match against Middlesex, during which the astonished Americans could overhear the bowling end umpire personally encouraging Hearne to take wickets.[89]

Returning home "entirely knocked out," and far short of their pre-tour expectations of "five or six" wins, the Philadelphians themselves attributed their poor showing to a lack of conditioning, soft English wickets, and most often, to the ubiquitous "hard luck" of the game, an excuse Caspar Whitney, for one, was no longer willing to buy. "'Hard luck' and 'uncertainties of the game,'" the *Harpers Weekly* sports editor claimed, "have been dragged forth so frequently by the Philadelphia cricketers . . . in extenuation of unexpectedly indifferent performances that the balm appears to have entirely lost its consoling virtues."[90]

Philadelphia's 1897 English tour had important long-term consequences for American cricket. Not only had the Philadelphians, with their unrealistic expectations against first-class opponents "run the risk (as they certainly have done) of losing their reputation as cricketers of the first rank," they seemed to have confirmed the perception that America would never achieve any sort of permanent standing in international cricket, something representative Philadelphia teams certainly did not do much to disprove over the next few years.[91]

The city lost both its matches against P. F. Warner's visiting English side in 1898, as it also did against Ranjitsinhji's strong English side a year later, the two matches against this team being so one-sided the English players were seen to go about their play "in a listless, don't care sort of fashion." Not that anyone could blame them since the Philadelphians were playing so poorly the English "all knew there was no hurry—our men would get out in a few minutes anyway." In all likelihood both English and Australian cricket authorities had by this time permanently discounted Philadelphia's first-class aspirations, with both showing a reluctance, from this point on, to send to the United States anything more than very moderate sides, such as the M.C.C. teams of 1905 and 1907, both composed largely of Oxbridge players, and the dissension-ridden Australians in 1912.[92]

It was a judgment English cricket seemed unwilling to modify even in the face of Philadelphia's unexpectedly successful English tour of 1903 and, to a lesser extent, its final first-class English tour five years after that.

Pretour predictions that the 1903 Philadelphians, a side that included eight members of the 1897 tour, "could not be other than a failure" seemed to be confirmed after another tour opening loss to Cambridge University, prompting the *Manchester Guardian* to declare "it cannot be said the Philadelphians have made a good impression."[93]

As it turned out, the *Guardian*'s coverage would be one of the more revealing barometers of how dramatically English cricket would change its estimation of this Philadelphia side. Following a creditable draw in its second match against Oxford and a win over Gloucestershire—discounted because the county's star batter Gilbert Jessup did not play—the *Guardian* slowly began to view these American cricketers more generously, quipping "we may have our visitors forthwith demanding a series of test matches." Only when Philadelphia won its next match, against previously unbeaten Nottinghamshire, did the paper seem willing to admit there was, perhaps, more to these Americans than it had assumed. "The mere respect which was at first felt for the Philadelphians has now given way to admiration."[94]

For the most part, the Philadelphians were able to uphold this newfound respect for the remainder of their visit. They overcame several noticeable lapses, such as a poor showing against the M.C.C. and several losses when King and Lester were temporarily out with injuries, to finish the tour with an impressive win against a full-strength Surrey side, over the course of which the Americans "had the pleasure of finding their cricket watched with the close attention that is usually reserved for Australian and county matches." Probably the most satisfying of the team's seven wins that summer (out of 16 played with 3 drawn) was the one over an improvised Lincolnshire 18, not so much because it represented the first time Americans had given odds to an English team at cricket, but because it seemed to symbolize the long-delayed fulfillment of Philadelphia's belief, ever since its loss to Shaw's English side 22 years earlier that "Patient continuance in well doing will, in time, bring deserved success."[95]

The critic's opinion that this Philadelphia side was comparable to some South African, maybe even Australian, sides did not, however, seem to be shared by either their opponents or the English public in general. As was the case with their predecessors six years earlier, this Philadelphia side also found themselves frequently opposed by less than full-strength county sides, such as the one they played at Old Trafford, a Lancashire team so weak it was "hardly better than a second eleven." Public interest in the Americans was also minimal, with barely a hundred spectators in attendance for their match with Lancashire, and "only a handful" for their one against Nottinghamshire.[96]

Interest wasn't any greater during Philadelphia's third, and final, first-class English tour in 1908, even though this squad was only slightly less successful than its immediate predecessor. With King "as individual in style and as persevering as ever" in his bowling, this Philadelphia side managed to win four of its 10 first-class matches, among them "a keenly fought and thoroughly interesting" win over the M.C.C., the first, and only, time a representative Philadelphia team managed to beat England's flagship cricket club. The team even seemed to play up well in many of its losses, Herbert Hordern believing their match with Kent, though lost, was one of the best the Americans played that summer.[97]

But again most county clubs fielded only modest sides against their American visitors, who proved to be no more popular with the British public than had earlier Philadelphia sides. Despite all their efforts, over the years, to gain recognition from the English cricket community, there seemed to be no avoiding the London *Daily News* conclusion that "the Philadelphians have never succeeded in making themselves an attraction in this country."[98]

To the Philadelphians themselves, however, it was more important that these international forays, whatever the perception they left with foreigners, should benefit the game back home. All of Philadelphia's first-class English tours had been undertaken in the confident expectation that the attendant notoriety and publicity would strengthen the game's grass roots appeal. It was assumed the "good results" of the 1897 tour would induce Philadelphians to "forswear the fascination of the links and the courts and return to . . . cricket," and that those of the 1903 tour would "stimulate enormously" cricket interest in other areas of the country. Even the normally skeptical New York press was convinced as a result of Philadelphia's good showing in 1903 that "the time seems to be ripe for a great development of cricket as played in the United States"; that would very likely lead to a "multiplication of bowlers, of wicket-keepers and of fielders in this country," a trend the *American Cricketer* seemed to think "there are many indications of" around the country.[99]

In fact, these international tours seemed to have only negligibly affected cricket's popularity in America, even in Philadelphia. The number of scheduled matches in that city did modestly rise for a couple of years after 1903, but then began to decline, to a point that the total number of matches played in 1914 was no greater than had been played 20 years earlier.[100]

Over time, some Philadelphia observers even began to question the wisdom of expending so much effort toward the apparently unattainable goal of consistent international success when this did not seem to appreciably benefit grass roots interest. Philadelphia Cricket Club captain John Mason believed Philadelphia's international decline after 1908 was actually something of a blessing in disguise since it allowed more resources to be shifted away from Halifax Cup matches (which had, after the 1897 tour, been extended throughout the summer in the hope of developing more international class players) to more broadly beneficial cricket activities, such as junior tournaments and overseas tours by individual clubs, which, after 1908, totally replaced those of representative Philadelphia sides.[101]

All this represented a broader organizational response to a problem that had troubled Philadelphia cricket throughout its history; namely, to what extent could an obligation to participant popularity—which demanded structural modifications to traditional cricket—be reconciled with an equally imposing obligation to competitive proficiency, which required a strict adherence to traditional cricket?

American cricketers at other times and places had struggled to come to terms with this problem, but Philadelphia had both the numbers and organizational independence to be able to openly declare, as George Newhall did in 1884, "If the MCC does not suit us, either we must go or the MCC must go." Probably the best example of this was Philadelphia's opposition to the M.C.C. interpretation of the LBW law (where a batter is judged out for blocking a ball from hitting his wicket with his body). At the 1885 United States Cricketers Association meeting, Philadelphia formally adopted, for its local competition, a simplified, more easily enforceable, interpretation of this law, a ruling clearly contrary to the M.C.C. law, but one so popular "there is probably no one playing of any standing on this side of the water who does not believe that the American rule is a fairer and wiser one."[102]

Philadelphia also seemed to be the first to act upon the widespread American dissatisfaction with the M.C.C. position on declarations (which allows a team to stop batting before all its players have gotten up). A number of widely publicized incidents had, over the years, demonstrated the absurdity of not having this option, such as the Alpha club batters who purposely hit their own wickets to end their innings against Harvard in 1873, or the Newark players who, ahead of the Manhattan club after one inning, deliberately dropped catches to avoid having to bat again in 1879. To once and for all eliminate such "farces" from their matches, Philadelphia formally permitted local teams, beginning in 1889, to declare their innings closed at any time, a rule that proved to be popular with clubs in other areas of the country as well.[103]

In their efforts to maximize participant interest, American cricket authorities in Philadelphia and elsewhere could hardly be blamed for looking to baseball for some ideas here. The suggestion, raised as early as 1859, that cricket adopt baseball's distinction between earned and unearned runs, as well as its statistical recognition of errors, was actually adopted by the Merion club during its match with the St. George in 1874. Other Philadelphia clubs, it appears, dropped this idea after a one-year trial period in 1888, but they did officially adopt, for their Halifax Cup matches, beginning in 1890, the baseball-inspired idea of allowing visiting teams choice of innings, something that proved more workable than the *Clipper*'s 1885 suggestion that players "take a shot at the wicket" to determine this.[104]

The more radical baseball-inspired idea of permitting double plays, proposed for the 1885 Halifax Cup matches, was never adopted, nor was the periodically recurring suggestion that cricket fielders be allowed to use gloves, an idea that was judged "a dismal failure" by the Chicago cricketers who tried it in 1911.[105]

All these modifications, however, were largely cosmetic, and did not directly resolve the long-standing complaints that cricket matches were too "drawn out" and tended to end in what the *Memphis Appeal* dubbed "that abortion of cricket"—the unfinished game.[106]

In an attempt to directly address these pivotal concerns, Philadelphia cricket officials, on separate occasions, authorized the adoption of two major structural modifications for local matches. The first, which came to be known as the "American Plan," had been suggested as early as 1882, but was not seriously considered until Merion cricketer John Thayer successfully lobbied on its behalf at the 1890 United States Cricketers Association meeting. Under this plan, teams would alternate batting and fielding on the fall of every third second innings wicket, an arrangement, it was hoped, that would not only liven up the later stages of the match, but also ensure a result.[107]

These same intentions were behind the second plan, also first suggested in the 1880s but not adopted until Philadelphia Cricket Club member John Mason pushed for it in 1911. Under Mason's plan, teams would continue to bat consecutively during their second innings along traditional lines, but each side could bat no longer than half the remaining second inning's time.[108]

Though the American Plan, heralded on its introduction as "a revolution in the cricket field" by Henry Chadwick himself, was used in several college matches, and the Mason plan was moderately popular with smaller clubs, neither innovation proved to be the magic formula for making cricket more attractive to Americans. Both plans had serious practical flaws that were soon exploited by local players, creating situations that prevented many of these matches from being satisfactorily completed, or, as turned out to be the case in many games played under the Mason plan, "the second innings quite frequently degenerated into a farce."[109]

Why did Philadelphia, for all its professed nationalism, fail to make cricket more structurally attractive to Americans?

It would be tempting to conclude, with the failure of such apparently radical modifications as the American and Mason plans, that perhaps there was simply no way to "Americanize" cricket. This would be correct if the many modifications Philadelphia proposed or implemented over the years reflected a truly American sensitivity to the game, something, however, that may not at all have been the case.[110]

Neither the American nor the Mason plans ever really addressed the critical issue of length determination, nor has any evidence come to light that the Philadelphians ever considered such potentially promising innovations as limited overs cricket, something that has proved to be popular in modern cricket.

This possibility, that the Philadelphians, despite their insistence that they built their cricket along American principles, may have, in fact, misjudged these very principles, seems even more evident in their long and misguided preoccupation with the over—the change of bowling direction every few pitches that requires fielders to constantly reposition themselves—a requirement Americans had long looked on as "a serious tax upon the game."[111]

The Philadelphians themselves tried to neutralize this drawback by reducing the number of overs per match, through either an increase in the number of balls per over (in some instances, as high as 10), or a prescribed time limit to each over (usually 30 minutes). In both instances, however, Philadelphia failed to recognize it wasn't the over *per se* that Americans found objectionable (the over in cricket, like the change of innings in baseball, actually provides a natural and welcome pause in the game's drama), but the "languid pedestrianism" of fielders having to do this over an indefinite period. By trying to simply adjust the length of the over, the Philadelphians, like Chadwick in his insistence upon "promptness," betrayed an inability to comprehend that cricket's inner action could simply not be invigorated without a willingness to alter the game's broader length determination.[112]

And the reason for this was fairly clear: behind Philadelphia's more visible attempts to "Americanize" cricket, to make it shorter or "quicker," there was an equally strong countercurrent that insisted only the traditional game, with two full innings played completely out, was "real cricket," never to be confused with the "chromo cricket" of the reformists. Even those Philadelphians who seemed more supportive of experimentation could never bring themselves to show any "sympathy with those who would reform cricket into a sort of dull copy of base ball," while more conservative players, like George Patterson, when pressed for ideas on how to improve the game, could do no more than fall back on Chadwick's scheme of "beginning matches with greater punctuality and not wasting so much time." From first to last, Philadelphians always looked upon their cricket as an "institution," with things about it that shouldn't be altered, that the game was, even in the face of popular discontent, "good enough for anybody as it stands and that any changes would be a mistake."[113]

In time, this posture would put Philadelphia cricket's never secure standing in jeopardy. Philadelphia may have been the "cricket capital" of America, but this grandiose title tended to obscure the fact that even here cricket rested upon a relatively limited participant base and the goodwill of a narrow nonparticipant social circle. Of the 2,000 and 1,300 members that belonged, respectively, to the Germantown and Merion clubs at the turn of the century, only some 100 and 75 of these members played cricket on a regular basis. A similar proportion probably existed in the city's other major cricket clubs.[114]

This relatively modest number of players was able to exert influence disproportionate to its size so long as it enjoyed the good graces of fashionable Philadelphia society. But the clientele that came to cricket matches, as Philadelphia cricket authorities well knew, "more because it was the social fad of the period than from the real love of the game," was clearly an insecure foundation. By the turn of the century such support was noticeably waning, eventually declining to such a low level that barely a handful of spectators were on hand, despite free admission, for Germantown's win over an Australian team in 1913, the last first-class match Philadelphia would ever play.[115]

Cricket did not fail in Philadelphia because the Americans who played it there loved their game any less. The long careers of such Philadelphia players as Frank Taylor's, which spanned some 50 years, and William Foulkrod's that saw an unbroken 20-year stretch of Halifax Cup matches, always "revealed the capabilities of men whose enthusiasm [for cricket] cannot be curbed." Cricket failed in Philadelphia because these Americans, for all their expressed devotion to the game, could never bring themselves to play it *like* Americans.

Incapable or unwilling to bring their cricket into conformity with broader American sporting tastes, Philadelphians eventually could only hold out, on the game's behalf, its "tradition" of moral benefits, or the "prestige" of international standing. These were acceptable motives for the two generations of proper Philadelphians that played the game after the Civil War. But by the turn of the century, the younger generation of proper Philadelphians, like Americans elsewhere, saw these motives as not only unacceptable substitutes for their basic play interests, but enticements to an emotional dishonesty toward them.[116]

Conclusion

Scholars have traditionally explained cricket's failure as an American sporting institution as a consequence of broad social or historical trends, such as the disruptive effects of the Civil War, class, or ethnic differences, or the emergence of American sporting nationalism.

I have tried to show that such macroanalytic interpretations, though valuable for a contextual understanding of the rise and development of American cricket, are inadequate for a satisfactory explanation of its decline.

The Civil War may stand as a convenient demarcation for cricket's cultural decline, vis-à-vis baseball, but it did not, in itself, materially contribute to this, nor did it represent any definitive break in America's antebellum sporting patterns.

I have also shown that antebellum cricket, though popular with all classes of Americans, was primarily supported by the middle class, the most formative social segment in the development of American team sports, then as now.

I have also shown that it was not so much cricket's identity as an English institution that retarded the game's acceptance by Americans as it was the inability of the immigrant English community to translate their game to Americans in the context of their own sporting culture.

The most popular explanation for the decline of American cricket, nationalism—the assertion that Americans settled upon baseball as an expression of a rather vague "need" for a national sporting identity—simply confuses cause and effect.

Early Americans preferred baseball because of its distinct appeal and attractiveness as a participant sport, not from any predetermined intellectual obligation, though once baseball became established, this exact relationship would, in time, become so blurred as to account for the peculiar strength of this explanation.

Only recently have scholars begun to recognize the importance of more narrowly focused, microanalytic, factors for explaining cricket's failure as an American sport, the most notable advocates of this approach being Melvin Adelman and George Kirsch.

The latter, for instance, believed cricket failed in America from a combination of inadequate coaching, playing grounds, and promotion, an explanation that, though partially correct, also comes up short.

Philadelphia, in its heyday, had cricket facilities second to none in the world, yet the game could not survive even in this favorable environment. And one certainly could not say cricket was underpromoted. Throughout the nineteenth century, the American sporting press was, if not outright supportive of, at least sympathetic toward, cricket. Yet this never seemed to affect, to any substantive degree, a shift in American grass roots attitudes toward the game. It is this episode in particular that stands as one of sports history's strongest refutations of the belief that popular sporting culture can be easily manipulated and redirected "from above."[1]

It was Adelman who more correctly recognized that a satisfactory explanation of cricket's failure as an American sport lies in an understanding of the more subtle interplay between culturally conditioned behavior and its expression through specific sporting structures. Working within this context, Adelman believed that baseball, with its shorter, rapid transition structure, and alternating periods of excitement and dramatic pauses, provided Americans with a cultural expression that cricket, at least within its traditional structural limitations, couldn't duplicate.

Adelman believed, however, that baseball's cultural dominance was a logically appropriate development for antebellum Americans within the broader trend of sport's modernizing process, while cricket, with its advanced technique and culturally unmalleable status, was "prematurely modern" for such a development.

While agreeing with Adelman that cricket's inability to come to terms with the cultural requirements of America's emerging bat-and-ball playing preferences (a tension that would resonate throughout the history of nineteenth-century American cricket) stands as the most attractive explanation for the game's demise as an American sport, I believe this tension does not so much represent a stage in the process of sports modernization as it does a pervasive cultural resistance to it.

I have tried to show that there is evidence that America's sporting culture seemed to be antithetical to the playing structure represented by cricket even in the premodern sporting era (prior to the 1830s), and that this sporting culture, in its eventual assertion of baseball, successfully resisted the broad rational forces that were working in cricket's favor.

In the two decades immediately before the Civil War, extensive media support, an appeal to established international standards, and the growing moral recognition of sports participation should have provided cricket with a strong, if not secure, basis for its popularity with Americans. But even the combined import of these modern trends could not neutralize the cultural inadequacies Americans felt toward the game, an inadequacy that relentlessly asserted itself in a persistent preference for baseball.

After the Civil War, cricket enjoyed something of a "second wind" as an alternative to sports of mass appeal, supporters building upon the game's perceived weaknesses (excessive length, lack of excitement, etc.) to enhance its appeal as a sport of character-building value, international prestige, and lifetime participation.

But neither could these highly rational inducements sustain the sport. Indeed, cricket progressively waned as the cultural expressions represented by baseball continued, over the nineteenth century, to solidify and deepen across class and social lines in America.

In sum, cricket did not fail in America because of any catastrophic social disruption. Nor did it fail from any premature technical development, foreign identity, or inadequacy of promotion. Cricket failed in America because it never established an American character.

This is a conclusion that raises some important issues for future sports scholarship. Are culturally determined sporting preferences so permanent and unalterable that they can resist, even offset, broader rational influences upon sports development? Nineteenth-century American cricket supporters were well aware that their sport, to flourish, had to be played under "American conditions," but they seemed incapable of bringing these about, even in Philadelphia.[2]

The problem this entailed could be clearly seen in the attempt, by Chicago Cricket Club secretary J. Wood, in 1870, to combine the best features of baseball and cricket into a hybrid sport. Projected to be "all the rage" that would once and for all resolve "the great international difficulty" between the two sports to the "satisfaction of both Englishmen and Americans," this contrived game proved to be culturally acceptable to no one and was quickly forgotten.[3]

Sports historians, in their preoccupation with the dynamics of broad rational trends (urbanization, social "dialectic," sporting "hegemony," etc.), have envisioned a sporting future where national, class, and cultural differences progressively give way to the forces of increased internationalism and competitive uniformity. But the history of cricket in America shows (as no doubt other episodes in sports history may) that this course may not be as relentless as it appears; that deeper, if harder to define, culturally preconditioned sporting preferences may not only continue to persist, they may be able to exert a resistance to, or even negation of, this course of modernization.

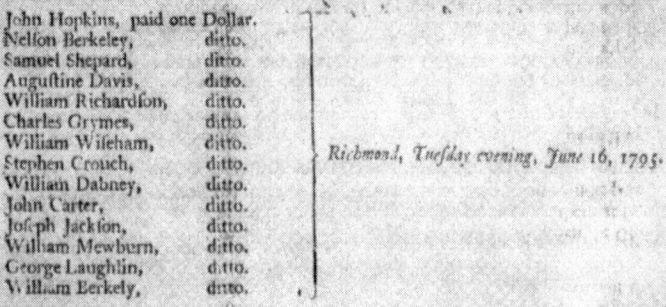

Fig. 1. The 1795 rules of the Richmond, Virginia, Cricket Club, the oldest-known cricket document in America. Courtesy of the Library of Virginia.

Photographs · 151

Fig. 2. The 1856 U.S.-Canada match played at Hoboken, when this event was at the height of its prestige and popularity. Courtesy of the *Clipper*.

Fig. 3. Because of his efforts to bring Americans into the game, New York Cricket Club president Henry Sharp, shown here in 1863, was probably most deserving of the title "Father of American Cricket." His inability, however, to get the American employees of even his own company to take up the game only underscored the difficulty English immigrants had in translating their game to American culture. Courtesy of *Wilkes Spirit of the Times*.

Fig. 4. A scene from the 1878 match between Philadelphia and Australia's national team at Nicetown. Though drawn, the controversy-marred match ended America's long string of losses against overseas teams. Courtesy of the *Daily Graphic*.

Fig. 5. The Paterson, New Jersey, Cricket Club, one of the New York area's more enduring cricket organizations, shown here in 1880. Among its members at this time were future Paterson mayor John Hinchliffe (bottom, fourth left) and former National League baseball pitcher Ed Nolan (top, extreme left). Courtesy of the American Labour Museum.

Fig. 6. The St. Paul's School cricket team, c.1890. With their histrionic poses and well-tailored uniforms, the team epitomized cricket's elitist image among late nineteenth-century private American schools. Courtesy of Dr. J. L. Pool.

156 · *The Tented Field*

Fig. 7. The rather somber looking members of the Hazen School girls cricket team of Pelham, New York. Their match with the Rosemary Hall girls cricket team in 1896 was one of America's earliest interscholastic girls sporting events. Courtesy of the Town of Pelham.

Fig. 8. Philadelphia's Belmont Cricket Club as seen through the eyes of water color artist Frank Taylor. Disbanded in 1913, this west Philadelphia club would be the only major nineteenth-century Philadelphia cricket club that has not survived to the present. Courtesy of the C. C. Morris Cricket Library.

158 · *The Tented Field*

Fig. 9. The spacious and imposing ground of the Merion Cricket Club, shown here during a match between Philadelphia and Lord Hawke's English team in 1894. Courtesy of the C. C. Morris Cricket Library.

Fig. 10. A youthful John Bartin King, shown here around 1897. By the end of his career, a decade and a half later, this Philadelphian had firmly secured a place for himself in cricket history as one of the game's greatest bowlers. Courtesy of the C. C. Morris Cricket Library.

Fig. 11. Nineteenth-century Philadelphia's most prominent cricket organization, the Germantown Cricket Club, shown here hosting a match between Pelham Warner's English side and a team of Philadelphia colts in 1897. Courtesy of the C. C. Morris Cricket Library.

Glossary of Cricket Terms and Phrases

This work was intended to be self-explanatory, but for the benefit of readers unfamiliar with cricket, the following glossary provides a layman's explanation of the more technical cricket terms that appear in the text.

"blocked ball after ball" Since the cricket batter doesn't have to run after hitting the ball, he will sometimes simply try to use his bat to block pitches from hitting his wicket to prevent being put out. This frequently results in long periods of inactivity, like a baseball batter fouling off several pitches.

bowler The cricket "pitcher."

"bowling outside the off stump" Cricket expression roughly equivalent to baseball's "pitching over the outside part of the plate."

"dead on the wicket" Cricket expression roughly equivalent to baseball's "pitching the ball right down the middle."

"fall of wicket(s)" The expression used in cricket for an out. It can also be used to designate each individual out; i.e., "the fall of the third [first, fourth, etc.] wicket" means the third batter in the lineup has been put out.

follow on A time-saving tactical option in a two innings cricket match whereby the team batting first, if ahead by a certain number of runs after each team's batted, can force the losing team to bat again (follow on) right after they've finished batting the first time. A team that has to follow on is usually in dire danger of losing the match.

"googly style of bowling" A type of bowling that first came into use at the end of the nineteenth century, where the ball is thrown to the batter slowly, but with a deceptive spin, making it bounce erratically.

gully A cricket fielding position situated to the cricket batter roughly equivalent to where the on-deck circle is to the baseball batter.

innings An innings (always used in the plural) in cricket is not completed after each team has made three outs, but only after each team has come to bat and ten of their eleven batters have been put out, one after another. An entire cricket match, therefore, lasts only one innings, or, at the most, two innings, in which case each team bats around twice.

M.C.C. Acronym for the Marylebone Cricket Club of London, an organization that, since the nineteenth century, has been recognized as the worldwide legislator of the official laws of cricket.

"playing back" Cricket expression roughly equivalent to baseball's "waiting back on the pitch."

round-arm bowling A type of bowling, popular from the 1830s to the 1860s, where the ball was thrown with a fast, sidearm motion.

"seven wicket margin" The team batting second, at the point it scored the winning run, still had seven of its batters yet to come up.

"soft English wickets" Because it rains a lot in England, the wicket (here used for the stretch of turf between the actual wickets) is often soft and spongy. Since the bowler in cricket can throw the ball to the batter on the bounce, having to bat on such a wicket, where the ball can bounce erratically, can be difficult for anyone unfamiliar with it.

"taken out the stumps" One way a bowler can get a batter out in cricket is to throw the ball past the batter and hit his wicket. With a very fast, powerful throw, the bowler can sometimes actually knock one of the three poles (each called a stump) completely out of the ground.

test match A match between two national cricket teams, the highest competitive level in cricket.

"32 for 7" An expression indicating the batting team, at the point in the game when its seventh batter was put out, had only 32 total runs. At high-level cricket, this would be a very poor batting performance.

wicket keeper The cricket "catcher."

wickets The two sets of three short, wooden poles situated twenty-two yards apart, that function something like bases in cricket. Also used as a colloquial expression for the stretch of turf between the wickets.

"wickets were pitched" The wickets were set up, indicating the game is about to start.

Notes

Introduction

1. Though somewhat outdated, Stephen Hardy's "The City and the Rise of American Sport: 1820-1920" (*Exercise and Sport Sciences Reviews* 9 [1983], 183-219), still provides the most useful summary of the various interpretations of American sport's urban origins.

2. Benjamin Rader, "The Quest for Sub Communities and the Rise of American Sport," *American Quarterly* 29 (1977), 355-69; Steven Gelber, "Their Hands Are All Out Playing: Business and Amateur Baseball, 1845-1917," *Journal of Sport History* 11, no. 1 (Spring 1984), 5-27.

3. For a predominantly ethnic interpretation of baseball's rise and cricket's decline, see Robert Lewis, "Cricket and the Beginnings of Organized Baseball in New York City," *International Journal of the History of Sport* 4 (December 1987), 315-21. For an analysis of this subject along the lines of social class, see Ian Tyrell, "The Emergence of Modern American Baseball, c.1850-1880," in Richard Cashman, ed., *Sport in History* (St. Lucia: Queensland University Press, 1979), 205-26.

4. George Kirsch, *The Creation of American Team Sports: Baseball and Cricket, 1838-1872* (Urbana: University of Illinois Press, 1989); Melvin Adelman, *A Sporting Time: New York City and the Rise of Modern Athletics, 1820-70* (Urbana: University of Illinois Press, 1986), 7, 135, 114.

Chapter 1

1. Allen Guttmann, *From Ritual to Record: The Nature of Modern Sports* (New York: Columbia University Press, 1978), 100; Adelman, *A Sporting Time*, 6.

2. William Byrd, *The Secret Diary of William Byrd of Westover, 1709-1712* (Richmond: Dietz, 1941), 144, 153, 155, 158; Nancy Struna, "The Formalizing of Sport and the Formation of an Elite: The Chesapeake Gentry, 1650-1720," *Journal of Sport History* 13, no. 3 (Winter 1986), 219.

3. John Lester, *A Century of Philadelphia Cricket* (Philadelphia: University of Pennsylvania Press, 1951), 4, 6; George Seymour, "The Old Time Game of Wicket and Some Old-Time Wicket Players," *Papers and Addresses of the Society of Colonial Wars in the State of Connecticut, 1903-1910*, 280; John Betts, "Mind and Body in Early American Thought," *Journal of American History* 54 (1968), 788.

4. *American Cricketer* 26 December 1878, 85; Henry Stiles, *A History of the City of Brooklyn* vol. 1 (New York: Heritage, 1993), 311, 313.

5. *American Cricketer* 26 December 1878, 85; 23 May 1889, 10; "Wicket in America," *Nation* 7 July 1910, 9; Lester, *A Century*, 5. Documents of the Richmond Cricket Club are held by the State Library of Virginia. In the face of this evidence, Struna's assertion that "British ball-games had no staying power among colonial adults" must be open to debate; Nancy Struna, *People of Prowess: Sport, Leisure and Labor in Early America* (Urbana: University of Illinois Press, 1996), 132.

6. *New York Weekly Gazette and Post Boy* 6 May 1751, 2; *American Cricketer* 26 December 1878, 85; Rowland Bowen, *Cricket: A History of Its Growth and Development Throughout the World* (London: Spottiswode, 1970), 54.

7. Quoted in Dale Somers, *The Rise of Sports in New Orleans* (Baton Rouge: Louisiana State University Press, 1972), 48; Harold Peterson, *The Man Who Invented Baseball* (New York: Scribner, 1969), 10-11; *Spirit of the Times* 31 May 1856, 187; 25 August 1838, 20.

8. *Wilkes Spirit of the Times* 5 December 1863, 211; Charles Peverelly, *The Book of American Pastimes* (New York: C. A. Peverelly, 1866), 532.

9. Henry Stiles, *A History of the City of Brooklyn*, vol. 1, 312, 313; "Wicket in America," *Nation* 7 July 1910, 9; *Forest and Stream* 26 June 1879, 410; *American Cricketer* 26 December 1878, 85; *New York Evening Post* 19 June 1820, 2; *Spirit* 27 October 1838, 292.

10. *Spirit* 31 May 1856, 187; John Woods, *Two Years Residence on the English Prairie of Illinois* (Chicago: Donnelley, 1968), 110, 211, 212. Click believes the cricket club organized in Norfolk, Virginia, in 1803 was in imitation of English customs; Patricia Click, *Spirit of the Times* (Charlottesville: University of Virginia Press, 1989), 73.

11. Alfred Bill, *Valley Forge; The Making of an Army* (New York: Harpers, 1952), 155; Bonnie Stadelman, "The Amusements of the American Soldiers During the Revolution" (Ph.D. Diss., Tulane University, 1969), 82-83; Bruce Daniels, *Puritans at Play* (New York: St. Martins, 1995), 174; Bonnie Ledbetter, "Sports and Games of the American Revolution," *Journal of Sports History* 6, no. 3 (Winter 1979), 3; *American Cricketer* 26 December 1878, 85; *American Farmer* 22 July 1825, 143.

12. Hamilton Bail, *Views of Harvard* (Cambridge: Harvard University Press, 1949), 94; Ralph Hill, ed., *College on the Hill* (Hanover: Dartmouth Pub., 1964), 265, 266, 267; George Seymour, "The Old-Time Game of Wicket," 285-86; Russell Nye, *The Cultural Life of the New Nation* (New York: Harper, 1966), 187.

13. Melvin Adelman, *A Sporting Time*, 98.

14. A. S. Rosenback, *Early Children's Books* (New York: Dover, 1971), 113-14; Robert Lewis, "Cricket and the Beginnings of Organized Baseball in

New York City," *International Journal of the History of Sport* 4 (December 1987), 318-19; Edward Everett Hale, *A New England Boyhood* (Boston: Little, Brown, 1910), 200-01.

15. Roberta Park, "The Attitudes of Leading New England Transcendentalists Toward Healthful Exercise, Active Recreations and Proper Care of the Body: 1830-1860," *Journal of Sport History* 4, no. 1 (Spring 1977), 40; John Betts, "Mind and Body in Early American Thought," *Journal of American History* 54 (1968), 802; Ruth Fink, "Recreational Pursuits of the Old South," *Research Quarterly* 23 (March 1952), 36; John Lester, *A Century*, 12; *Yankee* (Portland, ME) 6 February 1828, 42.

16. *True Sun* (New York) 24 September 1844, 2; *Clipper* 5 October 1878, 220.

17. Rowland Bowen, *Cricket: A History*, 35, 36, 85; *Cincinnati Commercial* 5 September 1869, 5; *Troy Times* 11 June 1860, 3.

18. George Seymour, "The Old-Time Game of Wicket," 272, 273; *New York Tribune* 28 August 1880, 2. Between the 1850s and 1870s wicket-playing was reported in such geographically dispersed locations as Rochester, New York; Elyria, Ohio; Clinton, Iowa; Madison, Wisconsin; Hiram and Kenyon colleges in Ohio, and Arkansas; *Rochester Union and Advertiser* 1 September 1857, 3; *Elyria Democrat* 16 August 1871, 3; *Clipper* 13 June 1857, 58; Merle Curti, *The University of Wisconsin: A History, 1848-1925* (Madison: University of Wisconsin Press, 1949), 195; *Porters Spirit of the Times* 9 May 1857, 156; Mary Treudley, *Prelude to the Future: The First Hundred Years of Hiram College* (New York: Association, 1950), 67; *University Quarterly*, July 1860, 198.

19. *Waterbury American* 31 August 1860, 2.

Chapter 2

1. *Spirit* 13 October 1838, 279; Henry Chadwick, *Chadwick's American Cricket Manual* (New York: DeWitt, 1873), 85-86; Henry Howard, *History of the City of Brooklyn* (Brooklyn: Daily Eagle, 1893), 1011; *Clipper*, 13 March 1858, 372.

2. *Spirit* 23 September 1837, 249; 7 October 1837, 272; *Clipper* 3 May 1856, 11.

3. *Albion* 7 July 1838, 215; *Spirit* 27 October 1838, 292; 26 October 1839, 397.

4. *By-Laws of the St. George Cricket Club of New York* (New York: Vinten, 1878), 31; *New York Morning News* 27 August 1845, 2; *Spirit* 26 October 1839, 397; *Spalding's Official Cricket Guide for 1907*, 15.

5. *Who Was Who: Historical Volume*, 482; *Albion* 29 June 1844, 316; *Spirit* 4 May 1844, 118; *True Sun* 16 September 1844, 2; *Clipper* 5 October 1878, 220.

166 · Notes to Chapter 2

6. *Anglo-American* 1 May 1847, 46. Over the course of the 19th century the St. George name would be adopted by English dominated cricket clubs in other American cities, among them Buffalo, Philadelphia, Toledo, St. Louis, and Chicago. But the name never seems to have been adopted by any predominantly working class immigrant English cricket club.

7. *Spirit* 27 October 1838, 292; 25 July 1840, 241; 31 July 1841, 258; *Albion* 17 October 1840, 343; 7 August 1841, 2; 6 August 1842, 380; *New York Morning News* 25 September 1844, 2.

8. *Clipper* 5 October 1878, 220. A match of this kind was first suggested in 1838; *Spirit* 26 October 1839, 397.

9. *Spirit* 26 August 1843, 306; *Albion* 12 September 1840, 299; 26 September 1840, 319; *American Turf Register and Sporting Magazine* October 1840, 554; John Hall, *Sixty Years of Canadian Cricket* (Toronto: Bryant, 1895), 13-15, 17.

10. *Albion* 4 September 1841, 317; 23 July 1842, 355; *Anglo-American* 23 September 1843, 524; *Albion* 3 August 1844, 358, 375-76; *True Sun* 30 July 1844, 2; John Hall, *Sixty Years of Canadian Cricket*, 49; *Spirit* 28 September 1844, 372.

11. *Anglo-American* 18 October 1845, 616; *Herald* (New York) 3 August 1845, 2; 4 May 1846, 2; *Montreal Gazette* 1 August 1845, 2; *Spirit* 8 November 1845, 434; *Herald* 14 May 1846, 2; 29 August 1846, 2; *Spirit* 5 September 1846, 327; *Anglo-American* 19 September 1846, 526; John Marder, *The International Series: The Story of the United States vs Canada at Cricket* (London: Kaye & Ward, 1968), 22.

12. *True Sun* 27 September 1844, 2; *Herald* 25 September 1844, 2.

13. *New York Morning News* 29 August 1845, 2; 30 August 1845, 2.

14. *Albion* 6 August 1842, 380; *Anglo-American* 4 November 1843, 44.

15. *Spirit* 4 December 1852, 498; 9 October 1847, 383; 7 July 1849, 353; *Albion* 29 June 1844, 316; *Anglo-American* 1 June 1844, 141; Francis Brinley, *Life of William T. Porter* (New York: Appleton, 1860), 97; *Spirit* 29 September 1855, 391; *Clipper* 5 October 1878, 220.

16. *Wilkes* 5 March 1864, 4; *True Sun* 16 September 1844, 2; *Clipper* 5 October 1878, 22; *Spirit* 25 May 1844, 150.

17. *Anglo-American* 6 July 1844, 262.

18. *Albion* 30 June 1855, 307; *Spirit* 23 July 1853, 270.

19. *Clipper* 5 October 1878, 220.

20. *Herald* 6 September 1845, 2; 7 April 1845, 2; *Spirit* 8 April 1848, 78; 20 April 1844, 20; 16 July 1844, 222; 27 May 1848, 163; 13 September 1845, 339; *Rochester Daily Advertiser* 18 August 1847, 2; *Chicago American* 4 September 1840, 2.

21. *Spirit* 14 June 1848, 207, 399; *Herald* 6 October 1845, 2; *Anglo American* 25 October 1845, 20; George Kirsch, "The Rise of Modern Sports: New

Jersey Cricketers, Baseball Players and Clubs, 1845-60," *New Jersey History* 101, no. 1-2 (1983), 57; *Anglo-American* 10 October 1846, 599; *Herald* 9 October 1845, 2; *Spirit* 1 August 1846, 267; *Cincinnati Enquirer* 25 September 1845, 3; *Spirit* 15 June 1850, 197. Phineas Moses, founder of Cincinnati's first synagogue, played for the Queen City club; Maurice Joblin, *Cincinnati Past & Present* (Cincinnati: Joblin, 1872), 111-12.

22. John Lester, *A Century*, 15; *Anglo-American* 16 September 1843, 502; *Public Ledger* (Philadelphia) 28 April 1907; *American Cricketer* 15 December 1902, 245; *Spirit* 22 August 1846, 303.

23. *Anglo-American* 14 October 1843, 598; *American Cricketer* 15 December 1902, 245.

24. *Anglo-American* 27 September 1845, 548; *Spirit* 27 September 1845, 363.

25. Melvin Adelman, *A Sporting Time*, 112.

26. *American Cricketer* 3 May 1893, 28; William R. Wister, *Some Reminiscences of Cricket in Philadelphia Before 1861* (Philadelphia: Allen, 1904), 15.

27. Barnet Phillips, "Cricket in the Forties," *Harper's Weekly* 22 September 1894, 909; Jones Wister, *Jones Wister's Reminiscences* (Philadelphia: Lippincott, 1920), 113.

28. *Anglo-American* 4 October 1845, 571; *Spirit* 4 October 1845, 380.

29. *Albion* 17 July 1847, 310; *Spirit* 8 July 1848, 234.

30. *Herald* 4 September 1850, 2; *Waterbury American* 27 September 1850, 2; *Milwaukee Sentinel* 30 April 1852, 3; *Spirit* 7 December 1850, 500.

31. *American Cricketer* 15 December 1902, 249; William R. Wister, *Some Reminiscences of Cricket*, 18.

32. *Herald* 19 October 1845, 2; *Brooklyn Daily Eagle* 15 June 1846, 2; Soeren Brynn, "Some Sports in Pittsburgh During the National Period, 1775-1860," *Western Pennsylvania Historical Magazine* 52 (January 1969), 71; *Wilkes* 6 September 1862, 4.

33. *Cincinnati Enquirer* 18 September 1846, 3; *Spirit* 26 October 1839, 397.

34. *Anglo-American* 1 June 1844, 302; *Spirit* 1 June 1844, 162; 12 September 1840, 330; John Hall, *Sixty Years*, 273; *Herald* 13 September 1844, 2; 5 August 1845, 2.

35. When the Union club of Philadelphia came to New York in 1844, both the St. George and the Union Star played them, but not each other; *New York Morning News* 5 October 1844, 2; *True Sun* 16 September 1944, 2; *Spirit* 31 July 1847, 263.

36. *Herald* 12 October 1845, 3; Douglas Branch, *The Sentimental Years* (New York: Appleton, 1934), 180; *Albion* 25 August 1855, 404; *True Sun* 16 September 1844, 2; *Saturday Evening Gazette* (Boston) 4 September 1858,

168 · Notes to Chapter 3

3. Only one Union Star player, Edward Hardy, seems to have held membership in New York's St. George Society during this period; *A History of the St. George Society of New York From 1770 to 1913* (New York: St. George, 1913), 265; Abram Dayton, *Last Days of Knickerbocker Life in New York* (New York: Putnam, 1897), 62-63.

37. *Herald* 10 September 1845, 2. The St. George also found no takers in its plans to organize a "gentlemen's" match in 1847; *Albion* 1 May 1847, 46.

38. Melvin Adelman, "The First Baseball Game, the First Newspaper References to Baseball, and the New York Club: A Note on the Early History of Baseball," *Journal of Sport History* 7, no. 3 (Winter 1980), 133-34; Dean Sullivan, ed., *Early Innings: A Documentary History of Baseball, 1825-1908* (Lincoln: University of Nebraska Press, 1995), 11-13. Though the matches played between the Brooklyn and New York clubs on 21 and 25 October 1845 are generally recognized as being the earliest baseball games of the "modern" era, they were, in fact, preceded by an even earlier game between these two clubs on 12 October; this one, curiously, won by the Brooklyn club, 22-1; *New York Morning News* 13 October 1845, 2.

39. *New York Morning News* 24 September 1845, 2; 7 August 1845, 2; *Porters Spirit of the Times* 30 April 1859, 132; 25 March 1859, 52.

40. *Spirit* 2 June 1855, 181; *Porters* 11 October 1856, 93; *Brooklyn Eagle* 18 August 1859, 3; *Sunday Mercury* 19 August 1860, 5.

41. *Anglo-American* 14 September 1844, 502.

Chapter 3

1. *Spirit* 14 May 1847, 137; 17 July 1847, 239; *Albion* 17 July 1847, 310.

2. *Herald* 25 August 1853, 4; Henry Chadwick, *Chadwick's American Cricket Manual* (New York: DeWitt, 1873), 87.

3. *Clipper* 16 March 1889, 11; *Spirit* 16 May 1840, 126; 3 August 1850, 288; Abram Dayton, *Last Days of Knickerbocker Life*, 335.

4. *Herald* 25 August 1853, 4; 15 September 1856, 2; 5 August 1856, 1; *Spirit* 13 May 1854, 150; *World* (New York) 15 September 1865, 8.

5. *Clipper* 20 September 1856, 174; *Spirit* 3 September 1853, 343.

6. *Herald* 6 November 1853, 4; *Clipper* 25 April 1857, 3; *Daily Evening Bulletin* (Philadelphia) 2 June 1857, 2; *Paterson Intelligencer* 18 July 1855.

7. *Clipper* 15 November 1856, 237; 12 December 1857, 268.

8. *American Cricketer* 5 February 1880, 85; *Clipper* 6 June 1857; 25 July 1857, 108; *Porters* 7 March 1857, 5. For other retrospective testimonies to cricket's popularity during this time see the *New England Base Ballist* 1 October 1868, 34, and the *New York Times* 20 September 1872, 4.

9. Melvin Adelman, *A Sporting Time*, 269-86; John Betts, "Sporting Journalism in Nineteenth Century America," *American Quarterly* (Spring 1953), 41-43; *Clipper* 13 April 1861, 410.

10. *Clipper* 17 January 1880, 840; *Herald* 8 May 1857, 7; *Sun* (New York) 22 September 1891, 4; *Sunday Mercury* 4 August 1861, 5; *Clipper* 5 October 1872, 210; Henry Chadwick, *Chadwick's American Cricket Manual*, 101-02; *Public Ledger* 23 June 1899, 14.

11. *Daily State Register* (Albany) 10 May 1855, 2; *Herald* 13 September 1855, 1; *Clipper* 3 May 1856, 11; *Argus* (Albany) 22 July 1879, 4; G. R. Howell, *History of the County of Albany, New York, from 1609 to 1886* (New York: Munsell, 1886), 747; *Milwaukee Sentinel* 6 July 1855, 2; 4 August 1870, 1.

12. *Clipper* 5 May 1860, 19; 24 May 1873, 58; *Daily Evening Express* (Lancaster) 27 July 1857, 2; Franklin Ellis, *History of Lancaster County, Pennsylvania* (Philadelphia: Everts, 1883), 504; *Monroe Sentinel* 27 July 1859, 3; *Ripon Weekly Times* 8 June 1860, 3. A number of post-Civil War journalists also took an active interest in cricket, such as David Alexander Munro, assistant editor of the *North American Review*, and Henry Whitney, editor of the *Hawaiian Gazette*; *World* (New York) 21 May 1893, 27; *Who Was Who in America* vol. 1, 879; *Daily Pacific Commercial Advertiser* (Honolulu) 3 October 1885, 2; Ralph Kuykendall, *Hawaiian Kingdom, 1874-1893*, vol. 3 (Honolulu: University of Hawaii, 1967), 19.

13. *New York Times* 28 June 1860, 5.

14. *Clipper* 13 June 1857, 205; *Saturday Evening Gazette* (Boston) 4 September 1858, 3; *Clipper* 26 July 1856, 107.

15. *Clipper* 13 June 1857, 61; *Chicago Tribune* 26 May 1857, 1; *Clipper* 28 November 1857, 252.

16. *Paterson Daily Press* 5 September 1878, 3; *Milwaukee Sentinel* 22 August 1865, 1; *History of Milwaukee County from Its First Settlement to the Year 1895*, vol. 3 (Chicago: American Biographical, 1896), 1111-13.

17. *Gazette & Courier* (Greenfield) 8 October 1855, 2; *Clipper* 11 September 1880, 195; *Milwaukee Sentinel* 6 July 1855, 2; Melinda Weaver, *Memoirs of Early Days* (Sussex: Hamilton School District, 1986), 64; Theron Haight, ed., *Memoirs of Waukesha County* (Madison: Western, 1907), 224; *Daily Argus and Democrat* (Madison) 12 November 1853, 2; *Black Earth Advertiser* 21 September 1871, 3; William Kittle, *History of the Township and Village of Mazomanie* (Madison: State Journal, 1900), 43.

18. *Oneida Morning Herald* (Utica) 3 August 1851, 2. *Ripon Home* 12 June 1857, 3; *Ripon Weekly Times* 13 July 1860, 3; "Henry Lambert," *Ripon Necrology*. For an analysis of cricket in Ripon, see Tom Melville, "From Ethnic Tradition to Community Institution: Nineteenth-Century Cricket in Small Town Wisconsin and a Note on the Enigma of a Sporting Discontinuity," *International Journal of the History of Sport* 11, no. 2 (August 1994), 281-84.

19. "Obituary: Robert Culpitt, 1904" at: Germantown Historical Society; *Clipper* 30 May 1857, 45; *Spirit* 7 December 1850, 500; *Public Ledger* 30 July 1897, 3; Jones Wister, *Jones Wister's Reminiscences*, 113.

170 · Notes to Chapter 3

20. George Newhall, "The Cricket Grounds of Germantown and a Plea for the Game," *Site and Relic Society of Germantown: Historical Address* 7 (1910), 170; John Lester, *A Century,* 9.

21. *Clipper* 5 October 1878, 220; *California Spirit of the Times* 8 October 1859, 1; *American Cricketer* 27 April 1898, 2; *Herald* 9 September 1855, 1; *American Cricketer* 11 August 1887, 105.

22. *Clipper* 18 August 1860, 140; 1 February 1873, 346; 17 December 1859, 275; 19 May 1860, 37; 18 October 1856, 264-65; 1 February 1873, 346; 15 September 1860, 17; 11 October 1856, 200. Sharp was also the cricket editor of *Wilkes* for a short period; *Wilkes* 14 February 1863, 380; John Marder, *The International Series,* 36.

23. *Albion* 27 August 1853, 416.

24. *Herald* 13 September 1855, 1; *Buffalo Courier* 7 August 1857, 3; *Newark Daily Advertiser* 3 May 1855, 2; Kristen Petersen, ed., *Waltham Rediscovered* (Portsmouth: Randall, 1988), 18; *Lowell Daily Citizen and News* 21 August 1858, 2; *Albion* 25 August 1855, 404.

25. *Spirit* 27 October 1855, 438; *Yonkers Statesman* 12 June 1870, 4; *Poughkeepsie Eagle* 13 October 1855, 2; *Clipper* 21 June 1856, 71; *Porters* 11 September 1858, 21; 8 August 1857, 356; *Daily Dispatch* (Richmond) 13 June 1857, 1. The club in Waterbury, Connecticut, was also largely American; Joseph Anderson, *The Town and City of Waterbury, Connecticut* (New Haven: Price, 1896), 1103.

26. *Clipper* 4 July 1857, 83; 17 July 1858, 101; *Spirit* 1 May 1858, 134; *Clipper* 14 November 1857, 240; *Detroit Free Press* 30 July 1858, 1; *Spirit* 6 June 1857, 199.

27. *Clipper* 23 October 1858, 213; *Miners Journal* (Pottsville), 15 May 1858, 2; 18 September 1858, 2; *Clipper* 14 August 1858, 136. There were six clubs in Pottsville alone during this period; *Clipper* 10 July 1858, 92; 1 August 1857, 119; 24 October 1857, 213; 14 November 1857, 239; 10 April 1858, 402; Alfred Spink, *The National Game* (St. Louis: National Game, 1910), 305; *Porters* 13 October 1858, 135.

28. Jones Wister, *Jones Wister's Reminiscences,* 115; *Daily Evening Bulletin* (Philadelphia) 2 June 1857, 2; *North American and United States Gazette* (Philadelphia) 1 June 1857, 1; Sally (Butler) Wister, *Walter S. Newhall: A Memoir* (Philadelphia: Sanitary Commission, 1864), 14.

29. *Clipper* 12 November 1853, 4; William R. Wister, *Some Reminiscences of Cricket in Philadelphia,* 23; *Spirit* 15 April 1854, 102; *American Cricketer* 1 March 1899, 11; John Lester, *A Century,* 16; *American Cricketer* 16 February 1903, 17; *The Young America Cricket Club of Germantown: Reports of the Directors and Treasurer for 1880,* 3.

30. *American Cricketer* 1 May 1884, 31; *Clipper* 31 May 1856, 46; J. Thomas Jable, "Latter Day Cultural Imperialism: The British Influence on the

Establishment of Cricket in Philadelphia, 1842-72," in J. A. Mangan, ed., *Pleasure Profit and Proselytism* (London: Cass, 1988), 184.

31. *American Journal of Education*, August 1827, 466.

32. *Clipper* 5 November 1853, 2; 7 October 1854, 3; *Herald* 9 September 1855, 1; Willis Rudy, *The College of the City of New York: A History, 1847-1947* (New York: Arno, 1977), 78.

33. *Spirit* 5 July 1856, 252; *Clipper* 5 July 1856, 86; 4 July 1857, 85; *Herald* 27 June 1857, 1; *Clipper* 15 May 1858, 28; Mary Greene, *Nathaniel T. Allen* (Privately printed, 1906), 117; Walter Havighurst, *The Miami Years, 1809-1969* (New York: Putnam, 1969), 104.

34. William Winn, "Tom Brown's Schooldays and the Development of 'Muscular Christianity,'" *Church History* 21 (1960), 64-71; Keith Sandiford, *Cricket and the Victorians* (Aldershot: Scholar, 1994), 35.

35. Quoted in Guy Lewis, "The Beginnings of Organized Collegiate Sport," *American Quarterly* vol. 22 (Summer 1970), 226. Thomas Hughes, "Recollections of American Universities," *Every Saturday* 25 March 25 1871, 286; *Clipper* 5 September 1857, 155; *New York Leader* 5 September 1857, 5; *Clipper* 3 October 1857, 188; 13 November 1858, 237; *Philo Mirror* (Phillips Academy) July 1858, 32; *Porters* 28 March 1857, 60. Hughes tried to transplant something of this English public school ethos to the ill-fated immigrant colony he established at Rugby, Tennessee during the 1880s, a location where a number of English sports, including cricket, were played. Edward Mack, *Thomas Hughes* (London: Benn, 1952), 230-50; *St. Louis Post-Dispatch* 12 October 1881, 8.

36. Adelman, *A Sporting Time*, 112; Kirsch, *The Creation of American Team Sports*, 111-37; *New Brunswick Daily News* 8 June 1855, 2; *Daily Missouri Democrat* 28 November 1859, 2; *Evening Picayune* (New Orleans) 19 May 1859, 1. The Buffalo cricket club was also composed primarily of young merchants and white collar workers, while the Utica Cricket Club, in 1845, had among its members a veterinarian, a variety store owner, a saw filer, a brewer, a physician, a news room manager, a lawyer, a merchant, a brass founder, and a cart man. David Gerber, *The Making of an American Pluralism: Buffalo, New York, 1825-1860* (Urbana: University of Illinois Press, 1989), 390; John Walsh, *Vignettes of Old Utica* (Utica: Utica Public Library, 1982), 265-66.

37. *Spirit* 7 July 1849, 235; 8 December 1849, 498; 7 August 1847, 275; *Porters* 25 September 1847, 359; *Clipper* 12 December 1857, 271; Frances Gruber, *William Ranney, Painter of the Early West* (New York: Potter, 1962), 11, 20-21.

38. *Brooklyn Eagle* 2 September 1859, 3; Alter Landersman, *A History of Newlots, Brooklyn* (Port Washington: Kennikat, 1977), 152; *Daily Evening Express* (Lancaster) 27 July 1857, 2; Franklin Ellis, *History of Lancaster County, Pennsylvania* (Philadelphia: Everts, 1883), 457; *Wisconsin Daily State Journal* 18 June 1859, 1; *Biographical Review of Dane County, Wisconsin*

(Chicago: Biographical, 1893), 178; *Goodhue County Republican* 27 July 1860, 3; Madeline Angell, *Red Wing, Minnesota* (Minneapolis: Dillon, 1978), 85, 132.

39. *Buffalo Courier* 7 September 1857, 3; 10 September 1857, 3; 15 September 1858, 3; H. R. Smith, *History of the City of Buffalo and Erie County* (Syracuse: Mason, 1884), 143; *Wisconsin Daily State Journal* 18 June 1859, 1; Daniel Durrie, *A History of Madison* (Madison: Atwood & Culver, 1874), 385; *Clipper* 9 October 1858, 197.

40. *Detroit Free Press* 30 July 1858, 1; Silas Farmer, *History of Detroit and Wayne County*, 3rd ed. (New York: Munsell, 1890), 137; *Clipper* 4 August 1860, 125; Madeline Angell, *Red Wing*, 125, 155.

41. Charles Peverelly, *Book of American Pastimes*, 534; *Wilkes* 19 July 1862, 307-08; 11 June 1864, 228; *Clipper* 9 April 1870, 5; *Milwaukee Sentinel* 6 August 1855, 2; *History of Waukesha County* (Chicago: Western, 1880), 983; *Milwaukee Sentinel* 6 July 1855, 2; James Buck, *Pioneer History of Milwaukee* vol. 3 (Milwaukee: Milwaukee News, 1876-1886), 293; vol. 4, 15; *Daily Missouri Democrat* 19 April 1859, 2; *St. Louis Democrat* 16 September 1873, 4; *Who Was Who* vol. 1, 637. A number of post-Civil War cricket players also went on to become mayors of their communities, among them William J. Broatch of Omaha, Robert M. McLane of Baltimore, John Hopkins of Chicago, John Hinchliffe of Paterson, New Jersey, Walter R. Vaughan of Council Bluffs, Iowa, Joseph Russell of Hoboken, John Saemann of Sheboygan, Wisconsin, N. W. Wheatley of Brainerd, Minnesota, and Arthur Cushing of Sandy, Utah; *Omaha Republican* 20 July 1889, 2; Alfred Sorenson, *The Story of Omaha* (Omaha: National, 1923), 445; *Illustrated Sporting News* 26 May 1906, 6; Wilma Pesavento, "'Men Must Play, Men Will Play'" Occupations of Pullman Athletes, 1880 to 1900," *Journal of Sport History* 12, no. 3 (Winter 1985), 246; *World* (New York) 1 June 1897, 5; *Paterson Morning Call* 19 March 1915, 4; *Omaha Republican* 3 June 1888, 2; Alfred Sorenson, *The Story of Omaha*, 445; *American Cricketer* 20 June 1889, 37; *Sheboygan Telegram* 12 July 1898, 5; *Portrait and Biographical Record of Sheboygan County, Wisconsin* (Chicago: Excelsior, 1894), 567, 568; *Pioneer Press* (St. Paul) 14 August 1892, 3; Carl Zapffe, *Brainerd, Minnesota, 1871-1946* (Minneapolis: Colwell, 1946), 190; *Salt Lake Daily Herald* 11 June 1874, 3; Martha Bradley, *Sandy City: The First 100 Years* (South, UT: Sandy City Corp., 1993), 47, 50.

42. *Clipper* 20 September 1856, 174; *Sunday Mercury* 18 March 1860, 5; Mary Treudley, *Prelude to the Future*, 67; Robert Gannon, *Up to the Present* (New York: Doubleday, 1967), 45. Wicket, cricket, and baseball were all being simultaneously played at Buffalo and Amherst College during the late 1850s; *Buffalo Courier* 14 September 1857, 3; 14 October 1858, 3; George Cutting, *Student Life at Amherst College* (Amherst: Hatche, 1871), 112.

43. Quoted in Kristen Petersen, *Waltham Rediscovered*, 75; *American Cricketer* April 1893, 18; *University Castalia 1867* (University of Michigan),

43; *New England Base Ballist* 10 September 1868, 22; James D'Wolf Lovett, *Old Boston Boys and the Games They Played* (Boston: Privately Printed, 1907), 75. Lovett actually returned to cricket later in his career, playing for a number of years with the Longwood Cricket Club; *Boston Globe* 7 September 1886, 1; 25 June 1887, 3.

44. *Milwaukee Sentinel*, 23 May 1855, 2.

45. *Herald* 29 August 1845, 2; *Porters* 10 September 1856, 37; *Albion* 20 September 1856, 452. For complaints about the English makeup of these American sides see also *Clipper* 29 July 1854, 3, and *Herald* 7 August 1859, 5.

46. *Porters* 20 December 1856, 261; *Clipper* 18 August 1860, 140; 13 August 1853 2; *New York Times* 10 August 1860, 8; *Sunday Mercury* 5 August 1860, 5.

47. *Clipper* 13 August 1859, 131; *Wilkes* 29 May 1860, 173; *Clipper* 28 July 1860, 114; 13 October 1860, 204.

48. *A History of the St. George Society of New York*, 32; *New York Leader* 10 July 1858, 5; *Herald* 6 November 1853, 4; *Clipper* 2 June 1860, 53; *New York Leader* 10 July 1858, 5.

49. *Porters* 9 April 1859, 84; Abram Dayton, *Last Days of Knickerbocker Life*, 125.

50. *North American and United States Gazette* 17 September 1857, 1; *Clipper* 7 September 1861, 164; 11 August 1860, 130; 25 July 1868, 125; *World* (New York) 17 September 1868, 10; *Wilkes* 21 September 1872, 81; *Clipper* 8 August 1863, 135.

51. *American Chronicle of Sports and Pastimes* 16 July 1868, 250; *New England Base Ballist* 10 September 1868, 22; *New York Times* 13 September 1868, 8.

52. Melvin Adelman, *A Sporting Time*, 111; *American Cricketer* 26 July 1877, 20; *Clipper* 16 May 1857, 26. Nonetheless, Americans and English in several areas seemed to show a marked preference for organizing separate cricket clubs. In St. Louis, Americans seemed to set up the St. Louis Cricket Club in opposition to that city's St. George Club. In Philadelphia, most of the English players gravitated toward the Wakefield and Girard clubs in the 1880s; *Daily St. Louis Democrat* 25 May 1874, 4; *St. Louis Globe-Democrat* 14 May 1876, 6; *Clipper* 29 May 1880, 75; *American Cricketer* 27 March 1884, 15; *Public Ledger* 12 July 1886, 3.

53. *Spirit* 22 September 1849, 6; *New York Times* 11 August 1854, 3; *Herald* 10 August 1854, 1; *Spirit* 12 August 1854, 306; *Clipper* 18 October 1856, 203; 16 June 1860, 67; Melvin Adelman, *A Sporting Time*, 111.

54. *Newark Daily Advertiser* 6 October 1856, 2; 7 November 1854, 2; *Spirit* 11 October 1856, 409; *Herald* 10 July 1856, 3; *Porters* 20 June 1857, 245; *Spirit* 7 July 1858, 271; 9 July 1859, 258; *Wilkes* 14 July 1860, 300; *Herald* 8 July 1860, 8.

55. *Sunday Mercury* 14 October 1860, 5; *Wilkes* 27 July 1861, 323; *Clipper* 2 October 1858, 189; 27 November 1858, 253; *Wilkes* 13 October 1860, 87; *Miners Journal* 13 August 1859, 2; *California Spirit of the Times* 27 May 1861, 2; *Spirit* 27 September 1852, 379. Though somewhat later, the local press in Reading, Pennsylvania, also found that "our home born young men are as well calculated to bat and bowl the ball as their more experienced English teachers." *Reading Daily Eagle* 26 May 1873, 4.

56. Sally (Butler) Wister, *Walter S. Newhall*, 20; *Spirit* 17 July 1858, 271; *Clipper* 11 September 1858, 165-66; Barnet Phillips, "Cricket in the Forties," 908; *Albion* 11 October 1856, 488; Fred Lillywhite, *The English Cricketers Trip to Canada and the United States in 1859* (London: Worlds Work, 1980), 41. All this tends to discredit Lester's claim that "The early Wisters were greater in organizing cricket than in playing it." John Lester, *A Century*, 26.

57. *Sunday Mercury* 8 July 1860, 8; *Clipper* 28 July 1860, 117.

58. *Clipper* 21 August 1858, 138; *Spirit* 6 June 1857, 199. French could also reportedly throw a cricket ball over one hundred yards; *Porters* 15 October 1859, 100; *American Cricketer* 15 July 1904; *Clipper* 4 September 1858, 158; *New York Leader* 28 August 1858, 6; *New York Times* 11 August 1854, 3; *Porters* 17 October 1857, 101. To contemporary observers, at least two Americans from Boston, a Wiswall and Tom Blanchard "were indeed very good" cricket players; *Wilkes* 1 October 1859, 52.

59. *Clipper* 30 June 1860, 85; *Cohoes Cataract* 16 July 1859, 3; *Wilkes* 4 May 1872, 185; Melvin Adelman, *A Sporting Time*, 113-14.

60. *Herald* 22 September 1855, 3.

61. *Chicago Times* 17 April 1889, 3. To the English sports periodical *Land and Water* as well, it was these "numberless varieties and changes" incidental to cricket batting that set the game apart from the one-dimensional nature of baseball batting; *World* (New York) 13 September 1874, 2.

62. *College Mercury* (Racine College) 31 May 1873, 550. The local press in Portland, Oregon, also believed the close, evenly matched games of the type played by local teams "will do more to render cricket popular than a dozen one-sided affairs," *Morning Oregonian* 8 September 1896, 8.

63. *Porters* 15 October 1859, 100; *Herald* 9 September 1855, 1.

64. *Spirit* 6 September 1851, 342. As a consequence of a match played along these lines in Detroit, years later, the local press declared, "It is the unanimous verdict that cricket is one of the most interesting sports in the world and that this game was a 'hummer,'" *Detroit Free Press* 16 September 1894, 6.

65. *Worcester Daily Spy* 6 October 1860, 3; *Clipper* 13 October 1860, 204.

66. We know that the total pitch count for some early baseball games ran as high as 700 or 800, a number that certainly equaled, if not exceeded, the total number of deliveries in a typical cricket match of that period; *Utica Morning Herald* 11 October 1860, 3; *Buffalo Courier* 11 October 1859, 3; 25 September

1860, 2. The cricket match between the Knickerbocker Base Ball Club and the Manhattan Cricket Club in 1872 was reportedly played over the same amount of time as "an old fashioned game of base ball"; *Sunday Mercury* 6 October 1872, 3.

67. *Daily Argus and Democrat* (Madison) 15 July 1857, 2; *Rochester Union and Advertiser* 18 October 1859, 4; *Washington Examiner* 4 November 1859, 1; *California Spirit of the Times* 31 December 1859, 1; Mortimer Neal Thompson, *Doesticks, What He Says* (Delmar: Scholars Facsimile, 1986), 3-5.

68. Phyllis Hill is one of the few historians who attempted to interpret American sports in this way, but the American characteristics she identifies— "high energy levels, a love of speed, and a need for power and self-determination"—are so general as to be of limited value for analyzing specific sports; Phyllis Hill, "Cultural History of Frontier Sport in Illinois, 1673-1820" (Ph.D. Diss., University of Illinois, 1966), 122.

69. *American Cricketer* 2 June 1881; *New York Tribune* 5 September 1880, 5; *Clipper* 8 September 1877, 187; *Herald* 27 May 1862, 3.

70. *Spirit* 28 August 1852, 330; *National Chronicle* 2 April 1870, 97, 100; *Clipper* 11 August 1860, 131; *College Mercury* 31 May 1873, 546; *Illustrated Sporting News* 17 October 1903, 14.

71. *Clipper* 5 May 1860, 19.

72. George Kirsch, *The Creation of American Team Sports*, 106.

73. *Porters* 9 May 1857, 156; *Clipper* 8 May 1858, 19; 28 May 1859, 37; 24 May 1862, 43; *Wilkes* 17 May 1862, 173.

74. *Newark Daily Advertiser* 5 May 1858, 2; *Porters* 9 May 1857, 156.

75. Barnet Phillips, "Cricket in the Forties," 909; *The Ichnolite* (Amherst College) May 1860, 338.

76. Melvin Adelman, *A Sporting Time*, 113; *Wilkes* 29 October 1864, 138; *Herald* 9 September 1855, 1; *Clipper* 3 April 1858, 396; *New York Leader* 22 September 1860, 8; *Clipper* 22 May 1858, 36; *Sunday Mercury* 14 April 1861, 8.

77. "Baseball and Cricket," *Our Young Folks* May 1867, 306.

78. Melvin Adelman, *A Sporting Time*, 322 n62; *American Chronicle of Sports and Pastimes* 27 February 1868, 65; *Oswego Commercial Advertiser and Times* 11 August 1868, 3. To some, the Massachusetts game was superior because it "requires more activity" than the New York game; *Buffalo Courier* 14 October 1858, 3. For a particularly harsh criticism of the New York game see *Racine Journal* 14 August 1867, 2.

79. Allen Guttmann, "The Diffusion of Sports and the Problem of Cultural Imperialism," in E. Dunning, ed., *The Sports Process* (Champaign: Human Kinetics, 1993), 125; Melvin Adelman, *A Sporting Time*, 135-36.

80. *Spirit* 31 May 1856, 187; *Porters* 15 November 1856, 176.

81. *New York Leader* 23 May 1857, 5.

Chapter 4

1. *Newark Daily Advertiser* 17 April 1855, 2; *Daily State Register* (Albany) 13 September 1855, 2; *Leslie's Illustrated* 15 October 1859, 306; *Clipper* 20 September 1856, 174.

2. *The International Cricket Match Played, October 1859, in the Elysian Fields of Hoboken on the Grounds of the St. George's Cricket Club* (New York: Vinten, 1859), vii-viii; Fred Lillywhite, *The English Cricketers Trip*, 1; *Sunday Mercury* 26 June 1859, 6.

3. *Wilkes* 10 September 1859, 9.

4. *Leslie's Illustrated* 15 October 1859, 305; *Clipper* 22 October 1859, 211; *Sunday Mercury* 10 October 1859, 5; *Atlas and Argus* (Albany) 17 October 1859, 3; *Baltimore American and Commercial Advertiser* 8 October 1859, 1; *Daily Missouri Democrat* 11 October 1859, 2. "Spectacles" in cricket terminology is when a batter fails to score in both his turns at bat.

5. *Sunday Mercury* 18 September 1859, 5; *Porters* 2 July 1859, 280; 8 October 1859, 85; *The International Cricket Match*, 5; *Brooklyn Eagle* 1 July 1858, 3.

6. William Caffyn, *Seventy-One Not Out* (Edinburgh: Blackwood, 1899), 145; *Porters* 15 October 1859, 100; *Herald* 4 October 1859, 10; 5 October 1859, 10; Fred Lillywhite, *The English Cricketers Trip*, 32.

7. *Porters* 15 October 1859, 100; William Caffyn, *Seventy-One Not Out*, 146; *Wilkes* 21 March 1860, 43.

8. *Clipper* 1 October 1859, 186; 22 March 1862, 388; John Marder, *The International Series*, 29, 34.

9. *Porters* 29 October 1859, 132; *The International Cricket Match*, 7.

10. *Clipper* 22 October 1859, 212; *Porters* 29 October 1859, 132; Jones Wister, *Jones Wister's Reminiscences*, 119; *Bells Life* 13 November 1859, 3.

11. *Pittsburgh Post* 28 June 1859, 1; 8 July 1859, 1; *Wisconsin Daily State Journal* 20 August 1859, 1; *California Spirit of the Times* 30 April 1859, 2; *Porters* 11 June 1859, 229.

12. *Daily Missouri Democrat* 19 October 1859, 2; *Wilkes* 21 June 1860, 308; *Sunday Mercury* 10 June 1860, 3; 30 October 1859, 5; *Detroit Free Press* 18 September 1859, 1; *Lowell Daily Citizen and News* 24 October 1859, 2; *Saturday Evening Gazette* (Boston) 12 May 1860, 2; *Daily Iowa State Democrat* 15 October 1859, 1.

13. *Clipper* 22 October 1859, 212; *Saturday Evening Gazette* (Boston) 12 May 1860, 2; *Clipper* 10 March 1860, 372 *Fitzgeralds City Item* (Philadelphia) 22 October 1859, 2.

14. *Porters* 29 January 1859, 341; *Herald* 30 July 1859, 1; *Maysville Eagle* 23 June 1860, 2; *Clipper* 15 September 1860, 173; *Goodhue County Republican* 25 May 1860, 3; *Detroit Free Press* 26 September 1860, 1; *California Spirit of the Times* 11 May 1860, 2; *Oswego Commercial Times* 1 October 1860, 3.

15. *Wilkes* 26 November 1859, 181; *Mobile Register* 16 May 1860, 3; *Evening Picayune* 19 May 1859, 1; *Spirit* 19 August 1854, 319.

16. *Encyclopedia of Southern Culture* vol. 3 (New York: Doubleday, 1989), 625; *Evening Picayune* 26 April 1866, 3; 27 April 1873, 3; *Louisville Democrat* 25 August 1868, 1.

17. *Clipper* 22 October 1859, 212; *New York Times* 9 July 1860, 1; Franklin Edmonds, *History of the Central High School of Philadelphia* (Philadelphia: Lippincott, 1902), 251; *Indianapolis Daily Journal* 1 July 1859, 3; *Clipper* 25 June 1859, 79; *Porters* 20 August 1859, 389.

18. *Clipper* 9 July 1859, 92; *Towns of the Nashaway Plantation* (Huson, MA: Lancaster League of Historical Societies, 1976), 92; Roland Mulford, *History of the Lawrenceville School, 1810-1935* (Princeton: Princeton University Press, 1935), 76; *Clipper* 19 May 1860, 37; *Wilkes* 22 June 1861, 245.

19. James Addison, *The Episcopal Church in the United States* (New York: Scribner, 1951), 210; Harold Wagner, *The Episcopal Church in Wisconsin, 1847-1947* (Waterloo: Courier, 1947), 64-65.

20. Harold Wagner, *The Episcopal Church in Wisconsin* 65, 155-57, 160; Sydney Croft, "A Hundred Years of Racine College and the DeKoven Foundation," *Wisconsin Magazine of History* vol. 35 (1951-52), 251.

21. William Pope, *Life of the Reverend James DeKoven* (New York: Pott, 1899), 19-20; *Weekly Racine Advocate* 27 June 1860, 3; *Daily Wisconsin* 5 July 1860, 2; *College Mercury* 15 June 1869, 3; 1 July 1867, 1; 15 June 1871, 289.

22. *College Mercury* 2 September 1877, 3; *Wilkes* 15 June 1861, 228; *College Mercury* 25 September 1874, 3; *Milwaukee Sentinel* 8 September 1854, 1; 31 May 1881, 7; *College Mercury* 1 July 1869, 10.

23. "Cricket Supplement," *Horae Scholasticae* (St. Paul's School) December 1886, 6; *Clipper* 16 June 1860, 68. For an analysis of cricket at St. Paul's School see Tom Melville, "'De Gustibus non est Disputandum': Cricket at St. Paul's School and a Note on the Structural/Character Debate in American Cricket," *International Journal of the History of Sport* 9 no. 1 (April 1992), 105-10.

24. *University Quarterly* July 1860, 169; *Bowdoin Bugle* June 1858; June 1859; November 1860; *University Quarterly* January 1860, 164; *Olio, 1861* (Amherst College), 30; *Ichnolite* (Amherst College) May 1860, 336-39; *Williams Quarterly* November 1859, 190; *Sunday Mercury* 22 April 1860, 5; Walter Meagher, *The Spires of Fenwick: A History of the College of the Holy Cross, 1843-1963* (New York: Vantage Press, 1966), 180; *University Quarterly* October 1860, 334; *University Palladium 1860/1* (University of Michigan), 46; *Students Monthly* (Oberlin College) July 1859, 361; *University Quarterly* October 1860, 391.

25. *Daily Evening Express* (Lancaster) 4 June 1860, 2; *Clipper* 8 September 1860, 165; William Dusenberry, *The Waynesburg College Story* (Kent State

University Press, 1975), 86-87. Dusenberry claims cricket remained the "most important intercollegiate sport" at Waynesburg up to 1880, 86-87; Ronald Smith, *Sports and Freedom: The Rise of Big-Time College Athletics* (New York: Oxford University Press, 1988), 219.

26. *Cohoes Cataract* 16 July 1859, 3.

27. *Wilkes* 15 October 1859, 89; *Clipper* 31 March 1860, 395; *Wilkes* 28 April 1860, 12; *Porters* 7 March 1857, 5.

28. *Spirit* 23 July 1859, 282; *Wilkes* 15 October 1859, 89; *Sunday Mercury* 13 May 1860, 5; *Clipper* 19 May 1860, 37.

29. *Clipper* 29 September 1860, 186; *Sunday Mercury* 23 September 1860, 5; *Wilkes* 21 June 1862, 244; *Clipper* 27 October 1860, 222; *New York Times* 20 October 1860, 8.

30. *Sunday Mercury* 23 September 1860, 5; 21 October 1860, 5; *Clipper* 31 August 1861, 159; *Wilkes* 28 June 1862, 269; *Clipper* 12 November 1864, 243.

31. *Bells Life* 4 December 1859, 6; *Union and Advertiser* (Rochester) 24 October 1859, 2; *Clipper* 28 May 1864, 50; *Porters* 19 November 1859, 180.

32. *Wilkes* 28 January 1860, 327; *Bells Life* 4 December 1859, 6; William Caffyn, *Seventy-One Not Out,* 146; *Herald* 5 October 1859, 10; *Wilkes* 28 January 1860, 327.

33. *Union and Advertiser* (Rochester) 8 October 1859, 2; 21 October 1859, 2; 22 October 1859, 2. Later English teams were courted just as heavily by such cities as Albany, Louisville, Minneapolis, and even Salt Lake City; *Argus* (Albany) 18 September 1879, 8; *Louisville Democrat* 14 August 1868, 1; *Pioneer Press* (St. Paul) 29 July 1994, 14; *Deseret Evening News* (Salt Lake City) 12 July 1879, 3.

34. *Clipper* 7 September 1861, 164. Quoted in *Washington Reporter* (Washington, PA) 12 October 1859, 3; *Albion* 5 November 1859, 538; Charles Haswell, *Reminiscences of an Octogenarian* (New York: Harper, 1896), 525; Fred Lillywhite, *The English Cricketers Trip*, 32.

35. *Porters* 15 October 1859, 101; *The International Cricket Match,* iv; *Spirit* 23 June 1849, 211.

36. *Herald* 16 October 1859, 1. The *New York Times* reiterated this sentiment some 20 years later (28 September 1878, 4). These statements seem to clearly run counter to Adelman's contention that had cricket only solidified its position before the rise of organized baseball it could have become America's dominant bat-and-ball sport; Melvin Adelman, "The Development of Modern Athletics; Sport in New York City, 1820-1870" (Ph.D. Diss.: University of Illinois, 1980), 285-86.

Chapter 5

1. For nineteenth-century claims that the Civil War fatally disrupted cricket see *Horae Scholasticae* (St. Paul's School) February 1868, 37; *New York Daily Tribune* 8 July 1883, 4; Frank Presbrey, *Athletics at Princeton: A History* (New York: Presbrey, 1901), 22, 23, 557 and *American Cricketer* 15 July 1904. For contemporary assertions to this effect see John Marder, *The International Series* 33; Melvin Adelman, *A Sporting Time*, 109; Keith Sandiford, *Cricket and the Victorians*, 148, and George Kirsch, ed., *Sports in North America*, vol. 4 (Gulf Breeze: Academic International, 1995), 131-32.

2. *Wilkes* 8 May 1861, 165; 13 July 1861, 291-92.

3. *Clipper* 27 April 1861, 10; *Outing* March 1886, 685; *Spirit* 25 May 1861, 244; *Wilkes* 31 May 1862, 195; 25 October 1865, 140; *Daily Missouri Democrat* 29 August 1866, 4; Sally (Butler) Wister, *Walter S. Newhall: A Memoir*, 17. See also John Betts, "Home Front, Battle Field and Sport During the Civil War," *Research Quarterly* 42, no. 2 (March 1971), 116, 127.

4. *Daily Evening Express* (Lancaster) 23 June 1857, 2; 27 July 1857, 2; Franklin Ellis, *History of Lancaster County, Pennsylvania*, 117, 132, 140, 143, 158, 201; John Marder, *The International Series*, 60; *Clipper* 8 October 1854, 204; *American Cricketer* 1 April 1880, D.97; *San Antonio Express* 26 February 1889, 3; *Detroit Free Press* 8 September 1894, 6; *University Palladium 1860/1*, 46; J. H. Kidd, *Personal Recollections of a Cavalryman* (Ionia: Sentinel, 1908), iii.

5. *American Cricketer* 15 May 1903, 67; Frank Taylor, *Philadelphia in the Civil War* (City of Philadelphia, 1913), 158, 159; J. H. Kidd, *Personal Recollections*, 17; *Clipper* 7 June 1862, 59; *Olio, 1862*, 28; *Amherst College, Class of 1863*, 108.

6. *Clipper* 29 February 1862, 364; John Betts, "Home Front, Battle Field, and Sport During the Civil War," 127; David S. Crockett, "Sports and Recreational Practices of Union and Confederate Soldiers," *Research Quarterly* 32 no. 3 (1962), 342.

7. Bell Wiley, *The Life of Billy Yank* (New York: Bobbs, 1951), 169; Bell Wiley, *The Life of Johnny Reb* (New York: Bobbs, 1943), 159; Hosea Rood, *Story of the Service of Company E and the 12th Wisconsin Regiment* (Milwaukee: Swain, 1893), 113; Donald Cole, *Immigrant City: Lawrence, Massachusetts, 1845-1921* (Chapel Hill: University of North Carolina Press, 1963), 140; *Clipper* 9 May 1863, 31; A. G. Spalding, *America's National Game* (Lincoln: University of Nebraska Press, 1992), 96.

8. *Clipper* 11 May 1861, 26; *Wilkes* 23 August 1862, 389; 27 August 1864, 402.

9. *Wilkes* 18 May 1861, 165; *Clipper* 6 July 1861, 95; *Wilkes* 2 August 1862, 340; 11 June 1864, 228; *Sunday Mercury* 22 September 1861, 5; *Brooklyn Daily Eagle* 11 September 1862, 2; *Clipper* 29 March 1862, 394.

10. William Ellis, ed., *Norwich University, 1819-1911*, vol. 1 (Montpelier: Capital, 1911), 123; *Gazette & Courier* (Greenfield, MA) 27 June 1864, 2; *Wilkes* 27 August 1864, 402; *Cincinnati Enquirer* 7 July 1863, 3; *Clipper* 18 July 1863, 11. The Peninsular Club of Detroit kept up a fairly regular cricket schedule with Canadian clubs during the war; *Detroit Free Press* 18 August 1863, 3; 6 August 1864, 1; *Deseret News* 9 July 1862, 16; 15 October 1862, 123; 24 June 1863, 410.

11. Melvin Adelman, *A Sporting Time* 116; *Clipper* 12 August, 1865, 140; *World* (New York) 26 June 1865, 5; "Baseball and Cricket," *Our Young Folks*, May 1867, 304; *Detroit Free Press* 21 April 1867, 1. See also *Wilkes* 16 November 1867, 243.

12. *American Chronicle of Sports and Pastimes* 13 February 1868, 49; 26 December 1867, 5; *New York Times* 28 March 1865, 2; Charles Peverelly, *The Book of American Pastimes*, 529; *Clipper* 20 April 1867, 10.

13. *Spirit* 19 September 1857, 373; 16 January 1858, 582; 27 February 1858, 30; 30 July 1859, 341; *World* (New York) 29 July 1869, 2; *Clipper* 12 August 1865, 138; 20 February 1858, 348; 19 May 1860, 37. The second elevens of these two clubs, however, continued to play each other over this period; *Wilkes* 19 September 1863, 36.

14. *World* (New York) 3 September 1865, 5; 13 September 1868, 5; 3 August 1865, 8; 29 July 1869, 2; *Clipper* 18 August 1866, 145; 7 August 1869, 140; *New York Times* 3 August 1865, 8.

15. *Clipper* 29 June 1867, 92; *Memphis Daily Appeal* 14 June 1867, 3; *Louisville Democrat* 4 August 1867, 1; *Wilkes* 19 May 1866, 77; *Clipper* 19 May 1866, 43; *Indianapolis Daily Journal* 4 June 1867, 2; Frederick Kershner, "A Social and Cultural History of Indianapolis, 1860-1914" (Ph.D. Thesis, University of Wisconsin, 1950), 227; *Clipper* 21 August 1869, 157; *Wilkes* 19 May 1866, 179; *Clipper* 20 April 1867, 10; *Daily Morning Chronicle* (Washington, D.C.) 29 May 1866, 4; *Ball Players Chronicle* 5 September 1867, 4. Young was on the all-New York team that played against Wilshire's English professionals in 1868 *Age* (Philadelphia) October 10, 1868, 1. Four cricket clubs were also using the Boston Common during this period; *Wilkes* 6 September 1873, 91.

16. Charles Peverelly, *The Book of American Pastimes*, 551; George Ellard, *Baseball in Cincinnati* (Cincinnati: Ohio Book Store, 1907), 43; *Wilkes* 17 April 1866, 85; *Ball Players Chronicle* 18 July 1867, 2; *Cincinnati Enquirer* 25 September 1864, 3; *Cincinnati Commercial* 19 May 1867, 8. According to Wright, cricket "was all the rage" in Cincinnati when he arrived there in 1866; *Cincinnati Daily Enquirer* 20 August 1875, 8.

17. Gregg Carter, "Baseball in St. Louis, 1867-1875: An Historical Case Study in Civic Pride," *The Bulletin, Missouri Historical Society* 31 (1975), 257-58; *St. Louis Democrat* 22 August 1874, 4; *St. Louis Dispatch* 8 August

1873, 4; *Forest and Stream* 5 March 1874, 60-63; *St. Louis Dispatch* 16 September 1873, 4. As late as 1895 the local press was demanding that "St. Louis certainly would not rank among the leading sporting and athletic cities without a good cricket club," *St. Louis Globe-Democrat* 23 June 1895, 11. For another example of cricket's association with civic pride, see *Buffalo Courier* 9 August 1877, 2.

18. *Ball Players Chronicle* 12 September 1867, 5; *Mohawk Daily Democrat* (Fonda, NY) 1 August 1865, 2; *Ripon Commonwealth* 9 June 1865, 5; *Waltham Free Press* 26 July 1867, 2; *Clipper* 12 May 1866, 36; *Wilkes* 16 June 1866, 247; *Black Earth Advertiser* (Black Earth, WI) 28 September 1871, 3; G. Clift, *History of Maysville and Mason County* (Lexington: Transylvania, 1936), 3, 205, 246; *Maysville Eagle* 30 August 1866, 3; *Maysville Bulletin* 13 June 1867, 3; *Clipper* 17 November 1866, 252. *Forest and Stream* claimed there was an "infinity" of smaller clubs in New England during the 1870s; *Forest and Stream* 14 August 1873, 11.

19. *Wilkes* 11 August 1866, 381; *Orange Journal* 29 April 1865, 2; *Cleveland Leader* 20 September 1865, 4; *Elyria Democrat* 15 June 1870, 3; *Port Huron Press* 26 July 1865, 3; *Galena Gazette* 21 August 1866, 3 *Grant County Witness* (Lancaster, WI) 23 August 1866, 3; *Sheboygan Journal* 25 May 1865, 1; *Northwestern* (Oshkosh, WI) 7 June 1866, 5.

20. *Deseret News* 9 August 1866, 285; 7 August 1872, 3; 4 June 1873, 3; Salt Lake *Daily Telegraph and Commercial Advertiser* 17 June 1869, 2; *Salt Lake Daily Herald* 9 July 1874, 3; *Ogden Junction* 29 July 1876, 3; *Windows of Wellsville* (Providence: Watkins, 1985), 428, 484, 576, 637; *Clipper* 27 September 1879, 211. Of Utah's population from the 1860s to the 1880s, 22 percent, had been born in England; 51 percent of Sandy's population alone being of English descent; Helen Papanikolas, ed., *The People of Utah* (Salt Lake City: Utah State Historical Society, 1976), 64; Martha Bradley, *Sandy City, The First 100 Years*, 34. It would be wrong to assume, however, that these Utah clubs were exclusively English. The cricket club of Plain City, for example, included several Americans and even a Danish missionary; *History of Plain City* (Plain City: Cook, 1979), 1, 21, 25, 28.

21. *Detroit Free Press* 1 August 1864, 1.

22. *New York Times* 28 March 1865, 2; *Clipper* 8 July 1871, 108; *Sunday Mercury* 9 June 1870, 6; *World* (New York) 17 September 1868, 10; 19 September 1872, 8.

23. *Detroit Free Press* 16 August 1865, 1; 21 April 1867, 1; *Milwaukee Sentinel* 14 August 1865, 1; *Clipper* 21 October 1865, 219; *Reporter & Tribune* (Washington, PA) 13 December 1865, 3; 11 July 1866, 3. So strong was baseball's popularity during this period that even in Philadelphia, "No one would join a cricket club" after the Civil War; Charles Peverelly, *The Book of American Pastimes*, 545.

24. *Miners Journal* (Pottsville) 27 May 1865, 2; 24 June 1865, 2; 2 September 1865, 2; 4 April 1868, 2. According to Peverelly, the Pottsville club alone played 15 matches in 1865; Charles Peverelly, *The Book of American Pastimes* 529.

25. *Wilkes* 16 August 1873, 19; *Cincinnati Commercial* 5 September 1869, 5; *Boston Globe* 6 September 1875, 4.

26. *New York Times* 8 March 1872, 4; *Wilkes* 26 October 1867, 190. For another criticism of baseball's claim to being the national game, see *Utica Morning Herald* 12 June 1874, 2. Thomas Atherr, "'The Most Summery, Bold, Free and Spacious Game,' Charles King Newcomb and Philadelphia Baseball, 1866-1871," *Pennsylvania History* 52, no. 2, 1985, 81-82. Newcomb was also an admirer of cricket; Charles Newcomb, *Journals of Charles King Newcomb* (Providence: Brown University Press, 1946), 285.

27. *New York Times* 20 October 1872, 3; *Forest and Stream* 14 August 1873, 8.

28. *Wilkes* 21 April 1860, 105; *New York Times* 27 October 1872, 1; *World* (New York) 19 September 1872, 4; *Wilkes* 3 December 1859, 205.

29. *National Chronicle* 5 June 1869, 85.

30. *Sporting Times* (Boston) 20 June 1868, 8; *Spirit* 16 June 1849, 193; *Clipper* 16 March 1889, 11; *Sporting Life* 26 October 1895, 2; *National Chronicle* 5 June 1869, 85. David Voigt, "The Boston Red Stockings: The Birth of Major League Baseball," *The New England Quarterly* December 1970, 546.

31. *Wilkes* 14 September 1867, 77; *Daily National Intelligencer* (Washington, D.C.) 9 September 1867, 3; *Forest and Stream* 12 August 1880, 34; Will Roffe, "Cricket in New England and the Longwood Club," *Outing* June 1891, 251; William Perrin, *Days of Greatness: Providence Baseball, 1875-1885* (Cooperstown, NY: Society for Baseball Research, 1984), 10; *San Francisco Chronicle* 30 September 1869, 3. For an analysis of the significance of this match, see Tom Melville, "Red Stockings at the Wicket," *Timeline* March/April 1994, 50-54; *New York Times* 27 October 1872, 1. For an advertisement featuring George Wright as a cricket player, see *Pioneer Press* (St. Paul) 17 May 1892, 6.

32. *Porters* 10 December 1859, 229; *Clipper* 20 July 1861, 106; *Wilkes* 16 June 1860, 229; 2 July 1864, 284; *Clipper* 18 November 1871, 257; *Sunday Mercury* 17 July 1870, 6; *Wilkes* 19 July 1862, 307-08; *Clipper* 10 June 1867, 77; 21 September 1872, 197; *Chicago Daily Tribune* 8 August 1874, 12; *Clipper* 22 October 1881, 498; *World* (New York) 9 September 1870, 2. Two other early baseballers, Lloyd Aspinwall and a Yeatman, also played cricket, as well as an early member of the Knickerbockers, R. F. Stevens, who "at one time bid fair to become one of the most finished cricketers in America," *Spirit* 25 May 1861, 244; *Clipper* 31 October 1868, 234; *National Republican* (Washington, D.C.) 29 August 1865, 3; *Porters* 6 December 1856, 229.

33. *Wilkes* 29 September 1860, 53; 16 August 1862, 37; 18 October 1862, 116; 6 September 1862, 4; 25 October 1862, 22; 7 March 1863, 11; *Clipper* 25 October 1862, 219.

34. *Wilkes* 19 September 1868, 69; 21 September 1872, 81; *Clipper* 18 October 1879, 234; 25 October 1879, 243; *Forest and Stream* 13 November 1879, 814.

35. *World* (New York) 19 September 1868, 7; *Wilkes* 24 October 1868, 148; *Clipper* 31 October 1868, 237; *Philadelphia Inquirer* 13 October 1868, 2; *Boston Herald* 2 October 1868, 2; *New England Base Ballist* 8 October 1868, 37; *World* (New York) 7 October 1879, 8; *Clipper* 25 October 1879, 243.

36. *Ball Players Chronicle* 19 September 1867, 6; *Beadles Dime Base Ball Player* (New York: Beadle, 1872), 10. Thomas Higginson noted before the Civil War how baseball "is every year becoming perfected into a sleight-of-hand like cricket," Thomas W. Higginson, "Gymnastics," *Atlantic Monthly* March 1861, 299; *Wilkes* 24 October 1868, 148.

37. *Porters* 18 October 1856, 11; *Sunday Mercury* 26 August 1863, 5; *Boston Herald* 22 July 1870, 2; *Providence Journal* 29 July 1889, 9.

38. *Clipper* 22 August 1874, 163; 5 September 1874, 183; 19 September 1874, 194. Baseball seems to have first been played in England by American students in 1868; *American Chronicle of Sports and Pastimes* 28 May 1868, 172.

39. Neil Stout, "1874 Baseball Tour Not Cricket to British," *Baseball Research Journal* 14 (1985), 85; *Clipper* 15 August 1874, 155; *St. Louis Democrat* 13 September 1874, 4; *Daily Inter-Ocean* (Chicago) 29 May 1887, 4; *Clipper* 21 June 1884, 210; 1 August 1885, 306; *Lillywhite's Cricketers Annual, 1885*, 45. For an overview of Spalding's later contacts with cricket, see Tom Melville, "Cricket and Mr. Spalding," *National Pastime* (1996), 8-10. In addition to Spalding, four other prominent nineteenth-century baseball organizers, Chris Von Der Ahe, Alfred Spink, S. M. Graffen (all of St. Louis), and R. C. Hall of Baltimore, were at one time associated with cricket; *American Cricketer* 21 April 1881, 103; *St. Louis Evening Post* 7 September 1878, 4; Alfred Spink, *The National Game* (St. Louis: National Game Pub., 1910), 344-45; *Clipper* 15 March 1873, 396; 9 January 1875, 322.

40. Allen Guttmann, *Games and Empires*, 179-80.

41. *St. Louis Globe-Democrat* 21 August 1875, 8; *Milwaukee Sentinel* 6 July 1878, 4; 24 August 1878, 4; *Chicago Daily Tribune* 15 July 1876, 5; *Providence Journal* 9 October 1882, 8. The professional baseball clubs in Baltimore and St. Louis also played some cricket against their local cricket clubs; *Baltimore Gazette* 7 August 1874, 1; *St. Louis Republican* 15 April 1875, 8.

42. *St. Louis Democrat* 10 August 1874, 4; *Meriden Daily Republican* 4 August 1873, 2; *Salt Lake Daily Herald* 28 August 1874, 3. In 1879 the baseball and cricket organizations of Salt Lake City even formed a joint association;

184 · Notes to Chapter 5

Ken Cannon, "Deserets, Red Stockings and Out-of-Towners," *Utah Historical Quarterly* 52, no. 2 (1984), 145; *Boston Globe* 10 September 1877, 2; *Grass Valley Union* 17 June 1884, 3; *Rochester Union and Advertiser* 12 July 1878, 2; *Forest and Stream* 31 October 1878, 264; *California Spirit of the Times* 13 July 1878, 223; *Morning Oregonian* (Portland) 10 August 1878, 3; *Forest and Stream* 23 October 1873, 173; *Clipper* 5 July 1873, 107; *Sunday Mercury* (New York) 6 October 1873, 3; *World* (New York) 17 October 1873, 2; 3 September 1875, 8.

43. *St. Louis Post Dispatch* 12 October 1881, 4; *Chicago Tribune* 8 October 1896, 8; *Daily Inter-Ocean* 10 October 1896, 10; *American Cricketer* 1 December 1881, 265; *California Spirit of the Times* 29 October 1881, 45.

44. *Wilkes* 20 December 1873, 435; *World* (New York) 29 July 1870, 5; Alfred Spink, *The National Game*, 4; *Herald* 19 September 1862, 5; *Paterson Daily Press* 2 October 1878, 3; *The Irish Cricketers in the United States, 1879* (Dublin: Lawrence, 1880), 27; *Clipper* 12 October 1878, 226; *New York Times* 2 October 1878, 2; *American Cricketer* 24 July 1879, 16.

45. *Forest and Stream* 3 July 1879, 435; William Ryczek, *Blackguards and Red Stockings: A History of Baseball's National Association, 1871-1875* (Jefferson, NC: McFarland, 1992), 32; *Clipper* 9 September 1882, 404; 14 May 1881, 122; *American Cricketer* 20 June 1889, 37; *New York Times* 28 September 1892, 9; *New York Times* 1 September 1885, 8; *Illustrated Sporting News* 22 July 1905, 8-9; *Forest and Stream* 25 March 1880, 149. Roller's amateur English cricketers were also given an exhibition of curveball pitching during their stop in Philadelphia in 1886; *Philadelphia Record* 3 October 1886, 7; R. A. Proctor, "Baseball and Cricket," *Longmans* 10 (1887), 181-82. The *Clipper* was also reporting, in 1879 (6 September, 187) that two former Philadelphia baseball professionals, Al Reach and John Radcliffe, were "now devoting all their spare time to cricket."

46. *Sunday Mercury* 8 September 1861, 5; *Clipper* 25 October 1879, 243; *Beadles Dime Base Ball Player* (New York: Beadle, 1880), 47; *Clipper* 11 October 1879, 227; 25 October 1879, 242. This idea had been raised as early as 1870; *National Chronicle* 19 March 1870, 82.

47. Lord Hawke, *Recollections and Reminiscences* (London: Williams, 1924), 230.

48. *Porters* 11 September 1858, 21; *University Chronicle* (University of Michigan) 16 March 1867, 1; *College Mercury* 12 February 1879, 2.

49. *St. Louis Globe-Democrat* 27 June 1875, 4. See also *Herald* 2 October 1872, 6.

50. *New York Times* 15 September 1872, 5; 30 August 1881, 4.

51. *New York Times* 30 August 1881, 4; *Clipper* 10 April 1869, 8; *American Chronicle of Sports and Pastimes* 18 June 1868, 202. For other post-Civil War assertions that cricket might still supersede baseball as a national game,

see *World* (New York) 22 October 1867, 5; *Louisville Democrat* 23 August 1868, 1.

52. *Clipper* 10 April 1869, 8; 18 May 1872, 53.

53. "Philosophy of the National Game, *Nation* 26 August 1869, 168.

54. *Clipper* 30 June 1860, 85. Complaints over a "lack of punctuality" had been raised during the very earliest organized American cricket matches; *Spirit* 9 November 1839, 423; 11 August 1849, 295; *Forest and Stream* 15 May 1879, 296. For instances of deliberate stalling, see *Newark Daily Advertiser* 18 September 1855, 2; *Clipper* 15 July 1865, 107; *Meriden Daily Republican* 6 September 1869, 2; *Toledo Blade* 15 August 1874, 3; *Boston Globe* 25 September 1888, 5.

55. *National Chronicle* 9 January 1869, 2; *Clipper* 8 June 1872, 75; 1 June 1878, 77; *Sunday Mercury* 25 August 1872, 6; *Outing* October 1884, 48; Henry Chadwick, *Chadwick's American Cricket Manual*, 3; *American Chronicle of Sports and Pastimes* 13 February 1868, 52; *Outing* June 1890, 228; *American Chronicle of Sports and Pastimes* 16 July 1868, 250.

56. *Wilkes* 24 August 1861, 389; *New York Times* 20 October 1860, 81; *Clipper* 27 October 1860, 22. Later baseball clubs suggested similar modifications for cricket; *Providence Journal* 9 October 1882, 8.

57. Henry Chadwick, *Chadwick's American Cricket Manual*, 82; *Clipper* 5 October 1872, 212; *Boston Herald* 27 September 1872, 1; R. A. Fitzgerald, *Wickets in the West* (London: Tinsley, 1873), 287-89. This match was characterized by such unorthodox technique and conditions that *Lillywhites Cricketers Annual* condemned it as a "mockery of cricket"; *Clipper* 18 January 1873, 333. Similar conditions also accounted for the brevity of the cricket match between the Knickerbocker Baseball Club and the Manhattan Cricket Club in 1872; *Clipper* 12 October 1872, 221.

58. *Wilkes* 2 February 1867, 357; *Clipper* 8 June 1878, 83.

59. Henry Chadwick, "Cricket in the Metropolis," *Outing* April 1891, 43; "American Cricket," *American* (Philadelphia) 7 May 1881, 58; "International Cricket," *American* 15 October 1881, 8; *American Cricketer* April 1913, 79; George S. Patterson, "Cricket in the United States," *Lippincott's Magazine* 50 (1892), 658; "Cricket Supplement," *Horae Scholasticae* December 1886, 8; *Spalding's Official Cricket Guide for 1913*, 87.

60. *Clipper* 10 April 1858, 402; 22 August 1874, 163.

Chapter 6

1. *Louisville Democrat* 25 August 1860, 1.

2. *New York Illustrated News* 4 August 1860, 196.

3. *Spirit of the Times* 18 July 1874, 572; *New York Times* 8 March 1872, 4.

4. *Forest and Stream* 14 August 1873, 8; Charles Newcomb, *The Journals of Charles King Newcomb*, 280-81.

5. *New York Times* 30 October 1881, 4.

6. *The International Cricket Match*, 24; *Union and Advertiser* (Rochester) 23 October 1858, 3; *Detroit Free Press* 29 July 1873, 1. See also *Beadles Dime Book of Cricket and Football* (New York: Beadle, 1866), 34.

7. *St. Louis Dispatch* 8 August 1874, 4; *Boston Herald* 19 August 1868, 2; *Cincinnati Commercial* 26 June 1869, 5; *Turf, Field and Farm* 24 November 1871, 330.

8. "Wickets in the West," *Canadian Monthly and National Review* 4 (July-December 1873), 38.

9. *New York Times* 30 August 1872, 8; *Clipper* 28 September 1872, 202, 204; *New York Times* 15 September 1872, 5.

10. R. A. Fitzgerald, *Wickets in the West*, 301; "Wickets in the West," *Canadian Monthly*, 41-42.

11. *American Cricketer* 20 September 1877, 51; *New York Times* 15 July 1877, 2; *By-Laws of the St. George Cricket Club of New York*, 2; *American Cricketer* 16 August 1883, 135; *The Irish Cricketers in the United States*, 28.

12. Charles Clay, "The Staten Island Cricket and Baseball Club," *Outing* November 1887, 104; *Clipper* 1 May 1880, 43; *Sporting Life* 13 April 1887, 4; *Clipper* 21 May 1887, 2; *New York Times* 17 May 1887, 2; *St. George Cricket Club of New York: 1888 Season* [1]; *St. George Cricket Club of New York: Season, 1891* [1]; *Brooklyn Daily Eagle* 24 August 1903, 7.

13. *Clipper* 11 May 1867, 35; *World* (New York) 29 July 1870, 5; *American Cricketer* 15 July 1904; *Clipper* 11 May 1872, 43; *New York Times* 23 July 1867, 8; *Clipper* 2 September 1882, 383. Another club by this name appeared in New York during the 1880s and 1890s, but it was not a direct descendent of the original New York Cricket Club; *World* (New York) 11 July 1884, 7; *New York Times* 6 July 1890, 5.

14. *Cincinnati Enquirer* 21 April 1871, 8.

15. *Forest and Stream* 5 March 1874, 63; *St. Louis Globe-Democrat* 14 May 1876, 6; 26 May 1876, 8.

16. *Anglo-American* 5 August 1843, 360; *New York Leader* 22 August 1857, 5; *Herald* 30 June 1856, 8; *The Staten Island Cricket and Base Ball Club: Constitution and By Laws* [1]; *Clipper* 11 May 1872, 43; 13 July 1872, 115; 13 June 1874, 83; Charles Clay, "The Staten Island Cricket and Baseball Club," 100; Randolph St. George Walker, *History of the Staten Island Cricket and Lawn Tennis Club, 1872-1917* (Staten Island: Privately printed, 1917), 1. To get to the St. George ground in Hoboken in 1869, one had to take a "horse car through bad smells on New Jersey flats," *Nation* 2 September 1869, 190; Charles Clay, "The Staten Island Cricket and Baseball Club," 100.

17. *Clipper* 30 March 1877, 3; Randolph St. George Walker, *History of the Staten Island Cricket and Lawn Tennis Club*, 2, 6; Charles Clay, "The Staten Island Cricket and Baseball Club," 110; *Clipper* 14 February 1880, 373; *Report*

of the Secretary of the Staten Island Cricket and Base Ball Club . . . February 6, 1888, 2; *Clipper* 31 May 1879, 77; 7 June 1879, 82; E. Digby Baltzell, *Sporting Gentlemen: Men's Tennis from the Age of Honor to the Cult of the Superstar* (New York: Free Press, 1995), 40; *Clipper* 10 May 1879, 50.

18. *Clipper* 22 July 1865, 115; *American Chronicle of Sports and Pastimes* 25 May 1868, 217; *Boston Herald* 29 August 1868, 4; Samuel Smith, *History of Newton, Massachusetts* (Boston: American, 1880), 669, 675, 697, 708, 753; Almon Hodges, *Genealogical Record of the Hodges Family of New England* (Boston: Higginson, 1896), 54-55; *Clipper* 4 July 1868, 103.

19. *Boston Globe* 31 May 1873, 5; Robert Minton, *One Hundred Years of Longwood* (Lynn: Zimman, 1977), 2; Will Roffe, "Cricket in New England and the Longwood Club," 251.

20. Will Roffe, "Cricket in New England and the Longwood Club," 251; *Boston Globe* 6 September 1885, 6; Will Roffe, "Cricket in New England and the Longwood Club," 251.

21. *Detroit Free Press* 3 October 1874, 1; *Spirit* 13 May 1876, 352; *Detroit Free Press* 6 August 1878, 1; 21 May 1882, 10; 3 May 1886, 4; *Forest and Stream* 6 May 1880, 276; *Detroit Free Press* 3 July 1887, 1; 31 May 1885, 7; 6 May 1894, 6; John Russell "The Detroit Athletic Club," *Outing* December 1888, 207.

22. *City of Detroit, Michigan* vol. 3 (Detroit: Clark, 1922), 93; vol. 4, 41; *Detroit Free Press* 15 October 1878, 1; 27 April 1867, 1; 3 May 1886, 4; Silas Farmer, *History of Detroit and Wayne County*, 176, 824.

23. *Daily Inter-Ocean* 7 September 1890, 3; John Russell, "The Detroit Athletic Club," 213; *Detroit Free Press* 10 July 1892, 17; 20 August 1897, 6; George Giffen, *With Bat and Ball* (London: Ward & Lock, 1897), 91; *Who Was Who in America* vol. 1, 236-37.

24. *Daily Inter-Ocean* 1 June 1890, 3; *Sporting Life* 13 January 1894, 6.

25. Randolph Downes, *Industrial Beginnings* (Toledo: Historical Society, 1954), 252; *Clipper* 12 July 1879, 124.

26. W. F. Mandle, "The Professional Cricketer in England in the Nineteenth Century," *Labour History* 23 (1972), 9. The professional cricketer at the Staten Island club was paid a salary of $501 in 1887, $61 more than the club paid its baseball professional; *Annual Report of the Staten Island Cricket and Base Ball Club for 1888*, 2; *Herald* 3 July 1859, 1; *Boston Herald* 10 September 1870, 4; *Sunday Mercury* 11 September 1870, 6; *Daily Inter-Ocean* 2 June 1889, 10; *Clipper* 4 June 1881, 171; 17 April 1886, 74; George Patterson, "Cricket in the United States," 653; Wilma Pesavento, "'Men Must Play: Men Will Play,'" 246; *Pioneer Press* (St. Paul) 3 May 1895, 6; *American Cricketer* 15 May 1902, 97.

27. George Patterson, "Cricket in the United States," 652; John Lester, *A Century* 79, 260; Robert Minton, *One Hundred Years of Longwood*, 8.

Notes to Chapter 6

28. *Daily Inter-Ocean* 14 August 1883, 2; *Clipper* 3 July 1880, 115; *St. Louis Globe-Democrat* 22 June 1880, 6; *Detroit Free Press* 5 June 1880, 6; 28 July 1881, 1.

29. *Boston Globe* 26 September 1886, 3; *Sun* (New York) 20 September 1895, 4; 23 August 1895, 4; *American Cricketer* 5 October 1895, 193; *Public Ledger* 18 July 1891, 8.

30. *Clipper* 27 August 1881, 363; John Hall, *Sixty Years of Canadian Cricket*, 416-19; Bernon Prentice, *History of the Seabright Lawn Tennis and Cricket Club* (Seabright, NJ: Privately Printed, 1937), 171; *Detroit Free Press* 11 July 1877, 1.

31. *Sun* (New York) 28 October 1882, 3; *Clipper* 4 November 1882, 531; *Detroit Free Press* 8 September 1878, 2; *Cricket* (London) 11 July 1889, 245; 10 June 1897, 194.

32. Charles Blancke, "The International Cricket Match at Manheim," *Harpers Weekly* 15 October 1892, 991; *Detroit Free Press* 27 September 1879, 1.

33. "Cricket in America," *Lippincott's Magazine* May 1873, 594.

34. *Chicago Tribune* 2 October 1878, 4; *Clipper* 28 September 1878, 210; *American Cricketer* 19 September 1878, 54; John Lester, *A Century*, 297.

35. *New York Times* 30 September 1878, 8; *Clipper* 28 September 1878, 210; *New York Times* 2 October 1878, 2; *New York Tribune* 2 October 1878, 8.

36. *Clipper* 12 October 1878, 226; John Lester, *A Century*, 59-65; *World* (New York) 6 October 1878, 1.

37. *Clipper* 18 January 1879, 341.

38. *Clipper* 10 May 1879, 50; *World* (New York) 8 May 1879, 8; *Forest and Stream* 8 January 1880, 977.

39. *Lillywhite's Cricketers Annual for 1880*, 1-12; *Forest and Stream* 20 November 1879, 837.

40. *Wisden's Cricketers Almanack for 1893*, 217-18; *Clipper* 15 October 1881, 486.

41. *New York Times* 10 October 1882, 8; *Clipper* 14 October 1882, 483.

42. *World* (New York) 14 October 1882, 8; *Clipper* 2 October 1882, 501.

43. *Detroit Free Press* 23 October 1879, 1; *Pittsburgh Post* 7 September 1888, 6; *Boston Globe* 16 September 1888, 6; *Lowell Daily Sun* 10 September 1892, 1; *American Cricketer* 27 September 1888, 92; *The Irish Cricketers in the United States* 7; *Forest and Stream* 1 May 1879, 256; *Clipper* 14 October 1882, 483.

44. *Public Ledger* 3 September 1886, 1; *American Cricketer* 19 October 1892, 177; *Public Ledger* 17 January 1888, 4.

45. *Public Ledger* 17 September 1879, 5; "Cricket Clubs of Philadelphia," *Harpers Weekly* 29 September 1894, 929.

46. *American Cricketer* 19 October 1892, 177; *New York Times* 15 September 1886, 2; 28 September 1886, 2; *New York Tribune* 5 September 1888, 8.

47. *Tribune Book of Open-Air Sports* (New York, 1887) 130; *Clipper* 11 October 1879, 227; *Sun* (New York) 11 October 1882, 3; *World* (New York) 29 July 1882, 8.

48. *World* (New York) 24 September 1896, 8; George Giffen, *With Bat and Ball*, 66; Francis Iredale, *33 Years of Cricket* (Sydney: Beatty, 1920), 137; *Boston Globe* 29 September 1886, 8.

49. *American Cricketer* 3 November 1899, 231; *American Cricket Annual for 1900*, 9; *London Times* 3 November 1899, 7; *Public Ledger* 7 October 1896, 19; George Giffen, *With Bat and Ball*, 97; *Public Ledger* 11 October 1901, 14; Lord Hawke, *Recollections and Reminiscences*, 222.

50. Andrew Davis, "College Athletics," *Atlantic Monthly* 51 (1883), 681; *New York Times* 1 May 1884, 4; 21 September 1907, 8; *New York Tribune* 8 July 1883, 4; "International Cricket," *American* 15 October 1881, 7; *Sporting Life* 10 August 1887, 7.

51. *New York Times* 20 September 1885, 8; *New York Tribune* 10 August 1903, 8.

52. *Clipper* 12 May 1860, 31; *The Cricket Players Pocket Companion* (Boston: Mayhew, 1859), 34; *Clipper* 27 April 1867, 20; 2 July 1864, 91; *World* (New York) 18 July 1873, 2; *Forest and Stream* 25 March 1880, 149; P. F. Warner, *Cricket in Many Climes* (London: Heinemann, 1900), 159.

53. *Age* (Philadelphia) 3 October 1868, 1; *Albion* 8 October 1859, 487.

54. *Outing*, September 1886, 689; *Sun* (Baltimore) 2 June 1883, 4; *Cincinnati Enquirer* 7 July 1863, 3; *American Chronicle of Sports and Pastimes* 16 April 1868, 124; *Forest and Stream* 9 September 1880, 114.

55. *World* (New York) 17 September 1868, 10; *American Cricketer* 28 October 1891, 205; Lord Hawke, *Recollections and Reminiscences*, 227.

56. *American Cricketer* 9 June 1881, 158; Robert Minton, *One Hundred Years of Longwood*, 3; *American Cricketer* 28 June 1877; *Providence Journal* 22 July 1888, 9; *Peoples Journal* (Greenwich, NY) 3 June 1886, 3; *Pioneer Press* (St. Paul) 28 May 1893, 2; *Omaha Daily Republican* 15 June 1884, 5; *Clipper* 24 November 1883, 590. By this time the St. George club had set up 20 tennis courts on its ground; "City Athletics," *Harpers New Monthly Magazine* January 1884, 304. Tennis was also affecting cricket at Staten Island by this time; *World* (New York) 29 July 1882, 8.

57. Quoted in the *American Cricketer* 27 January 1881, 84.

58. *American Cricketer* 27 January 1881, 84-85; 2 June 1881, 134; 29 April 1886, 1.

59. *Public Ledger* 17 September 1890, 6; *American Cricketer* 21 July 1887, 91; 23 September 1891, 184.

60. *Newark Daily Advertiser* 27 January 1891, 2; *New York Times* 17 June 1892, 3; *Sun* (New York) 31 May 1893, 8; *American Cricketer* 24 June 1891, 75; *Sun* (New York) 19 May 1893, 4; *Amateur Athlete* 13 May 1896, 11; *San*

Francisco Chronicle 27 April 1896, 4; Roberta Park, "British Sports and Pastimes in San Francisco, 1848-1900," *British Journal of Sports History* 1, no. 3 (1984), 316 n26.

61. *American Cricketer* 7 August 1879, 22; 8 August 1889, 73; 10 August 1885, 102; *Sporting Life* 4 June 1884, 7; *Boston Globe* 1 June 1886, 5; 9 September 1890, 7. Cricket also made only limited inroads into America's newly emerging country clubs, even though cricket supporters believed their game "should appeal most strongly" to such a clientele; H. Cornish "Cricket, a Game for American Gentlemen," *Country Life in America* July 1908, 278; *American Cricketer* 22 July 1891, 112; Douglas Rauschenberger, *Lost Haddenfield* (Haddenfield: Historical Society, 1989), 158; *San Francisco Chronicle* 13 August 1899, 25.

62. *Pittsburgh Post* 5 May 1888, 6; *Pioneer Press* (St. Paul) 11 May 1887, 2; *Daily Inter-Ocean* 1 June 1890, 3. Gerald Gems contends that most of Chicago's cricket clubs were middle class during this period; Gerald Gems, "Sports and Cultural Formation in Chicago, 1890-1940" (Ph.D. Diss., University of Maryland, 1989), 93; Mark Miller, *Mt. Washington: Baltimore Suburb* (Baltimore: GBS, 1980), 40; *Spalding's Official Cricket Guide for 1913*, 92. One of Sousa's relatives, an Anthony junior, seems to have been an active player with the Washington, D.C., cricket club; *Washington Post* July 5, 1913, 8; *Daily Inter-Ocean* 8 May 1883, 5; *American Cricketer* 25 April 1889, 4.

63. George Patterson, "Cricket in the United States," 658-59; *American Cricketer* 30 April 1900, 71.

64. Keith Sandiford, *Cricket and the Victorians*, 64, 71, 116; *St. Louis Post-Dispatch* 23 June 1895, 11; *Pioneer Press* (St. Paul) 2 September 1887, 2.

65. *Clipper* 23 April 1859, 5.

66. *American Cricketer* 27 January 1881, 85; *World* (New York) 26 June 1887, 13.

67. *Public Ledger* 21 September 1907, 2.

Chapter 7

1. *American* 26 July 1890, 286.

2. *American Athlete* 12 December 1890, 835. For other criticism of professional baseball during this period, see *World* (New York) 2 October 1891, 4; *America* (Chicago) 24 July 1890, 462.

3. *Pioneer Press* (St. Paul) 14 July 1895, 4.

4. *Daily Commonwealth* (Topeka, KS) 17 September 1887, 6; *New York Tribune* 6 May 1888, 4; *New York Times* 26 September 1891, 4; Ira Hollis, "Intercollegiate Athletics," *Atlantic Monthly* 90 (1902), 539; *New York Tribune* 5 May 1889, 18. At about the same time that this paper was declaring, "Where do you see a man over fifty years playing baseball?" (*New York Tribune* 15 June

1890, 12), the *New York Times* (12 August 1893, 2) was reporting that veterans cricket teams were "the craze in cricket circles." New York's Morris Park Cricket Club was made up entirely of players over 40; *World* (New York) 21 May 1893, 11.

5. Quoted in William Winn, "Tom Brown's Schooldays and the Development of 'Muscular Christianity,'" *Church History* 21 (1960), 70.

6. *Clipper* 25 October 1879, 242; *American Cricketer* 28 June 1877; *Forest and Stream* 26 February 1880, 75; 26 June 1879, 410. Philadelphia area merchants claimed they had sold more cricket equipment in 1878 than they had over the five previous years; *American Cricketer* 29 August 1878, 39.

7. *American Cricketer* 12 July 1883, 100.

8. *Daily True American* (Trenton) 26 August 1890, 4; *American Cricketer* 18 March 1891, 4; *World* (New York) 24 September 1893, 13.

9. *Milwaukee Sentinel* 29 August 1883, 2; *Detroit Free Press* 3 August 1888, 8; *Pioneer Press* (St. Paul) 12 October 1891, 1; *Butte Daily Miner* 27 June 1886, 1; *Boston Globe* 14 September 1886, 5. *Sporting Life* was also claiming cricket was "assuming gigantic proportions" in many areas of the country during this period; *Sporting Life* 2 May 1888, 10.

10. *Boston Globe* 13 September 1885, 3; 24 May 1885, 6; *American Cricketer* 27 April 1892, 26; *Public Ledger* 9 April 1895, 15; *World* (New York) 21 May 1893, 27; "Lord Hawke's Cricketers in Philadelphia," *Illustrated American* 17 October 1891, 394. Other indications of cricket's growing popularity were the seven active clubs in Hawaii (*Clipper* 19 February 1881, 378), the 5,000 spectators who attended a cricket match in Paterson, New Jersey (*World*, 8 September 1891, 8), and the "full supply" of cricket equipment New York's Peck and Snyder Department Store kept on hand, *Nineteenth Century Games and Sporting Goods-Peck & Snyder, 1886* (Princeton: Pyne, 1971), 28-29.

11. G. R. Howell, *History of the County of Albany, New York, from 1609 to 1886*, 747; *Daily Inter-Ocean* 7 June 1890, 3; *Newark Daily Advertiser* 3 June 1885, 3.

12. *Sun* (New York) 21 June 1889, 28; 29 August 1885, 3; 20 June 1893, 4; 21 July 1893, 4; *Brooklyn Daily Eagle* 28 July 1901, 9.

13. *Sun* (New York) 19 May 1891, 5; *Outing* May 1889, 21; *American Cricketer* 21 December 1898, 139; *Sun* (New York) 15 August 1896, 5; Henry Schnitzer, "A Glimpse of Bayonne in the 1880s," *Proceedings of the New Jersey Historical Society* vol. 80 (October 1962), 255; *Australasian* 7 November 1896, 902.

14. *Detroit Free Press* 12 July 1890, 8; *Cleveland Plain Dealer* 25 June 1899, 12; *American Cricketer* 21 April 1881, 103; *Omaha Daily Republican* 15 June 1884, 5; *Detroit Free Press* 6 July 1894, 2.

15. *Rocky Mountain News* (Denver) 5 July 1906, 8; *Morning Oregonian* (Portland) 10 June 1895, 8; *Daily Morning Astorian* 13 June 1895, 4.

192 · Notes to Chapter 7

16. *American Cricketer* 10 May 1893, 35; *Daily Inter-Ocean* 5 July 1891, 2; *Morning Oregonian* 30 August 1896, 9; *Philadelphia Press* 27 May 1904, 10.

17. *American Cricketer* 8 September 1894, 165; April 1895, 12; *San Francisco Chronicle* 24 July 1899, 8; *Milwaukee Sentinel* 29 July 1878, 8; *Milwaukee Directory for 1878*, 109.

18. *Clipper* 16 September 1876, 195; *American Cricketer* 1 July 1882, 51; William Wilson, *History of the Pennsylvania Railroad Company*, vol. 2 (Philadelphia: Coates, 1895), 35.

19. *American Cricketer* 27 May 1886, 24; *Pioneer Press* (St. Paul) 26 July 1891, 2; 14 August 1892, 6; Carl Zapffe, *Brainerd, Minnesota*, 74-75.

20. *Clipper* 17 November 1883, 575; 12 April 1887, 43; *Metropolitan District Cricket League: Minute Book, 1890-1899*, 6; *American Cricketer* April 1895, 12; *New York Times* 28 May 1899, 25; *American Cricketer* September 9, 1898, 98; *Brooklyn Daily Eagle* 16 July 1903, 10. The New York Association seems to have disbanded in 1908, but the Metro League survived until 1934. Brooklyn's Prospect Park also had its own league; *Spalding's Official Cricket Guide for 1908*, 51; *Brooklyn Daily Eagle* 1 July 1901, 13. Urban cricket leagues were also set up during this time in San Francisco and Pittsburgh; *San Francisco Call* 11 May 1891, 7; *Outing* July 1893, 84.

21. *Daily Inter-Ocean* 11 October 1891, 9; *Chicago Tribune* 20 September 1891, 7. The smaller cricket clubs in Boston also discussed setting up their own league in 1894; *Boston Globe* 4 June 1894, 7.

22. *Sporting Life* 16 August 1890, 12; *Pottsville Republican* 29 July 1890, 4; *American Cricketer* 27 October 1894, 198; *Outing* May 1896, 31-32; Albert Prosser, ed. *Sanford, Maine* (Sanford: Historical Committee, 1968), 333. A number of Wisconsin cricket clubs also planned, at one time, to form a state league; *Milwaukee Sentinel* 29 July 1888, 2.

23. *Chicago Times* 13 October 1881, 5; *Pioneer Press* (St. Paul) 9 September 1887, 2; 5 August 1897, 3; *Spalding's Official Cricket Guide for 1909*, 97. The ground used for the 1898 tournament in Omaha "was evidently a cornfield until a short time ago," *Pioneer Press* (St. Paul) 31 July 1898, 11.

24. *Clipper* 13 September 1856, 165; *Sunday Mercury* 28 April 1861, 8.

25. *Sunday Mercury* 28 April 1861, 8; Sidney Foreman, *West Point* (New York: Columbia, 1950), 179; James L. Morrison, *"The Best School in the World:" West Point, the Pre-Civil War Years, 1833-1866* (Kent, OH: Kent State University Press, 1986), 76; *Wilkes* 3 December 1859, 205; Park Benjamin, *The United States Naval Academy* (New York: Putnam, 1900), 267; *American Journal of Education* March 1865, 31.

26. *Army and Navy Journal* 15 April 1884, 727; *Louisville Democrat* 10 October 1868, 1; 1 November 1868, 1; *Deseret Evening News* 10 September 1879, 3; 20 September 1879, 3; 8 August 1881, 3.

27. *San Antonio Express* 25 August 1889, 3; 6 October 1889, 7; *Herald* 7 August 1860, 2; *San Antonio Express* 18 February 1889, 7.

28. *American Cricketer* 4 March 1880, 90; *Hawaiian Gazette* 26 March 1895, 5; *American Cricketer* 31 May 1900, 125.

29. *Cincinnati Enquirer* 7 July 1863, 3. There is even one instance on record of a cricket match being temporarily stopped so its players could go to church; *Washington Examiner* (Washington, PA) 27 October 1859, 3.

30. *Clipper* 31 May 1873, 67. A cricket team composed entirely of clergymen from Wisconsin's Episcopal Diocese played a match with Racine College in 1872; *College Mercury* 6 July 1872, 476.

31. James Tuttleton, *Thomas Wentworth Higginson* (Boston: Twayne, 1978), 33; Thomas Wentworth Higginson, *Cheerful Yesterdays* (New York: Arno, 1968), 195; *Clipper* 24 April 1858, 4; *Worcester Daily Spy* 6 July 1858, 2; Mary Higginson, *Thomas Wentworth Higginson* (Port Washington: Kennikot, 1971), 139.

32. *Who Was Who in America*, vol. 2, 185; *Wilkes* 30 July 1864, 340; *Clipper* 3 May 1879, 43; *American Cricketer* 7 July 1881, 163.

33. *History of Milwaukee, Wisconsin* (Chicago: Western, 1881), 880; *Milwaukee Sentinel* 2 March 1880, 5.

34. *Canadian Cricket Guide* (Toronto: Toronto News Co., 1877), 4-5; *Forest and Stream* 10 August 1876, 11; *Daily Inter-Ocean* 5 July 1896, 10; John Marder, *The International Series*, 55; *Spalding's Official Cricket Guide for 1911*, 124. Other cricket playing American clergymen included Rev. C. Dalies of Ripon's German Lutheran Church, and Rev. Charles Wood of Buffalo's Central Presbyterian Church; *Ripon Commonwealth* 15 May 1891, 3; Samuel Pedrick, *A History of Ripon, Wisconsin* (Ripon: Historical Society, 1964), 207; *Buffalo Courier* 25 May 1877, 2; H. R. Smith, *City of Buffalo*, 279.

35. *Sun* (New York) 16 May 1891, 4; W. S. Rainsford, *The Story of a Varied Life* (New York: Doubleday, 1922), 302; James Addison, *The Episcopal Church in the United States* 282.

36. *Sun* (New York) 26 May 1896, 4; 1 September 1898, 5; *Omaha Republican* 11 August 1889, 2; *American Cricketer* 13 July 1895, 103; Randolph Downes, *Industrial Beginnings* 269, 276, 277.

37. William Baker, "Disputed Diamonds: The YMCA Debate Over Baseball in the Late 19th Century," *Journal of Sport History* 19(3), 257-62; *Amateur Athlete* 12 August 1897, 16; *Outing* December 1890, 62; *New York Times* 21 August 1887, 3; *Spalding's Official Cricket Guide for 1913*, 61; *Spalding's Official Cricket Guide for 1908*, 54; *New York Tribune* 3 August 1890, 3.

38. Patrick Scott, "Cricket and the Religious World in the Victorian Period," *Church Quarterly* vol. 3, no. 2 (October 1970), 136; *Meriden Daily Republican* 6 September 1869, 2; *St. Louis Post Dispatch* 30 August 1891, 6.

39. Patrick Scott, "Cricket and the Religious World in the Victorian Period," 144; *American Cricketer* 25 November 1885, 151; *Academy Scholium for 1888*, 5; *Sun* (New York) 27 September 1885, 7; *Amateur Athlete* 8 April 1897, 5-6; *American Cricketer* 13 June 1889, 27; *Westonian* (Westtown School) vol. 1 (1895), 81; vol. 4 (1898), 46.

40. *College Mercury* 15 June 1875; Sydney Croft, "A Hundred Years of Racine College and the DeKoven Foundation," 253; *Daily Racine Journal* 9 June 1886, 3; *Yearbook for 1902* (Racine College), 56.

41. Peter Ingeman, *The Role of the Episcopal Church and of Nashotah House in the Establishment of St. Johns Military Academy, Delafield, Wisconsin* (1986), 3, 6, 8; Harold Wagner, *The Episcopal Church in Wisconsin*, 163; *Portrait and Biographical Record of Waukesha County, Wisconsin* (Chicago: Excelsior, 1894), 816-17; *St. Johns Call* November 1885, 1.

42. *St. Johns Military Academy, 17th Annual Announcement, 1900* 153; *Register of St. Johns Military Academy, 1889*, 39; *Catalogue of St. Johns Military Academy, 1894*, 59; *Milwaukee Sentinel* 15 July 1894, 7; *Daily Inter-Ocean* 4 October 1892, 6.

43. *Forest and Stream* 29 June 1876, 344; *Clipper* 14 July 1877, 125; 30 June 1883, 235; *New York Times* 1 July 1899, 11; *American Cricketer* 26 September 1889, 93; John Hall, *Sixty Years of Canadian Cricket*, 483-87.

44. *Pioneer Press* (St. Paul) 26 September 1897, 8; *Milwaukee Sentinel* 17 November 1879, 8; *American Cricketer* 25 November 1885, 152-53. The Detroit public high school was also playing some cricket in 1878; *Spirit* 6 November 1878, 397.

45. *The Record of the Class of 1900, Central High School, Philadelphia*, 165; *Spalding's Official Cricket Guide for 1906*, 22; John Lester, *A Century*, 371; Horace Lippincott, *A History of Germantown Academy* (Camden: Hadden Craftsmen, 1935), 19; *American Cricketer* 15 April 1901, 80; John Lester, "Another Cricket Invasion of England," *Outing* October 1902, 122; *Index: The Haverford Grammar School, 1901*, 31.

46. *Boston Globe* 13 June 1888, 6; *Illustrated Sporting News* 12 May 1906, 12, 26.

47. Archibald Graham, *Cricket at the University of Pennsylvania* (Burlington, PA: Privately printed, 1930), 15; Ronald Smith, *Sports and Freedom*, 125; D. A. Sargent, "History of the Administration of Intercollegiate Athletics in the United States," *American Physical Education Review* April 1910, 253; *New York Times* 15 May 1885, 4,

48. *Boston Daily Evening Transcript* 30 September 1867, 4; *Clipper* 17 April 1880, 26; D. A. Sargent, "The Regulation and Management of Athletic Sports," *Proceedings of the American Association for the Advancement of Physical Education*, 7th proceedings, 1892, 113.

49. Henry Chadwick, "Cricket at Harvard," *Outing* August 1890, 415; *New York Times* 15 May 1885, 3; *Clipper* 24 January 1885, 717; *American Cricketer* 18 May 1898, 13; *Boston Globe* 13 June 1888, 6.

50. *Boston Globe* 26 June 1887, 5; *American Cricketer* 24 May 1894, 43; 10 May 1894, 27; *Boston Globe* 10 May 1894, 5; *Amateur Athlete* 27 May 1897, 13; *Cricket Club Life* 1 January 1898, 8; *New York Tribune* 12 June 1898, 6.

51. *Spirit* 20 September 1851, 366; *Forest and Stream* 9 July 1874, 339; *American Cricketer* 29 December 1887, 177; 13 May 1891, 29; John Lester, *A Century* 7; Richard Hurd, *A History of Yale Athletics* (New Haven: Yale University Press, 1888), 153.

52. *World* (New York) 12 June 1879, 8; *Forest and Stream* 11 March 1880, 109; *Acta Columbiana* (Columbia University) 1 June 1880; 23 June 1880; *American Cricketer* 6 April 1882, 22; *Acta Columbiana* 28 April 1882.

53. Frank Presbrey, *Athletics at Princeton: A History*, 23, 30; *Nassau Monthly* (Princeton University) October 1874, 11; *Clipper* 3 July 1880, 269; *American Cricketer* 14 July 1881, 167; *Boston Globe* 12 July 1885, 8.

54. Archibald Graham, *Cricket at the University of Pennsylvania* 10; *Public Ledger* 20 September 1878, 1; *Clipper* 20 September 1879, 203; *American Cricketer* 12 September 1878, 47.

55. "Cricket at Haverford," *Harpers Weekly* 3 October 1896, 989; John Lester, *A Century*, 11; *American Cricketer* 15 December 1902, 248.

56. *A History of Haverford College for the First Sixty Years of Its Existence* (Philadelphia: Porter & Coates, 1892), 126; *American Cricketer* 14 July 1893, 76; Henry Hubbart, *Ohio Wesleyan's First Hundred Years* (Delaware: Ohio Wesleyan, 1943), 24, 280; Robert Gannon, *Up to the Present: The Story of Fordham* (New York: Doubleday, 1967), 45.

57. Allen Thomas, "Haverford College Cricket," *Outing* June 1896, 236, 237.

58. Allen Thomas, "Haverford College Cricket," 238; Lester, "Another Cricket Invasion," 123; *A History of Haverford College*, 442.

59. John Lester, *A Century*, 95; "Cricket at Haverford," *Harpers Weekly* 989; *Illustrated Sporting News* 26 November 1904, 9. The idea of sending Philadelphia school teams to England had been raised as early as 1879; *American Cricketer* 23 October 1879, 65.

60. Archibald Graham, *Cricket at the University of Pennsylvania*, 14; *American Cricketer* 17 February 1900, 28; 15 April 1902, 78.

61. *American Cricketer* February/March 1895, 4; *Public Ledger* 14 September 1895, 1.

62. *Spalding's Official Cricket Guide for 1908*, 7-24; H. V. Hordern, *Googlies* (Sydney: Angus & Robertson, 1932), 32-34. The university cricket team also undertook an extensive tour to Canada in 1911; *American Cricketer* July 1911, 149-50.

63. *New York Times* 26 April 1881; *Acta Columbiana* 18 May 1881.

64. *Horae Scholasticae* 4 April 1881, 91; *Trinity Tablet* (Trinity College) 22 May 1880; Glenn Weaver, *The History of Trinity College* (Hartford: Trinity, 1967), 210; *World* (New York) 22 May 1881, 2.

65. John Lester, *A Century,* 94, 379. Cricket was actually played at Cornell as early as 1869, its appearance possibly inspired by Thomas Hughes' visit to the college that year; *National Chronicle* 4 June 1870, 172; W. T. Hewett, *Cornell University: A History* (New York: University Publishing, 1905) vol. 3, 146, 270; *American Cricketer* 6 July 1895, 91-92; *Public Ledger* 6 July 1899, 13.

66. Roland Bowen, *Cricket: A History of Its Growth,* 70, 94; *Clipper* 21 June 1856, 71; *Cricket Players Pocket Companion,* 6; *Ball Players Chronicle* 6 June 1867, 5.

67. *Spirit* 6 November 1847, 431.

68. *Spirit* 5 September 1846, 327; *Herald* 31 August 1846, 2; *Anglo-American* 19 September 1846, 526. It was later revealed that Helliwell was not the "gentleman" army officer he claimed to be but a lawyer's clerk; *Brooklyn Evening Star* 2 September 1846, 2.

69. *Forest and Stream* 14 August 1879, 556; *Daily Inter-Ocean* 26 August 1889, 3.

70. *National Chronicle* 9 January 1869, 2; *Milwaukee Sentinel* 27 April 1880, 8.

71. *Waterbury American* 4 October 1853, 2; Constance Green, *History of Naugatuck, Connecticut* (New Haven: Yale University Press, 1948), 136; *Clipper* 21 June 1856, 71; *Waterbury American* 26 August 1859, 2; *Hartford Daily Courant* 5 October 1859, 2; *Clipper* 19 July 1856, 101; Ruth Bridge, ed., *The Challenge of Change: Three Centuries of Enfield, Connecticut, History* (Canaan: Phoenix, 1977), 195, 196.

72. *Daily Evening Express* (Lancaster) 18 May 1857, 2; 24 October 1857, 2; *Oswego Commercial Times* 3 September 1860, 3; *Cohoes Cataract* June 18, 1859, 3; *Herald* 22 June 1856, 1; J. Murphy, *Paterson & Passaic County* (Northridge: Windsor, 1987), 39. All this calls into question Goldstein's assertion that antebellum cricket gave way to baseball because the English game was "less rooted in metropolitan neighborhoods or particular workplaces"; Warren Goldstein, *Playing for Keeps: A History of Early Baseball* (Ithaca: Cornell University Press, 1989), 170 n2.

73. *Waltham Free Press* 20 July 1864, 3; *Boston Globe* 3 May 1885, 6; *World* (New York) 18 July 1873, 2; Kristen Petersen, *Waltham Rediscovered,* 18; Howard Gitelman, *Workingmen of Waltham* (Baltimore: Johns Hopkins University Press, 1974), 154; E. C. Alft, *Elgin, An American History* (Elgin: Crossroads, 1984), 49, 50, 67, 98; *American Cricketer* 13 September 1893, 181; *Daily Inter-Ocean* 31 May 1896, 11.

74. Rowland Berthoff, *British Immigrants in Industrial America* (New York: Russell, 1953), 5.

75. *Meriden Daily Republican* 28 July 1873, 2; 4 August 1873, 2; *Boston Globe* 24 August 1884, 6.

76. *Boston Globe* 24 August 1884, 6; *Providence Journal* 10 June 1888, 9; *Boston Globe* 4 July 1886, 6; 3 May 1885, 6; *Sporting Life* 25 March 1885, 2; *Boston Globe* 3 May 1885, 6; 3 September 1889, 8; *Sporting Life* 25 March 1885, 2; Orra Stone, *History of Massachusetts Industries* (Boston: Clarke, 1930), 587, 588, 989.

77. *Boston Globe* 3 May 1885, 6; Rowland Berthoff, *British Immigrants* ?°; *Boston Globe* 16 August 1891, 7; 13 August 1888, 5; Orra Stone, *History of Massachusetts Industries*, 333, 730.

78. *Field and Stream* 3 October 1874, 339; *American Cricketer* 13 June 1884, 96; *Amsterdam Recorder* 10 July 1910, 2; *American Cricketer* 15 July 1899, 118; October 1897, 143; *Milwaukee Sentinel* 2 September 1883, 3; 15 March 1884, 3; Bernard Korn, *The Story of Bay View* (Milwaukee: Historical Society, 1980), 69. Other well-known manufacturing companies that supported cricket teams included the Remington Typewriter Company of Ilion, New York, and the General Electric Company of Schenectady; *Spalding's Official Cricket Guide for 1907*, 92; *American Cricketer* 15 September 1902, 198.

79. *Daily Inter-Ocean* 8 September 1895, 10; Wilma Pesavento, "Sport and Recreation in the Pullman Experiment, 1880-1900," *Journal of Sport History* 9, no. 2 (Summer 1982), 49, 57.

80. *Clipper* 10 July 1858, 92; *Salt Lake Daily Herald* 31 July 1874, 3; *Uinta Chieftain* (Evanston, WY) 30 August 1884, 3; Elizabeth Stone, *Uinta County, Its Place in History* (Glendale, CA: Clark, 1924), 125; *Deseret News* 2 October 1878, 3.

81. *Butte Daily Miner* 22 June 1886, 4; *Livingston Enterprise* 14 July 1888, 1; *Helena Daily Herald* 24 May 1889, 8; *Tribune Review* (Butte) 19 August 1899, 3; John Rowe, *Hard Rock Men: Cornish Immigrants and the North American Mining Frontier* (New York: Barnes & Noble, 1974), 241. Cornish miners were also most likely behind the cricket organized in the little California mining community of Grass Valley; *Grass Valley National* 24 September 1861, 2; Ralph Mann, *After the Gold Rush: Society in Grass Valley and Nevada City, California, 1849-1878* (Palo Alto: Stanford University Press, 1982), 86.

82. *Pipestone County Star* 24 July 1891, 5; Wayne Fanebust, *Where the Sioux River Bends* (Freeman: Pine Hill, 1984), 206, 211, 242; *Ripon Press* 6 August 1906, 8; *Waushara Argus* (Lohrville, WI) 7 August 1907, 5; *Redgranite, Wisconsin* (Redgranite, 1986), 2; *Rocky Mountain Daily News* 23 July 1888, 6; *American Cricketer* 25 October 1888, 100; *Denver Times* 4 March 1900, 8.

83. *Copper Country Evening News* (Calumet) 10 May 1906, 7; 14 May 1906, 7; *Evening Journal* (Hancock, MI) 26 April 1909, 6; 6 August 1908, 8;

Paul Steele, *Tamarack Town* (Calumet, 1982), 21-23; Clarence Monette, *Upper Peninsula's Wolverine* (Lake Linden, 1992), 28-31.

84. Wayne Fanebust, *Where the Sioux River Bends,* 214; Paul Steele, *Tamarack Town,* 86; *Copper Country Evening News* 23 May 1906, 7; Andrea Kluge, "Creating Corporate Culture: Welfare Work in Industrial America, 1890-1921" (Ph.D. Diss., Emory University, 1992), 3.

85. *Sporting Life* 18 March 1885, 11; *Boston Globe* 12 July 1885, 8; *Copper Country Evening News* 17 June 1907, 5; Paul Steele, *Tamarack Town,* 52-53; *Racine Daily Journal* 13 August 1888, 3; *Portrait and Biographical Album of Racine and Kenosha Counties* (Chicago: Lake, 1892) 427; *Daily Inter-Ocean* 12 June 1887, 2; Wilma Pesavento, "'Men Must Play; Men Will Play,'" 237 n10, 240, 241, 242.

86. *Daily Morning Union* (Grass Valley) 4 June 1905, 2; *Providence Journal* 18 July 1888, 3; *Boston Globe* 14 June 1885, 6.

87. *Boston Globe* 20 July 1887, 2; *Evening Journal* 12 April 1909, 6; *Spalding's Official Cricket Guide for 1914,* 144; Arthur Thurner, *Rebels on the Range* (Linden: Forster, 1984), 7.

88. *San Francisco Call* 23 July 1894, 4.

89. *Daily Inter-Ocean* 5 August 1888, 17; *Pioneer Press* (St. Paul) 18 August 1890, 8; *Chicago Times* 4 November 1888, 19; *Daily Inter-Ocean* 25 May 1890, 22; *Milwaukee Sentinel* 28 July 1895, 15; John White, "The New Athletics," *Proceedings of the American Association of the Advancement of Physical Education* no. 3 (1889), 52; Theodore Knauff, *Athletics for Physical Culture* (New York: Tait, 1894), 398.

90. *New York Times* 2 September 1888, 8; *Public Ledger* 30 July 1888, 6; Bernon Prentice, *History of the Seabright Lawn Tennis and Cricket Club,* 11. The *Clipper* (31 October 1857, 220) had recommended women take up the game as early as 1857. Some American women reportedly umpired matches and held positions as cricket reporters during this period; *Wilkes* 16 September 1863, 52; *American Cricketer* 2 August 1893, 129.

91. *Sun* (New York) 23 August 1895, 4; *Amateur Athlete* 29 June 1897, 18; *Philadelphia Inquirer* 18 July 1891, 1; *Public Ledger* 13 October 1898, 20; 13 June 1899, 15.

92. *Public Ledger* 28 April 1898, 16; *Cricket Club Life* 16 May 1898, 4; *Choate Alumni Bulletin* Spring 1964, 12; *World* (New York) 15 November 1896, 4; Adelia Brainerd, "The Outdoor Woman," *Harpers Bazaar* 28 November 1896, 995. Sophia Richardson, "Tendencies in Athletics for Women in Colleges and Universities," *Appleton's Popular Science Monthly* February 1897, 522.

93. Robert Reinders, *End of an Era: New Orleans 1850-1860* (New Orleans; Pelican, 1964), 161-62; *Philadelphia Tribune* 3 May 1913, 4; J. Thomas Jable, "Sport in Philadelphia's African-American Community," in

George Eisen, ed., *Ethnicity and Sport in North American History* (Westport: Greenwood, 1994), 166; *Washington Reporter* (Washington, PA) 18 August 1869, 1.

94. *Spalding's Official Cricket Guide for 1908*, 71; *Spalding's Official Cricket Guide for 1910*, 19.

95. *San Francisco Call* 27 June 1896, 11. The St. George Club of New York had adopted something of an "affirmative action" hiring policy for its own organization as early as the 1870s. It is doubtful, however, that these cricket contacts between blacks and whites altered the typical American's racial attitudes during this time; *The Irish Cricketers in the United States*, 30; "The Crack Bat," *Harpers Weekly* 31 October 1908, 31.

96. *World* (New York) 13 September 1903, 11; *Brooklyn Daily Eagle* 13 September 1903, 6.

97. *Morning Oregonian* 11 August 1901, 8; *American Cricketer*, March 1925, 56; *Spalding's Official Cricket Guide for 1911*, 87. Another ethnic group that took an interest in cricket was the Portuguese immigrants of Fall River and New Bedford, Massachusetts. In all likelihood this explains the popularity of "bowlywicket" among the Portuguese descendants of that area; *Spalding's Official Cricket Guide for 1911*, 95; Alan Powers, "Bowlywicket: the Provenance of a New England Street Game," *Folklore* 93, no. 2 (1982), 165.

98. Clarence Monetta, *Early Days in Mohawk, Michigan* (Lake Linden: Curtin, 1980), 75. Shirley Ewart claims the descendants of Cornish miners continued to play cricket in Grass Valley up to the Second World War; Shirley Ewart, *Cornish Mining Families of Grass Valley, California* (New York: AMS, 1989), 155.

99. *Cricket Club Life* 1 April 1898, 5. It should not be assumed all working-class American cricket clubs were exclusively English. With the exception of its three English members, the Butte, Montana, team was made up entirely of novices. Some eastern Europeans also played for the Keweenaw Peninsula's Mohawk Club; *Butte Daily Miner* 26 August 1887, 2; *Copper Country Evening News* 1 July 1907, 5; Clarence Monette, *Early Days of Mohawk, Michigan*, 75.

100. *Racine Journal* 13 September 1865, 2; *Horae Scholasticae* 4 April 1881, 91; *College Mercury* 11 April 1874, 15; *American Cricketer* 31 May 1900, 114; *Harvard Crimson* 2 June 1903.

101. *American Cricketer* 20 June 1882, 80; *Public Ledger* 1 February 1888, 5; *Syracusaean for 1878* (Syracuse University) 77; *Sun* (Baltimore) 29 April 1884, 6; Edgar Kiracote, "Athletics and Physical Education in the Colleges of Virginia" (Ph.D. Diss., University of Virginia, 1932), 9; *Columbia Spectator* 5 May 1882, 83.

102. Clarence Rainwater, *The Play Movement in the United States* (Chicago: University of Chicago Press, 1922), 249, 346; *American Cricketer*

15 January 1904, 55-56; *Illustrated Sporting News* 21 May 1904, 23; *Wellesley College Catalogue for 1909,* 108.

103. The most egregious example of this was the decision by the St. Paul's school authorities, at the turn of the century, to ban student participation in all competitive sports except cricket; *Illustrated Sporting News* 22 August 1903, 2; *New York Times* 28 September 1878, 4.

Chapter 8

1. *New York Times* 21 August 1903, 8.
2. *American Cricketer* April 1894, 17.
3. *American Cricketer* 30 April 1900, 71; "International Cricket" *American* 15 October 1881, 8; John Lester, *A Century,* 17.
4. *Philadelphia Evening Bulletin* 19 August 1872, 4; Patrick Scott, "Cricket and the Religious World in the Victorian Period," 140; John Lester, "Another Cricket Invasion of England," 123.
5. George Newhall, "The Cricket Grounds of Germantown and a Plea for the Game," 175; *Public Ledger* 23 September 1872, 2.
6. *American Cricketer* 14 July 1881, 171; 27 January 1888, 5; February 1893, 5.
7. George Patterson, "Cricket in the United States," 653-54. Staten Island, Paterson, New Jersey, and Chicago all promoted junior cricket; *Forest and Stream* 30 August 1877, 69; *New York Times* 5 August 1893, 3; 19 August 1893, 3; *Daily Inter-Ocean* 24 July 1892, 6; 31 August 1890, 2; E. Digby Baltzell, *The Philadelphia Gentleman* (Glencoe: Free Press, 1958), 60; Robeson Perot, *A History of Athletics at the Germantown Academy* (Philadelphia: Jenkins, 1910), 72.
8. *New York Times* 31 October 1879, 4. At least one organized fathers vs sons match was played in Philadelphia in 1895; *American Cricketer,* 6 July 1895, 92.
9. J. Thomas Jable, "Social Class and the Sport of Cricket in Philadelphia, 1850-1880," *Journal of Sport History* 18, no. 2 (Summer 1991), 218; David Contosta, *Suburb in the City: Chestnut Hill, Philadelphia, 1850-1990* (Columbus: Ohio State University Press, 1992), 87; *Philadelphia Record* 18 September 1886, 7; *American Cricketer* 7 September 1892, 155; John Lester, "Another Cricket Invasion of England," 123.
10. A. G. Bradley, *Other Days* (London: Constable, 1913), 415; P. F. Warner, *Cricket in Many Climes,* 155. Quoted in *Cricket Club Life* 1 September 1897, 4.
11. *American Cricketer* 30 August 1893, 164; *Harpers Weekly* 26 September 1891, 735.
12. George Newhall, "The Cricket Grounds of Germantown and a Plea for the Game," 185; *World* (New York) 20 September 1865, 3; *Outing* October 1884, 47. The *Public Ledger* also insisted there were no "All Muggletons" or

"Dingley Dellers" among Philadelphia cricketers; *Public Ledger* 3 October 1878, 2; *Australasian* 7 October 1893, 633; *New York Times* 10 October 1878, 5; 26 January 1879, 8; *American Cricketer* 23 January 1879, 91.

13. *American Cricketer* 24 November 1884, 221; *Chicago Tribune* 29 June 1884, 10.

14. Thomas Wharton, "Inter-City and International Cricket in America," *Outing* June 1892, 180; *American Cricketer* 17 May 1894, 33.

15. Francis Iredale, *33 Years of Cricket* 140; Arthur Mailey, *10 for 66 and All That* (London: Phoenix, 1958), 152.

16. *American Cricketer* 30 September 1898, 103; 1 March 1899, 11.

17. "Cricket Clubs of Philadelphia," *Harpers Weekly* 29 September 1894, 929; *American Cricketer* 11 August 1887, 105; David Contosta, *Suburb in the City* 87-88; *American Cricketer* 29 June 1895, 86.

18. David Contosta, *A Philadelphia Family: The Houstons and Woodwards of Chestnut Hill* (Philadelphia: University of Pennsylvania Press, 1988), 28.

19. *The City of Philadelphia as It Appears in the Year 1893* (Trade League of Philadelphia, 1893), 127; John Lester, *A Century*, 252.

20. John Lester, *A Century*, 247-48.

21. *American Cricketer* 30 September 1898, 103; George Newhall, "The Cricket Grounds of Germantown and a Plea for the Game," 184.

22. *Forest and Stream* 11 September 1879, 635.

23. *New York Leader* 22 September 1860, 8; *Chicago Times* 2 August 1881, 5; *National Chronicle* 7 May 1870, 142.

24. *The Young America Cricket Club of Germantown: Reports of the Directors and Treasurer for the Year 1880*, 6; George Newhall, "The Cricket Grounds of Germantown and a Plea for the Game," 188; *World* (New York) 6 October 1878, 1.

25. *American Cricketer*, Thanksgiving Day 1887, 170; George Newhall, "The Cricket Grounds of Germantown and a Plea for the Game," 173; "Lord Hawke's Cricketers in Philadelphia," *Illustrated American* 17 October 1891, 391.

26. "Cricket Clubs of Philadelphia," *Harpers Weekly* 29 September 1894, 929; *Merion Cricket Club: Charter, By-Laws, Officers and Members* (Philadelphia, 1917), 3, 5, 7.

27. Mabel Priestman, "The Merion Cricket Club of Philadelphia," *International Studio* (April 1908), 80.

28. John Lester, *A Century* 54, 55; J. Thomas Jable, "Social Class and the Game of Cricket in Philadelphia, 1850-1880," 218; E. Digby Baltzell, *Philadelphia Gentleman*, 194.

29. *Clipper* 20 March 1880, 413; *Philadelphia Record* 12 June 1885, 3; *American Cricketer* 28 December 1892, 195; March 1894, 10; 30 August 1893, 164.

Notes to Chapter 8

30. *Public Ledger* 3 May 1903, 17; *Clipper* 25 August 1877, 170; 12 July 1879, 124; John Lester, *A Century*, 334.

31. *American Cricketer* 30 November 1880, 75.

32. *American Cricketer* 15 January 1902, 8.

33. *American Cricketer* 26 April 1888, 1; 17 February 1900, 19; 1 October 1905, 215; *Illustrated Sporting News* 17 October 1903, 14.

34. *American Cricketer* 1 April 1880, 99; March 1894, 9; *Public Ledger* 4 July 1894, 15.

35. *The Irish Cricketers in the United States*, 24; *American Cricketer* December 1895, 216; 1 June 1895, 49; 17 August 1895, 142.

36. *American Cricketer* 28 June 1877, 2.

37. *Australasian* 7 October 1893, 633; *American Cricketer* 31 January 1880, 2; *Clipper* 9 May 1885, 115; John Lester, *A Century*, 178.

38. *New York Times* 22 June 1865, 2; *Clipper* 27 October 1866, 237; 6 October 1866, 203; *World* (New York) 22 September 1865, 5; *Sunday Mercury* 18 September 1870, 6.

39. *The City of Philadelphia as It Appears in 1893*, 126; *American Cricketer* 25 December 1884, 231; *New York Times* 15 July 1884, 4.

40. *Clipper* 9 May 1885, 115; *Detroit Free Press* 14 July 1887, 8; *Pittsburgh Post* 11 April 1888, 6; *Chicago Tribune* 17 July 1885, 2; *Public Ledger* 8 August 1899, 12.

41. Thomas Wharton, "Inter-City and International Cricket in America," 172, 178; *American Cricketer* 16 September 1891, 169.

42. *Ball Players Chronicle* 30 June 1867, 5; *Clipper* 27 April 1878, 37; *The Cricketers Association of the United States: Proceedings of Convention Held in Philadelphia, April 17, 1878 and Constitution and Rules Adopted Thereat*, 4.

43. *World* (New York) 5 May 1878, 5; *Clipper* 14 April 1883, 155; *Sporting Life* 6 May 1885, 9; *World* (New York) 12 July 1903, 10.

44. *Daily Inter-Ocean* 21 June 1887, 6; *Public Ledger* 16 April 1890, 8; *American Cricketer* 27 January 1892, 2.

45. *Clipper* 9 May 1885, 115; *American Cricketer* 25 December 1884, 231; *Sporting Life* 23 August 1890, 10.

46. *Wilkes* 1 October 1859, 52; *Forest and Stream* 15 June 1876, 306.

47. Robert Viele, *First Annual Report on the Improvement of the Central Park, New York, January 1, 1857*, 39; Roy Rosenzweig, *The Park and the People: A History of Central Park* (Ithaca: Cornell University Press, 1992), 100, 116, *Clipper* 14 June 1856, 63.

48. *Clipper* 8 May 1858, 19.

49. *The Irish Cricketers in the United States* 89; *World* (New York) 12 May 1865, 5; *Clipper* 13 May 1865, 34. Chicago also forbade cricket playing in its public parks before the Civil War; Bessie Pierce, *A History of Chicago* vol. 2 (New York: Knopf, 1937), 340.

50. *Forest and Stream* 12 June 1879, 376; *Sun* (New York) 6 September 1885, 7; *Sporting Life* 16 September 1885, 5. It was claimed that the North Meadow area of the park had actually been part of the St. George's old Red House cricket ground; *Forest and Stream* 20 May 1880, 319.

51. *Nation* 2 September 1869, 191; *New York Times* 26 August 1893, 3; *World* (New York) 19 July 1896, 5; *Sun* (New York) 26 May 26, 1897, 9.

52. *Clipper* 12 September 1885, 414; *Outing* May 1886, 244; *Sun* (New York) 19 September 1885, 3; *Boston Globe* 8 May 1886, 2. Cricket seems to have first been played in Prospect Park in 1869; *World* 2 September 1869, 5; Henry Chadwick, "Cricket in the Metropolis," *Outing* April 1891, 43; *American Cricketer* 5 August 1898, 83

53. *World* (New York) 1 September 1865, 5. I have not found any evidence, at least from American sources, to support Cooper's belief that a dispute over the use of professionals disrupted the series after 1865; David Cooper, "Canadians Declare 'It Isn't Cricket.' A Colonial Rejection of the Imperial Game" (Master's Thesis: University of Toronto, 1995), 116.

54. *Oswego Commercial Advertiser and Times* July 24, 1867, 3; *Buffalo Courier* May 25, 1877, 2; *World* (New York) 1 September 1874, 8; *Clipper* 30 June 1877, 109; 1 August 1868, 13; *Detroit Free Press* 11 July 1877, 1.

55. *Clipper* 12 August 1876, 155, 157; *Sporting Times* 25 July 1868, 9; *Montreal Herald* 27 July 1868, 2; *American Cricketer* 25 September 1884, 177; *Outing* October 1886, 86; *Philadelphia Record* 8 August 1886, 7. There also seems to be no compelling reason why the 1921 match between Philadelphia and an eastern Canadian team should not qualify as an official match in this series; *American Cricketer* October 1921, 232; John Marder, *The International Series*, 318-19.

56. *American Cricketer* 25 August 1879, 35; *Clipper* 9 August 1879, 157; 11 September 1880, 195; *Forest and Stream* 9 September 1880, 415; *American Cricketer* 7 August 1879, 22; 9 July 1885, 65.

57. *American Cricketer* 10 October 1900, 284; 15 August 1904, 184.

58. *Clipper* 6 May 1875, 42; *Spalding's Official Cricket Guide for 1906*, 41; John Marder, *The International Series*, 99; *New York Times* 14 August 1886, 2; G. L. Jessop, *A Cricketers Log* (London: Hodder & Stoughton, 1926), 134; John Marder, *The International Series*, 221; T. C. Turner, "Cricket," *Outing* October 1895, 14; *American Cricketer* 15 October 1902, 212.

59. *Public Ledger* 30, 31 August 1898, 1; *Clipper* 23 September 1882, 431; 21 August 1886, 363.

60. *American Cricketer* 8 September 1887, 121; 25 April 1889, 3; 26 September 1889, 89; 5 October 1892, 170.

61. Fred Lillywhite, *The English Cricketers Trip to Canada and the United States*, 42-43; *Clipper* 17 October 1868, 22; *World* (New York) 25 September 1872, 8; 6 October 1878, 1; *American Cricketer* 10 October 1878, 68; John Lester, *A Century*, 67.

Notes to Chapter 8

62. *Lillywhite's Cricketers Annual for 1885*, 45, 47; *The Tour of the "Gentlemen of Philadelphia" in Great Britain in 1884* (Philadelphia: Allen, 1897), 43.

63. *New York Times* 18 August 1884, 5; *Outing* August 1888, 459; *Sporting Life* 9 July 1884, 10; 16 July 1884, 9.

64. Lord Hawke, *Recollections and Reminiscences*, 219; *Harper's Weekly* 26 September 1891, 735; *American Cricketer* 23 September 1891, 178.

65. *American Cricketer* 30 September 1891, 187; *Public Ledger* 28 September 1891, 3.

66. *New York Times* 18 September 1875, 2; Charles Blancke, "The International Cricket Match at Manheim," 991; *American Cricketer* 14 October 1891, 194.

67. *American Cricketer* 30 September 1891, 187; 14 October 1891, 193.

68. *Lillywhite's Cricketers Annual for 1897*, 25; *American Cricketer* 20 June 1889, 33; George Patterson, "Cricket in the United States," 657; *The Tour of the "Gentlemen of Philadelphia,"* 8.

69. *Public Ledger* 10 June 1903, 10; *Cricket* (London) 28 December 1893, 475; *Manchester Guardian* 20 July 1903, 4; Andrew Davis, "College Athletics," *Atlantic Monthly* 51 (1883), 681.

70. *Cricket* (London) 12 April 1888, 49-50; Charles Blancke, "Cricket in America," *Harper's Weekly* 26 September 1891, 732; *American Cricket Annual for 1893*, 17; John Lester, *A Century* 309.

71. *American Cricketer* 15 October 1895, 192; P. F. Warner, *Cricket in Many Climes*, 82; George Giffen, *With Bat and Ball* 97; Henry Lanier, "In the Field of International Sport," *Review of Reviews* November 1895, 578; John Lester, *A Century* 157; *Harpers Weekly* 12 October 1895, 978.

72. *American Cricketer* May 1896, 13; *Cricket* (London) 23 July 1903, 289; *Cricket Club Life* 15 October 1897, 5.

73. *Manchester Guardian* 10 July 1903, 4; John Lester, *A Century* 204-05; *Cricket* (London) 23 July 1903, 289.

74. "Obituary: John Barton King," *Cricket Quarterly* 4 (1966), 62; *Cricket* (London) 29 July 1897, 309-10; *Public Ledger* 1 August 1888, 6; F. M. Gilbert, "What Makes a Cricket Ball Curve in the Air?" *Strand Magazine* 15 (1899), 730.

75. "The Cricket Season of 1908," *Fortnightly Review* September 1908, 486; H. V. Hordern, *Googlies*, 55-56. Sandiford claims Hirst was the better practitioner of this type of bowling, but this wasn't the view of contemporary players; K. Sandiford, *Cricket and the Victorians*, 133; S. M. J. Woods, *My Reminiscences* (London: Chapman, 1925), 92; Arthur Mailey, *10 for 66 and All That*, 112; *New York Times* 16 August 1903.

76. John Lester, *A Century*, 166; *Public Ledger* 21 September 1896, 16; *Sheffield Daily Telegraph* 28 June 1897, 11; *Public Ledger* 5 August 1897, 3.

77. P. F. Warner, *Cricket in Many Climes*, 84; G. L. Jesso, *A Cricketers Log*, 60; *Manchester Guardian* 8 July 1903, 3; 27 June 1903, 5.

78. *American Cricketer* 15 July 1903, 123; *Manchester Guardian* 7 July 1903, 5.

79. *American Cricketer* 18 May 1895, 35; *Public Ledger* 21 September 1896, 16; *American Cricketer* 21 September 1892, 162; John Lester, *A Century*, 241; *Manchester Guardian* 9 July 1903, 4.

80. *American Cricketer* 15 October 1903, 187; *Illustrated Sporting News* 5 September 1903, 8-9.

81. *Public Ledger* 25 September 1894, 1; 1 October 1894, 1.

82. *Public Ledger* 19 September 1898, 17; *Harpers Weekly* 12 October 1895, 978.

83. *Public Ledger* 2 October 1893, 13; *American Cricketer* 4 October 1893, 204; *Sun* (New York) 30 September 1893, 3; *Public Ledger* 6 October 1896, 1.

84. *Public Ledger* 2 October 1893, 13, *Australasian* 18 November 1893, 902; *Sheffield Daily Telegraph* 28 June 1897, 11; *Public Ledger* 7 June 1897, 19; 21 August 1895, 5.

85. *Wisden's Cricketers Almanack for 1898*, 308; *Manchester Guardian* 8 June 1897, 7; *Public Ledger* 18 June 1897, 6; *Wisdens Cricketers Almanack for 1898*, 302, 313, 315. Nottingham even enrolled 55-year-old Alfred Shaw into their lineup against the Philadelphians; *Wisden's Cricketers Almanack for 1898*, 315.

86. *Manchester Guardian* 18 June 1897, 11; *Wisden's Cricketers Almanack for 1898*, 314; *Public Ledger* 10 July 1897, 17.

87. *Sussex Daily News* June 18, 1897; *Cricket* (London) 5 August 1897, 334; *Cricket Club Life* 1 September 1897, 5; *Sheffield and Rottingham Independent* 29 June 1897, 8.

88. "The Tour of the Philadelphia Cricketers," *Harper's Weekly* 14 August 1897, 816; *Manchester Guardian* 2 August 1897, 9; *Lillywhite's Cricketers Annual for 1897*, 26; *New York Times* 8 June 1897, 5.

89. *Lillywhite's Cricketers Annual for 1897*, 25; *Wisden's Cricketers Almanack for 1898*, 303; *Public Ledger* 12 July 1897, 16.

90. *New York Times* 1 August 1897, 13; *Public Ledger* 3 June 1897, 17; "The Tour of the Philadelphia Cricketers," *Harper's Weekly*, 816; *Harper's Weekly* 24 July 1897, 746.

91. *Public Ledger* 26 July 1897, 15.

92. *Public Ledger* 11 October 1899, 18; T. C. Turner, "International Cricket in America," *Harper's Weekly* 19 August 1905, 1192; John Lester, *A Century*, 217, 240.

93. *American Cricketer* 12 September 1903, 166; *Manchester Guardian* 11 June 1903, 5.

94. *Manchester Guardian* 18 June 1903, 4; 20 June 1903, 5.

95. *Public Ledger* 23 June 1903, 10; *American Cricketer* 15 August 1903, 129; *London Times* 10 August 1903, 1; *Public Ledger* 13 August 1903, 10; *American Cricketer* 13 October 1881, 246.

96. *American Cricketer* 15 July 1903, 123; *Manchester Guardian* 22 June 1903, 4; 7 July 1903, 5; *American Cricketer* 15 July 1903, 111; *Manchester Evening News* 7 July 1903, 3; *Nottingham Evening Post* 20 June 1903.

97. *Wisden's Cricketers Almanack for 1909,* 351, 362; H. V. Hordern, *Googlies,* 87.

98. *Wisden's Cricketers Almanack for 1909,* 350; *Daily News* (London) 31 July 1908, 2.

99. *Public Ledger* 5 April 1897, 18; *London Times* 10 April 1903, 5; *New York Times* 16 August 1903, 8; *New York Tribune* 10 August 1903, 8; *American Cricketer* 15 August 1903, 160.

100. John Lester, *A Century,* 207.

101. *Public Ledger* 4 June 1911, 3; *American Cricketer* 17 February 1900, 19; July 1911, 148, 156; John Lester, *A Century,* 239, 251.

102. *American Cricketer* 24 November 1884, 221; 26 April 1888, 2-3; 25 May 1895, 44; *Public Ledger* 6 April 1896, 21. According to the LBW rule adopted by the Philadelphians, an umpire could declare a batter out so long as he believed the ball would have hit the wicket, regardless of where it pitched; *American Cricketer* 15 January 1903, 8.

103. *World* (New York) 30 July 1879, 2; *Boston Globe* 19 May 1873, 5; *Public Ledger* 12 April 1889, 6; *Daily Inter-Ocean* 10 June 1889, 3.

104. *Porters* 7 May 1859, 149; *Clipper* 30 May 1874, 67; *Sporting Life* 12 April 1890, 13; *Clipper* 17 January 1885, 700.

105. *American Cricketer* 21 May 1885, 19; *Omaha World Herald* 19 September 1897, 20; *Spalding's Official Cricket Guide for 1912,* 79.

106. *Memphis Daily Appeal* 19 September 1867, 3.

107. *American Cricketer* 5 October 1882, 181; *New York Times* 6 March 1890, 3; 21 March 1890, 1.

108. *American Cricketer* 24 November 1884, 221; *Public Ledger* 28 March 1911, 6.

109. *Outing* June 1890, 228; *Boston Globe* 6 June 1890, 2; 12 June 1890, 3; *American Cricketer* March 1927, 101; *Cricket* (London) 26 November 1903, 450; *American Cricketer* July 1911, 147.

110. As far back as 1849, the *Spirit of the Times* (11 August 1849, 295) claimed that no matter how unsatisfactory unfinished matches were, there seemed to be no practical alternative.

111. "American Cricket," *American* 7 May 1881, 57; *Detroit Free Press* 20 July 1882, 1.

112. *American Cricketer* 18 May 1895, 34; *Clipper* 8 June 1872, 75. Other suggestions included changing overs only at the fall of a wicket or after twenty deliveries; *American Cricketer* 5 October 1882, 176; *American Chronicle of Sports and Pastimes* 18 June 1868, 202; *New York Times* 20 September 1885, 8.

113. *American Cricketer* 24 March 1881, 96; 22 August 1878, 38; 16 July 1885, 73; "American Cricket," *American*, 57; George Patterson, "Cricket in the United States," 658; *American Cricketer* April 1913, 75; *Cricket* (London) 26 November 1903, 450.

114. *The City of Philadelphia as It Appears in the Year 1893*, 127; *Cricket* (London) 29 October 1903, 433.

115. *Public Ledger* 28 February 1895, 15; 3 August 1913, 4.

116. John Lester, *A Century* 268; *American Cricketer* March 1926, 243; *Public Ledger* 4 September 1920, 13. Other Americans who enjoyed long associations with cricket included Daniel Baker, the antebellum Newark cricketer who, in 1888, was still serving as that club's vice-president, and the antebellum president of the Amsterdam, New York, Cricket Club, Isaac Jackson, who, as late as 1906, was still umpiring matches in his community; *Outing* June 1888, 283; *Clipper* 16 April 1859, 410; *Amsterdam Evening Recorder* 17 July 1906, 2. Philadelphia's mind-set on this point was so ingrained that even Lester, writing in 1951, could only reiterate, on cricket's behalf, the old nineteenth-century ethical arguments; John Lester, *A Century*, 282.

Conclusion

1. An example of this misconception can be seen in Steven Pope's argument that baseball became America's dominant nineteenth-century team sport not because of national characteristics or modernization but because "certain groups of people" were able "to legitimize particular values and activities and to discount competing alternatives"; S. W. Pope, *Patriotic Games: Sporting Traditions in the American Imagination, 1876-1926* (New York: Oxford University Press, 1997), 179.

2. *Omaha World Herald* 19 September 1897, 20.

3. *Clipper* 3 December 1870, 277; *Turf, Field and Farm* 11 November 1870, 300; *College Mercury* (Racine College) 1 December 1870, 190.

Bibliographic Essay

Any student of American cricket history must begin with a debt of gratitude for Melvin Adelman's *A Sporting Time* (Urbana: University of Illinois Press, 1986) and George Kirsch's The *Creation of American Team Sports* (Urbana: University of Illinois Press, 1989). Not only do these two studies represent the first extensive analytical examinations of this subject, they are indispensable for understanding the broader mid-nineteenth century social and cultural context within which early American sports arose.

Both these studies work within the analytical framework of urban modernism in explaining the rise of early American sports, but students of this subject should also consult Carl Stempel's "Towards a Historical Sociology of Sport in the United States: 1825-1875" (Ph.D. Diss., University of Oregon, 1992), which argues, as an alternative theory, that American sports developed through a historical dialectic between social classes.

Until now John Lester's *A Century of Philadelphia Cricket* (Philadelphia: University of Pennsylvania Press, 1951) and John Marder's *The International Series* (London: Kaye & Ward, 1968) were the only full-length works on American cricket history. Lester's work provides valuable firsthand accounts and pen portraits of late nineteenth-century Philadelphia cricket, while Marder's stands as a useful documentary resource but neither treats his subject in a critical or analytical manner.

The most valuable primary sources for American cricket history are the major nineteenth-century sports periodicals. In the pre-Civil war years these included the *Spirit of the Times,* the *Clipper, Porter's Spirit of the Times* and *Wilkes Spirit of the Times*.

For the 1860s and 1870s, the best sources were the *Spirit of the Times and New York Sportsman,* the *Ball Players Chronicle* (and its successor the *National Chronicle), Turf Field and Farm* and the *New England Base Ballist*.

During the 1880s and 1890s, cricket was most extensively covered by *Outing, Sporting Life, Forest & Stream,* the *Amateur Athlete* and the *Illustrated Sporting News*.

Dozens of newspapers were consulted for this study, from communities both large and small throughout the United States. In the pre-Civil War era, the papers that provided the best cricket coverage were the *New York Morning News*, the *Albion*, the *Anglo-American* and the New York *Herald*.

During the 1860s and 1870s the best papers were the New York *World*, the Philadelphia *Sunday Mercury* and the New York *Sunday Mercury*.

A number of papers carried fairly extensive cricket reports over the last decades of the nineteenth century, among them the Philadelphia *Public Ledger*, the Chicago *Daily Inter-Ocean*, the *Boston Globe*, the *Detroit Free Press*, the St. Paul *Pioneer Press*, the *San Francisco Call* and the *Omaha World Herald*.

Of the sports-specific publications, by far the most valuable was the *American Cricketer*, though its coverage was always heavily slanted toward Philadelphia cricket. The *American Cricket Annual*, which after 1904 became *Spalding's Official Cricket Guide*, provided useful documentary material on late nineteenth-century and early twentieth-century American cricket.

Dozens of institutional histories were consulted for information on school, college, and university cricket, but most valuable were student publications themselves. Here the most useful were the *University Quarterly*, the Racine *College Mercury*, the St. Paul's *Horae Scholasticae*, the Westtown School *Westonian*, the Columbia University *Acta Columbiana*, the Harvard University *Crimson*, the *Trinity Tablet*, the Princeton University *Nassau Monthly*, the Amherst College *Olio*, and the University of Michigan *University Chronicle*.

Inquiries were also made to dozens of historical societies throughout the country for cricket-related material, a search that uncovered valuable and, in some instances, previously undocumented items, such as the handwritten constitution of Boston's Crescent Cricket Club (Lynn Historical Society), the constitution and by-laws of the Cranston, Rhode Island, Mechanics Cricket Club (Rhode Island Historical Society), some late nineteenth-century yearbooks of the St. George Cricket Club (New York Historical Society), several annual reports of the Staten Island Cricket Club (Staten Island Institute of Arts and Sciences), as well as a near complete run of yearbooks for the Baltimore Cricket Club (Maryland Historical Society).

Appendix
Directory of American Cricket Clubs, 1837-1914

State	Community	Club/Organization	Reference
ALABAMA	Mobile	Mobile	*Evening Picayune* 16 May 1860, 1
ARIZONA	Clifton	Clifton	*Spalding's Official Cricket Guide for 1909*, 119
	Phoenix	Phoenix	*Arizona Weekly Journal* 30 Oct. 1895, 2
	Prescott	Prescott	*Arizona Weekly Journal* 30 Oct. 1895, 2
CALIFORNIA	Alameda	Alameda	*Spalding's Official Cricket Guide for 1912* 85
	Auburn	Auburn	*American Cricketer* June 1897, 103
	Azusa	Azusa	*American Cricketer* 15 July, 1898, 57
	Bakersfield	British Club	*San Francisco Call* 2 Sept. 1894, 18
	Calistoga	Lake County	*San Francisco Call* 1 July 1894, 18
	Duarte	Duarte/Covena	*Los Angeles Times* 25 May 1899, 10
	Grass Valley	Athletic	*Grass Valley Union* 1 May 1888, 3
		Grass Valley	*California Spirit of the Times* 27 May 1861, 2
		North Banner	*Grass Valley Union* 3 May 1888, 3
		Union	*Grass Valley Union* 18 May 1884, 3
		Victoria Lodge	*Daily Morning Union* 24 May 1905, 2
	Kenswick	Kenswick	*Outing* Dec. 1899, 326

211

212 · The Tented Field

Lakeport	Lakeport	*San Francisco Chronicle* 9 July 1899, 24
Loomis	Lake County	*American Cricketer* Dec. 1896, 80
	Citrus Colony	*San Francisco Call* 24 Nov. 1893, 10
	Placer County	*Outing* Dec. 1896, 302
Los Angeles	Arden Rugby Club	*Spalding's Official Cricket Guide for 1914*, 147
	Los Angeles	*Los Angeles Times* 25 May 1899, 10
Lower Lake	Burrs Valley	*San Francisco Call* 23 May 1891, 3
Mill Valley	Mill Valley	*San Francisco Call* 23 May 1896, 10
Nevada City	Capital	*Sporting Life* 17 Dec. 1884, 10
	Nevada County	*American Cricketer* May 1896, 14
	Prince Albert Lodge	*Daily Morning Union* 24 May 1905, 2
Oakland	Oakland	*Clipper* 17 May 1879, 61
Pomona	Pomona	*American Cricketer* 15 July 1898, 57
Sacramento	Sacramento	*American Chronicle of Sports and Pastimes* 19 March 1868, 92
San Diego	San Diego	*San Diego Union* 18 Nov. 1899, 5
San Francisco	All-Comers	*San Francisco Chronicle* 24 July 1899, 8
	Bankers & Insurance	*San Francisco Chronicle* 24 July 1899, 8
	Barbarians	*Spalding's Official Cricket Guide for 1913*, 89
	Bohemian Club	*Outing* June 1895, 64
	California	*San Francisco Chronicle* 16 April 1869, 3
	City College	*California Spirit of the Times* 16 March 1861, 3
	Eagle	*California Spirit of the Times* 6 Oct. 1860, 3
	Excelsior	*California Spirit of the Times* 16 March 1861, 2
	Golden State	*Spalding's Official Cricket Guide for 1913*, 89

	Knickerbocker Athletic Club	*Outing* Dec. 1899, 326
	Mercantile Marine	*San Francisco Chronicle* 16 Aug. 1896, 24
	Merian	*San Francisco Bulletin* 14 July 1881, 2
	Occident	*Clipper* 24 Sept. 1878, 205
	Pacific	*San Francisco Call* 22 March 1891, 2
	Pioneer	*California Spirit of the Times* 2 July 1859, 2
	Presidio	*Outing* Jan. 1896, 68
	St. George	*Alta California* 12 July 1874, 1
	San Francisco	*Porters* 8 Nov. 1856, 105
	San Francisco County	*Spalding's Official Cricket Guide for 1909*, 109
	Trinity School	*American Cricketer* 18 Dec. 1892, 194
	Union	*California Spirit of the Times* 2 July 1859, 2
	Young America	*Clipper* 24 May 1873, 58
	Young Eagle	*California Spirit of the Times* 6 April 1861, 2
	Wanderers	*Spalding's Official Cricket Guide for 1912*, 89
	Western Addition	*Clipper* 21 April 1879, 18
San Jose	San Jose	*Outing* Nov. 1898, 217
	Santa Clara County	*Outing* Dec. 1897, 306
	Country Club	*Outing* Oct. 1899, 108
Santa Cruz		*Spalding's Official Cricket Guide for 1908*, 97
San Mateo	San Mateo	*Spalding's Official Cricket Guide for 1912*, 85
Santa Monica	Santa Monica	*American Cricketer* 3 June 1891, 49
Santa Rosa	Santa Rosa	

COLORADO

Central City	Central City	*American Cricketer* 25 Oct. 1888, 100
Colorado Springs	Colorado Springs	*American Cricketer* 24 Oct. 1889, 99

214 · *The Tented Field*

	Cripple Creek	*Spalding's Official Cricket Guide for 1906*, 70
Cripple Creek	Denver	*Denver Times* 26 Feb. 1899, 6
Denver	Denver Athletic Club	*Rocky Mountain News* 5 July 1906, 8
	Thistles	*American Cricketer* 25 Dec. 1884, 226
Nevadaville	Bald Mountain	*Rocky Mountain Daily News* 23 July 1888, 6
	Mountain Daisy	*Denver Times* 17 June 1899, 3
Sedalia	Douglas County	*American Cricketer* 25 Dec. 1884, 226

CONNECTICUT

Ansonia	Ansonia	*Spirit* 7 Nov. 1857, 458
Bridgeport	Bridgeport	*Spirit* 7 Nov. 1857, 458
	Calthrops School	*Herald* (New York) 13 June 1856, 8
	Wheeler & Wilson Co.	*Clipper* 9 July 1859, 92
Danielsonville	Quinnebauge	*Clipper* 1 Aug. 1857, 119
Derby	Derby	*Spalding's Official Cricket Guide for 1911*, 99
Hanover	Hanover	*Clipper* 22 July 1871, 124
Hartford	Hartford	*Clipper* 18 July 1857, 99
	Trinity College	*Trinity Tablet* 22 May 1880, 66
Hazardville	Hazardville	*Clipper* 18 July 1857, 99
	Scitico	*Clipper* 12 Dec. 1857, 268
Meriden	Britannia Co.	*Boston Globe* 3 May 1885, 6
	Meriden	*Clipper* 11 Sept. 1869, 181
	Meriden Silver Plate	*Meriden Daily Republican* 28 July 1873, 2
Middletown	Agallian	*Sunday Mercury* (Philadelphia) 22 July 1866, 4
	United Mechanics	*Sunday Mercury* (Philadelphia) 22 July 1866, 4
	Wesleyan University	*University Quarterly* Oct. 1860, 3

Naugatuck	Naugatuck	*Spirit* 29 Oct. 1853, 432
	Union Knife Co.	*Waterbury American* 14 Oct. 1853, 2
New Britain	New Britain	*Waterbury American* 30 Sept. 1859, 2
New Haven	Ben Franklin	*Spirit* 4 Oct. 1851, 396
	New Haven	*Clipper* 5 Sept. 1885, 394
	Sons of St. George	*Clipper* 12 March 1887, 829
	Yale University	*Sun* (New York) 4 May 1891, 4
Northfield	Northfield	*Clipper* 2 Oct. 1875, 213
Norwalk	Norwalk	*Outing* Sept. 1890, 93
Plainfield	Plainfield	*Clipper* 9 Oct.1858, 197
Plymouth	Young America	*Spirit* 13 Oct. 1855, 409
Plymouth Hollow	Plymouth Hollow	*Clipper* 16 Oct. 1858, 205
Rockville	Rockville	*Sunday Mercury* 2 Sept. 1860, 5
South Meriden	Meriden Britannica	*Clipper* 26 April 1873, 29
	South Meriden	*Clipper* 11 Sept. 1875, 187
	Union	*Clipper* 11 Sept. 1869, 181
	Wilcox Silver Plate Co.	*Meriden Daily Republican* 4 Aug. 1873, 2
Southington	Southington	*Clipper* 11 Sept. 1875, 187
Stamford	Stamford	*New York Times* 30 July1899, 8
Thomaston	Young America	*Clipper* 26 April 1873, 29
Vernon	Vernon	*Spirit* 17 Sept. 1853, 367
Wallingford	Rosemary Hall	*New York Times* 6 June 1898, 12
	Wallingford	*Clipper* 29 July 1871, 131
Waterbury	Naugatuck Valley	*Clipper* 12 Dec. 1857, 265
	Waterville Knife Co.	*Waterbury American* 14 Oct. 1853, 2

216 · *The Tented Field*

Waterville	Waterville	*Spirit* 21 Sept. 1850, 367
West Winstead	West Winsted	*Clipper* 16 Oct. 1858, 205
Westerly	Granite	*Providence Daily Journal* 29 Aug. 1879, 1
Windsor	Windsor	*Spirit* 11 Sept. 1858, 368
Winsted	Eagle	*Waterbury American* 8 July 1853, 2
	Winsted	*Clipper* 16 Oct. 1858, 205

DELAWARE

Newcastle	Olympian	*Clipper* 28 July 1860, 117
Wilmington	Delaware	*Sporting Life* 18 May 1887, 8
	St. George	*American Cricketer* 11 Oct. 1883, 193

DISTRICT OF COLUMBIA

	American	*Clipper* 4 Oct. 1865, 212
	Howard University	*Public Ledger* 1 Feb. 1888, 5
	National Peverelly	Peverelly, *Book of American Pastimes*, 492
	Washington, D.C.	*Clipper* 10 Oct. 1863, 204

FLORIDA

Acton	Acton	*Florida Times Union* 5 Jan. 1887, 2
Ft. Meade	Ft. Meade	*Florida Times Union* 5 Jan. 1887, 2
Jacksonville	Jacksonville	*Florida Times Union* 25 March 1898, 2

GEORGIA

Atlanta	Atlanta	*Spalding's Official Cricket Guide for 1911*, 125
Macon	Muscogee	*Spirit* 20 April 1844, 90
Savannah	Savannah	*Wilkes* 26 Nov. 1859, 181

Appendix · 217

HAWAII

Honolulu Honolulu *Hawaiian Gazette* 4 Feb. 1874, 3
Pacific *Clipper* 19 Feb. 1881, 378
Wide-Awakes *Clipper* 19 Feb. 1881, 378

ILLINOIS

Albion Albion *Outing* Jan. 1887, 374
Aurora Aurora *Daily Inter-Ocean* 28 July 1889, 2
Bloomington Bloomington *Daily Pantagraph* 31 July 1857, 3
Calumet Calumet *Spalding's Official Cricket Guide for 1906*, 55
 Abstract *American Cricketer* 15 Sept. 1894, 172
Chicago Albion *Daily Inter-Ocean* 7 June 1886, 2
 Austin *Chicago Tribune* 17 May 1885, 14
 Bankers Athletic Club *Daily Inter-Ocean* 27 Aug. 1891, 2
 Bessemer Steel *Chicago Tribune* 29 Sept. 1874, 8
 British Consul *Chicago Tribune* 25 May 1857, 1
 British Public Schools *Daily Inter-Ocean* 24 May 1896, 10
 Chicago *Chicago Tribune* 20 May 1876, 5
 Columbian *Chicago Tribune* 6 Aug. 1893, 7
 Douglas Park *Daily Inter-Ocean* 9 Aug. 1896, 11
 Emeralds *Daily Inter-Ocean* 29 June 1890, 2
 Garfield *Daily Inter-Ocean* 27 May 1887, 2
 Haddock, Valitte & Rickords *Chicago Tribune* 6 Sept. 1891, 4
 Handy Co. *Chicago Tribune* 6 Sept. 1891, 4
 Hobson *Chicago Tribune* 13 June 1891, 6
 Hyde Park *Chicago Tribune* 21 June 1908, 3
 Lake Shore *American Cricketer* 13 July 1895, 103

Lawndale   *Chicago Tribune* 13 June 1891, 6
Lincoln Park   *Chicago Tribune* 1 Sept. 1868, 1
Metropolitan   *Spalding's Official Cricket Guide for 1906*, 55
Northern Trust Co.   *Chicago Tribune* 3 Oct. 1897, 4
Ogden   *Chicago Tribune* 23 May 1871, 4
Oplain   *Chicago American* 4 Sept. 1840, 3
Phenix   *Daily Inter-Ocean* 18 May 1892, 6
Prairie   *Chicago Tribune* 16 Sept. 1857, 1
Rovers   *Chicago Tribune* 13 June 1891, 6
St. George   *Daily Inter-Ocean* 27 May 1887, 2
St. James   *Daily Inter-Ocean* 25 July 1896, 6
St. Lawrence   *Daily Inter-Ocean* 25 May 1896, 4
South Park   *Spalding's Official Cricket Guide for 1910*, 101
Swifts   *Chicago Tribune* 13 June 1891, 6
Thistles   *Chicago Tribune* 13 June 1891, 6
Tinkhams   *Chicago Tribune* 27 June 1857, 1
Union   *Chicago Tribune* 11 Aug. 1857, 1
Union Stockyards   *American Cricketer* 25 May 1882, 46
United   *Daily Inter-Ocean* 24 May 1896, 11
Wanderers   *Daily Inter-Ocean* 6 June 1886, 4
West Chicago   *Daily Inter-Ocean* 5 July 1883, 6
Wonders   *Daily Inter-Ocean* 5 July 1883, 6
Worlds Fair   *Chicago Tribune* 31 Aug. 1893, 6
Zingari   *Daily Inter-Ocean* 31 May 1893, 10

Appendix · 219

Cicero	Cicero	*Daily Inter-Ocean* 29 June 1890, 2
Elgin	Elgin	*Daily Inter-Ocean* 7 Aug. 1887, 6
Freeport	Freeport	*Clipper* 10 July 1858, 91
Galena	Galena	*Galena Gazette* 21 Aug. 1866, 3
Joliet	Joliet	*Clipper* 22 Nov. 1856, 244
La Grange	La Grange	*American Cricket Annual for 1899*, 68
Lake Forest	Lake Forest	*Spalding's Official Cricket Guide for 1914*, 141
Lockport	Lockport	*Clipper* 22 Nov. 1856, 244
Oak Park	Oak Park	*Chicago Tribune* 2 Aug. 1874, 16
Pullman	Pullman	*Daily Inter-Ocean* 19 June 1882, 6
Rockford	Rockford	*Clipper* 14 May 1859, 28
Waukegan	Waukegan	*Spalding's Official Cricket Guide for 1914*, 141
Zion	Zion	*American Cricketer* 10 July 1903, 123

INDIANA

Elkhart	St. George	*Democratic Union* 22 May 1874, 3
Indianapolis	Indianapolis	*Clipper* 11 Nov. 1865, 242
	Pioneer	*Indianapolis Daily Journal* 1 July 1859, 3
	St. George	*American Cricket Annual for 1899*, 68

IOWA

Akron	Akron	Van der Zee, *British in Iowa*, 191
Cherokee	Cherokee	*Milwaukee Sentinel* 9 Oct. 1881, 2
Clinton	Clinton	*Porters* 20 June 1857, 245
Council Bluffs	Council Bluffs	*Omaha Republican* 3 June 1888, 2
Davenport	Blackhawk	*Clipper* 6 Nov. 1858, 229
	Davenport	*Daily Iowa State Democrat* 30 June 1859, 1

Decorah	Decorah	*Forest and Stream* 4 Dec. 1873, 266
Des Moines	Des Moines	*Iowa State Journal* 27 June 1857, 3
Independence	Independence	*Weekly Independence Civilian* 10 May 1860, 3
LeMars	LeMars	*Clipper* 13 May 1882, 128
Lyons	Lyons	*Clipper* 15 Aug. 1857, 153
Muscatine	Muscatine	*Clipper* 21 June 1862, 7
Portlandville	Portlandville	R. Smith, "Sports and Games in Western Iowa," *Palimpsest* vol. 65 (1984), 25
Sibley	Sibley	*Osceola County Tribune* 1 Aug. 1884
Sioux City	Sioux City	*Pioneer Press* 3 Aug.1896, 3
West Fork	West Fork	Van der Zee, *British in Iowa*, 191

KANSAS

Emporia	Emporia	*Emporia News* 28 June 1886
Topeka	Santa Fe	*Spalding's Official Cricket Guide for 1914*, 145
	Topeka	*Emporia News* 28 June 1886
Victoria	Victoria	Raish, *Victoria*, 52
Wyandotte City	Wyandotte City	*Ball Players Chronicle* 19 Sept. 1867, 7

KENTUCKY

Frankfort	Kentucky Military Institute	*Porters* 28 March 1857, 60
Lexington	Lexington	*Porters* 11 June 1859, 229
Louisville	Kentucky	*Louisville Democrat* 4 Aug. 1867, 1
	2nd U.S. Infantry	*Louisville Democrat* 10 Oct. 1868, 1
Maysville	Maysville	*Maysville Eagle* 23 June 1860, 2
	Hoit Junior	*Clipper* 4 July 1868, 103
Newport	Kentucky	*Wilkes* 18 May 1861, 165

LOUISIANA

	Paris	*Wilkes* 12 Nov. 1859, 145
	Vanceburg	*Maysville Eagle* 18 Sept. 1866, 3
New Orleans	Cotton Exchange	*Evening Picayune* 3 April 1898, 8
	Crescent	*Evening Picayune* 19 May 1859, 1
	Louisiana	*Evening Picayune* 27 April 1873, 3
	New Orleans Lawn Tennis Club	*Evening Picayune* 14 Aug. 1898, 8
	Pelican	*Evening Picayune* 25 Aug. 1859, 2
	Victoria	*Evening Picayune* 3 April 1898, 8

MAINE

Bangor	Bangor	*Porters* 30 July 1859, 341
Biddeford	Biddeford	*Clipper* 12 June 1858, 60
Brunswick	Bowdoin College	*Bowdoin Bugle* June 1859
	Olympic	*Bowdoin Bugle* Nov. 1860
Portland	Columbian	*Ball Players Chronicle* 30 June 1867, 5
Sanford	Sanford	*Boston Globe* 7 May 1885, 6

MARYLAND

Annapolis	Naval Academy	*Wilkes* 3 Dec. 1859, 205
Baltimore	Atlantic	*Clipper* 1 Aug. 1860, 132
	Baltimore	*Baltimore American* 8 Oct. 1859, 1
	Catonsville Country Club	*American Cricketer* 10 Aug. 1895, 133
	Chesapeake	*Porters* 16 July 1859, 309
	Franklin	*Porters* 11 June 1859, 229
	Hygeia	*Clipper* 28 July 1860, 117
	Ivanhoe	*Sun* (Baltimore) 25 Oct. 1860, 1

222 · *The Tented Field*

	Johns Hopkins University		*American Cricketer* 8 May 1884, 38
	Maryland		*Porters* 8 Oct. 1859, 89
	Monumental		*Sun* (Baltimore) 25 Oct. 1860, 1
	Pastime		*Sun* (Baltimore) 30 Aug. 1865, 1
	Patapsco		*Clipper* 28 July 1860, 117
	Pickwick		*Porters* 8 Oct. 1859, 89
	Sons of St. George		*Washington Post* 14 July 1913, 6
MASSACHUSETTS	Amesbury	Amesbury	*Clipper* 12 May 1860, 31
	Amherst College	Amherst	*Olio for 1861*, 30
	Andover	Andover	*Boston Globe* 2 Aug. 1875, 5
	Andover Theological Seminary		*University Quarterly* Oct. 1860, 334
	Olympic		*Porters* 23 July 1859, 324
	Phillips Academy		*Philo Mirror* July 1858, 32
	Primitive Methodist		*Amateur Athlete* 20 May 1897, 113
	Merrimack	Belvidere	*Lowell Citizen & News* 28 Sept. 1859, 2
	United Shoe Machinery	Beverly	*Spalding's Official Cricket Guide for 1913*, 61
	Bay State	Boston	*Porters* 13 Aug. 1859, 373
	Boers		*American Cricket Annual for 1897*, 107
	Boston		*Herald* 8 Aug. 1845, 2
	Boston Athletic Assoc.		*New York Tribune* 14 June 1890, 3
	Boston Belting Co.		*Boston Globe* 3 Sept. 1889, 8
	Boston Juniors		*Clipper* 15 June 1872, 83
	Bunker Hill		*Clipper* 7 May 1859, 19
	Cambridge		*Clipper* 24 July 1875, 130

Caribbean	*Spalding's Official Cricket Guide for 1913*, 61
City Points	*Boston Globe* 18 June 1890, 10
East Boston	*Boston Globe* 27 May 1894, 6
East Boston Reserves	*Boston Globe* 12 July 1903, 4
East Cambridge	*Spirit* 13 Oct.1855, 409
Franklin	*American Cricket Annual for 1901*, 72
Guinise	*Boston Globe* 23 Aug. 1896, 7
Harvard University	*Boston Evening Transcript* 30 Sept. 1867, 4
Hearts of Oak	*Daily Evening Transcript* 4 Aug. 1890, 2
Hyde Park	*Boston Globe* 31 May 1888 3
Longwood	Minton, *One Hundred Years of Longwood* (1977)
Mayflower	*Clipper* 29 Aug. 1874, 173
Millbury	*Boston Globe* 3 May 1885, 6
St. Mary	*Boston Globe* 5 July 1898, 4
Sefton	*Boston Globe* 30 Aug. 1891, 5
Shamrocks	*Boston Globe* 2 June 1889, 3
South End	*Spirit* 5 June 1858, 200
Star & Thistle	*Saturday Evening Gazette* 1 Nov. 1856, 8
Suffolk	*Boston Evening Transcript* 30 Sept. 1867, 4
Temple School	*Boston Globe* 19 June 1886, 8
Terra Nova	*Boston Globe* 3 Aug. 1884, 8
Victoria	*American Cricketer* 15 May 1884, 43
West End	*Boston Globe* 18 June 1889, 10
West India	*Boston Globe* 31 May 1894, 14
West Indian Athletics	*Spalding's Official Cricket Guide for 1913*, 61

	Young Boston	Lovett, *Old Boston Boys*, 75
	Zingari	*Boston Globe* 3 May 1885, 6
Braintree	Braintree	*Boston Herald* 10 Sept. 1860, 4
	Monatiquot	*Clipper* 16 Sept. 1854, 3
Brockton	Brockton	*Boston Globe* 3 May 1885, 6
	Herbert & Rapp Co.	*Boston Globe* 28 June 1885, 6
	South Enders	*Boston Globe* 28 June 1885, 6
Canton	Canton	*Spalding's Official Cricket Guide for 1910*, 7
Centerville	Centerville	*Boston Globe* 17 Aug. 1890, 7
Charlestown	Independent	*Boston Herald* 28 July 1870, 4
	Mystic	*Clipper* 12 July 1862, 103
Chelsea	Amateur	*Boston Herald* 8 July 1868, 4
	Chelsea	*Saturday Evening Gazette* 2 Oct. 1858, 3
	Eagle	*Boston Globe* 5 July 1873, 1
	Mt. Hope	Peverelly, *Book of American Pastimes* (2nd ed.), 592
	Mutual	*Clipper* 17 July 1869, 115
	Mystics	*Boston Evening Transcript* 10 Oct. 1867, 4
	Stella	*New England Base Ballist* 27 Aug. 1868, 15
	Winnisimet	*Clipper* 17 Sept. 1870, 189
Chicopee	Chicopee	*Springfield Daily Republican* 18 June 1859, 8
Clinton	Clinton	*Porters* 26 June 1858, 261
Concord	Concord	*Clipper* 4 June 1859, 52
Dedham	Dedham	*Dedham Transcript* 24 July 1886, 3
	East Dedham	*Dedham Transcript* 26 June 1886, 3
	Walnut Hill	*Dedham Transcript* 28 Aug. 1886, 3

Dorchester	Dorchester	*Saturday Evening Gazette* 2 Oct. 1858, 3
Easthampton	Hampton County	*Spalding's Official Cricket Guide for 1913*, 69
Everett	Everett	*Boston Globe* 16 Aug. 1875, 5
Fall River	Athletic	*Boston Herald* 3 July 1872, 4
	Baysides	*Boston Globe* 2 Aug. 1903, 9
	Border City	Peverelly, *Book of American Pastimes* (2nd ed.), 592
	Bowenville	*Clipper* 4 Aug. 1877, 147
	Brooklawn	*Spalding's Official Cricket Guide for 1906*, 49
	Cascade	*Ball Players Chronicle* 3 Oct. 1867, 7
	Excelsior	*Ball Players Chronicle* 3 Oct. 1867, 7
	Fall River	*Wilkes* 13 Sept. 1862, 53
	King Philip	*Clipper* 15 June 1872, 83
	Lincoln	*Clipper* 21 Aug. 1867, 188
	Mayflower	*Boston Globe* 7 July 1875, 2
	Mount Hope	*Ball Players Chronicle* 19 Sept. 1867, 7
	Nightingale	*Spirit* 29 Oct. 1881, 355
	North End	*Clipper* 15 July 1882, 271
	Pacific	*Clipper* 24 July 1875, 130
	Rovers	*Boston Globe* 27 Aug. 1891, 4
	South End	*Boston Globe* 22 Sept. 1889, 2
	Suffolk	*Clipper* 27 Oct. 1866, 237
	Union	*Boston Herald* 10 Sept. 1860, 4
	Washington	*Spalding's Official Cricket Guide for 1906*, 49
Fitchburg	Fitchburg	*Boston Globe* 14 May 1882, 12
Foxboro	Foxboro	*Boston Globe* 5 July 1887, 2

226 · *The Tented Field*

Grantville	Albion	*Boston Herald* 17 Sept. 17, 1872, 4
Greenfield	Greenfield	*Clipper* 19 July 1856, 99
Hanover	Hanover	*Clipper* 30 Sept. 1865, 194
Harrisville	Harrisville	*Clipper* 18 Dec. 1858, 197
Highlandville	Albion	*Boston Globe* 4 July 1886, 6
Holyoke	Farr Alpaca Co.	*Boston Globe* 3 May 1885, 6
	Holyoke	*Clipper* 13 Sept. 1879, 197
Hopewell	Hopewell	*Clipper* 20 Sept. 1856, 174
Ipswich	Ipswich	*National Chronicle* 28 May 1870, 163
Lawrence	Albion	*Boston Globe* 4 Aug. 1889, 3
	Arlington	*Clipper* 31 Aug. 1881, 331
	Methuen	*Boston Globe* 29 May 1898, 2
	National	*American Cricketer* 28 Sept. 1882, 170
	Pacific	*Porters* 23 July 1859, 324
	Parkvale	*Boston Globe* 26 June 1898, 6
	St. John Athletic Assoc.	*Boston Globe* 12 June 1898, 3
	Union	*National Chronicle* 28 Aug. 1869, 183
Lenox	Lenox	*Spalding's Official Cricket Guide for 1906*, 47
Leominster	Leominster	*Boston Globe* 26 July 1903, 2
Lowell	Bleachery	*Clipper* 7 Sept. 1861, 165
	Blue Stars	*Clipper* 10 June 1876, 85
	Boot Mill	*Boston Globe* 13 Aug. 1888, 5
	Excelsior	*Lowell Citizen & News* 24 Oct. 1859, 2
	Independence	*Clipper* 10 Oct. 1857, 197
	International	*Boston Globe* 3 May 1885, 6

Appendix · 227

	Lowell	*Lowell Citizen & News* 25 Aug. 1856, 2
	Lowell Carpet Works	*American Cricketer* 9 Aug. 1893, 142
	Merrimack	*Spirit* 27 Oct. 1855, 439
	Mohair Plush	*Spalding's Official Cricket Guide for 1910*, 7
	Nationals	*Boston Globe* 17 Sept. 1882, 2
	Pawtucket	*Clipper* 16 Oct. 1858, 205
	Pioneer	*Clipper* 16 Oct. 1858, 205
	Union	*Clipper* 7 Nov. 1857, 229
	United	*Lowell Citizen & News* 28 Sept. 1859, 2
	U.S. Bunting	*Spalding's Official Cricket Guide for 1914*, 53
	Washington	*Clipper* 7 Nov. 1857, 229
	Zion	*Spalding's Official Cricket Guide for 1910*, 11
Ludlow	Ludlow	*Boston Globe* 7 June 1903, 9
Lynn	Bay State	*Sunday Mercury* 22 April 1860, 5
	Crescent	*Clipper* 28 April 1860, 13
	Eagle	*Porters* 3 July 1860, 293
	Essex	*Lynn Weekly Reporter* 5 May 1860
	Lynn	*Boston Globe* 6 May 1894, 5
	Wanderers	*Spalding's Official Cricket Guide for 1910*, 7
Maynard	Maynard	*Boston Globe* 12 July 1903, 4
Medford	British-American	*Boston Globe* 10 June 1888, 3
	Medford	*Boston Globe* 5 Sept. 1886, 8
	Mystics	*Boston Globe* 1 June 1886, 5
Menotomy	Menotomy	*Clipper* 7 May 1859, 19
Millsbury	Millsbury	*Outing* July 1885, 503

228 · *The Tented Field*

Mount Vernon	Mount Vernon	*Clipper* 14 May 1859, 27
Nahant	Atalanta	*Lynn Weekly Reporter* 14 May 1860
	Nahant	*Boston Daily Advertiser* 20 Sept. 1872, 1
	Yankee	*Porters* 3 July 1860, 293
Needham	Albion	*Clipper* 24 June 1871, 91
	Lincoln	*Clipper* 3 Sept. 1870, 235
	YMCA	*Spalding's Official Cricket Guide for 1913*, 61
Newton	Nonantum	*Boston Herald* 29 Aug. 1868, 4
Newtonville	Newtonville	*Boston Globe* 3 Aug. 1884, 8
New Bedford	Bay View	*Spalding's Official Cricket Guide for 1913*, 65
	Hathaway Portuguese	*Spalding's Official Cricket Guide for 1913*, 67
	New Bedford	*Boston Globe* 3 May 1885, 6
	North End	*Spalding's Official Cricket Guide for 1907*, 81
	West Indians	*Spalding's Official Cricket Guide for 1914*, 5
North Adams	North Adams	*Peoples Journal* 8 July 1886, 3
North Attleboro	Pickwick	*Clipper* 29 Aug. 1874, 173
North Billerica	North Billerica	*American Cricket Annual for 1901*, 73
Northampton	Bay State	*Boston Globe* 3 May 1885, 6
Northfield	Knife Co.	*Clipper* 2 Oct. 1875, 213
Peabody	Peabody	*Boston Globe* 16 Aug. 1896, 3
Quincy	Quincy	*Boston Globe* 26 Sept. 1886, 3
Rockland	Rockland	*Boston Globe* 13 May 1894, 5
Roxbury	Albion	*Clipper* 5 May 1860, 19
	Roxbury	*Spirit* 13 Oct. 1855, 409
	Roxbury Carpet Works	*Boston Globe* 14 July 1886, 6

	Roxbury Latin School	Jarvis, *Schola Illustris*, 289
Salem	West Roxbury	*Dedham Transcript* 26 June 1886, 3
	Alpha	*Clipper* 27 Oct. 1866, 237
	Centennial	*Clipper* 11 Sept. 1875, 187
	Essex	*Clipper* 27 Oct. 1866, 237
	Lafayette	*Spirit* 3 Oct. 1857, 451
	Franklin	*Boston Evening Transcript* 18 Sept. 1860, 2
	United	*Sunday Mercury* 15 April 1860, 5
	Washington	*Lowell Citizen & News* 2 Oct. 1858, 2
Salisbury	Salisbury	*Clipper* 12 May 1860, 31
Sandwich	Assumption College	*Clipper* 13 Nov. 1858, 237
	Cape Cod	*Clipper* 20 April 1861, 2
Saxonville	Albion	*Waltham Free Press* 18 Oct. 1872, 2
Shelbourne Falls	Eagle	*Gazette & Courier* 29 Aug. 1860, 2
	Franklin	*Clipper* 21 July 1860, 107
	Monitor	*Gazette & Courier* 17 Aug. 1863, 3
Somerville	British-American	*Boston Globe* 3 June 1888, 6
South Barre	South Barre	*Spalding's Official Cricket Guide for 1914*, 69
South Danvers	Franklin	*Spirit* 3 Oct. 1857, 451
	Washington	*Wilkes* 21 April 1860, 100
Springfield	Hampden	*Springfield Daily Republican* 18 June 1859, 8
Sterling	Allendale Academy	*Clipper* 26 May 1860, 44
	Sterling	*Clipper* 19 Sept. 1857, 172
	Williams Academy	*Clipper* 25 Sept. 1858, 182
Sutton	Empire	*Clipper* 3 Sept. 1859, 157

Taunton	Taunton	*Clipper* 20 Sept. 1856, 174
Waltham	Bleachery	Petersen, *Waltham Rediscovered*, 75
	Boston Manufacturing Co.	*Boston Globe* 12 Aug. 1873, 1
	Marylebone	*National Chronicle* 16 April 1870, 116
	Massasoit	Petersen, *Waltham Rediscovered*, 75
	New Church School	Petersen, *Waltham Rediscovered*, 75
	Rumford	*Spirit* 5 Sept. 1857, 356
	Star	*Clipper* 13 Oct. 1860, 204
	United	*Spirit* 5 Sept. 1857, 356
	Waltham	*Clipper* 18 July 1857, 101
	West End	Petersen, *Waltham Rediscovered*, 75
Webster	East Village	*National Chronicle* 11 June 1870, 180
	Union	*National Chronicle* 11 June 1870, 180
Ware	Ware	*Clipper* 8 Sept. 1877, 187
Warren	Warren	*Clipper* 18 Dec. 1858, 197
Watertown	Massasoit	*Ball Players Chronicle* June 1867, 5
	Stars	*Boston Globe* 6 Sept. 1873, 1
Wellesley	Wellesley College	*Wellesley College Catalogue for 1909*, 108
Westfield	Westfield	*Clipper* 13 Sept. 1979, 197
West Warren	West Warren	*American Cricketer* 6 Sept. 1877, 43
West Newton	English & Classical School	Greene, *Nathaniel T. Allen*, 117
Whitinsville	Whitinsville	*Boston Globe* 22 June 1890, 5
Williamsburg	Williams College	*Williams Quarterly* Nov. 1859, 190
Worcester	College of the Holy Cross	*Clipper* 28 April 1860, 3
	Globe Village	*Worcester Daily Spy* 3 Oct. 1860, 3

	Lincoln	*Porters* 26 June 1858, 261
	Olympic	*Clipper* 4 July 1863, 90
	South Worcester	*Boston Globe* 19 July 1882, 2
	Worcester	*Porters* 25 April 1857, 125
	Worcester County	*Boston Globe* 5 July 1888, 3
MICHIGAN		
Ahmeek	Ahmeek	*Evening Journal* 4 May 1908, 4
Ann Arbor	University of Michigan	*University Palladium 1861/2*, 55
Baltic	Baltic	*Evening Journal* 4 May 1908, 4
Bay City	Bay City	*Detroit Free Press* 21 Sept. 1883, 4
Boston	Boston	*Evening News* 10 Sept. 1908, 8
Calumet	Tamarack	*Spalding's Official Cricket Guide for 1912*, 91
Detroit	Belle Isle	*Detroit Free Press* 8 July 1894, 6
	Clan Cameron	*Detroit Free Press* 4 Sept. 1892, 7
	Crawford Ave.	*Spirit* 3 Sept. 1881, 140
	Detroit	*Detroit Free Press* 8 Aug. 1857, 1
	Detroit Athletic Club	*Detroit Free Press* 16 May 1891
	Empire	*Detroit Free Press* 18 Sept. 1859, 1
	Hamtramack	*Porters* 1 Oct. 1859, 69
	High School	*Spirit* 16 Nov. 1878, 397
	Michigan Athletic Assoc.	*Detroit Free Press* 16 May 1891
	Olympic	*Detroit Free Press* 16 May 1891
	Peninsular	*Detroit Free Press* 15 Sept. 1858, 1
	Phoenix	*Detroit Free Press* 30 July 1867, 1
	Pontiac	*Detroit Free Press* 19 Aug. 1857, 1

232 · *The Tented Field*

	St. George	*Detroit Free Press* 10 Sept. 1861, 1
	Union	*Detroit Free Press* 18 Sept. 1859, 1
	Wolverine	*Detroit Free Press* 24 June 1860, 1
East Saginaw		*Clipper* 4 July 1874, 107
Grand Rapids		*Daily Morning Democrat* 6 May 1874, 4
Hancock		*Copper Country Evening News* 22 July 1907, 7
Jackson		*Wilkes* 29 Oct. 1859, 116
Kearsarge		*Copper Country Evening News* 4 May 1908, 4
	North Kearsarge	*Spalding's Official Cricket Guide for 1912*, 91
	South Kearsarge	*Spalding's Official Cricket Guide for 1913*, 83
Kalamazoo		*Detroit Free Press* 16 June 1896, 6
Mesnard		*Evening Journal* 12 April 1909, 6
Mohawk		*Copper Country Evening News* 6 Aug. 1906, 7
Negaunee		*Evening News* 28 Sept. 1908, 6
Niles		*Detroit Free Press* 16 June 1896, 6
Painsdale		*Copper Country Evening News* 3 May 1906, 8
Port Huron	Grand Trunk	*Detroit Free Press* 29 July 1871, 1
	Port Huron	*Detroit Free Press* 26 Sept. 1860, 1
Portage Lake		*Copper Country Evening News* 8 May 1906, 7
	Pewabic Heroes	*Evening Journal* 18 Aug. 1908, 6
	Quincy	*Copper Country Evening News* 29 July 1907, 4
Trimountain		*Copper Country Evening News* 14 May 1906, 3
Ypsilanti		*Detroit Free Press* 13 Aug. 1873, 1

MINNESOTA

Brainerd	Brainerd	*Pioneer Press* 14 June 1891, 2
Como	Como	*Pioneer Press* 16 May 1891, 2
Duluth	Duluth	*Pioneer Press* 23 Aug. 1897, 5
	Union Jack	*Minneapolis Tribune* 28 Aug. 1886, 2
Faribault	Faribault	*Minneapolis Tribune* 26 Sept. 1874, 4
Minneapolis	Great Northern	*Pioneer Press* 21 June 1891, 3
	Minneapolis	*Minneapolis Tribune* 22 May 1884, 8
	Northern Pacific	*Pioneer Press* 26 July 1891, 2
Pipestone	Pipestone	*Pipestone County Star* 6 July 1888, 5
Red Wing	Olympic	*Goodhue County Republican* 27 July 1860, 3
	Red Wing	*Goodhue County Republican* 27 July 1860, 3
St. Paul	High School	*Pioneer Press* 26 Sept. 1897, 8
	Minnesota	*Pioneer Press* 16 May 1897, 7
	St. Paul	*St. Paul Daily Press* 18 June 1861, 1
	Young Americans	*American Cricketer* 22 June 1892, 89
Tyler	Coon Creek	*Pipestone County Star* 21 June 1889, 5
	Island Lakes	*Pipestone County Star* 4 July 1890, 5
Windon	Windon	*Pipestone County Star* 25 July 1890, 5

MISSISSIPPI

Natchez	Natchez	*Spirit* 20 April 1844, 90

MISSOURI

Crystal City	Crystal City	*St. Louis Globe Democrat* 10 April 1881, 7
	British-Americans	*Spalding's Official Cricket Guide for 1913*, 82
	Country Club	*Spalding's Official Cricket Guide for 1913*, 82
Kansas City	Kansas City	*Clipper* 23 Sept. 1871, 197

234 · *The Tented Field*

St. Joseph	St. George	*St. Joseph Daily Gazette* 19 Sept. 1869, 4
St. Louis	Benton	*Clipper* 3 March 1860, 362
	Jackson	*Daily Missouri Democrat* 28 Nov. 1859, 2
	Missouri	*Clipper* 3 March 1860, 362
	Mound City	*Daily Missouri Democrat* 3 May 1859, 2
	Old Hickory	*Porters* 7 May 1859, 149
	Olympian	*Clipper* 3 March 1860, 362
	Railroad	*St. Louis Globe-Democrat* 7 Aug. 1895, 5
	St. George	*Clipper* 2 Aug. 1873, 138
	St. Louis	*Daily Missouri Democrat* 19 Oct. 1859, 2
	Triple A	*St. Louis Globe-Democrat* 24 July 1904, 14
	Union	*Clipper* 3 March 1860, 362
	Victoria	*St. Louis Post Dispatch* 7 May 1881, 9
	Western American	*Daily Inter-Ocean* 31 May 1882, 5
Springfield	Springfield	*St. Louis Democrat* 9 Oct. 1874, 4

MONTANA

Burlington	Burlington	*Butte Daily Miner* 13 Sept. 1886, 4
Butte	Butte	*Sporting Life* 24 June 1885, 2
	Colorado Mining Co.	*Tribune Review* 8 July 1899, 1
	Sons of St. George	*Tribune Review* 5 Aug. 1899, 1
Centerville	Centerville	*Tribune Review* 17 June 1899, 1
Great Falls	Great Falls	*Tribune Review* 5 Aug. 1900, 1
Helena	Helena	*Livingston Enterprise* 14 July 1888, 1
Livingston	Livingston	*Livingston Enterprise* 14 July 1888, 1
Marysville	Marysville	*Tribune Review* 19 Aug. 1899, 3

	Moreland	*Butte Daily Miner* 27 June 1886 1
	Sand Coulee	*Tribune Review* 5 Aug. 1899, 1
	Three Forks	*Butte Daily Miner* 20 June 1887, 1
	Walkerville	*Anaconda Standard* 8 Sept. 1897
NEBRASKA	Buffalo	*Omaha Republican* 30 July 1889, 2
	Hastings	*Omaha Republican* 18 Oct. 1884, 8
	Lincoln	*Omaha Republican* 27 July 1884, 4
	Omaha	*Omaha Republican* 11 Aug. 1889, 2
	Burlington-Misssouri Railroad	*American Cricketer* 27 May 1886, 24
	High School	*American Cricketer* 25 Nov. 1885, 152
	Omaha	*Sporting Life* 23 April 1884, 2
	Randalites	*Omaha Republican* 10 June 1889, 1
	Trinity Cathedral	*Omaha Republican* 11 Aug. 1889, 2
	Plattsmouth	*Omaha Republican* 25 Aug. 1889, 2
NEVADA	Reno	*Nevada State Journal* 21 Oct. 1871, 3
NEW HAMPSHIRE	Concord	*Horae Scholasticae*, Dec. 1865, 6
	Dover	*Boston Globe* 5 July 1888, 3
	Fisherville	*Concord Daily Monitor* 26 Aug. 1870
	Hanover	Bartlett, *Dartmouth Athletics*, 4
	Manchester	*Clipper* 21 June 1856, 71
	Nashua	*Boston Globe* 28 June 1885, 6
	Portsmouth	*Clipper* 26 Aug. 1871, 164

Appendix · 235

Gallatin Valley / Sand Coulee / Three Forks / Walkerville

Buffalo / Hastings / Lincoln / All Saints / Burlington-Misssouri Railroad / High School / Omaha / Randalites / Trinity Cathedral / Plattsmouth

Mary Pines School

St. Paul's School / Dover / Dustin Island / Dartmouth College / Manchester / Nashua / Portsmouth

236 · *The Tented Field*

Suncook	Rockingham	*Clipper* 17 July 1869, 115
	Strawberry Bank	*American Cricketer* 10 May 1893, 35
	Suncook	*Concord Daily Monitor* 26 Aug. 1870

NEW JERSEY

Bayonne	New Jersey Athletic Club	*New York Tribune* 17 July 1890, 2
Belleville	Essex	*Clipper* 10 May 1884, 115
Beverley	Beverley	*Clipper* 1 Aug. 1857, 155
Boonton	Boonton	*Clipper* 8 May 1858, 2
Bordertown	Independent	*Wilkes* 12 Nov. 1859, 145
Bound Brook	Bound Brook	*Spalding's Official Cricket Guide for 1911*, 81
Camden	Albion	*Washington Post* 1 Sept. 1913, 6
	Camden Athletic Assoc.	*American Cricketer* 17 May 1893, 48
	Highland	*Philadelphia Record* 29 Aug. 1886, 7
Comminipaw	Elm	*American Cricketer* 1 June 1895, 51
Cranford	Cranford	*New York Times* 18 Sept. 1892, 11
Eagleswood	Leather Stocking	*Porters* 26 Nov. 1859, 196
	Pioneer	*Porters* 26 Nov. 1859, 196
Elberon	Elberon	*Clipper* 5 Sept. 1885, 394
Elizabeth	Elizabeth	*Sun* (New York) 21 May 1893, 8
	Pioneer	*World* 6 Sept. 1891, 8
	Union County Cricket and Tennis Club	*Spalding's Official Cricket Guide for 1910*, 89
Franklin	YMCA	*Spalding's Official Cricket Guide for 1908*, 55
	Franklin	*Herald* 7 July 1855, 1
Guttenburg	Guttenburg Athletic Club	*World* 24 June 1892, 5

Appendix · 237

Hackensack	Beaconsfield	*New York Times* 29 June 1892, 3
	British-Americans	*American Cricketer* 15 May 1902, 93
Hightstown	Hightstown	*Wilkes* 1 Oct. 1859, 53
Hoboken	Americus Athletic Club	*Sun* (New York) 20 June 1893, 4
	Hoboken	*Sun* (New York) 5 Sept. 1893, 6
	Minnetonka	*Illustrated Sporting News* 5 Sept. 1903, 23
	Stevens Institute	*Clipper* 23 May 1874, 59
Jersey City	Chadwick Co.	*American Cricketer* 15 April 1901, 82
	Claremont	*Clipper* 17 Sept. 1881, 418
	Hudson County	*Spalding's Official Cricket Guide for 1908*, 77
	Jersey City	*New York Times* 19 June 1872, 2
	MDCL	*American Cricket Annual for 1899*, 68
	Peter Henderson Co.	*World* 19 July 1892, 4
Kearny	Linoleum Works	*Newark Daily Advertiser* 30 June 1890, 3
	Marshall Co.	*New York Tribune* 18 Aug. 1889, 2
	Mile End	*Newark Daily Advertiser* 30 June 1890, 3
Lafayette	Claremont	*Clipper* 15 July 1882, 271
Lambertville	Delaware	*Clipper* 16 June 1860, 67
Lawrenceville	Lawrenceville School	Mulford, *History of the Lawrenceville School*, 76
Long Branch	Long Branch	*Clipper* 24 Aug. 1861, 151
Merchantville	Merchantville	*Clipper* 8 July 1882, 251
Middletown Point	Middletown Point	*Clipper* 11 March 1854, 3
Montclair	Montclair	*Spalding's Official Cricket Guide for 1910*, 89
	Montclair Athletic Club	*American Cricketer* 5 Aug. 1899, 83
Mount Hope	Mount Hope	*Sporting Life* 6 May 1885, 9

238 · *The Tented Field*

New Brunswick	New Brunswick	*Spirit* 2 Oct. 1858, 404
	St. George	*New York Times* 18 Sept. 1892, 11
New Durham	New Durham	*Clipper* 26 Sept. 1857, 183
Newark	Alina	*Clipper* 5 Sept. 1885, 394
	Alma	*Clipper* 10 May 1884, 115
	American	*Herald* 1 June 1855, 8
	Arbroath Wanderers	*Clipper* 3 Sept. 1881, 381
	Branch Brook	*Illustrated Sporting News* 29 May 1903, 23
	Christ Church	*Newark Daily Advertiser* 24 July 1855, 2
	Clark Thread Works	*Clipper* 10 May 1884, 115
	Colonial	*Spalding's Official Cricket Guide for 1910*, 89
	Electric	*Sun* (New York) 21 May 1893, 8
	English	*Clipper* 30 Jan. 1886, 730
	Essex	*Spirit* 18 July 1857, 267
	Forest Hill	*Sun* (New York) 13 Sept. 1896, 8
	Mechanics	*Spirit* 25 Aug. 1855, 330
	Mile End	*American Cricketer* 2 Oct. 1884, 187
	Mt. Washington	*Newark Daily Advertiser* 7 Oct. 1858, 2
	New Jersey	*Newark Daily Advertiser* 6 Sept. 1858, 2
	Newark	*Herald* 6 Oct. 1845, 2
	Newark Amateur Football and Cricket Club	*American Cricketer* 19 July 1883, 110
	ONT	*Clipper* 30 Jan. 1886, 730
	Peoples Park	*New York Times* 17 June 1893, 12
	Philanthropic	*Clipper* 30 Jan. 1886, 730

Appendix · 239

	Pioneer	*New York Times* 18 Aug. 1892, 3
	Tiffany Athletic Club	*Sun* (New York) 22 Sept. 1895, 8
	Union	*Clipper* 23 July 1864, 115
Orange	Old Mountain	*Forest and Stream* 17 April 1879, 209
	Orange	*Clipper* 24 Sept. 1864, 186
	Mountain	*World* 16 July 1869, 3
	Roseville	*Amateur Athlete* 26 Aug. 1897, 16
Passaic	Passaic	*Clipper* 29 May 1869, 58
Paterson	Juvenile	*Paterson Daily News* 2 July 1878, 3
	Passaic County	*Sun* (New York) 30 July 1893, 4
	Paterson	*Herald* 18 July 1855, 1
	Perseverance	*Clipper* 30 Jan. 1886, 730
	St. George	*Wilkes* 3 Sept. 1864, 4
	Sexagenarian	*Spirit* 5 Oct. 1878, 237
	Texas	*Herald* 22 June 1856, 1
	Union	*Paterson Daily Press* 8 July 1878, 3
Perth Amboy	Perth Amboy	*Outing* May 1896, 31
Plainfield	Plainfield	*Sporting Life* 9 Aug. 1890, 12
Princeton	Princeton University	*Clipper* 5 Sept. 1857, 155
Rockaway	Rockaway	*Clipper* 30 Jan. 1886, 730
Roseville	Roseville	*Sporting Life* 17 March 1894, 8
Seabright	Seabright Lawn Tennis and Cricket Club	Prentice, *History of the Seabright Lawn Tennis and Cricket Club* (1937)
Susquehanna Depot	Susquehanna Depot	*Clipper* 22 July 1865, 116
Trenton	Excelsior	*Wilkes* 12 Nov. 1859, 145

240 · *The Tented Field*

	Juniors	*Clipper* 4 Sept. 1858, 158
	Trenton	*Daily True American* 29 May 1858, 3
	Union	*Clipper* 7 June 1862, 59
	YMCA	*Sun* (New York) 8 Sept. 1891, 4
Upper Montclair	Bellvue	*New York Times* 19 July 1908, 2
Westwood	Westwood	*New York Times* 10 Sept. 1875 3
Woodcliff	Albion	*Sun* (New York) 7 May 1893, 5
	Bergen County	*Sun* (New York) 31 May 1893, 8

NEW YORK

Albion	Albion	*Syracuse Standard* 30 Sept. 1889, 4
Albany	Albany	*Spirit* 23 Sept. 1837, 249
	Albany Academy	*Argus* (Albany) 2 Oct. 1880, 4
	Excelsior	*Clipper* 4 July 1857, 83
	Jeffersonian	*Albany Atlas & Argus* 4 July 1860, 3
	Ridgefield Athletic Club	Howell, *History of the County of Albany*, 747
	Social Club	*Albany Atlas & Argus* 31 Aug. 1859, 3
Amsterdam	Amsterdam	*Amsterdam Evening Recorder* 16 May 1906, 4
	Jackson	*Clipper* 14 Aug. 1858, 133
	Sons of St. George	*Amsterdam Evening Recorder* 6 Aug. 1906, 4
	Star	*Clipper* 22 May 1858, 35
	Union	*Clipper* 22 May 1858, 35
Auburn	Auburn	*Spalding's Official Cricket Guide for 1913*, 3
Bedford	Bedford	*Spirit* 8 April 1848, 78
Belvidere	Belvidere	*Spirit* 2 Oct. 1858, 404
Brockport	Brockport	*Sunday Mercury* 22 July 1860, 5

Buffalo	Buffalo	*Buffalo Courier* 25 May 1877, 2
	Junior	*Clipper* 18 Sept. 1875, 194
	Parks	*Buffalo Morning Express* 12 July 1875, 4
	Queen City	*Buffalo Courier* 20 July 1860, 2
	Railtons	*Buffalo Morning Express* 12 July 1875, 4
	St. George	*Clipper* 29 Aug. 1857, 148
Canandaigua	Canandaigua	*Rochester Union & Advertiser* 19 July 1860, 2
Canastota	Canastota Knife Co.	*Oswego Palladium* 30 July 1880, 1
Clarks Mills	Clarks Mills	*American Cricketer* 1 Oct. 1905, 219
Cohoes	Cohoes	*Porters* 4 Oct. 1856, 85
	Harmony Mills	*Clipper* 18 Sept. 1858, 173
Dobbs Ferry	Greenburg	*Clipper* 6 Sept. 1862, 163
Elmira	Elmira	*Daily State Register* 20 May 1855, 2
Fultonville	Fultonville	*Clipper* 24 Oct. 1857, 213
Genesee Valley	Genesee Valley	*Spirit* 25 Sept. 1852, 379
Geneva	Palmyra	*Wilkes* 27 Sept. 1873 163
Gloversville	Gloversville	*Clipper* 11 July 1857, 93
	Star	*Clipper* 26 Aug. 1865, 156
Grassy Point	Minnesseongo	*Sunday Mercury* 14 Aug. 1870, 4
Greenwich	Greenwich	*Clipper* 12 July 1884, 263
Hamilton	Norwich	*Clipper* 7 Sept. 1861, 162
Ilion	Ilion	*Wilkes* 11 Aug. 1866, 381
	Remington Typewriter Co.	*Utica Observer* 4 Sept. 1905, 2
Ithaca	Cornell University	*National Chronicle* 4 June 1870, 172
Jamaica	Eclipse	*Spirit* 14 June 1848, 207

242 · *The Tented Field*

Jamestown	Chautauqua Sons of St. George	*Jamestown Evening Journal* 14 Aug. 1899, 1
	Columbia Sons of St. George	*Jamestown Evening Journal* 14 Aug. 1899, 1
	Worsted Mills	*Spalding's Official Cricket Guide for 1913*, 37
Johnstown	Johnstown	*Herald* 25 May 1856, 4
	Union	*Clipper* 26 Aug. 1865, 156
Kingston	Empire	*Sunday Mercury* 24 June 1860, 5
Lansingburg	Lansingburg	*Clipper* 22 Oct. 1859, 212
	Lansingburg Academy	*National Chronicle* 20 Feb. 1869, 26
	Union	*Clipper* 22 Oct. 1859, 212
Lockport	Niagara	*Clipper* 5 Oct. 1867, 205
Marcellus	Marcellus	*Spalding's Official Cricket Guide for 1913*, 35
Middle Village	Middle Village	*Clipper* 8 Aug. 1863, 135
Middletown	Middletown	*Clipper* 18 July 1857, 99
	Orange County	*Yonkers Statesman* 21 June 1866, 5
Mt. Morris	Mt. Morris	*Spirit* 25 Sept. 1852, 379
New Rochelle	New Rochelle	*Outing* Oct. 1890, 17
New Windsor	New Windsor	*New York Leader* 17 July 1858, 5
New York	All Angels	*Brooklyn Daily Eagle* 20 Sept. 1903, 4
	Alpha	*Brooklyn Eagle* 4 Aug. 1860, 2
	Amateur League	*Sun* (New York) 15 July 1888, 7
	American	*Clipper* 21 Sept. 1861, 186
	American Meter Co.	*Sun* (New York) 20 Aug. 1890, 3
	Amicus	*World* (New York) 10 Aug. 1881, 6
	Anglo-American	*Clipper* 11 Oct. 1862, 203
	Antilles	*Brooklyn Daily Eagle* 16 June 1901, 10

Appleton	*World* (New York) 2 May 1880, 2
Astoria	*Sun* (New York) 22 Sept. 1893, 6
Athens	*Spalding's Official Cricket Guide for 1913*, 1
Atlantic	*Spirit* 16 May 1857, 162
Beaconsfield	*World* (New York) 28 Aug. 1892, 5
Bensonhurst Field Club	*Spalding's Official Cricket Guide for 1912*, 25
Berkeley Athletic Club	*Sun* (New York) 21 June 1891, 28
Bermuda	*World* (New York) 19 July 1896, 5
Bloomingdales	*Sun* (New York) 20 June 1893,
British Public Schools	*New York Times* 23 June 1896, 8
Broadway	*Clipper* 12 May 1860, 31
Bronxville	*Clipper* 8 Oct. 1864, 31
Bronx United	*New York Times* 16 Aug. 1908,
Brooklyn	*New York Times* 5 June 1887, 3
Brooklyn Nomads	*Spalding's Official Cricket Guide for 1906*, 33
Camden	*Sun* (New York) 9 July 1893, 4
Cameron	*Spalding's Official Cricket Guide for 1913*, 20
Canal Street	*Herald* 7 May 1855, 1
Caribbeans	*New York Times* 30 July 1899, 8
Central Park	*Sun* (New York) 7 Sept. 1897, 4
Chadwick	*American Cricketer* 15 Feb. 1902, 32
Clinton Institute	*Clipper* 17 Dec. 1859, 275
Colonial	*Spalding's Official Cricket Guide for 1909*, 69
Columbia University	*Acta Columbiana* 29 Oct. 1880
Continental	*New York Times* 20 Sept. 1885, 3

Cosmopolitan	*New York Tribune* 18 Aug. 1889, 2
County Down	*World* (New York) 6 Sept. 1892, 4
Crescent Athletic Club	*Amateur Athlete* 24 June 1896, 7
Danish West Indies	*Spalding's Official Cricket Guide for 1913*, 19
Deaf and Dumb Institution	*New York Daily Express* 26 April 1855, 1
East New York	*Spirit* 28 Nov. 1857, 498
East Williamsburgh	*Spirit* 18 May 1861, 229
Elm Flax Mills	*World* (New York) 29 July 1894, 10
Faustus	*Turf Field and Farm*, 1865, 171
Flatbush	*Clipper* 25 June 1860, 77
Free Academy	*Spirit* 15 Oct. 1853, 409
Fordham University	Gannon, *Up to the Present*, 45
Fort Hamilton	*New York Tribune* 6 July 1890, 5
Galway	*Sun* (New York) 7 Sept. 1897, 4
Grace	*World* (New York) 20 Sept. 1891, 6
Hamilton	*Outing* April 1890, 44
Harlem	*Spirit* 20 May 1854, 162
Harlem YMCA	*New York Tribune* 3 Aug. 1890, 3
Hampshire	*New York Times* 19 July 1908, 2
Hudson Street	*Herald* 7 May 1855, 1
Independent	*Sunday Mercury* 18 Dec. 1859, 5
International	*Porters* 17 March 1860, 66
International Athletic Club	*World* (New York) 29 May 1896, 10
International Tile Company	*Sporting Life* 18 May 1885, 11
Irish-American	*American Cricketer* 25 April 1889, 5

John Mathews	*New York Times* 10 July 1893, 2
Kilkenny Confederation	*Sun* (New York) 30 June 1893, 4
Kings County	*Herald* 25 Oct. 1846, 2
Knickerbocker	*Herald* 9 Sept. 1853, 4
Lexington	*World* 21 Aug. 1892, 5
Long Island	*Spirit* 4 Oct. 1851, 390
Manhattan	*Spirit* 19 Dec. 1857, 529
Manufacturers	*Sun* (New York) 20 Aug. 1893, 4
Marshall & Co.	*American Cricketer* 6 June 1889, 22
Melbourne	*Spalding's Official Cricket Guide for 1913*, 19
Metropolitan	*Clipper* 11 June 1887, 303
Metropolitan Life Insurance Co.	*Sun* (New York) 12 Aug. 1895, 9
Morris Park	*Sun* (New York) 7 May 1893, 5
Mt. Vernon	*Herald* 25 Oct. 1846, 2
Municipal	*Clipper* 17 Sept. 1881, 59
Musical and Social	*American Cricketer* 9 Oct. 1884, 192
Nelson Lodge	*New York Times* 29 June 1892, 3
New Amsterdam	*New York Times* 5 July 1899, 8
New Brighton	*Spirit* 15 Sept. 1855, 367
New York	*Spirit* 4 May 1844, 118
New York Adult School	*Spalding's Official Cricket Guide for 1910*, 57
New York Arbroath	*Sun* (New York) 11 July 1897, 9
New York Athletic Club	*New York Times* 17 June 1892, 3
New York County	*Spalding's Official Cricket Guide for 1913*, 19
New York Jockey Club	*Sun* (New York) 31 May 1893, 8

New York Printing Co.   *New York Times* 15 July 1893, 3
New York Racquet and   *Sun* (New York) 19 May 1893, 4
  Tennis Club
New York University   *Clipper* 20 Nov. 1879, 285
North Shore   *Clipper* 21 Aug. 1858, 141
Occidental   *World* (New York) 5 June 1892, 3
Oceania   *American Cricketer* 15 July 1901, 164
Orient   *World* (New York) 5 June 1892, 3
Picayune   *Turf Field and Farm* 1865, 171
Pickwick   *Spalding's Official Cricket Guide for 1914*, 41
Pioneer   *World* (New York) 28 Aug. 1892, 5
Polytechnic Institute   *Forest and Stream* 16 June 1878, 350
Prospect Park   *Clipper* 5 Oct. 1872, 210
Queens   *Clipper* 12 May 1860, 31
Queens County   *American Cricket Annual for 1899*, 68
Riverside   *Clipper* 16 Jan. 1886, 698
Royal   *World* (New York) 18 June 1878, 8
St. Agnes Church   *Sun* (New York) 26 May 1896, 4
St. Austin School   *American Cricketer* 13 June 1889, 27
St. Christopher   *Sun* (New York) 13 Aug. 1893, 4
St. James Church   *Sun* (New York) 1 Sept. 1898, 5
St. Thomas   *Spalding's Official Cricket Guide for 1913*, 19
Satellite   *Porters* 31 March 1860, 90
Sheffield   *Herald* 10 Sept. 1845, 2
Sons of St. George   *Sun* (New York) 14 Aug. 1895, 4

South Brooklyn	*History of Brooklyn* (1893), 1030
Spartans	*Spalding's Official Cricket Guide for 1914*, 41
Staten Island	Walker, *History of the Staten Island Cricket and Lawn Tennis Club* (1917)
Staten Island Athletic Club	*Sun* (New York) 21 July 1893, 4
Stone Cottage	*Sun* (New York) 23 July 1885, 6
Thespians	*New York Times* 16 Aug. 1893, 6
Thistles	*Brooklyn Daily Eagle* 10 May 1903, 7
Underhill	*Clipper* 28 June 1884, 227
Union Star	*Herald* 13 Sept. 1844, 2
United Laceworkers	*American Cricketer* 12 Sept. 1889, 83
Van Courtland	*Spalding's Official Cricket Guide for 1913*, 20
Vernon Lodge	*Spalding's Official Cricket Guide for 1913*, 20
Veterans	*Spalding's Official Cricket Guide for 1913*, 17
Victor Albion	*World* (New York) 20 May 1893, 7
Victoria	*World* (New York) 10 June 1897, 5
Wallabout Bay	*Herald* 5 Aug. 1845, 2
Wanderers	*Spalding's Official Cricket Guide for 1913*, 19
Washington	*Herald* 9 Oct. 1845, 2
Weary Foot Common	*Clipper* 18 Aug. 1860, 140
West Brighton	*World* (New York) 27 May 1883, 3
West Indian	*Spalding's Official Cricket Guide for 1913*, 26
West Side Athletic Club	*World* (New York) 9 Aug. 1891, 9
West Side YMCA	*Spalding's Official Cricket Guide for 1913*, 26
Williamsburg	*Spirit* 2 Sept. 1854, 342

	Williamsburg Athletic Club	*Sun* (New York) 29 Aug. 1885, 3
	Willow	*Wilkes* 18 Oct. 1862, 99
	Windsor Terrace	*American Cricketer* 17 Aug. 1895, 141
	World	*Spalding's Official Cricket Guide for 1907*, 71
	Yorkville	*Amateur Athlete* 16 Sept. 1897, 11
	Young New York	*Turf Field and Farm* 1865, 189
	Zingari	*Sun* (New York) 10 July 1885, 3
Newburgh	Newburgh	*World* (New York) 4 Aug. 1883, 6
Nyack	Eureka	*Wilkes* 11 Aug. 1866, 381
	Mechanics	*Wilkes* 18 Aug. 1866, 397
Oswego	Excelsior	*Oswego Commercial Times* 25 July 1860, 3
	Iron Bound	*Syracuse Standard* 3 Sept. 1860 3
	Ontario	*Oswego Commercial Times* 5 June 1860, 3
	Oswego	*Oswego Palladium* 30 Sept. 1880, 3
	St. George	*Syracuse Standard* 28 June 1859, 3
	Washington	*Sunday Mercury* 16 Aug. 1861, 8
Oswego Falls	Oswego Falls	*Forest and Stream* Aug. 14, 1879, 556
Pelham Manor	Hazen School	*New York Times* 15 Nov. 1896, 8
Port Washington	Castlegould Estate	*Spalding's Official Cricket Guide for 1913*, 39
Poughkeepsie	Poughkeepsie	*Poughkeepsie Eagle* 13 Oct. 1855, 2
Rouses Point	Rouses Point	*Clipper* 4 July 1857, 85
Rochester	British-American	*Spalding's Official Cricket Guide for 1913*, 35
	Eagle	*Rochester Union & Advertiser* 23 Aug. 1860, 2
	Rochester	*Rochester Union & Advertiser* 12 June 1857, 3
Schenectady	American Locomotive	*Amsterdam Recorder* 11 July 1910, 2

Appendix · 249

Syracuse	Schenectady	*Albany Journal* 18 Aug. 1858, 3
	Shendoah	*Porters* 14 May 1859 164
	Lillywhite	*Clipper* 21 Sept. 1867, 180
	Onondaga	*Syracuse Standard* 1 June 1880, 4
	Outdoor Amusement Club	*Clipper* 5 Aug. 1882, 319
	Renwick Castle	*Clipper* 21 Sept. 1867, 180
	Sanderson Steel Works	*American Cricketer* 3 July 1884, 96
	Syracuse	*Spirit* 6 July 1844, 222
	Syracuse University	*Syracusaean for 1878*, 77
Troy	Albany County	*Troy Times* 13 Oct. 1866, 3
	Aurora	*Porters* 4 Oct. 1856, 85
	Ida Hill	*Clipper* 7 Dec. 1861, 267
	Rensselaer Polytechnic	*Clipper* 7 June 1856, 51
	Rensselaer	*Clipper* 8 Oct. 1864, 202
	Rensselaer County	*Clipper* 23 Oct. 1858, 214
	Stirling	*Porters* 11 April 1857, 92
	Watervliet	*Clipper* 12 May 1860, 31
Tuxedo Park	Tuxedo Ramblers	*Spalding's Official Cricket Guide for 1913*, 39
Utica	Oneida	*Utica Morning Herald* 12 Sept. 1860, 3
	Union	*Utica Morning Herald* 12 Sept. 1860, 3
	Utica	*Utica Daily Gazette* 12 July 1848, 2
Walden	Walden	*Clipper* 1 Oct. 1870, 204
Wappingers Falls	Wappingers Falls	*Clipper* 2 Oct. 1875, 213
Waterville	Waterville	*Daily State Register* 23 May 1855, 2
West Farms	Independent	*Spirit* 15 Sept. 1855, 367

250 · *The Tented Field*

	West Point	Forman, *West Point* 179
		U.S. Military Academy
		Spalding's Official Cricket Guide for 1913, 20
		St. George
		New York Times 21 Aug. 1887, 3
	Yonkers	YMCA
		Yonkers
		Spirit 9 June 1855, 200
NORTH CAROLINA	Asheville	Asheville
		Cricket Club Life 15 Oct. 1897, 2
NORTH DAKOTA	Fargo	Fargo
		Sporting Life 2 May 1888, 10
OHIO	Aberdeen	Aberdeen
		Maysville Eagle 23 June 1860, 2
	Akron	Akron
		Spalding's Official Cricket Guide for 1906, 61
	Altoona	Altoona
		American Cricketer 1 June 1882, 51
	Amherst	Amherst
		Forest and Stream 6 Nov. 1879, 788
	Ashtabula	Ashtabula
		Forest and Stream 6 Nov. 1879, 788
	Avon	Avon
		Elyria Democrat 31 Aug. 1870, 3
	Beechwold	Beechwold
		Clipper 8 Dec. 1866, 275
	Canton	Canton
		Spalding's Official Cricket Guide for 1914, 142
	Cincinnati	Buckeye
		Cincinnati Enquirer 22 May 1858, 3
		Cincinnati
		Cincinnati Enquirer 31 Oct. 1856, 1
		Eagle
		Wilkes 1 Oct. 1864, 68
		Queen City
		Cincinnati Enquirer 25 Sept. 1845, 3
		Sheffield
		Spirit 15 June 1850, 197
		Star
		Clipper 3 April 1858, 396
		Union
		Cincinnati Enquirer 9 May 1857, 3
		Western
		Cincinnati Enquirer 25 Sept. 1845, 3

Appendix · 251

Circleville	Aurora	*Circleville Watchman* 8 June 1860, 3
Cleveland	Britannica	*Spalding's Official Cricket Guide for 1913*, 77
	Buckeye	*Wilkes* 8 Sept. 1866, 13
	Citizens	*Spirit* 24 Sept. 1853, 384
	East End	*Plaindealer* 20 Sept. 1899, 6
	Excelsior	*Forest and Stream* 6 Nov. 1879, 788
	Forest City	*Clipper* 10 April 1858, 405
	Forest Park	*Forest and Stream* 6 Nov. 1879, 788
	High School	*Spirit* 15 Aug. 1857, 320
	Ivanhoe	*Cleveland Leader* 19 June 1858, 1
	Live Oak	*Cleveland Leader* 15 Sept. 1866, 4
	Mecnanics	*Forest and Stream* 6 Nov. 1879, 788
	Rising Sun	*Forest and Stream* 6 Nov. 1879, 788
	St. George	*Spirit* 24 Sept. 1853, 384
	Union	*Clipper* 4 Aug. 1860, 125
	Western Reserve	*Spalding's Official Cricket Guide for 1914*, 142
	Worsted Mills	*Spalding's Official Cricket Guide for 1914*, 142
Columbus	Columbus	*Wilkes* 28 July 1866, 34
	Ohio State University	*American Cricketer* 20 June 1882, 80
Delaware	Ohio Wesleyan University	Hubbart, *Ohio Wesleyan's First Hundred Years*, 24
	Delaware	*New York Daily Express* 26 April 1856, 4
East Liverpool	East Liverpool	*Pittsburgh Post* 16 July 1884, 4
Elyria	Elyria	*Elyria Democrat* 15 June 1870, 3
Lancaster	Lancaster	*Clipper* 15 Aug. 1857, 153
Leetonia	Washington	*Pittsburgh Post* 18 Aug. 1884, 5

Lodi	Lodi	*University Palladium*, 1872, 77
Maumee	Maumee	*Wilkes* 5 May 1860, 143
	Maumee Valley	*Toledo Blade* 6 Oct. 1880, 3
Newburg	Excelsior	*Clipper* 21 June 1879, 98
Oberlin	Oberlin	*Clipper* 17 Aug. 1859, 148
	Oberlin College	*Students Monthly* July 1859, 361
Oxford	Miami University	Havighunt, *The Miami Years*, 104
Ripley	Ripley	*Clipper* 15 Sept. 1860, 173
Springfield	Springfield	*Clipper* 10 Aug. 1872, 146
Steubenville	Steubenville	*Pittsburg Dispatch* 6 Sept. 1881, 8
Toledo	East Toledo	*Toledo Daily Blade* 24 Aug. 1880, 3
	Forest	*Ypsilanti Commercial* 11 July 1885, 1
	Toledo	*Toledo Blade* 24 Aug. 1860, 3
	Toledo Outing Club	*Detroit Free Press* 20 May 1894, 7
	St. George	*Clipper* 23 May 1874, 59
	Wagon Works	*American Cricketer* 25 Sept. 1884, 180
University Heights	University Heights	*Clipper* 4 Aug. 1860, 125
Walnut Hills	Eagle	*Cincinnati Enquirer* 13 July 1865, 2
Youngstown	Youngstown	*Clipper* 21 June 1856, 71
Zanesville	Zanesville	*Clipper* 4 July 1857, 85

OREGON

Astoria	Astoria Football Club	*Morning Oregonian* 10 June 1895, 8
Corvalis	Corvalis	*American Cricketer* 1 April 1880, 97
Portland	Associated Bank	*Morning Oregonian* 22 July 1895, 8
	Mercantile	*Morning Oregonian* 27 July 1884, 6

Appendix · 253

	Mt. Tabor	*Morning Oregonian* 17 Aug. 1894, 3
	Multnomah Amateur Athletic Club	*Morning Oregonian* 10 June 1895, 8
	Portland	*Morning Oregonian* 9 July 1878, 3
	Portland Amateur Athletic Club	*Morning Oregonian* 10 June 1895, 8
	Wanderers	*Morning Oregonian* 7 Sept. 1896, 10
PENNSYLVANIA		
Allegheny City	Atalanta	*Pittsburgh Post* 28 June 1859
	Eureka English Athletic and Cricket Club	*Sporting Life* 31 May 31, 1890, 15
Allentown	Allentown	*Spalding's Official Cricket Guide for 1911*, 41
Altoona	Altoona	*Clipper* 27 Sept. 1879, 24
	St. George	*American Cricketer* 16 Aug. 1883, 137
Amity	Excelsior	*Clipper* 16 April 1859, 410
Ashley	Ashley	*American Cricketer* 18 June 1877, 3
Banksville	Banksville	*American Cricketer* 20 July 1882, 100
Beaver Falls	St. George	*Pittsburg Dispatch* 5 Sept. 1882, 5
Bedford	Bedford	*American Cricketer* 8 Sept. 1881, 211
Bellefonte	Farmers High School	*Porters* 20 Aug. 1859, 389
Blairsville	Blairsville	*Blairsville Enterprise* 7 May 1880, 5
Bloomsburg	Bloomsburg	*Public Ledger* 28 Aug. 1905, 4
Bradford	Bradford	*American Cricketer* 18 March 1880, 93
Bristol	Bristol	*Fitzgeralds City Item* 11 Aug. 1860, 3
	Worsted Mills	*Spirit* 10 Sept. 1881, 174
Brushton	Brushton	*Pittsburgh Post* 5 May 1884, 4

254 · *The Tented Field*

Bryn Mawr	Bryn Mawr	*American Cricketer* 22 Aug. 1878, 36
	Bryn Mawr College	Ainsworth, *History of Physical Education*, 29
Canonsburg	Jefferson	*Clipper* Aug. 11, 1860, 131
	Keystone	*Clipper* 6 Oct. 1860, 197
Easton	Easton	*Spirit* 1 July 1854, 235
Farmington	Farmington	*Clipper* 22 Nov. 1862, 253
Glenshaw	Glenshaw	*Pittsburgh Post* 17 Aug. 1891, 6
Grimsby	Grimsby	*American Cricketer* 28 Oct. 1880, 72
Harrisburg	Bessemer	*Sunday Mercury* (Philadelphia) 12 Sept. 1869, 4
	Harrisburg	*Clipper* 23 July 1859, 111
Hazelton	Hazelton	*Pottsville Republican* 29 July 1890, 4
Hestonville	Amicus	*American Cricketer* 9 Sept. 1880, 43
	Chippewa	*Clipper* 1 Oct. 1864, 199
	Jefferson	*Clipper* 1 Oct. 1864, 199
Homestead	Homestead	*American Cricketer* Oct. 1897, 243
Homewood	Homewood	*Outing* July 1893, 84
Jeanette	Jeanette	*Pittsburgh Post* 3 Aug. 1891, 6
Kittaning	Kittaning	*Pittsburgh Post* 29 July 1859, 1
Lancaster	Conestoga	*Clipper* 29 May 1858, 44
	Franklin & Marshall College	*Daily Evening Express* 7 July 1860, 2
	Independence	*Daily Evening Expres* 7 July 1857, 2
	Keystone	*Porters* 20 June 1857, 245
Lebanon	Lebanon	*Public Ledger* 18 Feb. 1891, 2
McKeesport	McKeesport	*Pittsburg Dispatch* 21 July 1882, 2
Meadville	Excelsior	*Cleveland Leader* 20 Sept. 1865, 4

Appendix · 255

Mechanicsville	United	*Miners Journal* 22 June 1867, 2
Media	Chestnut Grove	*Sunday Mercury* (Phil) 25 July 1869, 4
	Media	*Spirit* 30 June 1860, 252
Millersville	Normal School	*Daily Evening Express* 4 June 1860, 2
Newcastle	Newcastle	*Spalding's Official Cricket Guide for 1913*, 77
Norristown	Norristown	*Pottsville Republican* 9 Aug. 1890
Oakland	St. George	*Pittsburgh Post* 28 June 1859, 1
Orwigsburg	Orwigsburg	*Miners Journal* 25 Aug. 1866, 2
Philadelphia	[Note: The following includes only those Philadelphia cricket clubs not listed in Lester, *A Century of Philadelphia Cricket*, 371-75]	
	Alhambra	*North American & U.S. Gazette* 2 June 1857, 1
	All United	*Wilkes* 14 July 1860, 299
	Alphean	*Clipper* 25 July 1857, 109
	America	*Clipper* 24 May 1856, 39
	American Gentlemen	*Clipper* 12 Nov. 1853, 4
	Amicus	*World* (New York) 10 Aug. 1881, 6
	Ashland	*Sunday Mercury* 22 April 1860, 5
	Atalanta	*Fitzgeralds City Item* 19 May 1860, 4
	Bolivar	*Clipper* 3 Dec. 1859, 260
	Cadwalader	*Clipper* 2 June 1860, 53
	Century Wheelman	*American Cricketer* 28 June 1893, 94
	Chippewa	*Sunday Mercury* 27 May 1860, 5
	Christ Church	*Philadelphia Inquirer* 8 June 1902, 4
	Columbia	*Spirit* 29 Oct. 1881, 355
	Columbus	*Wilkes* 22 Dec. 1860, 245

256 · *The Tented Field*

Commercial Exchange	*American Cricketer* 5 June 1879, 122
Commercial Trust Co.	*Philadelphia Press* 27 May 1904, 10
Continental	Peverelly, *Book of American Pastimes*, 542
Crescentville	*Sunday Mercury* (Philadelphia) 18 July 1869, 4
Decatur	*North American & U.S. Gazette* 26 May 1857, 1
Delaware	*Daily Evening Bulletin* 18 May 1857, 3
Diligente	*Philadelphia Tribune* 3 May 1913, 4
Enterprise	*Sunday Mercury* (Philadelphia) 27 May 1866, 3
Evergreen	*Sunday Mercury* (Philadelphia) 21 July 1872, 3
Mr. Faire's School	*Wilkes* 22 June 1861, 245
Forest	*Clipper* 3 Dec. 1859, 260
Franklin	*Philadelphia Record* 29 Aug. 1886, 7
Franklin National Bank	*Philadelphia Press* 27 May 1904, 10
Hamilton	*North American & U.S. Gazette* 12 May 1857, 1
Harrison	*Clipper* 2 June 1860, 53
Hiawatha	*Fitzgeralds City Item* 19 May 1860, 4
Jackson	*Sunday Mercury* 22 April 1860, 5
Jamestown	*American Cricketer* Oct. 1886, 59
John Quincy Adams	*Clipper* 19 May 1860, 37
Grammar School	
Johnson	*Wilkes* 18 Aug. 1860, 379
Knights of the Pencil	*Spirit* 29 Oct. 1881, 358
Lafayette	*Times* (Philadelphia) 19 June 1881, 2
Larchmont	*Times* (Philadelphia) 21 June 1881, 2
Leona	*Clipper* 2 June 1860, 53

Appendix · 257

Lincoln	Sunday Mercury (Philadelphia) 27 May 1866, 3
Mr. Lyons School	"Haverford College Cricket," Outing June 1896, 236
Madison	Spirit 29 Oct. 1881, 355
Magnolia	Clipper 11 April 1857, 403
Maple	Spirit 25 June 1881, 556
Mechanics	Sunday Mercury 29 April 1860, 5
Merry Athlete	Times (Philadelphia) 16 Oct. 1881, 2
Metamora	Philadelphia Tribune 3 May 1913, 4
Meteor	St. Louis Globe-Democrat 17 Aug. 1882, 8
Mohegan	Sunday Mercury 29 April 1860, 5
Monroe	Sunday Mercury 29 April 1860, 5
Morphy	Wilkes 28 July 1860, 332
Niagara	Fitzgeralds City Item 2 June 1860, 4
No name	Wilkes 14 May 1864, 173
Oakland County	American Cricket Annual for 1899, 68
Oak Lane	American Cricket Annual for 1901, 73
Olive	Philadelphia Tribune 3 May 1913, 4
Ontario	Fitzgeralds City Item 12 May 1860, 2
Oregon	Clipper 26 Aug. 1858, 150
Osceola	Wilkes 14 July 1860, 299
Panola	Daily Evening Bulletin 3 June 1857, 4
Penn Knitting Mills	Spirit 10 Sept. 1881, 174
Pennsylvania	Wilkes 1 Sept. 1860, 405
Pennsylvania Hospital	Public Ledger 15 Sept. 1879, 1
Powelton	Sunday Mercury (Philadelphia) 18 March 1866, 3

	Putnam	*Sunday Mercury* 13 May 1860, 4
	Quid Nunc	Peverelly, *Book of American Pastimes*, 543
	Resolute	*Sunday Mercury* (Philadelphia) 10 Oct. 1869, 4
	Saranac	*Clipper* 5 Nov. 1859, 227
	Senior	*Fitzgeralds City Item* 16 June 1860, 4
	Social Art	*World* (New York) 20 June 1882, 8
	Strathaven	*American Cricket Annual for 1899*, 68
	Sumter	*Clipper* 4 May 1861, 19
	Sussex	*Clipper* 12 May 1860, 29
	Thalian	*Clipper* 21 Nov. 1857, 244
	Tracy	*Spirit* 25 June 1881 556
	Typographical	*Clipper* 16 Oct. 1858, 205
	Ury College	*American Cricketer* 1 June 1882, 53
	Valparaiso	*Clipper* 28 Nov.1857, 252
	Vernon	*Wilkes* 28 July 1860, 352
	Vesper	*Spirit* 25 June 1881, 556
	Yorkshire Society	*Spalding's Official Cricket Guide for 1910*, 50
Pittsburgh	Buena Vista	*Pittsburgh Post* 3 Aug. 1891, 6
	Chartiers	*Pittsburgh Post* 17 June 1859, 1
	Chartiers Valley	*Sporting Life* 19 April 1890, 16
	Crescent	*Pittsburgh Post* 16 Aug. 1888, 6
	Duquesne	*Pittsburgh Post* 15 Aug. 1859, 1
	Ebenezer	*Pittsburgh Post* 8 July 1859, 1
	Exchange	*Wilkes* 23 June 1866, 263
	Linden	*Pittsburgh Post* 16 Aug. 1888, 6

	Nimrod	*Pittsburgh Post* 8 July 1859, 1
	Oliver Roberts	*Sporting Life* 16 April 1884, 2
	Olympic	*Pittsburgh Post* 17 June 1859, 1
	Pittsburgh	*Spirit* 17 Dec. 1850, 500
	Pittsburgh Field Club	*American Cricketer* 15 July 1899, 118
	Petroleum Exchange	*Pittsburgh Post* 11 Oct. 1886, 6
	St. Andrews	*American Cricketer* 14 June 1888, 37
	Twin City	*American Cricketer* 15 June 1886, 73
	Westinghouse Electric	*American Cricketer* 15 July 1899, 118
	Young America	*Pittsburgh Post* 26 Aug. 1859, 1
Plymouth	Olympic	*Clipper* 6 Oct. 1883, 469
Port Carbon	Shawnees	*Clipper* 5 Sept. 1874, 181
	Port Carbon	*Miners Journal* 24 July 1858, 2
	Sherman	*Miners Journal* 1 July 1863, 2
Pottsville	American	*Miners Journal* 22 June 1867, 2
	Athletic	*Miners Journal* 22 June 1867, 2
	Atlantic	*Miners Journal* 14 Aug. 1858, 2
	Grant	*Miners Journal* 1 July 1863, 2
	Junato	*Miners Journal* 31 Aug. 1867, 2
	Keystone	*Miners Journal* 24 July 1858, 2
	Lillywhite	*Miners Journal* 3 July 1858, 2
	Mechanics	*Miners Journal* 16 July 1858, 2
	Miners	*Miners Journal* 29 July 1865, 2
	New Philadelphia	*Miners Journal* 23 July 1859
	No Name	Peverelly, *Book of American Pastimes*, 549

	Olympian	*Miners Journal* 3 July 1858, 2
	Osceola	*Miners Journal* 24 July 1858, 2
	Pioneer	*Miners Journal* 4 Nov. 1865, 2
	Pottsville	*Miners Journal* 15 May 1858, 2
	Rough & Ready	*Miners Journal* 8 July 1865, 2
	Schuylkill	*Miners Journal* 2 Sept. 1865, 2
	Slow Boys Mutual	*Miners Journal* 16 June 1866, 2
	UECC	*Miners Journal* 23 June 1866, 2
	United	*Miners Journal* 13 June 1858, 2
	U.S. Grant	*Miners Journal* 26 Aug. 1865, 2
Reading	Reading	*Reading Daily Eagle* 20 May 1873, 4
Rochester	Rochester	*Clipper* 13 Sept. 1873, 187
St. Clair	St. Clair	*Miners Journal* 7 Aug. 1858, 2
	Senior	*Clipper* 2 Oct. 1858, 189
	Starlight	*Clipper* 2 Oct. 1858, 189
Schuylkill Haven	Geary	*Miners Journal* 25 Aug. 1866, 2
	Perseverance	*Miners Journal* 14 Aug. 1858, 2
Scranton	Albion	*Clipper* 13 Sept. 1873, 187
	Pittston	*Clipper* 13 Sept. 1873, 187
Silver Creek	Anthracite	*Miners Journal* 15 July 1865, 2
Stonesboro	Stonesboro	*Titusville Morning Herald* 26 June 1873, 3
Strasburg	Constitution	*Daily Evening Express* 8 Oct. 1857, 2
Susquehanna Depot	Susquehanna Depot	*Porters* 6 Aug. 1859, 357
Tamaqua	Hiawatha	*Miners Journal* 29 July 1865, 2
	Tamaqua	*Miners Journal* 30 July 1859, 2

Titusville	Amateur	*Titusville Morning Herald* 16 April 1873, 3
Tuscarora	Excelsior	*Miners Journal* 16 June 1866, 2
Wadesville	Miners	*Miners Journal* 7 Aug. 1858, 2
	Wadesville	*Sporting Life* 16 Aug. 1890, 12
Washington	Anglo	*Washington Reporter* 18 Aug. 1869, 1
	African	*Washington Reporter* 18 Aug. 1869, 1
	Excelsior	*Washington Reporter* 13 July 1859, 2
	Grange	*Pittsburgh Post* 27 June 1860, 1
	OK Club	*Reporter & Tribune* 15 Nov. 1865, 3
	Victoria	*Clipper* 16 April 1859, 410
	Washington	*Porters* 25 June 1859, 261
	Washington College & Jefferson	Coleman, *Banners in the Wilderness*, 183
Waynesburg	Washington County Lockyer	*Clipper* 21 Oct. 1965, 219
	Philopaizans	*Clipper* 8 Sept. 1860, 165
West Chester	Brandywine	*Clipper* 8 Sept. 1860, 165
Wilkensburg	Wilkensburg	*Clipper* 2 June 1860, 53
Wilkes Barre	Hazelton	*Outing* July 1893, 84
Williamsport	Williamsport	*Clipper* 6 Oct. 1883, 469
		Sun and Lycoming Democrat 1 Sept. 1875, 5
York	York	*Sunday Mercury* 3 June 1860, 4

RHODE ISLAND

Ashaway	Lillywhite	*Clipper* 19 July 1856, 99
	Union	*Clipper* 3 May 1856, 11
Ashton	Ashton	*Clipper* 11 Oct. 1879, 227

262 · *The Tented Field*

Berkeley	Centennial	*Clipper* 8 May 1880, 50
Cranston	Mechanics	*Clipper* 6 Oct. 1866, 203
Greystone	Benns Mohair	*Spalding's Official Cricket Guide for 1913*, 71
Lonsdale	Union	*Clipper* 21 Sept. 1867, 188
Narragansett	Narragansett	*Boston Globe* 20 Aug. 1899, 2
Newport	Newport	*Sporting Life* 4 June 1884, 7
	Newport Casino	*Boston Globe* 17 Sept. 1885, 2
	Old Haverford	*Clipper* 9 Aug. 1879, 157
	Summer Tourist	*Boston Globe* 9 Sept. 1890, 7
Olneyville	Thorntons	*Boston Globe* 4 July 1886, 1
Pawtucket	Free Wanderers	*Boston Globe* 21 June 1886, 3
	Lorraines	*Boston Globe* 21 June 1886, 3
	Pawtucket	*Clipper* 8 Oct. 1856, 205
	YMCA	*Boston Globe* 2 Aug. 1903, 9
Providence	Brown University	*Boston Globe* 12 July 1885, 8
	Broadway Baptist Brotherhood	*Spalding's Official Cricket Guide for 1913*, 73
	Central Falls	*Clipper* 15 Sept. 1866, 180
	Potter & Johnson	*Spalding's Official Cricket Guide for 1913*, 73
	Providence	*Clipper* 10 Aug. 1867, 141
	Providence Valley	*Clipper* 15 Sept. 1866, 180
	River Points	*Boston Globe* 16 July 1888, 3
	South Providence	*Spalding's Official Cricket Guide for 1907*, 90
	Spragueville Mechanics	*Clipper* 10 Aug. 1867, 141
	Wanskuck	*Clipper* 28 June 1879, 106
	Willow Park	*Spalding's Official Cricket Guide for 1909*, 92

Appendix · 263

	Richmond	Shamrock	*Clipper* 31 May 1856, 11
	River Point	Clyde	*Providence Journal* 17 June 1888, 9
	Rumford	Rumford	*Boston Globe* 27 Aug. 1885, 5
	Saylesville	Saylesville	*Boston-Globe* 16 July 16, 1888, 3
	Slatersville	Slaters	*Spalding's Official Cricket Guide for 1914*, 73
	Warren	British-Americans	*Boston Globe* 9 Aug. 1891, 3
	Westerly	Westerly	*Clipper* 10 Sept. 1856, 183
	Woonsocket	Blackstone	*Providence Journal* 27 May 1888, 9
		Worsted Mills	*Spalding's Official Cricket Guide for 1914*, 73
SOUTH CAROLINA	Charleston	Charleston	*Spirit* 27 May 1848, 163
SOUTH DAKOTA	Clark	Clark	*Clipper* 2 Aug. 1884, 311
	Dell Rapids	Dell Rapids	Farnbust, *Where the Sioux River Bends*, 211
	Sioux Falls	East Sioux Falls	*Pipestone County Star* 24 July 1891, 5
	Watertown	Watertown	*Dakota News* 30 June 1883, 5
	Waverly	Waverly	*Dakota News* 30 June 1883, 5
TENNESSEE	Memphis	Chelsea	*Memphis Daily Appeal* 14 June 1867, 3
		St. George	*Memphis Daily Appeal* 14 June 1867, 3
	Nashville	Nashville	*Turf Field and Farm*, 1865, 189
	Rugby	Rugby	*St. Louis Post-Dispatch* 12 Oct. 1881, 8
TEXAS	Austin	Austin	*Austin American Statesman* 24 Dec. 1874, 3
	Boerne	Boerne	*San Antonio Express* 8 Aug. 1889, 3

264 · *The Tented Field*

Galveston	Galveston	*Galveston Daily News* 19 Oct. 1884, 3
Houston	Houston	*Galveston Daily News* 19 Oct. 1884, 3
Kerrville	Kerrville	*San Antonio Daily Light* 20 May 1892
San Antonio	Garrison	*American Cricketer* 6 June 1889, 22
	San Antonio	*San Antonio Express* 26 Feb. 1889, 3

UTAH

Coalville	Coalville	*Deseret News* 26 July 1875, 3
Hennefer	Hennefer	*Ogden Junction* 29 July 1876, 3
Hyrum	Hyrum	*Windows to Wellsville*, 309
Logan	Cache County	*Deseret News* 9 Oct. 1867, 316
	Logan	*Windows to Wellsville*, 309
Ogden	Ogden	*Deseret News* 24 June 1863, 410
Paradise	Paradise	*Windows to Wellsville*, 309
Plain City	Plain City	*Salt Lake Daily Telegraph* 17 June 1869, 2
Salt Lake City	Deseret Union	*Deseret News* 4 Sept. 1867, 287
	Eleventh Ward	*Deseret News* 9 July 9, 1862, 16
	Ft. Douglas	*Deseret News* 16 Aug. 1879, 3
	Great Salt Lake	*Deseret News* 9 Oct. 1867, 316
	Metropolitan	*Deseret News* 17 Sept. 1862, 90
	Walker Bros. Dept. Store	*Deseret News* 13 Nov. 1879, 3
Sandy	Sandy	*Deseret News* 29 July 1875, 3
Smithfield	Smithfield	*Deseret News* 9 Aug. 1866, 285
Springville	Springville	*Deseret News* 15 Oct. 1862, 123
Wellsville	Wellsville	*Deseret News* 9 Aug. 1866, 285
West Weber	West Weber	*Salt Lake Daily Telegraph* 17 June 1869, 2

VERMONT	Barre	*Boston Globe* 5 July 1888, 3
	Northfield	Ellis, *Norwich University*, vol. 1, 123
VIRGINIA	Charlottesville	University of Virginia Kiracofe, "Athletics and Physical Education in the Colleges of Virginia," 9
	Norfolk	*Clipper* 20 Nov. 1858, 243
	Portsmouth	*American Cricketer* 6 Aug. 1900, 223
	Richmond	*Spirit* 6 June 1857, 199
	Roanoke	*American Cricketer* 21 Sept. 1892, 182
WASHINGTON	Seattle	*Spalding's Official Cricket Guide for 1912*, 91
	Spokane	*Spokane Falls Review* 28 March 1890, 6
	Tacoma	*Morning Oregonian* 23 June 1901, 3
WEST VIRGINIA	Wheeling	*Pittsburg Dispatch* 5 Sept. 1882, 5
WISCONSIN	Albion	*Wisconsin State Journal* 25 May 1871, 4
	Arena	*Daily Argus & Democrat* 12 Nov. 1853
		Black Earth Advertiser 15 June 1871, 3
	Bay View	*Milwaukee Sentinel* 22 Sept. 1879, 8
	Beloit	*Milwaukee Sentinel* 22 Oct. 1888, 3
	Delafield	*Milwaukee Sentinel* 15 July 1894, 7
		Milwaukee Sentinel 15 Oct. 1888, 1
	Dodgeville	*Dodgeville Chronicle* 20 June 1867, 1
	Eagle	*Milwaukee Sentinel* 23 Oct. 1855, 3

Barre — Barre
Northfield — Norwich University
Charlottesville — University of Virginia
Norfolk — Norfolk
Portsmouth — Portsmouth
Richmond — Richmond
Roanoke — Roanoke
Seattle — Seattle
Spokane — Spokane
Tacoma — Tacoma
Wheeling — Wheeling
Albion — Prairie Clippers
Arena — Iowa County
— Union
Bay View — Bay View
Beloit — Beloit
Delafield — Delafield
— St. Johns Academy
Dodgeville — Badger
Eagle — Eagle

Green Bay	Green Bay	*Green Bay Advocate* 23 Aug. 1883, 3
Green Lake	Green Lake	*Milwaukee Sentinel* 26 July 1856, 2
Janesville	Janesville	*Chicago Tribune* 28 Sept. 1873, 13
Kenosha	Kenosha	*Spalding's Official Cricket Guide for 1910*, 111
Lisbon	Lisbon	*Milwaukee Sentinel* 7 June 1852, 2
Madison	Madison	*Wisconsin State Journal* 18 June 1859, 1
	Washington	*Wisconsin State Journal* 27 Aug. 1859, 1
Markesan	Markesan	*Milwaukee Sentinel* 26 July 1856, 2
Mazomanie	Mazomanie	*Daily Argus & Democrat* 12 Nov. 1853
Milwaukee	Cream City	*Milwaukee Sentinel* 17 May 1888, 3
	East Side	*Milwaukee Sentinel* 20 June 1880, 5
	Fourth District School	*Milwaukee Sentinel* 17 Nov. 1879, 8
	Ironside	*Milwaukee Sentinel* 23 July 1887, 9
	Milwaukee	*Milwaukee Sentinel* 20 April 1852, 2
	St. Andrews	*Milwaukee Sentinel* 11 May 1889, 3
	West Side	*Milwaukee Sentinel* 20 June 1880, 5
	Willow	*Milwaukee Sentinel* 19 May 1879, 3
	Young America	*Milwaukee Sentinel* 17 April 1879, 8
Mineral Point	Mineral Point	*Monroe Sentinel* 20 July 1859, 3
Monroe	Monroe	*Monroe Sentinel* 20 July 1859, 3
Nashotah	Nashotah House Seminary	*Racine Daily Journal* 7 July 1860, 1
Oshkosh	Oshkosh	*Northwestern* 12 July 1866, 5
Platteville	Platteville	*Grant County Witness* 23 Aug. 1866, 3
	Grove	*Milwaukee Sentinel* 30 Aug. 1866, 1
Racine	Horlick Athletic Assoc.	*Spalding's Official Cricket Guide for 1910*, 111

	Racine	*Racine Daily Journal* 12 July 1860, 1
	Racine College	*Racine Daily Journal* 30 June 1860, 1
Red Granite	Red Granite	*Ripon Commonwealth* 25 Aug. 1905, 5
Ripon	Ripon	*Milwaukee Sentinel* 26 July 1856, 2
Sheboygan	Chair City	*Sheboygan Telegram* 21 July 1898, 5
	Sheboygan	*Sheboygan Journal* 25 May 1865, 1
Superior	Superior	*Pioneer Press* 23 Aug. 1897, 5
Sussex	Sussex	*Spirit* 9 Sept. 1854, 355
Waukesha	Waukesha	*Milwaukee Sentinel* 27 Sept. 1859, 1

WYOMING

Almy	Almy	*Deseret News* 1 June 1885, 3

Index

Ackworth School, England 135
Adelman, Melvin 2, 3, 8, 9, 16, 19, 22, 29, 33, 34, 35, 36, 37, 40, 41, 55, 147, 148, 178n36
Ahmeek, Michigan 112
Albany, New York 11, 17, 27, 44, 178n33
All-England cricketers; American tour, 1859 43, 44-45, 50, 86, 133
Allen, Nathaniel 29
Allen, Thomas 47
All Saints Church, Omaha 102
Almy, Wyoming 58, 112
Alpha Cricket Club, Salem, Massachusetts 78, 143
Altoona, Pennsylvania 98
American Cricket Club, New York 23, 50, 62, 69
American Cricketer 127
American Gentleman's Cricket Club, Philadelphia 28
"American plan" 143-44
American vs English cricket matches 34-35
American Watch Company, Waltham, Massachusetts 110
America's Cup 87
Americus Athletic Club, Hoboken, New Jersey 96
Amherst College 40, 49, 172n42
Amsterdam, New York 27, 54, 57
Anderson, William C. 29
Andover Theological Seminary 49
Andrews, Dr., New York cricketer 35
Anson, Cap 65
Ardmore, Pennsylvania 125
Arkansas School of Theology, Winslow, Arkansas 101

Arlington Mill, Lawrence, Massachusetts 111
Armitage, Tom 81
Armour, Phillip 90
Ashton, Rhode Island 113
Aspinal, Lloyd 182n32
Associated Bank Cricket Club, Portland, Oregon 97
Assumption College, Sandwich, Massachusetts 29
Astoria (Oregon) Football Club 97
athletic clubs, and cricket 98-99
Auburn, New York 99
Australia 64, 119
Australian cricketers in America: in 1878, 66, 83, 86, 125, 133; in 1882, 84; in 1893, 80, 126; in 1896, 65, 86, 97, 138; in 1912, 137, 140; in 1913, 146

Bage, Robert 12
Baker, Thomas 40, 207n16
Baltimore 7, 44, 46, 53, 58
Baltimore Cricket Club 66, 87, 90, 126
Bankers Athletic Club, Chicago 97
Barclay, A. Charles 35, 45
Barclay, Delancey 14
barn ball 6
baseball 10, 20, 22, 23, 26, 31, 34, 36-38, 49, 56, 59, 60, 62, 63, 68, 69, 73-74, 93-94, 136, 143, 148, 174n66, 175n78, 184n45, 190n2
baseballers as cricketers 50, 61-62, 65-66, 67
baseball tour to England, 1874 63-64
basketball 93
Bay View, Wisconsin 48, 111

Bedford, Long Island 15
Belmont Cricket Club, Philadelphia 80, 98, 124, 125-26, 128
Berkeley Athletic Club, New York 96
Bessemer Steel Company, Chicago 111
Bixby, C. L. 79
blacks and cricket 114-15
Blanchard, Tom 174n58
Bloomington, Illinois 27
Bohemian Club, San Francisco 90
Bohlen, Frank 135
Bond, Hugh 90
Bonner, George 85
Booker, W. R. 24
Boot Hill Mill, Lowell, Massachusetts 111
Bosanquet, Bernard 86
Boston Belting Company 111
Boston common 180n15
Boston Cricket Club (1809) 7
Boston Red Stockings 64
Bowdoin College 49
Bowen, Roland 9
Boys Own Book 8
Bradley, A. G. 121
Bradshaw, William 26, 28, 123
Brainerd, Asa 50
Brainerd, Minnesota 98
Branch Brook Cricket Club, New Jersey 115
Brewster, Captain, U.S. Military Academy 99
Bridgeport, Connecticut 29
Brientnall, R. Heber 66
Bristol, J. I. D. 97
British Temperance Society 25
Broach, W. J. 172n41
Brockton, Massachusetts 111
Bromhead, George 81
Brooklyn Baseball Club (1845) 19, 168n38
Brooklyn, New York 5, 12, 34, 36
Brown family, Philadelphia 124
Brown, Hazen 105
Brown, Henry 127

Brown University 106
Buffalo Cricket Club 26, 171n36
Buffalo, New York 26, 58, 81, 99
Burlington & Missouri Railroad 98
Butte, Montana 112, 199n99
Byrd, William 5

Calder, F. C. 100
Calthrop, Samuel 29, 101
Calumet, Michigan 112
Calvert, Charles 79
Camac estate, Philadelphia 45
Cambridge University 138, 140
Camden, New Jersey 123
Carnegie, Andrew 89, 90
Carnegie, T. M. 89
Carnegie, W. C. 89
Carpenter, Robert 45
Carpenter, William 30
Cartwright, Alexander 9
Carvill, William 106-07
Cass Baseball Club, Detroit 82
Cater, Aymr 78
Central City, Colorado 112
Central High School, Philadelphia 47, 104
Central Park, New York 90, 130-31
Centerville, Montana 112
Chadwick, Henry 23, 49, 61, 69-71, 100, 133, 144
Chambers, Isaac 81
Champion, Aaron 57
Charleston, South Carolina 15
Chartist movement 26
Chestnut Hill Cricket Club, Philadelphia 123
Chestnut Hill, Pennsylvania 120
Chicago 15, 24, 58, 81, 98, 99, 143, 202n49
Chicago Cricket Club 80, 82, 90, 149
Chicago White Stockings 65
Christ Episcopal Church, Milwaukee 101
Christian Brothers College, St. Louis 102
Church, Judge 9

Churchman, Joseph 30
Cicero, Illinois 102
Cincinnati 15, 17, 57
Cincinnati Red Stockings 57, 59, 61
Circleville, Ohio 34
Civil War, and cricket 53-55, 147
Clark family, Philadelphia 124
clergymen as cricketers 6, 100-02
Cleveland 24, 128
Cleveland Cricket Club 24
Cleveland Cricket and Golf Club 97
Clinton, Massachusetts 101
Clipper 23
clown cricketers 97
Club Record Cup, Philadelphia 126
Coalville, Utah 58, 112
Cobb, M. R. 97, 132
Codd, George P. 80
Coit, Henry 48
College of the Holy Cross 49
Colles, C. H. T. 53
Columbia Athletic Club, New York 96
Columbia University 106, 108, 117
Comery, New York cricketer 45
Commercial Trust Company, Philadelphia 97
Connecticut 5, 9, 17
Connecticut Mutual Insurance Company 97
Connecticut State Reform School 102
Conover, F. S. 106
Conover, J. P. 106
conventions, national cricket 40, 53
Conway, John 122
Cooper, David 203n53
Cope, Henry 127
Coquette, H.M.S. 100
Cornell University 108
country clubs, and cricket 190n61
Cregar, Eddie 126
Creighton, James 50, 62
Crescent Athletic Club, New York 96
Cress, New York cricketer 132
Cricket Club Life 127
cricket, in colonial America 5-7; on ice 70

Cricketers Association of the United States 129
Cripple Creek, Colorado 112
Crocket, J. Frank 30
Croswell, Harry 8
Cushing, Arthur 172n41
Custer, George A. 54

Daft, Richard 62, 67, 84, 86, 133
Dakin, Thomas 50
Dale, Tam 81
Dalies, C. 193n34
Dana, Richard Henry 8
Dartmouth College 8
Davenport, Iowa 46
Davidge, William 78
Davis, Ebenezer 8
Davis, Free Academy student 35
Dedham, Massachusetts 113
DeKoven, James 47, 48, 103
Delafield estate, Staten Island 78
Denver 99
Denver Athletic Club 97
Detroit 27, 46, 58
Detroit Athletic Club 79, 97
Detroit Sporting & Recreation Company 79
Dorian Cricket Club, Haverford College 107
Dudson, Sam 109

Eastern Elastic Company, Chelsea, Massachusetts 111
Eastern Pennsylvania Cricket League 98
East New York Cricket Club 30, 55
East Sioux City, South Dakota 112
East Williamsburg Cricket Club, New York 61
Elgin Watch Company 110
Elliot, Charles 104
Elyria, Ohio 57
Elysian fields, Hoboken, New Jersey 14, 21, 44, 58, 130
Emerson, Ralph W. 8
Emery, Stanley 108

Empire Baseball Club, New York 66
Empire Mining Company, Grass Valley, California 113
Enterprise, U.S.S. 100
Episcopal Church 47
Essex Cricket Club, New Jersey 130
Eureka Baseball Club, New York 66
Ewing, Marshall 125
Excelsior Baseball Club, Brooklyn 62, 66

Faire's School, Mr., Philadelphia 47
Fall River, Massachusetts 113
Farley, James 78
Farmers High School, Bellefonte, Pennsylvania 47
Farr Alpaca Company, Holyoke, Massachusetts 111
"father of American cricket" 25-26
Fay, H. F. 78
Ferry House Tavern, Brooklyn 5, 7, 11
Field, Marshall 90
Fitzgerald, Robert 58, 61, 62, 70, 75-76, 133
Flatbush Cricket Club, New York 63
Folkes, Reuben 112
folk games 8, 30
football 42, 60, 78
Fordham University 107
Ft. Douglas, Utah 100
Ft. Greene, Brooklyn 18
Ft. Leavenworth, Kansas 54
Foulkrod, William 146
Fourth District School, Milwaukee 104
Fox, Joe 135
Franklin & Marshall College 49
Franklin National Bank, Philadelphia 97
Franklin, New Jersey 26
Free Academy, New York 28, 32
Free Church, Worcester, Massachusetts 101
French, John G. 35
Friends Select School, Philadelphia 103

Galena, Illinois 57
gambling 75
"Garrison Knickerbocker" 131
Gems, Gerald 190n62
General Electric Company 197n78
Georgia 5
Germantown Academy, Philadelphia 104
Germantown Cricket Club 25, 28, 53, 91, 114, 124, 127, 145, 146
Germantown, Pennsylvania 16, 119
Giffen, George 135
Girard Cricket Club, Philadelphia 173n52
Gloucestershire County Cricket Club 140
Gloversville, New York 27
Goldstein, Warren 196n72
golf 60, 88
Grace, W. G. 75
Graffen, S. M. 183n39
Grass Valley, California 34, 46, 65, 197n81, 199n98
Greenfield, Massachusetts 55
Green, John P. 98, 125
Greenwich, New York 5, 89
Groom, Harry 25

Haire, Norma 113
Hale, Edward E. 8
Halifax Cup 124, 126, 142, 143, 146
Halifax Tournament, 1874 126, 131
Hall, E. P. 75
Hall, R. C. 183n39
Hammond, William 81
Hand, George E. 79
Hardy, Edward 168n36
Hardy Tavern, Philadelphia 15
Hargreaves brothers 121
Harper, Alex 113
Harrington, Elliot 31
Harris, Lord 84
Harvard University 8, 29, 48, 81, 105, 107, 108, 116, 143
Hatch, E. W. 102
Hatfield, John 61

Haverford College 49, 105, 106-07
Haverford Station, Pennsylvania 125
Hawke, Lord 67, 87, 88, 134, 137
Hazelton, Myron 29
Hazelton, Pennsylvania 98
Hazen School, Pelham Manor, New York 114
Hearne, J. T. 139
Heaton, Eliza 114
Heigho, George 79
Helena, Montana 112
Helliwell, T. 109
Herbert & Rapp Company, Brockton, Massachusetts 111
Higginson, T. W. 100-01
Higham, Dick 61
Higham, James 56
Hill, Phyllis 175n68
Hinchliffe, John 172n41
Hinchman, Ford 79
Hines, John 30
Hirst, George 136, 204n75
Hodges family 78
Hodges, John 35
Holmes, American cricketer 35
Homestead Steel Mill, Homestead, Pennsylvania 111
Hopkins, J. P. 172n41
Hordern, Herbert 108, 141
Horlick, William 113
horse racing 91
Houston, Henry H. 123
Howard University 117
Hubbard, Chelsea W. 113
Hubbard, John 78
Hughes, Thomas 29
Hyde-Clark, G. 106

Illinois 7
India 64
Indianapolis 56
Indianapolis High School 47
Inter-Academic Athletic League, Philadelphia 104
Inter-City Cricket Championship, 1891 129
Inter-City Cricket League, Philadelphia 126
Intercollegiate Cricket Association 106, 107, 108-09
International Tile Company, New York 113
Iredale, Frank 123, 138
Irish cricketers, in America 66, 85, 86, 137
Irvine, F. C. 132
Irving, John 51, 74
Isthmian Cricket Club, St. Paul's School 48

Jable, J. Thomas 28
Jackson Cricket Club, St. Louis 30, 53
Jackson, George 44
Jackson, Isaac 27, 207n116
Jackson, John 44
Jackson, Michigan 57
Jamaica 115
Jamaica Cricket Club, New York 15
Jamestown, New York 99
Jarvis Field, Harvard University 105
Jarvis, William 25, 26
Jessup, Gilbert 132, 136, 140
Jessup, Henry 12
Jewell, Herbert S. 66
John Quincy Adams Grammar School, Philadelphia 47
Johns Hopkins University 117
Johnson, C. P. E. 30
Johnstown, New York 27

Kankakee, Illinois 81
Kansas City 99
Kearsarge, Michigan 112
Kelly, F. F. 97
Kent County Cricket Club 141
Kentucky Military Institute 29
Kephardt, Philadelphia cricketer 35
Keweenaw copper mining strike, 1913 113
King, John B. 126, 136-37, 138, 139, 141
King, Rufus 23

274 · Index

Kings County Cricket Club, New York 41
Kirsch, George 2, 3, 29, 40, 147
Knickerbocker Athletic Club, New Jersey 126
Knickerbocker Baseball Club 9, 20, 65
Krebs, William 78

Lacey, William 23
lacrosse 78
Lambert, Henry 25
Lambertville, New Jersey 57
Lancashire County Cricket Club 138, 141
Lancaster, Pennsylvania 23, 100
Lawrence, Massachusetts 54, 85
Lawrenceville School, New Jersey 47
laws, cricket *see* rules, cricket
Law, Sutherland 31
Lebanon, Pennsylvania 98
leisure class 87
LeMars, Iowa 99
Leonard, Andy 70
Lester, John 105, 122, 135-36
Lexington, Kentucky 46
Lincoln, Abraham 53
Lincoln Cricket Club, Worcester, Massachusetts 101
Lincolnshire, England 141
Linder family 78
Linder, George 79
Livingston, Montana 112
Lockyer, Tom 44, 50
Long Island Cricket Club, New York 20, 54
Longwood Cricket Club 48, 61, 78-79, 86, 173n43
Lonsdale, Rhode Island 63
Lords Cricket Ground, England 130
Louisville, Kentucky 56, 100, 178n33
Lovett, James D. 31
Lowell Cricket Club, Massachusetts 7, 26, 65
Lowell, Massachusetts 46, 63
Lyon, Dr. 107

Macon, Georgia 15
MacLaren, Archie 86
Madison, Wisconsin 30, 46
Mailey, Arthur 123
Maine 99
Mallinkrodt, K. W. 132
Manhattan Cricket Club, New York 65, 66, 70, 143
Marsh, New York cricketer 45
Marylebone Cricket Club *see* MCC
Mary Memorial Church, Syracuse, New York 101
Marysville, Montana 112
Mason, John 142, 144
Massachusetts State Cricket Conventions 30, 55
Massie, H. H. 85
Mayers, Charles 30
Maysville, Kentucky 46, 57
Mazomanie, Wisconsin 25, 57
McBride John D. 61
MCC 69, 75, 129, 140, 141, 142
McCartys; Tavern, New York 14
McClure, Charles 30
McKean, Henry P. 124
McKean, Thomas 90
McLane, Robert M. 90, 172n41
McNutt, Howard 134
McVey, Cal 70
Meadville, Pennsylvania 57
Medway Baseball Club 38
Memphis, Tennessee 56
Meriden, Connecticut 111
Merion Cricket Club, Philadelphia 125, 127, 143, 145
Merrigan, Thomas 30
Metropolitan District Cricket League, New York 98, 102, 192n20
Metropolitan Life Insurance Company 97
Miami College 29
Michigan Athletic Association, Detroit 97
Middlesex County Cricket Club 139
Millersville Normal School 49
Milner, Thomas P. 12, 14, 25

Milwaukee 17, 24, 95, 99
Minneapolis 89, 91, 95, 99
Minneapolis Cricket Club 90
Mitchell, Frank 108, 135, 137, 138
Mitchell, John K. 16, 20
Mixer, Charles 79
Mobile, Alabama 46
Mohawk, Michigan 112
Mold, Arthur 137
Monitor Cricket Club, Greenfield, Massachusetts 55
Montreal 13, 32, 43, 131
Moore, William C. 54
Morgan, William 45
Morley, Sam 104
Morris Park Cricket Club, New York 191n4
Moses, Phineas 167n21
Mudie, English cricketer 44
Multnomah Amateur Athletic Club, Portland, Oregon 97
Munro, David A. 169n12
"muscular Christianity" 100
Mutual Baseball Club, New York 61, 66

Nashotah House Seminary 48, 101
Natchez, Mississippi 15
National Association of Professional Baseball Players 64
National Baseball League 27
Naugatuck Valley, Connecticut 110
Nevadaville, Colorado 112
Newark Cricket Club 15, 21, 26, 34, 66, 96, 143
Newark, New Jersey 22, 58
Newark Orphan Asylum 82
New Bedford, Massachusetts 199n97
New Brunswick, New Jersey 29
Newcomb, Charles K. 60, 74
Newhall, Dan 127
Newhall family 120
Newhall, George 35, 122, 142
Newhall, Robert 83
Newhall, Walter 35, 45, 54
New Jersey 99

New Jersey Athletic Club 97, 114
New Orleans 8, 46-47, 58
Newport, Rhode Island 90, 99
New York Athletic Club 90
New York Baseball Club (1845) 19, 168n38
New York Cricket Association 98
New York Cricket Club 9, 12, 14, 15, 17, 19, 26, 32, 34, 37, 56, 77
New York, cricket in colonial, 6-7; in the 1890s 95
New York Jockey Club 90
New York Racquet Club 90
Nicetown, Philadelphia 91, 124
Nineteenth Massachusetts Colored Regiment 54
Ninety-Fifth Pennsylvania Regiment 54
Nonantum Cricket Club, Newton, Massachusetts 78
Norfolk, Virginia 164n10
Norley, John 81
Norristown, Pennsylvania 98
Northeast Manual Training School, Philadelphia 104
Northern Pacific Railroad 98
North, G. T. C. 23
Northwestern Cricket Association 99
Norwich University 55
Nottingham County Cricket Club 139, 140, 141
Novel, Duncan 78
Nyack, New York 57
Nymph, H. M. S. 100

Oberlin College 49
Ogden, Utah 55
Ohio State University 117
Ohio Wesleyan College 107
Old Hundred Cricket Club, St. Paul's School 48
Olmstead, Frederick 130
Olympics, 1904, St. Louis 117
Omaha 89, 99
Omaha Cricket & Athletic Association 97

276 · Index

Omaha High School 104
Opposition Baseball Club, Meriden, Connecticut 65
Orange, New Jersey 57
Original Lady Cricketers, England 114
Oshkosh, Wisconsin 57
Oswego, New York 46, 55
Outerbridge, Albert E. 78
Outerbridge, Mary 78
Oxford-Cambridge cricket match 106
Oxford movement 47
Oxford University 106, 108, 138, 140

Painsdale, Michigan 112
Parker, John 23
Parr, George 44
Paterson, New Jersey 24, 26, 191n10
Patterson, George 135, 139, 145
Paull, James 113
Pawtucket, Rhode Island 89
Pearson, Henry 15
Peck & Snyder Department Store 191n10
Peninsular Cricket Club, Detroit 59, 79-80, 82, 131, 180n10
Pennell, Christopher 54
Penn State University 47
Pennsylvania Railroad 98
Pfeffer, Fred 65
Phelps, Francis 30
Philadelphia 15-17, 25, 27-28, 46, 67, 71, 87, 96
Philadelphia Athletics Baseball Club 61, 62
Philadelphia Cricket Club 25, 28, 53, 58, 123-24, 131
Philadelphia Cup 126
Philadelphians, English tour: 1884, 128, 133-34; 1889, 82; 1897, 135, 138-39; 1903, 140-41; 1908, 141
Philadelphia, U.S.S. 100
Philippine Islands 100
Phillipps, T. D. 101, 131
Phillips Andover Academy 29
Phillips, Barnet 16-17, 40

physical education, and cricket 28, 117
Pickering, W P. 43
Piercy, A. J. 65
pigeon shooting 51
Pillsbury, C. A. 90
Piraeus, Greece 100
Pittsburgh 17, 18, 46, 58, 85, 129
Pittsburgh Cricket Club 80, 89
Plain City, Utah 58, 181n20
Platteville, Wisconsin 57
playground movement 117
Plumley, A. S. 30
polo 88, 90
Polytechnic School, Brooklyn 70
Pool, E. A. 105
Pool, J. L. 132
Pope, S. W. 207n1
Port Carbon, Pennsylvania 27, 59, 98
Porters Spirit of the Times 22
Porter, William 14
Port Huron, Michigan 46
Portland Amateur Athletic Club 97
Portland, Oregon 65, 174n62
Portuguese immigrants, and cricket 199n97
Pottsville Athletic Club 59
Pottsville, Pennsylvania 27, 34, 59, 98, 182n24
Poughkeepsie, New York 27
Prairie Cricket Club, Chicago 53
Presidents Cup 98
Price & Littell estate, Philadelphia 125
Princeton University 29, 39, 105, 106, 108
prisoners base 30
professionalism 73-74, 75, 83, 94
Prospect Park, Brooklyn 131, 192n20
Prospect Park Cricket Club 23, 100
Protestant Episcopal Academy 47, 103
Providence Grays Baseball Club 61, 62, 65
Provost, American cricketer 35
Pullman Cricket Club, Chicago 81, 109, 112

Queen City Cricket Club, Cincinnati 167n21
Queen, Frank 23
Queens County Cricket Club, New York 39
Quincy, Massachusetts 111

Racine College, Wisconsin 37, 39, 47, 67, 103, 115, 193n30
Radnor High School 104
Rainsford, W. S. 101-02
Ranjitsinhji, Kumar S. 86, 136, 140
Ranney, William 14, 30
Reach, Al 184n45
Reading, Pennsylvania 174n55
Redgranite, Wisconsin 112
Red House Tavern, New York 13, 21, 203n50
Redwing, Minnesota 30, 46
Reese, P. R. 66
Reff, E. A. 136
Reid, P. H. 30
Remington Typewriter Company 197n78
Richard, B. 17
Richards, John 14
Richardson, Tom 137
Richmond, Virginia 6, 27
Ridgeland Athletic Club, Albany, New York 96
Ripley, Ohio 46
Ripon, Wisconsin 25, 57
Rittenhouse Club, Philadelphia 90
Riverside Cricket Club, New York 130
Roanoke, Virginia 98
Rochester Cricket Club 75
Rochester, New York 14, 43, 50, 51, 65, 99
Rockafield, H. A. 23, 30
Roller, E. W. 86
Rosemary Hall, Wallingford, Connecticut 114
Rouse, New York cricketer 18
Roxbury Carpet Works 111
Rugby, Tennessee 171n35

rules, cricket 40, 69, 129; choice of innings 143; declarations 143; LBW 142, 206n102; overs 144-45
Rumford Cricket Club, Waltham, Massachusetts 26
Russell, Henry 18, 19, 20
Russell, Joseph 172n41
Russell, William 18, 19, 20
Ruutz-Rees, Caroline 114

Saemann, John 172n41
St. Agnes Church, New York 102
St. Austin School, New York 103
St. Clair, Pennsylvania 27, 59
St. George Cricket Club, New York 11, 12-13, 15, 19, 21, 24, 32-33, 51, 53, 56, 58, 62, 76, 89, 126, 128, 129, 130, 143, 186n16, 199n95
St. George Episcopal Church, New York 101
St. George Society, New York 168n36
St. James Church, Brooklyn 102
St. Johns Academy, Delafield, Wisconsin 103
St. Louis 29, 44, 46, 57, 77, 91, 99, 181n17
St. Louis Browns Baseball Club 65
St. Paul's School, Concord, New Hampshire 47, 71, 85, 103-04, 105, 200n103
Salt Lake City 55, 112, 178n33
Salt Lake City Baseball Club 65
Samuels, G. F. 115
San Antonio, Texas 54, 100
Sanderson Steel Company 111
Sandy, Utah 58
San Francisco 24, 46, 61, 65, 71
Sanitary Commission 54
Savannah, Georgia 46
Sawyer, English cricketer 14
Scadding, Charles 102
Scattergood, Henry 135
Schenck, William G. 66
Schenectady Locomotive Works 111
Schulkyll Haven, Pennsylvania 27, 59
Scott family, Philadelphia 124

278 · Index

Seabright Lawn Tennis and Cricket Club 82, 114, 132
Sears estate, Boston 78
Sebring, Frank 66
Second U.S. Infantry 100
Senior, Tom 28
Seventh New York Regiment 53
Seymour, George 9
Sharp, Henry 26, 45, 77
Shaw, Alfred 65, 133, 205n85
Sheboygan, Wisconsin 57
Sheffield, Lord 91
Shelbourne Falls, Massachusetts 24
Sherman, Richard 106
Shober, J. B. 106
Shonnard, E. F. 14, 27
Shrewsbury, Arthur 84
Silliman, Benjamin 9
Sivyer family, Milwaukee 24
Smith, Horatio 6
Smythe, S. T. 103
Soldier Field, Harvard University 105
Sousa, Anthony 190n62
Sousa, John P. 90
South Africa 141
Soutter, James T. 76
Spalding, Albert G. 63, 98
Spalding Cup 98
Sparkhawk, G. 113
Spink, Alfred 183n39
Spirit of the Times 22
Sprague, Joseph E. 66, 83
Springville, Utah 55
Star Baseball Club, New York 66
Star Cricket Club, Philadelphia 25
Staten Island Athletic Club 98
Staten Island Cricket Club 66, 77-78, 86, 97, 114, 129
Stempel, Carl 209
Stenton, Philadelphia 125
Sterling, Massachusetts 47
Stevens, Edward A. 14, 44
Stevens, R. F. 182n32
Strawberry Bank, Portsmouth, New Hampshire 97
Struna, Nancy 164n5

Suffolk Cricket Club, Boston 105
Surrey County Cricket Club 140
Sussex County Cricket Club 138
Sussex, Wisconsin 24, 30, 48
Sweney, William 30
Syracuse, New York 15, 17, 21, 81, 98
Syracuse University 117

Tallcott & Underhill Company 110
Tamaqua, Pennsylvania 59
Tamarack, Michigan 112
Tamarack Mining Company 113
Taylor, Frank 146
Taylor, John 12
Tenney, George 23
tennis 78, 88-89, 91, 189n56
Texas Cricket Club, Paterson, New Jersey 110
Thayer, John B. 108, 143
Third Pennsylvania Cavalry 54
Thirty-Second New York Regiment 54
Thompson, Mortimer Neal 39
Thornton, E. T. 85, 87
Thornton, Rhode Island 111
Thorp, James 25
Tibbets, J. K. 106
Tichnor, George 15
Tinson, Henry 25
Tioga Cricket Club, Philadelphia 126, 136
Toledo Outing Club 80, 97
Tom Brown's Schooldays 29
trap ball 30
Treloar, A. S. 97
Tri-Mountain Baseball Club, Boston 62
Trimountain, Michigan 112
Trinity Cathedral, Omaha 102
Trinity College, Hartford, Connecticut 39, 108
Trinity Episcopal Church, Toledo 102
Trott, George 65, 138
trotting 68
Trumble, Hugh 80
Tuscarora, Pennsylvania 59
Twelfth Wisconsin Regiment 54
Tynge, Jimmy 66

Union Baseball Club, New York 62, 81
Union Cricket Club, Cincinnati 55, 77
Union Cricket Club, Philadelphia 13, 15, 16, 18
Union Star Cricket Club, Brooklyn 18-20
United States Military Academy 99
United States National Tennis Association 89
United States Naval Academy 99
United States vs Canada cricket series 13, 14, 21-22, 31-32, 34, 43, 55, 101, 131-32, 137, 203n53
University of Michigan 31, 49, 67
University of Pennsylvania 16, 29, 49, 108
University of Virginia 117
Upton Baseball Club 38
Utah 55, 58, 181n20
Utica Cricket Club 171n36
Utica, New York 65, 99

Valley Forge, Pennsylvania 7
Van Buren, Frank 35
Vanceburg, Kentucky 57
Vaughan, W. R. 172n41
Verdi, Giuseppe 88
Vernou, Charles A. 53, 100
Viele, Robert 130
Von der Ahe, Chris 183n39

Wadesville, Pennsylvania 98
Wakefield Cricket Club, Philadelphia 173n52
Walker, Isaac 54
Walker, V. E. 44
Waller, Robert 15, 16, 43, 56
Waltham, Massachusetts 26, 31, 57
Wanderers Cricket & Athletic Club, Chicago 96
Ward, Edward R. 101
Ward, John M. 65
Warner, P. F. 87, 121, 136, 137, 140
Warren, Massachusetts 27
Warwickshire County Cricket Club 138

Washington Cricket Club, Pennsylvania 25
Washington, D.C. 56, 90
Washington & Jefferson College 49
Washington Nationals Baseball Club 61
Washington, Pennsylvania 59, 114
Waterbury, Connecticut 10, 170n25
Waters, Ed 113
Watervliet, New York 110
Waynesburg, College 49, 178n25
Weaver family, Sussex, Wisconsin 25
Weaver, Richard 30
Webster, William 30
Wellesley College 117
Wellsville, Utah 58
Wesleyan College, Middletown, Connecticut 49
Western Church 101
Western Cricket Association 99
West Indian Benevolent and Social League 115
West Indies 64, 82, 85, 86, 115
Westinghouse Electric Company 111
Westinghouse, George 90
Westtown School 103
Wharton, George 125
Wheatcroft, George 15
Wheatley, N. W. 172n41
Wheeler & Wilson Company 110
White Lead Paint Company 79
White Oak Church, Virginia 54
Whitney, Caspar 134, 135, 139
Whitney, Henry 169n12
Whitney, John 50
wicket 6, 7, 9-10, 30, 165n18
Wilkes Spirit of the Times 22
William Penn Charter School, Philadelphia 104
Williamsburg Athletic Club, New York 96
Williams College 49
Wilshire, Edgar 58, 62, 88, 133
Wilson, Cyril 113
Winnipeg, Canada 99
Wisconsin 57, 192n22

Wisden, John 44
Wister family, Philadelphia 120
Wister, Jones 17, 25, 35
Wister, William R. 16, 17, 18, 25, 27, 35
Wiswall, Boston cricketer 174n58
Wolters, Rynie 66
women's cricket 114, 198n90
Wood, A. M. 122
Wood, Charles 193n34
Woodcock, Arthur 107
Worcester, Massachusetts 38
Wright, George 36, 61, 70, 79, 96, 115, 116, 182n31
Wright, Harry 50, 57, 61, 64, 70, 77
Wynnewood, Pennsylvania 125

yachting 43, 90, 91
Yale University 8, 105-06
Yeatman, baseball player 182n32
YMCA 93, 102
Yonkers, New York 27
Yorkshire County Cricket Club 139
Young America Cricket Club, Milwaukee 101, 110
Young America Cricket Club, Philadelphia 14, 25, 28, 53, 78, 84, 100, 122, 124, 128
Young, Nicholas E. 27, 57
Young, Sidney 127

CPSIA information can be obtained at www.ICGtesting.com
Printed in the USA
LVOW11s0215040314

375869LV00002B/563/P